Rick Steves'
FRANCE
BELGIUM & THE NETHERLANDS
2000

Rick Steves and Steve Smith

John Muir Publications
Santa Fe, New Mexico

Other JMP travel guidebooks by Rick Steves
Rick Steves' Europe Through the Back Door
Europe 101: History and Art for the Traveler (with Gene Openshaw)
Rick Steves' Postcards from Europe
Rick Steves' Mona Winks: Self-Guided Tours of Europe's Top Museums
    (with Gene Openshaw)
Rick Steves' Best of Europe
Rick Steves' Germany, Austria & Switzerland
Rick Steves' Great Britain & Ireland
Rick Steves' Italy
Rick Steves' Scandinavia
Rick Steves' Spain & Portugal
Rick Steves' London (with Gene Openshaw)
Rick Steves' Paris (with Steve Smith and Gene Openshaw)
Rick Steves' Rome (with Gene Openshaw)
Rick Steves' Phrase Books: German, French, Italian,
    Spanish/Portuguese, and French/Italian/German
Asia Through the Back Door (with Bob Effertz)

Thanks to Steve's wife, Karen Lewis, for her help on covering the cuisine of France.

John Muir Publications, P.O. Box 613, Santa Fe, NM 87504
Copyright © 2000, 1999, 1998, 1997, 1996 by Rick Steves and Steve Smith
Cover copyright © 2000 by John Muir Publications
All rights reserved.

Printed in the United States of America
Second printing March 2000

For the latest on Rick's lectures, guidebooks, tours, and public television series, contact Europe Through the Back Door, Box 2009, Edmonds, WA 98020, tel. 425/771-8303, fax 425/771-0833, www.ricksteves.com, or e-mail: rick@ricksteves.com.

ISSN 1084-4406
ISBN 1-56261-497-5

Europe Through the Back Door Editor Risa Laib
John Muir Publications Editors Laurel Gladden Gillespie,
    Krista Lyons-Gould
Production & Typesetting Kathleen Sparkes, White Hart Design
Design Linda Braun
Cover Design Janine Lehmann
Maps David C. Hoerlein
Printer Banta Company
Cover Photo Arc d' Triomphe, Paris, France; © Jeff Greenberg/Unicorn
    Stock Photos

Distributed to the book trade by
Publishers Group West
Berkeley, California

CONTENTS

Top Destinations in France, Belgium, and the Netherlands

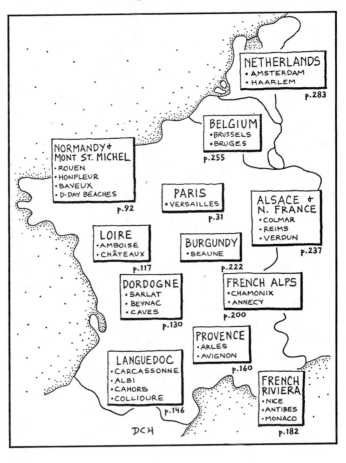

INTRODUCTION

Our compliments. You've made a great choice. France is Europe's most diverse, tasty, and, in many ways, exciting country to explore And for extra travel thrills, this book takes you north through the best of Belgium and the Netherlands.

France is nearly as big as Texas, with 58 million people and 460 different cheeses. *Diversité* is a French forte: This country features three distinct mountain ranges (the Alps, the Pyrénées, and the Massif Central), remarkably different Atlantic and Mediterranean coastlines, cosmopolitan cities, and sleepy villages. From its Swisslike Alps to its Italianesque Riviera and from the Spanish Pyrénées to das German Alsace, you can stay in France, feel like you've sampled much of Europe, and never be more than a short stroll from a good *vin rouge*.

Belgium and the Netherlands, called the Low Countries because nearly half their land is below sea level, are easy to overlook, surrounded by mega-Europe. We've spliced these into our France guide so that your memories can include some Bruges lace, Belgian waffles, a dike hike, and a few Dutch masters. If ever an area was a travel cliché come true, it's the Low Countries.

After years of researching and tour guiding together, Rick Steves and Francophile Steve Smith have teamed up to write this book. Together we give you the region's top destinations and tips on how to use your time and money most efficiently. France, Belgium, and the Netherlands are a many-faceted cultural fondue. Each of our recommended destinations is a dripping forkful (complete with instructions on how to enjoy the full flavor without burning your tongue).

This book covers the predictable biggies and mixes in a healthy dose of "Back Door" intimacy. Along with the Eiffel Tower, Mont St. Michel, and the French Riviera, you'll take a bike tour of the Loire, marvel at 15,000-year-old cave paintings, and walk the walls of a medieval fortress city. You'll find a *magnifique* castle perch to catch a Dordogne Valley sunset, ride Europe's highest mountain lift, and touch the quiet Romanesque soul of village Burgundy.

Rick Steves' France, Belgium & the Netherlands is a tour guide in your pocket—actually, two tour guides in your pocket. Places covered are balanced to include the most famous cities and intimate villages, from jet-setting beach resorts to the traditional heartland. We've been very selective, including only the most exciting sights. For example, there are *beaucoup* beautiful châteaus surrounding the Loire. We recommend the best three. The best is, of course, only our opinion. But after more than 25 busy years of travel writing, lecturing, tour guiding, and Francophilia between us, we've developed a sixth sense for what tickles the traveler's fancy.

This Information Is Accurate and Up-to-Date

This book is updated every year. Most publishers of guidebooks that cover a region from top to bottom can afford an update only every two or three years (and even then it's often by letter). Since this book is selective, covering only the places we think make the top month of sightseeing, we can update it each summer. Even with an annual update, things change. But if you're traveling with the current edition of this book, we guarantee you're using the most up-to-date information available. This book will help you have an inexpensive, hassle-free trip. *Use this year's edition.* Saving a few bucks by traveling on old information is not smart. If you're packing an old book, you'll learn the seriousness of your mistake...in Europe. Your trip costs at least $10 per waking hour. Your time is valuable. This guidebook saves lots of time.

Planning Your Trip

This book is organized by destinations. Each of these destinations is a minivacation on its own, filled with exciting sights and homey, affordable places to stay. For each chapter, you'll find the following:

Planning Your Time, a suggested schedule with thoughts on how to best use your limited time.

Orientation material, including tourist information, city transportation, and an easy-to-read map designed to make the text clear and your arrival smooth.

Sights with ratings: ▲▲▲—Don't miss; ▲▲—Try hard to see; ▲—Worthwhile if you can make it; No rating—Worth knowing about.

Sleeping and **Eating**, with addresses and phone numbers of our favorite budget hotels and restaurants.

And **Transportation Connections** to nearby destinations by train and route tips for drivers.

The handy **Appendix** includes a climate chart, campground listings, telephone tips, and French survival phrases.

Browse through this book, choose your favorite destinations, and link them up. You'll travel like a temporary local, getting the absolute most out of every mile, minute, and dollar. You won't waste time on mediocre sights because, unlike other guidebooks, we cover only the best. Since your major financial pitfall is lousy, expensive hotels, we've worked hard to assemble the best accommodation values for each stop. As you travel the route we know and love, we're happy you'll be meeting some of our favorite European people.

Trip Costs

Five components make up your total trip cost: airfare, surface transportation, room and board, sightseeing/entertainment, and shopping/miscellany.

Airfare: Don't try to sort through the mess. Find and use a good travel agent. A basic round-trip United States-to-Paris flight costs $700 to $1,100, depending on where you fly from and when. Always consider saving time and money in Europe by flying "open jaws" (into one city and out of another). Flying into Amsterdam and out of Paris costs roughly the same as flying round-trip to Paris. You can get cheaper round-trip flights to London or Amsterdam, but the cost of additional train tickets (to get you back to London or Amsterdam for your flight home) will eliminate most of your savings.

Surface Transportation: For a three-week whirlwind trip of our recommended destinations in France, allow $500 per person for public transportation (trains and key buses), or $650 per person (based on two people sharing) for a three-week car rental, tolls, gas, and insurance. Car rental is cheapest if arranged from the United States. Train passes are normally available only outside of Europe. You may save money by simply buying tickets as you go (see "Transportation," below).

Room and Board: You can thrive in France and the Low Countries on $60 a day per person for room and board (allow $70 a day for Paris). A $60-a-day budget allows $10 for lunch, $15 for dinner, and $35 for lodging (based on two people splitting the cost of a $70 double room that includes breakfast). That's doable. Students and tightwads do it on $35 to $40 ($20 per bed, $15–20 for meals and snacks). But budget sleeping and eating require the skills and information covered later in this chapter (and in far more depth in *Rick Steves' Europe Through the Back Door*).

Sightseeing and Entertainment: In big cities, figure $5 to $8 per major sight (Louvre-$8, Anne Frank House-$6), $2 for minor ones (climbing church towers), $10 for guided walks, and $25 for bus tours and splurge experiences (concerts in Paris' Sainte-Chapelle or the Chamonix gondola). An overall average of $15 a day works for most. Don't skimp here. After all, this category directly powers most of the experiences all the other expenses are designed to make possible.

Shopping and Miscellany: Figure $2 per ice-cream cone, coffee, or soft drink. Shopping can vary in cost from nearly nothing to a small fortune. Good budget travelers find that this category has little to do with assembling a trip full of lifelong and wonderful memories.

Prices, Times, and Discounts

The prices in this book, as well as the hours and telephone numbers, are accurate as of late 1999. Europe is always changing, and we know you'll understand that this, like any other guidebook, starts to yellow even before it's printed.

In Europe—and in this book—you'll be using the 24-hour clock. After 12:00 noon, keep going—13:00, 14:00, and so on.

For anything over 12, subtract 12 and add p.m. (for example, 14:00 is 2 p.m.).

This book lists spring, summer, and fall hours for sightseeing attractions. Off-season, expect generally shorter hours and more lunchtime breaks. Virtually all sights covered in this book remain open in winter.

While discounts for sights and transportation are not listed in this book, seniors (60 and over), students (with International Student Identification Cards), and youths (under 18) often get big discounts—but only by asking.

Exchange Rates
We've priced things in this book in the local currency:

About $1 equals...
6 French francs (F). One franc is worth about 17 cents.
40 Belgian francs (BF). One Belgian franc is worth less than 3 cents.
2 Dutch guilders (f). One guilder is worth about 50 cents.

To convert prices in francs into dollars divide by six (160F = about $27). To convert Belgian francs very roughly into dollars, knock off the last digit and divide the rest by four (235BF = about $6). For Dutch guilders, divide by two (f98 = about $50).

When to Go
Late spring and fall are best. Wildflowers proliferate in May and June, while September brings the grape harvest and drier weather. In late October France glistens in fall colors. Europeans vacation in July and August, jamming the Riviera and the Alps (August is worst), leaving the rest of the country reasonably tranquil. And while many French businesses close in August, the traveler hardly notices. Winter travel is OK—you'll find gray, generally mild weather in the south (unless the wind is blowing), cold weather in the north, and rain everywhere. While Holland is a festival of flowers in the spring, the Low Countries have considerably shorter summers and drearier winters than southern France. Sights and tourist information offices keep shorter hours, and some tourist activities (like English-language castle tours) vanish altogether.

Sightseeing Priorities
Depending on the length of your trip, here are our recommended priorities. The material in this book could keep you wonderfully entertained for a month in France, Belgium, and the Netherlands.

France:

3 days: Paris and maybe Versailles
5 days, add: Normandy
7 days, add: The Loire
10 days, add: Dordogne, Carcassonne
14 days, add: Provence, the Riviera
18 days, add: Burgundy, Chamonix
21 days, add: Alsace, Champagne

(This includes everything on the following three-week route to match the map on page 7.)

Belgium and the Netherlands: With cheap flights from the United States, minimal culture shock, almost no language barrier, and a super-well-organized tourist trade, the Low Countries are a good place to start a European trip.

2 days: Amsterdam, Haarlem
3–4 days, add: Bruges
5–6 days, add: Brussels
7 days, add: Side trips from Amsterdam
(e.g., Enkhuisen, The Hague)

Whirlwind (Kamikaze) Three-Week Tour of France by Car or Train

Day By Car

1 Fly into Paris, pick up car, visit Giverny and/or Rouen, overnight in Honfleur (save Paris sightseeing for end of trip).

2 9:00–Depart Honfleur, 10:00–Caen World War II Museum, 12:00–Drive to Arromanches for lunch and museum, 15:00–American cemetery, 16:00–Point du Hoc, 17:00–German cemetery, dinner and overnight in Bayeux.

3 9:00–Bayeux tapestry and church, 13:30–Mont St. Michel, 16:00–Drive to Dinan, 17:00–Arrive in Dinan for one Brittany stop, sleep in Dinan.

4 10:00–Depart Dinan and drive to Loire, 14:00–Tour Chambord, 17:00–Arrive in Amboise, sleep in Amboise.

5 8:45–Depart Amboise, 9:00–Chenonceau, 11:30–Cheverny château and lunch, 14:00–Possible stop in Chaumont, back in Amboise for Leonardo's house and free time in town, sleep in Amboise.

6 8:30–Depart Amboise, morning stop in Chauvigny, lunch at Mortemart, 13:30–Oradour-sur-Glane, 14:30–Drive to Beynac, 17:30–Wander Beynac or tour its castle, dinner and overnight in Beynac.

7 9:00–Browse the town and market of Sarlat, 12:00–Font de Gaume tour, 14:00–More caves, castles, or canoe extravaganza, dinner and sleep in Beynac.

8   9:00–Depart Beynac, 10:00–Short stop at Cahors bridge, 12:30–Arrive in Albi, couscous lunch, 14:00–Tour church and Toulouse-Lautrec Museum, 16:00–Depart for Carcassonne, 18:00–Explore, have dinner, and sleep in Carcassonne.

9   10:30–Depart Carcassonne, 11:00–Lastours castles or Minerve, 15:30–Pont du Gard, 16:30–Drive to Arles, 17:30–Set up for evening in Arles.

10   All day for Arles and Avignon, evening back in Arles.

11   8:30–Depart Arles, 9:00–Les Baux, 11:00–Depart Les Baux, 12:00–Lunch and wander in Isle sur la Sorgue, 14:00–Luberon hilltown drive, 16:00–Depart for the Riviera, 19:00–Arrive in Nice or Antibes.

12   Sightsee in Nice and Monaco, sleep in Nice or Antibes.

13   Morning free, 12:00–Drive north, sleep at Clelles.

14   Morning drive north, long stop in Annecy, in afternoon arrive in Chamonix. With clear weather do Aiguille du Midi.

15   All day for the Alps.

16   9:00–Depart Chamonix, 12:00–Lunch in Brancion, 14:00–Depart, 15:00–Arrive in Beaune for Hotel Dieu and wine tasting, sleep in Beaune.

17   9:00–Depart for Burgundy village treats or get to Alsace early. Arrive in Colmar after 3.5-hour drive.

18   9:00–Unterlinden Museum, 10:00–Free in town, 14:00–Wine Road villages, evening back in Colmar.

19   8:00–Depart Colmar, 12:00–Lunch, tour Verdun battlefield, 15:00–Depart, 16:00–Arrive Reims, church and champagne, 18:00–Turn in car at Reims, picnic dinner celebration on train, 21:00–Collapse in Paris hotel.

20   Sightsee Paris.

21   Sightsee Paris, tour over.

Day By Train and Bus

All times are approximate. Fewer buses and trains run on Sunday; be careful.

1   Fly into Paris, find your hotel, go for an afternoon walk.

2   All day to sightsee in Paris.

3   Head to Giverny in morning (about 8:00, depart Paris by train to Vernon, check bags at station, then bus or taxi to Giverny), early afternoon train to Rouen (check bags at station), sightsee there, then head to Honfleur (from Rouen take late afternoon train to Le Havre—about 16:15—then catch bus to Honfleur—about 17:30), sleep in Honfleur.

4   Morning in Honfleur, midday bus to Caen, then train to Bayeux, see tapestries in the afternoon (or visit the World War II museum in Caen and take a later train to Bayeux), sleep in Bayeux.

5   All day for D-day beaches by minivan excursion or day car

Whirlwind Three-Week Tour of France

rental (or split day between D-day beaches and tapestries), late afternoon train (about 17:00) to Pontorson, taxi to Mont St. Michel, sleep on Mont St. Michel, tour abbey at night (sound-and-light show).

6 Early morning walk around the island, 9:00–Bus to Pontorson, about 10:00–Train to Caen, transfer there to Tours, transfer there to Amboise, sleep in Amboise.

7 All day to tour the Loire by minivan excursion, bike, or day car rental, sleep in Amboise.

8 Early morning train to Sarlat (with transfers at Tours and Bordeaux St. Jean), afternoon walking tour of Sarlat, sleep in Sarlat or Beynac (note: it's possible to visit Oradour sur Glane on this day; see Sarlat and Amboise "Transportation Connections").

9 All day in the Dordogne, morning train to Les Eyzies (Grotte de Font de de Gaume), taxi back, afternoon canoe trip, sleep in Sarlat or Beynac.

10 Morning train to Carcassonne (transfer in Souillac or Bordeaux and in Toulouse), afternoon wall walk, sleep in Carcassonne.

11 Morning train to Arles, sleep in Arles.

12 Morning train to Nîmes, late morning bus to Pont du Gard (about 11:00), early afternoon bus from Pont du Gard to Avignon (about 13:30), afternoon in Avignon, evening train back to Arles, sleep in Arles.

13 Morning bus to Les Baux (about 8:30), midday return to Arles, afternoon train to Nice, stroll the promenade, sleep on the Riviera.

14 Morning in Nice's old city, then bus to Monaco, see changing of the guard and casino, return to Nice for beach time or Chagall museum, sleep in Nice.

16 Choose between urban or rural: Morning train to Lyon, visit Lyon, sleep there. Or take the scenic train to Digne/Grenoble and sleep in a remote mountain village en route (see "Transportation Connections—Nice").

17 Morning in Lyon, midday train to Annecy, visit Annecy, late afternoon train to Chamonix, sleep in Chamonix. Or train from your remote village to Grenoble and Annecy (visit if time allows), then train to Chamonix.

18 All day to hike in the Alps, sleep in Chamonix.

19 Train to Colmar, sleep in Colmar.

20 All day in Alsace, sleep in Colmar (or evening train to Paris if you must leave the next day).

21 Train to Paris.

Red Tape and Business Hours

You need a passport but no visa or shots to travel in France, Belgium, and the Netherlands.

You'll find much of rural France closed weekdays from 12:00 to 14:00 (lunch is sacred). On Sunday most French businesses are closed (family is sacred), though small markets such as *boulangeries* (bakeries) are open Sunday morning until 12:00, and museums are open all day. On Mondays many businesses are closed until 14:00 and often all day. Saturdays are like weekdays. Beware: Many sights stop admitting people 30 to 60 minutes before they close.

PTT (Postal, Telegraph, and Telephone) offices' hours vary, though most are open weekdays from 8:00 to 19:00 and Saturday from 8:00 to 12:00. (Small-town PTTs close for lunch 12:00–14:00.) Stamps and phone cards are also sold at the *tabac* (tobacco shop). It costs 4.40F to mail a postard to the United States.

Banking

Bring your ATM, credit, or debit card and some traveler's checks in dollars. Listed hotels rarely accept American Express.

The best and easiest way to get cash in French francs is to use the omnipresent French bank machines (always open, lower fees, quick processing; you'll need a four-digit PIN—numbers only, no letters—with your Visa or MasterCard). Some ATM bankcards will work at some banks, though Visa and MasterCard are more reliable. Before you go, verify with your bank that your card will work. Bring two cards; demagnetization seems to be a common problem. "Cash machine" in French is "*distributeur automatique des billets*," or *D.A.B.* (day-ah-bay).

Regular banks have the best rates for cashing traveler's checks. For a large exchange it pays to compare rates and fees. The Bank of France (Banque de France) offers the best rates but is generally located only in larger cities. French banking hours vary, though most are open Tuesday through Friday from 9:00 to 16:30. Some branches open Saturday morning, and many are closed on Monday. Post offices, train stations, and tourist offices usually change money if you can't get to a bank. Post offices (which take cash or American Express traveler's checks) give a fair rate, have longer hours, and charge no fee. Don't be petty about changing traveler's checks. The greatest avoidable money-changing expense is having to waste time every few days returning to a bank. Change 10 days' or two weeks' worth of money, get big bills, stuff them in your money belt, and travel!

Just like at home, credit (or debit) cards work easily at hotels, restaurants, and shops, but small businesses (like bed-and-breakfasts) accept payment only in local currency. Smart travelers function with hard local cash.

The Language Barrier

You've no doubt heard that the French are "mean and cold and refuse to speak English." This is an out-of-date preconception left over from the de Gaulle days. The French are as friendly as any other people. Parisians are no more disagreeable than New Yorkers. And, without any doubt, the French speak more English than Americans speak French. Be reasonable in your expectations: Waiters are paid to be efficient, not chatty. And small-town French postal clerks are every bit as speedy, cheery, and multilingual as ours are back home.

With an understanding of French culture, you're less likely to misinterpret the French people. The French take great pride in their culture, clinging to their belief in cultural superiority despite the fact that they're no longer a world superpower. Let's face it—it's tough to keep on smiling when you've been crushed by a Big Mac, lashed by Levis, and drowned in instant coffee. To the French, Americans must seem a lot like Ross Perot in a good mood. The French are cold only if you decide to see them that way. Polite and formal, they respect the fine points of culture. In France, strolling down the street with a big grin on your face is a sign of senility, not friend-liness (seriously). The French think that Americans, while friendly, are hesitant to pursue more serious friendships. Recognize sincerity and look for kindness. Give the French the benefit of the doubt.

Communication difficulties in France are exaggerated. To hurdle the language barrier, bring a small English/French dictio-nary, a phrase book (look for ours), a menu reader, and a good supply of patience. If you learn only five phrases, learn and use these: *bonjour* (good day), *pardon* (pardon me), *s'il vous plaît* (please), *merci* (thank you), and *au revoir* (goodbye). The French place great importance on politeness.

The French are language perfectionists—they take their language (and other languages) seriously. Often they speak more English than they let on. This isn't a tourist-baiting tactic but is timidity on their part to speak another language less than fluently. Start any conversation with *"Bonjour, madame/monsieur. Parlez-vous anglais?"* and hope they speak more English than you speak French. In transactions, a small notepad and pen minimize misunderstand-ings about prices—have vendors write the price down.

In Belgium and the Netherlands, forget the language barrier. Except in smaller, untouristy towns, most young or well-educated people speak English (along with other languages). In southern Belgium, French is foremost; in northern Belgium and the Netherlands it's Dutch, but English is a close second.

Travel Smart

Upon arrival in a new town, lay the groundwork for a smooth depar-ture. Reread this book as you travel and visit local tourist informa-tion offices. Buy a phone card and use it for reservations and confirmations. Begin every encounter with *"Bonjour madame/mon-sieur"* and end every encounter with *"Au revoir madame/monsieur."* Enjoy the friendliness of the local people. Ask questions. Most locals are eager to tell you about their town's history and point you in their idea of the right direction. Wear your money belt and see simplicity as a virtue. Those who expect to travel smart, do. Plan ahead for banking, laundry, post office chores, picnics, and Sundays (particu-larly if traveling by train). Train travelers should read the tips on trains and buses later in this chapter; drivers should read our driving tips and study the examples of road signs in this chapter. Everyone should maximize rootedness by minimizing one-night stands. Mix intense and relaxed periods. Every trip (and every traveler) needs at least a few slack days. Pace yourself. Assume you will return.

As you read through this book, note special days (festivals, market days, and days when sights are closed). Sundays have pros and cons, as they do for travelers in the United States (special events and weekly markets, limited hours, shops and banks closed, limited public transportation, no rush hours). Saturdays are virtu-

ally weekdays. Popular places are even more popular on wee~
and inundated on three-day weekends (most common in May).

Tourist Information

The tourist information office is your best first stop in any new
city. If you're arriving in town after the office closes, try calling
ahead or picking up a map in a neighboring town. In this book we
refer to tourist offices as TIs (for Tourist Information). Throughout France and the Low Countries you'll find TIs are usually well
organized and have English-speaking staffs. Most will help you
find a room by calling hotels (for a small fee) or giving you a complete listing of available bed-and-breakfasts. Towns with a lot
of tourism generally have English-speaking guides available for
private hire (about $100 for a 90-minute guided town walk).

The French call their TIs by different names. Office de
Tourisme and Bureau de Tourisme are used in cities, while
Syndicat d'Initiative or Information Touristique are used in small
towns. French TIs are often closed from 12:00 to 14:00.

Tourist Offices, U.S. Addresses

Each country's national tourist office in the United States is a
wealth of information. Before your trip, request any specific
information you may want (such as city maps and schedules of
upcoming festivals). The Web offers much more information for
travelers adept in cyberspace (note Web site info below).

French Tourist Office: For information, call 410/286-8310
or write to the nearest office: 444 Madison Avenue, 16th floor,
New York, NY 10022; 676 North Michigan Avenue #600,
Chicago, IL 60611; 9454 Wilshire Boulevard, #715, Beverly Hills,
CA 90212. www.francetourism.com. For the latest on Paris, log on
to www.pariscope.fr/.

Belgian National Tourist Office: 780 Third Avenue, #1501,
New York, NY 10017, tel. 212/758-8130, fax 212/355-7675,
www.visitbelgium.com. Good country map.

Netherlands National Tourist Office: 225 North Michigan
Avenue, #1854, Chicago, IL 60601, tel. 888/GO-HOLLAND
(automated) or 312/819-1500 (live), fax 312/819-1740, www
.goholland.com. Send a $3 check to receive information within
one week (call first to request). Great country map.

Recommended Guidebooks

Consider some supplemental travel information, especially if you're
traveling beyond our recommended destinations. Considering the
improvements they'll make in your $3,000 vacation, $25 or $35 for
extra maps and books is money well spent. One simple budget tip
can easily save the price of an extra guidebook.

France: Lonely Planet's *France* is well researched and packed with good maps and hotel recommendations for low- to moderate-budget travelers but is not updated annually. The highly opinion-ated, annually updated *Let's Go: France* (St. Martin's Press) is great for students and vagabonds. The popular skinny green Michelin guides are dry but informative, especially if you're driving. They're known for their city and sightseeing maps and for their concise and helpful information on all major sights. English editions, covering most of the regions you'll want to visit, are sold in France for about $12 (or $20 in the United States). Consider another of our recent books, *Rick Steves' Paris* (see below). Of the multitude of other guidebooks on France and Paris, many are high on facts and low on opinion, guts, or personality. For background reading, consider *French or Foe* (by Polly Platt), *Fragile Glory* (by Richard Bernstein), and *The Course of French History* (by Pierre Gourbet).

Belgium and the Netherlands: For the same reason that this region only appears as an add-on to our France book, the Low Countries seem to fall through the cracks in most travel publishers' catalogs. You'll find skimpy chapters in the big all-Europe books or too much information in the various city or country guidebooks covering the region.

Rick Steves' Books and Videos

Rick Steves' Europe Through the Back Door 2000 (John Muir Publications) gives you budget travel tips on minimizing jet lag, packing light, planning your itinerary, traveling by car or train, finding budget beds without reservations, changing money, avoiding rip-offs, outsmarting thieves, hurdling the language barrier, staying healthy, taking great photographs, using your bidet, and lots more. The book also includes chapters on 34 of Rick's favorite "Back Doors."

Rick Steves' Country Guides are a series of seven guide-books—including this book—covering Europe; Britain and Ireland; Germany, Austria, and Switzerland; Italy; Scandinavia; and Spain and Portugal. All are updated annually and come out in January.

Rick Steves' City Guides feature Paris, London, and Rome. These easy-to-read, annually updated guides offer thorough cover-age of the best of these grand cities. Enjoy self-guided, illustrated tours of the top sights, with a focus on the great art.

Europe 101: History and Art for the Traveler (cowritten with Gene Openshaw, John Muir Publications, 1996) gives you the story of Europe's people, history, and art. Written for smart people who were sleeping in their history and art classes before they knew they were going to Europe, *101* really helps Europe's sights come alive.

Rick Steves' Mona Winks (also cowritten with Gene Openshaw, John Muir Publications, 1998) gives you fun, easy-to-follow self-guided tours of Europe's top 20 museums, including Amsterdam's Rijksmuseum and Van Gogh Museum and Paris' Louvre, Orsay, and Palace of Versailles, and a walk through historic Paris.

My rigorously researched *Rick Steves' French Phr*
Muir Publications, 1999) gives you the words and sur
you'll need while traveling in France and much of Belgium.

My television series, *Travels in Europe with Rick Steves*,
includes 10 half-hour shows on France, Belgium, and the Netherlands. A new series of 13 shows—including one on Paris—airs in
2000, and earlier shows are still airing on both public television
and the Travel Channel. They're also available as information-
packed videotapes along with my two-hour slideshow lecture on
France (call us at 425/771-8303 for our free newsletter/catalog).

Rick Steves' Postcards from Europe (John Muir Publications,
1999), my autobiographical book, packs more than 25 years of
travel anecdotes and insights into the ultimate European adventure.
Through my guidebooks, I share my favorite European discoveries
with you. *Postcards* introduces you to my favorite European friends.

Maps

The maps in this book, drawn by Dave Hoerlein, are concise and
simple. Dave, who is well traveled in France and the Low Countries,
has designed the maps to help you locate recommended places and
get to the TIs, where you'll find more in-depth maps (often free) of
the cities or regions. For ease of navigation in France, keep in mind
that a *rue* is a street, a *place* is a square, and a *pont* is a bridge.

Don't skimp on maps. Excellent Michelin maps are available
throughout France at bookstores, newsstands, and gas stations (for
26F, half the U.S. price). Train travelers can do fine with Michelin's #989 France map (1:1,000,000). For serious navigation, pick
up the yellow 1:200,000-scale maps as you travel. Drivers should
consider the soft-cover Michelin France atlas (the entire country
at 1:200,000, well organized in a $20 book with an index and maps
of major cities). Learn the Michelin key to get the most sightseeing value out of their maps.

Transportation

By Car or Train?

Cars are best for three or more traveling together (especially
families with small kids), those packing heavy, and those scouring
the countryside. Trains and buses are best for solo travelers, blitz
tourists, and city-to-city travelers. We have significantly improved
information for train travelers in this edition.

Trains

Train stations are almost always centrally located in cities, making
hotel hunting and sightseeing easier. Schedules change by season,
weekday, and weekend. Verify train schedules shown in this book
(to study ahead on the Web: http://bahn.hafas.de/english).

The French Rail System

France's rail system (SNCF) sets the pace in Europe. Its super TGV system has inspired bullet trains throughout the world. The TGV runs at 170 to 220 mph. Its rails are fused into one long, continuous track for a faster and smoother ride. The TGV has changed commuting patterns in much of France and put most of the country within day-trip distance of Paris. The Eurostar English Channel tunnel train to Britain and the new Thalys bullet train to Brussels are two more links in the grand European train system of the 21st century.

While Eurailpasses and Europasses work well, those traveling solely within France will save money with a France Railpass (available outside of France only, through your travel agent or Europe Through the Back Door; call us at 425/771-8303 to get our free railpass guide or download it at www.ricksteves.com). For about the cost of a Paris–Avignon–Paris ticket, the France Railpass offers three days of travel (within a month) anywhere in France. You can add up to six additional days for the cost of a two-hour ride each.

(The Flexi Saver gives two traveling together a 25 perc
count.) Each day of use allows you to take as many trip:
want in a 24-hour period (you could go from Paris to Cnartres, see
the cathedral, then continue to Avignon, stay a few hours, and end
in Nice). Buy second-class tickets in France for shorter trips and
spend your valuable railpass days wisely.

If traveling sans railpass, inquire about the many point-to-
point discount fares possible (for youths, those over 60, married
couples, families, travel during off-peak hours, and more).

Reservations are generally unnecessary for local trains but are
required for any TGV train (generally 20–60F) and for *couchettes*
(berths, 100F) on night trains. Even railpass holders need reservations for the TGV trains. To avoid the more expensive reservation
fees, avoid traveling at peak times; ask at the station. Validate (*com-
poster*) all train tickets and reservations in the orange machines
located before the platforms. (Watch others and imitate.)

Cars, Rail 'n' Drive Passes, and Buses

Car rental is cheapest if arranged in advance through your hometown travel agent. The best rates are weekly with unlimited
mileage or leasing (see below). You can pick up and drop off just
about anywhere, anytime. Big companies have offices in most
cities. Small rental companies can be cheaper but aren't as flexible.

When you drive a rental car you are liable for its replacement
value. CDW (Collision-Damage Waiver) insurance gives you the
peace of mind that comes with a zero- or low-deductible coverage
for about $15 a day. A few "gold" credit cards provide this cover-
age for free if you use their card for the rental; quiz your credit-
card company on the worst-case scenario. Or consider the $6/day
policy offered by Travel Guard (U.S. tel. 800/826-1300).

For a trip of three weeks or more, leasing is a bargain. By
technically buying and then selling back the car, you save lots of
money on tax and insurance (CDW is included). Leasing, which
you should arrange from the United States, usually requires a
22-day minimum contract, but Europe by Car leases cars in
France for as few as 17 days for $500 (U.S. tel. 800/223-1516).

You can rent a car on the spot just about anywhere. In many
cases this is a worthwhile splurge. All you need is your American
driver's license and money (about 330F, or $60, for a day, with
100 kilometers included).

In the Netherlands, Campanje rents and sells used VW
campers fully loaded for camping through Europe. Rates vary from
$500 to $600 per week (less for long-term rentals), including tax and
insurance. (For a brochure, write P.O. Box 9332, 3506 GH Utrecht,
Netherlands; tel. 31/30-244-7070, fax 31/30-242-0981, e-mail: cam-
panje@xs4all.nl). They have a creative program offering short-term,
long-term, camping-gear-inclusive, rental, and buy/sell-back deals.

Cost of Public Transportation

2000 FRANCE FLEXIPASS

	1st class	2nd class
Any 3 days in a month*	$210	$180
France Flexi Saver**	171	146
Any 4 days in 2 months Youth (2nd cl)***		164

*Extra days $30 (6 max). Kids 4-11: half fare.

**3 days in a month, per person for 2 or more people traveling together on all journeys (no kids discounts). Extra days $30 (6 max).

***Must be under age 26. Extra days $20 (6 max).

1999 FRANCE RAIL & DRIVE PASS
(2000 prices may vary)

Any 3 days of rail and 2 days of Avis rental car in a month.

Car category	1st class	2nd class	Extra car day
Economy	$204	$187	$50
Compact	232	214	75
Intermediate	249	232	95
Small automatic	247	232	89

Rail & Drive prices are approximate per person, two traveling together. Solo travelers pay about $100 extra, 3rd & 4th members of a group need only buy the equivalent flexi railpass. Extra rail days (6 max) cost $30 per day for first or second class. You can add up to 6 extra car days.

France: The map shows approximate point-to-point one-way 2nd-class rail fares in $US. Add up fares for your itinerary to see whether a railpass will save you money.

Note: For a France Flexipass order form, or for Rick's Railpass Guide, visit www.ricksteves.com or call us at 425/771-8303. To order France Rail & Drive passes, call your travel agent or Rail Europe at 800/438-7245.

Rail 'n' drive passes let you economically mix car and train travel (available outside of France only, from your travel agent). Generally, big-city connections are best done by train, and rural regions are best scoured with the freewheeling mobility of a car. With a rail 'n' drive pass you get an economic "flexi" railpass and the chance to add on a few "flexi" car days at the cheaper weekly rate rather than the budget-busting daily rate. This allows you to combine rail and drive into one pass—you can take advantage of the high speed and comfort of the TGV trains for longer trips and rent a car for as little as one day at a time for those regions that are difficult to get around in without a car (like the Loire, the Dordogne, and Provence), all for a very reasonable package price. Within the same country, you can pick a car up in one city and drop it off in another city with no problem. While you're only required to reserve the first car day, it's safer to reserve all days, as cars are not always available on short notice.

Another good car/train solution is combining a one-way car rental from Paris to Nice (seeing Normandy, the Loire, the Dordogne, Carcassonne, and Provence) with, if you have more time, a return to Paris with a railpass (via Chamonix, Burgundy,

Train Tips

- Arrive at the station with plenty of time before your departure to find the right platform, confirm connections, and so on.
- Always check schedules in advance for the next few days of your trip; don't leave a station without knowing departure possibilities. Large stations have a separate information window or office; at small stations, the regular ticket office gives information. Ask for departures near the time you want to go (i.e., day of the week, morning or afternoon) and they'll give you a printout of your options.
- Write the date on your "flexi" pass each day you travel.
- Validate tickets (not passes) and reservations in orange machines before boarding. If you're traveling with a pass and have a reservation for a particular trip (e.g., TGV), you must validate the reservation.
- When getting on a train, confirm that it's going where you think it is. For example, ask the conductor or any local passenger on the platform, "Ah Bayeux?" (To Bayeux?).
- Some trains split cars en route. Make sure your train car is continuing to your destination by asking, "Set vwa-ture vah ah Bayeux?" ("This car goes to Bayeux?").
- If a seat is reserved, it will be labeled *réservé*, with the cities to and from which it is reserved.
- Verify with the conductor all transfers you must make ("Correspondance ah?" means "Transfer where?").
- To guard against theft, keep your bags right overhead; don't store them on the racks at the end of the car.
- Note your arrival time so you'll be ready to get off.
- Use the trains' free WCs before you get off (a bird in the hand).

Bus Tips

- Wednesday bus schedules are often different during the school year; remember to double-check schedules if you're taking a bus on Wednesday. Year-round, service is sparse on Sunday.
- Be at stops five minutes ahead of time. Buses can be early.
- On schedules, *"en semaine"* means Monday through Saturday.

Key Phrases

- *Bonjour, monsieur/madame, parlez vous anglais?* Phonetics: bohn-zhoor, muhs-yur/mah-dahm, par-lay-voo ahn-glay? Meaning: Hello, sir/madame, do you speak English?
- *Je voudrais un depart pour* ___ (destination), *pour le* ___ (date), *vers* ___ (general time of day), *la plus direct possible*. Phonetics: zhuh voo-dray day-par poor ___ (destination), poor luh ___ (date), vayr ___ (time), lah ploo dee-rek poh-see-bluh. Meaning/Example: I would like a departure for Amboise, on 23 May, about 9:00, the most direct way possible.

). This allows you to take advantage of weekly car-
~~r~~ the parts of France most deserving of a car) and
~~France's cheap~~ railpass deals.

Regional buses take over where the trains stop. You can get
almost anywhere by rail and bus if you're well organized and
patient. Review our bus schedule information and always verify
times at the tourist office or bus station, calling ahead when possible. A few bus lines are run by SNCF (France's rail system) and
are included with your railpass, but most bus lines are independent
of the rail system and are not covered by railpasses. Train stations
often have bus information where train-to-bus connections are
important—and vice versa for bus companies. On Sunday regional
bus service virtually disappears.

Regional minivan excursions offer organized day tours of
regions where bus and train service is virtually useless. For the
Dday beaches, châteaus of the Loire Valley, sightseeing in the
Dordogne Valley, and wine tasting in Burgundy, we identify small
companies providing this extraordinarily helpful service at reasonable rates. Some of these minivan excursions offer just transportation between the sights; others add a running commentary and
regional history.

Driving

The hardest thing about driving in France is not stopping at every
mouthwatering bakery and *pâtisserie* you pass.

An international driver's license is not necessary. Seat belts
are mandatory, and children under age 10 must be in the back
seat. Gas is expensive: over $4 per gallon. It's most expensive on
autoroutes (you'll save about $4 a tank by filling up at a supermar-
ket). Many gas stations close on Sunday.

Go metric. A liter is about a quart, four to a gallon. A kilometer is six-tenths of a mile. I figure kilometers to miles by cutting
them in half and adding back 10 percent of the original (120 km:
60 + 12 = 72 miles, 300 km: 150 + 30 = 180 miles).

Four hours of autoroute tolls cost about $20, but the alterna-
tive to these super "feeways" is often being marooned in rural
traffic. Autoroutes usually save enough time, gas, and nausea to
justify the splurge. Mix scenic country-road rambling with high-
speed "autorouting."

Roads in France are classified into departmental (D), national
(N), and autoroutes (A). D routes (usually yellow lines on maps)
are slow and often the most scenic. N routes (usually red lines) are
the fastest after autoroutes (orange lines). Green road signs are for
national routes; blue are for autoroutes. There are plenty of good
facilities, gas stations, and rest stops along most French roads.

Here are a few French road tips: In city centers, traffic merg-
ing from the right normally has the right of way (*priorité à droite*).

Standard European Road Signs

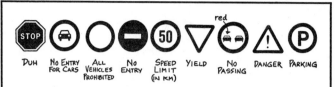

| STOP | No Entry For Cars | All Vehicles Prohibited | No Entry | Speed Limit (in km) | Yield | No Passing | Danger | Parking |

Approach intersections cautiously. When navigating through cities, stow the map and follow the signs to *centre-ville* (downtown) and from there to the tourist information office. When leaving (or just passing through), follow the *Toutes Directions* or *Autres Directions* (meaning anywhere else) signs until you see a sign for your specific destination. Be careful of sluggish tractors on country roads. While the French are eating (12:00–14:00), many sights (and gas stations) are closed, so you can make great time driving. The French drive fast and love to tailgate.

Parking is a headache in the larger cities, and theft is a problem throughout France. Ask your hotelier for ideas, and pay to park at well-patrolled lots or use the parking meters, which are usually free 12:30 to 14:00 and 19:00 to 9:00 and in August. Keep a pile of 1F and 2F coins in your ashtray for parking meters, public restrooms, and Laundromat dryers.

Biking
Throughout France and the Low Countries you'll find areas where public transportation is limited and bicycle touring is an excellent idea. We've listed bike-rental shops where appropriate. The TI will always have addresses. For a good touring bike, allow about $12 for a half day and $18 for a full day. You're always better off paying a bit more for better equipment; generally the best is available through bike shops, not at TIs or train stations. Before committing to an extensive ride, think how long it's been since you've spent all day on a bike. It can make sense to start with an easy ride.

Telephones and Mail
An efficient card-operated system has virtually replaced coin-operated public phones throughout Europe. Each country offers phone cards good for use only in telephones within its borders (though you can use it for international calls). Insert the card in the phone and dial away.

France: Buy a phone card (*une télécarte*) from any post office or train station or from most newsstands and tobacco shops (*tabac*). There are two denominations of phone cards in France: *Une petite* costs 42F; *une grande* is 98F. When you use the *télécarte* (simply take the phone off the hook, insert the card, and wait for a dial tone) the price of the call (local or international) is automatically deducted. Buy a *télécarte* at the beginning of your trip and use it for hotel reservations, calling TIs, and phoning home. France's newest phone card (KOSMOS) is not inserted into the phone but allows you to dial from the comfort of your hotel (or anywhere) and charge the call to the card for lower rates than with a *télécarte*. It's simple to use, instructions are provided in English, and the card is sold wherever *télécartes* are sold. And while per-minute rates are cheaper with KOSMOS than a *télécarte*, it's slower to use (more numbers to dial), so local calls are quicker with a *télécarte* from a phone booth.

Despite the expense, some travelers prefer to use American calling cards (AT&T, MCI, and Sprint numbers listed in Appendix). Calling-card calls were a fine deal until direct-dial rates were cut in half. Now it's cheaper to make your international calls using a European phone card (French or KOSMOS, Belgian, or Dutch). Definitely avoid using your calling card for calls between European countries; it's far cheaper to call direct.

France has a dial-direct 10-digit telephone system. There are no area codes. To call to or from anywhere in France, including Paris, you dial the 10 numbers directly. To dial out of France you must start your call with its international code: 00. To call France from another country, start with the international access code of the country you're calling from (00 for European countries and 011 from the United States and Canada), dial France's country code (33), and then drop the initial zero of the 10-digit local number and dial the remaining nine digits. For example, the phone number of one of our favorite hotels in Paris is 01 47 05 49 15. To call it from home, dial 011-33-1 47 05 49 15. For a list of international access codes and country codes, see the Appendix. European time is six/nine hours ahead of the east/west coast of the United States.

Belgium and the Netherlands: Both countries use area codes throughout. For instance, Bruges' area code is 050. To call Bruges long distance from within Belgium, dial 050 then the local number. When calling from another country, drop the first zero in the area code. Calling Bruges from Amsterdam, you'd dial 00 (the Netherlands' international access code), 32 (Belgium's country code), 50 (Bruges' area code without the zero), then the local number.

Mail: To arrange for mail delivery, reserve a few hotels along your route in advance and give their addresses to friends or you can use American Express Company's mail services (available to anyone who has at least one American Express traveler's check). Allow 10 days for a letter to arrive. Phoning is so easy that we've dispensed with mail stops altogether.

Sleeping

In France and the Low Countries, accommodations are a good value and easy to find. Choose from one- or two-star hotels, bed-and-breakfasts, hostels, and campgrounds. We like places that are clean, small, central, traditional, inexpensive, friendly, and not listed in other guidebooks. Most places we list have at least five of these seven virtues.

Hotels

In this book the price for a double room will normally range from $30 (very simple, toilet and shower down the hall) to $140 (maximum plumbing and more), with most clustering around $60. Rates are higher in Paris and other popular cities. A triple and a double are often the same room, with a small double bed and a sliver single, so a third person sleeps very cheaply. Most hotels have a few singles, triples, and quads. While groups sleep cheap, traveling alone can be expensive—a single room usually costs about the same as a double.

French receptionists are often reluctant to mention the cheaper rooms. Study the room price list posted at the desk. Understand it. You'll save an average of $15 if you get a room with a shower "down the hall" rather than in your room; ask for a room without a shower (*sans douche*) rather than with a shower (*avec douche*). A room with a bathtub (*salle de bain*) costs $5 to $10 more than a room with a shower (*douche*) and is generally larger. A double bed (*grand lit*) is $5 to $10 cheaper than twins (*deux petits lits*), though rooms with twin beds tend to be larger and French double beds are generally smaller than American double beds. Queen-size beds are rare. Hotels often have more rooms with tubs than showers and are inclined to give you a room with a tub (which the French prefer). If you prefer a double bed and a shower, you need to ask for it—and you'll save up to $20. If you'll take twins or a double, ask for a *chambre pour deux* (room for two) to avoid being needlessly turned away.

The French have a simple hotel rating system (zero through four stars) that depends on the amenities offered. We like the one- or two-star hotels and the occasional three-star hotel. More than two stars generally gets you expensive and unnecessary amenities. Unclassified hotels (no stars) can be bargains or depressing dumps. Look before you leap and lay before you pay (upon departure). You'll almost always have the option of breakfast at your hotel, which is pleasant and convenient, but paying an average of 35F for coffee, croissant, and bread is not a great value. Some hotels now offer a buffet breakfast (about 50F), adding cereals, fruit, cheese, and yogurt alongside the bread and croissants; while it's more than you'd pay at home, this seems a better value and a good way to start the day. While hotels hope you'll spring for their

Sleep Code

To give maximum information in a minimum of space, we use these codes to describe accommodations listed in this book. Prices listed are per room, not per person.

S = Single room (or price for one person in a double).

D = Double or Twin. French double beds can be very small.

T = Triple (generally a double bed with a single).

Q = Quad (usually two double beds).

b = Private bathroom with toilet and shower or tub.

t = Private toilet only. (The shower is down the hall.)

s = Private shower or tub only. (The toilet is down the hall.)

CC = Accepts credit cards (Visa, MasterCard, American Express). If CC isn't mentioned, assume you'll need to pay cash.

SE = Speaks English. This code is used only when it seems predictable that you'll encounter English-speaking staff.

NSE = Does not speak English. Used only when it's unlikely you'll encounter English-speaking staff.

* = French hotel rating system, ranging from zero to four stars.

According to this code, a couple staying at a "Db-450F, CC:V, SE" hotel would pay a total of 275 French francs (or about $75) for a double room with a private bathroom. The hotel accepts Visa or French cash in payment, and the staff speaks English.

breakfast, this is optional unless otherwise noted. Many travelers enjoy their coffee and croissant for less at the corner café.

Many traditional French hotels strongly encourage their peak-season guests to take half-pension; that is, breakfast and either lunch or dinner. By law, they can't require you to take half-pension unless you are staying three or more nights, but in effect, many do. While the food is usually good, it limits your ability to shop around. We've indicated where we think *demi-pension* (half-pension) is a good value. The yellow *logis de France* sign posted at the door indicates a particularly good value.

France is littered with inexpensive, sterile, ultramodern hotels, usually located on cheap land just outside of town, providing drivers with low-stress accommodations. The antiseptically clean and cheap Formule 1 chain (140–220F per room for up to 3 people) and the

more hotelesque IBIS hotels (330–400F for a double) are 1
ular. While far from quaint, these can be a fine value.

Rooms are safe. Still, keep cameras and money out of sight.
Towels aren't routinely replaced every day; drip-dry and conserve.
If that French Lincoln-log pillow isn't your idea of comfort,
American-style pillows (and extra blankets) are usually in the closet
or available on request. For a pillow, ask for *"un oreiller, s'il vous
plaît"* (un oar-ray-yay, see-voo-play).

Making Reservations

It's possible to travel at any time of year without reservations, but
given the high stakes, erratic accommodations values, and the quality of the gems we've found for this book, we'd highly recommend
calling ahead for rooms several days in advance as you travel.

If you know exactly which dates you need and really want a
particular place, reserve a room well in advance before you leave
home. This is especially important for Paris, which can be jammed
during conventions (May, June, September, and October are worst).

When tourist crowds are down, you might make a habit of
calling between 10:00 and 11:00 on the day you plan to arrive,
when the hotelier knows who'll be checking out and just which
rooms will be available. We've taken great pains to list telephone
numbers with long-distance instructions (see "Telephones and
Mail," above, and the Appendix). Use the telephone and convenient phone cards. Most hotels listed are accustomed to English-
only speakers. A hotel receptionist will trust you and hold a room
until 16:00 without a deposit, though some will ask for a credit-
card number. *Please honor (or cancel by phone) your reservations.*
These family-run businesses lose money if they turn away customers while holding a room for someone who doesn't show up.
Long distance is cheap and easy from public phone booths. Don't
let these people down—we promised you'd call and cancel if for
some reason you won't show up. Don't needlessly confirm rooms
through the tourist office; they'll take a commission.

To reserve from home, call, fax, e-mail, or write the hotel.
Phone and fax costs are reasonable, e-mail costs are a steal, and
simple English is usually fine. To fax, use the form in the Appendix (online at www.ricksteves.com/reservation). If you're writing a
letter, add the zip code and confirm the need and method for a
deposit. A two-night stay in August would be "two nights, 16/8/00
to 18/8/00"—Europeans write the date as day/month/year, and
European hotel jargon uses your day of departure. You'll often
receive a letter back requesting one night's deposit. A credit card
will usually be accepted as a deposit, though you may need to send
a signed traveler's check or a bank draft in the local currency.
If you give your credit-card number for the deposit, the hotel
may bill one night's stay to your card (most let you know this in

advance). Don't give your credit card number as a deposit unless you're sure you want to stay there on the dates you requested. If you don't show up, you'll be billed for one night, and if you cancel in advance, you may not receive your entire deposit back. Reconfirm your reservations a few days in advance for safety.

Bed-and-Breakfasts

B&Bs offer double the cultural intimacy for a good deal less than most hotel rooms. TIs have listings for each town.

France: *Chambres d'hôte* (CH) are found mainly in the smaller towns and the countryside. They are listed by the owner's family name. While some post small *"Chambres"* or *"Chambres d'hôte"* signs in their front windows, many are found only through the local tourist office. We list reliable CHs that offer a good value and/or unique experience (such as CHs in renovated mills, châteaus, and wine *domaines*). Doubles with breakfast cost around 200F (breakfast may or may not be included—ask), though the truly exceptional ones will run twice that. This is a great way to get beneath the surface with French locals. While your hosts will rarely speak English, they will almost always be enthusiastic and a delight to share a home with.

Belgium and the Netherlands: B&Bs in the Low Countries are common in well-touristed areas. Hosts are usually English-speaking and interesting conversationalists. Local TIs can book you into a B&B much cheaper than a hotel (though it's even cheaper to use our B&B listings and book direct). B&Bs are more important for budget travelers here than in France.

Hostels

Hostels charge about $14 per bed. Get a hostel card before you go (Hostelling International, tel. 202/783-6161, www.hiayh.org). Travelers of any age are welcome if they don't mind dorm-style accommodations or meeting other travelers. Travelers without a hostel card can generally spend the night for a small extra "one-night membership" fee. Cheap meals are sometimes available, and kitchen facilities are usually provided for do-it-yourselfers. Expect youth groups in spring, crowds in the summer, snoring, and incredible variabiliy in quality from one hostel to the next. Family rooms are sometimes available on request, but it's basically boys' dorms and girls' dorms. You usually can't check in before 17:00 and must be out by 10:00. There is often a 23:00 curfew. Official hostels are marked with a triangular sign that shows a house and a tree. In France ask for an *auberge de jeunesse*.

Camping

In Europe camping is more of a social than an environmental experience. It's a great way for American travelers to make European friends. Camping costs about $12 per campsite per night, and almost every destination recommended in this book has a camp-ground within a reasonable walk or bus ride from the town center and train station. A tent and sleeping bag are all you need. Many campgrounds have small grocery stores and washing machines, and some even come with discos and miniature golf. Hot showers are better at campgrounds than at many hotels. Local TIs have camp-ing information. You'll find more detailed information in the *Michelin Camping Guide*, available in most French bookstores; or in the thorough *Guide Officiel Camping/Caravaning* (Fédération Française de Camping et de Caravaning).

Eating in France

The French eat long and well. Relaxed lunches, three-hour dinners, and endless hours sitting in outdoor cafés are the norm. They have a legislated 35-hour workweek and a self-imposed 36-hour eat-week. The French spend much of their five annual weeks of paid vacation at *la table*. Local cafés, cuisine, and wines become a high-light of any French adventure—sightseeing for your palate. Even if the rest of you is sleeping in cheap hotels, let your tastebuds travel first-class in France. (They can go coach in England.) You can eat well without going broke—but choose carefully: You're just as likely to blow a small fortune on a mediocre meal as you are to dine wonderfully for $15.

Restaurants

If you want to see a menu, ask for *la carte*; if you ask for the *menu*, you'll get a fixed-price meal. This fixed-price *menu* gives you your choice of soup, appetizer, or salad (*entrée*); your choice of three or four main courses (*plat principal*) with vegetables; plus a cheese course and/or a choice of desserts. Service is included, but wine or drinks are generally extra.

In France an *entrée* is the first course and *le plat principal* is the main course. *Le plat du jour* (plate of the day) is usually a one-course (main) daily special served with vegetables (usually 50–70F) and, when available, is served only at lunch at restaurants but all day at bistros and cafés. For a light, healthy, fast, and inexpensive option in a pricey café, the various salads are 40F to 60F well spent. Soft drinks and beer cost 8F to 20F ($1.50–3.50), and a bottle or carafe of house wine—which is invariably good enough for Rick, if not always Steve—costs 30F to 70F ($6–14). Service is always included. To get a waiter's attention, simply say, "*S'il vous plaît.*"

French Café Culture

French cafés (or brasseries) provide light meals and a refuge from museum and church overload. They are carefully positioned spots from which to watch the river of local life flow by. It's easier to sit and feel comfortable in a café when you know the system.

Check the price list first. Prices, which must be posted prominently, vary wildly between cafés. Cafés charge different prices for the same drink depending upon where you want to be seated. Prices are posted: *comptoir* (counter/bar) and the more expensive *salle* (seated). Don't pay for your drink at the bar and then take it to a table (as you might do at home).

Your waiter probably won't overwhelm you with friendliness. Notice how hard they work. They almost never stop. Cozying up to clients (French or foreign) is probably the last thing on their minds.

The standard menu items are the *croque monsieur* (grilled ham and cheese sandwich) and *croque madame* (*monsieur* with a fried egg on top). The *salade composée* (com-po-zay) is a hearty chef's salad. Sandwiches are least expensive but plain unless you buy them at the *boulangerie* (bakery). To get more than a piece of ham (*jambon*) on a baguette, order a sandwich *jambon-crudité* (crew-dee-tay), which means garnished with lettuce, tomatoes, cucumbers, and so on. Omelettes come lonely on a plate with a basket of bread. The *plat du jour* (daily special) is your fast, hearty 50F-to-60F hot plate. Regardless of what you order, bread is free; to get more, just hold up your bread basket and ask, *"Encore, s'il vous plaît."*

If you order coffee, here's the lingo:
- *un express* (uh nex-press) = shot of espresso
- *une noisette* (oon nwah-zette) = espresso with a shot of milk
- *café au lait* = coffee with lots of milk. Also called *un grand crème* (uh grahn krem; big) or *un petit crème* (uh puh-tee krem; average)
- *un café allongé* (uh kah-fay ah-low-zhay) = cup of coffee, closest to American-style
- *un décaffine* (uh day-kah-fee-nay) = decaf; can modify any of the above drinks

Note: By law the waiter must give you a glass of tap water with your coffee if you request it; ask for *"Un verre d'eau, s'il vous plaît"* (uh vayr dough, see voo play).

House wine at the bar is cheap (5–14F per glass, cheapest by the larger *pichet*, or jug), and the local beer is cheaper on tap (*une pression*) than in the bottle (*bouteille*). While prices include service, tip, and tax, it's polite to round up for a drink or meal well served (e.g., if your bill is 24F, leave 25F).

Breakfast

Petit déjeuner (puh-tee day-zhu-nay) is typically *café au lait*, hot chocolate, or tea; a roll with butter and marmalade; and a croissant. Don't expect much variety. While they're available at your hotel (about 35F), breakfasts are cheaper at corner cafés (but you get no coffee refills). It's entirely acceptable to buy a croissant or roll at a nearby bakery and eat it with your cup of coffee at a café. If your hotel offers a buffet breakfast (usually cereal, yogurt, cheese, fruit, and bread), spring for it. If the morning egg urge gets the best of you, drop into a café and order *une omelette* or *oeufs sur le plat* (fried eggs). You could also buy or bring plastic bowls and spoons from home, buy a box of French cereal and a small box of milk, and eat in your room before heading out for coffee. We carry fruit and a package of Vache Qui Rit (Laughing Cow) cheese to supplement the morning jelly.

Lunch

For most lunches—*déjeuner* (day-zhuh-nay)—we picnic or munch a take-away sandwich from a *boulangerie* (bakery).

French picnics can be first-class affairs and adventures in high cuisine. Be daring. Try the smelly cheeses, ugly pâtés, sissy quiches, and minuscule yogurts. Local shopkeepers are accustomed to selling small quantities of produce. Try the tasty salads to go and ask for *une fourchette en plastique* (a plastic fork).

Gather supplies early; you'll probably want to visit several small stores to assemble a complete meal, and many close at noon. Look for a *boulangerie*, a *crémerie* (cheeses), a *charcuterie* (deli items, meats, and pâtés), an *épicerie* or *alimentation* (small grocery with veggies, drinks, and so on), and a *pâtisserie* (delicious pastries). Open-air markets (*marchés*) are fun and photogenic and close about noon (local TIs have details). Local *supermarchés* offer less color and cost, more efficiency, and adequate quality. Department stores often have supermarkets in the basement. On the outskirts of cities you'll find the monster *hypermarchés*. Drop in for a glimpse of hyper-France in action.

If not picnicking, look for food stands and bakeries selling take-out sandwiches and drinks or *crêperies* or brasseries for fast and easy sit-down restaurant food. Brasseries are cafés serving basic fare, such as omelets, hearty salads, chicken, fries, and simple sandwiches. Look for their *plat du jour* (daily special). Many French restaurants offer good-value three- to five-course *menus* at lunch only. The same *menu* is often 40F more at dinner. Drivers find roadside *frites* trailers selling fries, hot snacks, drinks, and so on. (Also see "Café Culture," above.)

Dinner

For *dîner* (dee-nay) choose restaurants filled with locals, not places with big neon signs boasting, "We Speak English." Consider our suggestions and your hotelier's opinion but trust your instinct. If the menu (*la carte*) isn't posted outside, move along. Also look for set-price *menus* and restaurants serving regional specialities. Refer to our restaurant recommendations at least to get a sense of what a reasonable meal should cost where you are. Ask the waiter for help deciphering *la carte*. Go with his or her recommendations and anything *de la maison* (of the

it's organ meat (*tripes, rognons, andouillette*).
    ....mets should bring a menu translator (the *Marling*
_____ ..._____ster is excellent). Remember, if you ask for *un menu*,
you'll get a meal (*la carte* is the list of what's cooking); and if you
ask for an *entrée*, you'll get a first course (soup, salad, or appetizer). The wines are often listed in a separate *carte des vins*; ask
for un *vin ordinaire* (van or-din-air) if all you want is table wine.
Tipping (*pourboire*) is unnecessary, though if you enjoyed the
service it's polite to leave a few francs (10F per person if you
really appreciated the service, none if you didn't). When you're
on the road, look for the red and blue Relais Routier decal,
indicating that the place is recommended by the truckers' union.
Restaurants are generally a far better value in the countryside
than in Paris.

Drinks

In stores, unrefrigerated soft drinks and beer are one-third the
price of cold drinks. Milk and boxed fruit juice are the cheapest
drinks. Avoid buying drinks to go at streetside stands; you'll find
them far cheaper in a shop. Try to keep a water bottle with you.
Water quenches your thirst better and cheaper than anything
you'll find in a store or café. We drink tap water throughout
France and the Low Countries.
    The French often order bottled water with their meal (*eau
minérale*; oh mee-nay-rahl). If you'd rather get a free pitcher of tap
water, ask for *une carafe d'eau*. Otherwise, you may unwittingly buy
bottled water. To save money when ordering a beer at a café or
restaurant, ask for *une pression* or *un demi* (draft beer), which is
cheaper than bottled. When ordering table wine at a café or restaurant, ask for a pitcher, *un pichet* (pee-shay), again cheaper than a
bottle. If all you want is a glass of wine, ask for *un verre de vin*. You
could drink away your children's inheritance if you're not careful.
The most famous wines are the most expensive, while lesser-known
taste-alikes remain a bargain (see our regional suggestions in each
chapter). If you like brandy, try a *marc* (regional brandy, e.g., *marc
de Bourgogne*) or an Armagnac, cognac's cheaper twin brother.
Pastis, the standard *apéritif*, is a sweet anise or licorice drink that
comes on the rocks with a glass of water. Cut it to taste with lots
of water. France's best beer is Alsatian; also try Krônenburg or the
heavier Pelfort. *Une panaché* (pan-a-shay) is a very refreshing
French shandy (lemonade and beer). For a fun, bright, nonalco-
holic drink, order *un diabolo menthe* (7-Up with mint syrup). The
ice cubes melted after the last Yankee tour group left.

Stranger in a Strange Land

We travel all the way to Europe to enjoy differences—to become
temporary locals. You'll experience frustrations. Certain truths that

we find "God-given" or "self-evident," like cold beer, ice in drinks, bottomless cups of coffee, hot showers, body odor smelling bad, and bigger being better, are suddenly not so true. One of the benefits of travel is the eye-opening realization that there are logical, civil, and even better alternatives. The fact that Americans treat time as a commodity can lead to frustrations when dealing with other cultures. For instance, while an American "spends" or "wastes" time, a French person merely "passes" it. A willingness to go local (and at a local tempo) ensures that you'll enjoy a full dose of European hospitality.

If there is a negative aspect to the European image of Americans, we can appear big, loud, aggressive, impolite, rich, and a bit naive. While Europeans look bemusedly at some of our Yankee excesses—and worriedly at others—they nearly always afford us individual travelers all the warmth we deserve.

Back Door Manners

While updating this book, we heard over and over again that our readers are considerate and fun to have as guests. Thank you for traveling as temporary locals who are sensitive to the culture. It's fun to follow you in our travels.

Tours of France by Rick Steves and Steve Smith

At Europe Through the Back Door, we organize and lead tours covering the highlights of this book. Choose among a 14-day *Feast of the East*, a 14-day *Best of the West*, or the 20-day *Best of Village France*. These depart each year from April through October, are limited to 26 people per group, and have two guides and big buses with lots of empty seats. We also offer new one-week winter getaways to Paris. For details call us at 425/771-8303.

Send Us a Postcard, Drop Us a Line

If you enjoy a successful trip with the help of this book and would like to share your discoveries, please fill out and send the survey at the end of this book to us at Europe Through the Back Door, Box 2009, Edmonds, WA 98020. We personally read and value all feedback. Thanks in advance—it helps a lot.

For our latest travel information, tap into our Web site: www.ricksteves.com. For any updates to this book, check www.ricksteves.com/update. Rick's e-mail address is rick@ricksteves.com. Anyone is welcome to request a free issue of our *Back Door* quarterly newsletter.

Judging from all the positive feedback and happy postcards we receive from travelers who have used this book, it's safe to assume you'll enjoy a great, affordable vacation—with the finesse of an independent, experienced traveler.

From this point, "we" (your coauthors) will shed our respective egos and become "I."

Thanks, and *bon voyage*!

BACK DOOR TRAVEL PHILOSOPHY
As Taught in *Rick Steves' Europe Through the Back Door*

Travel is intensified living—maximum thrills per minute and one of the last great sources of legal adventure. Travel is freedom. It's recess, and we need it.

Experiencing the real Europe requires catching it by surprise, going casual . . . "Through the Back Door"

Affording travel is a matter of priorities. (Make do with the old car.) You can travel—simply, safely, and comfortably—anywhere in Europe for $70 a day plus transportation costs. In many ways, spending more money only builds a thicker wall between you and what you came to see. Europe is a cultural carnival; time after time you'll find that its best acts are free and the best seats are the cheap ones.

A tight budget forces you to travel close to the ground, meeting and communicating with the people, not relying on service with a purchased smile. Never sacrifice sleep, nutrition, safety, or cleanliness in the name of budget. Simply enjoy the local-style alternatives to expensive hotels and restaurants.

Extroverts have more fun. If your trip is low on magic moments, kick yourself and make things happen. If you don't enjoy a place, maybe you don't know enough about it. Seek the truth. Recognize tourist traps. Give a culture the benefit of your open mind. See things as different but not better or worse. Any culture has much to share.

Of course, travel, like the world, is a series of hills and valleys. Be fanatically positive and militantly optimistic. If something's not to your liking, change your liking. Travel is addicting. It can make you a happier American as well as a citizen of the world. Our Earth is home to nearly 6 billion equally important people. It's humbling to travel and find that people don't envy Americans. They like us but, with all due respect, they wouldn't trade passports.

Globe-trotting destroys ethnocentricity. It helps you understand and appreciate different cultures. Travel changes people. It broadens perspectives and teaches new ways to measure quality of life. Many travelers toss aside their hometown blinders. Their prized souvenirs are the strands of different cultures they decide to knit into their own character. The world is a cultural yarn shop. And Back Door Travelers are weaving the ultimate tapestry. Come on, join in!

Db-300F, CC:VM, take elevator down to boutique level or walk down from departure level, tel. 01 48 62 06 16, fax 01 48 62 56 97). You get 16 hours of silence buried under the check-in level with TV and toilet. Hôtel IBIS, at the Roissy Rail station, is comfortable (Db-420F, CC:VMA, free shuttle bus to airport takes 2 minutes, tel. 01 49 19 19 19, fax 01 49 19 19 21).

Orly Airport

This airport has two terminals: Sud and Ouest. International flights arrive at Sud. After you exit baggage claim (near gate H), signs will direct you to city transportation, car rental, and so on. Turn left to enter the main terminal area and you'll find exchange offices with barely acceptable rates, an ATM, the ADP (a quasi-tourist office that offers free city maps and basic sightseeing information), and an SNCF French rail desk (sells train tickets and Eurailpasses). Downstairs is a sandwich bar, a bank (lousy rates), a newsstand (sells *télécartes*), and a post office (great rates for cash or Amex traveler's checks). For flight info call 01 49 75 15 15.

Transportation between Paris and Orly Airport: Three public-transportation routes, taxis, and a couple of airport shuttle services link Orly and central Paris. The Air France bus (outside gate F) runs to Paris' Invalides Métro stop (40F, 4/hrly, 30 min) and is best for those staying in or near the rue Cler neighborhood (from Invalides terminal, take the Métro 2 stops to École Militaire). The Jetbus #285 (outside gate F, 24F, 4/hrly) is the quickest way to the Métro and the best way to the recommended hotels in the Marais and Contrescarpe neighborhoods (take Jetbus to Villejuif Métro stop, buy a *carnet* of 10 tickets, then take the Métro to the Sully Morland stop for Marais or the Cardinal Lemoine stop for Contrescarpe). The Orlybus (outside gate H, 30F, 4/hrly) takes you to the Denfert-Rochereau RER-B line and the Métro. The Orlyval trains are overpriced (57F). Allow 150F for a taxi into central Paris.

Consider airport shuttle minivans (see "Charles de Gaulle Airport," above). From Orly, figure about 120F for one person, 80F per person for two, or less for larger groups and kids.

Sleeping near Orly Airport: IBIS is cheaper (Db-420F, CC:VMA, tel. 01 46 87 33 50, fax 01 46 87 29 92) than the more comfortable Hilton (Db-680F, tel 01 45 12 45 12, fax 01 45 12 45 00). Both offer free airport shuttle service.

NORMANDY

These are lands of lush, green, rolling hills; apple orchards; dramatic coastlines; half-timbered homes; and thatched roofs. Parisians call Normandy "the 21st *arrondissement*." It's their escape—the nearest beach. The British call this area close enough for a weekend away.

Viking Norsemen settled here in the ninth century, giving Normandy its name. William the Conqueror invaded England from Normandy in the 11th century. To see his victory commemorated in a remarkable tapestry, weave Bayeux into your trip. In Rouen, France's all-time inspirational leader, Jeanne d'Arc (Joan of Arc), was convicted of heresy and burned at the stake by the English, against whom she had rallied France during the Hundred Years' War. (For more information, see the Appendix.)

The rugged coast of Normandy harbors tiny fishing villages, such as little Honfleur, which today has more charm than fish. The cliff-hanger coast, two hours south of Honfleur, was the scene of a WWII battle that changed the course of history. South of the D-day beaches, on the border of Brittany, is the almost surreal island abbey of Mont St. Michel, rising serene and majestic, oblivious to its tides of tourists.

Planning Your Time

Honfleur, the D-day beaches, and Mont St. Michel each merit an overnight stop. Visit Giverny and Rouen between Paris and Honfleur, see the Caen Battle of Normandy museum/memorial between Honfleur and the D-day beaches, and arrive late in the day or very early at Mont St. Michel. Dinan, only 40 minutes from Mont St. Michel (one hour by train), offers an enchanting introduction to Brittany. Many see Mont St. Michel on a day trip from Dinan.

Normandy

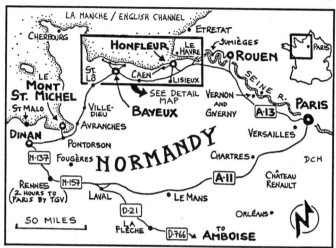

Getting around Normandy

Trains serve Rouen, Caen, Bayeux, Mont St. Michel, and Dinan, with good service from Paris but less service between these sights (e.g., there are only 2 trains/day between Rouen and Bayeux and 2 trains/day between Bayeux and Pontorson, near Mont St. Michel). Plan ahead and you'll do fine. Buses connect Giverny with Rouen or Paris (via Vernon), Honfleur with Paris (via Lisieux), Bayeux (via Caen or Lisieux) with Rouen (via Le Havre), and Arromanches with Bayeux. Sundays see little if any bus service.

Cuisine Scene—Normandy

Known as the land of the four Cs (Calvados, Camembert, cider, and *crème*), Normandy specializes in cream sauces, organ meats (kidneys, sweetbreads, and tripe—"the gizzard salads" are great), and seafood (*fruits de mer*). Dairy products are big here. Local cheeses are Camembert (mild to very strong), Brillat-Savarin (buttery), Livarot (spicy and pungent), Pavé d'Auge (spicy and tangy), and Pont l'Evêque (earthy flavor). Normandy is famous for its powerful Calvados apple brandy, Benedictine brandy (made by local monks), and three kinds of alcoholic apple ciders (*cidre* can be *doux*—sweet, *brut*—dry, or *bouche*—sparkling and the strongest).

ROUEN

This 2,000-year-old city of 100,000 people mixes dazzling Gothic architecture, exquisite half-timbered houses, and contemporary bustle like no other in France. A one-time powerhouse, medieval Rouen walked a political tightrope between England and France. It was an English base during the Hundred Years' War. William the Conqueror lived here 900 years ago; 300 years later, Joan of Arc was burned here.

Tourist Information: The TI, in a fine Renaissance building, faces the cathedral. Pick up their map highlighting an ideal walking tour (Mon–Sat 9:00–19:00, Sun 9:00–13:00, 14:30–18:00; mid-Sept–Apr Mon–Sat 9:00–18:30, Sun 10:00–13:00, tel. 02 32 08 32 40).

Arrival in Rouen

By Train: Rue Jeanne d'Arc cuts down from Rouen's station (24-hr lockers available) straight through the town center to the Seine River. Leave the station, walking straight down rue Jeanne d'Arc to rue du Gros Horloge, the medieval center's pedestrian mall that connects the Old Market and Jeanne d'Arc church (to the right) with the cathedral and TI (to the left). To go directly to the start of the Rouen walking tour, described below, turn right on rue du Gros Horloge (you'll see the sweeping roof of the modern Église Jeanne d' Arc). Rouen's new subway will take you effortlessly from the train station to the Palais de la Justice in one stop (8f), one block above the rue du Gros Horloge.

By Car: Follow signs to *"centre-ville"* and *"rive droite"* and park along the river (metered until 19:00) or in one of many underground lots (near the cathedral is best).

Sights—Rouen

▲▲**Rouen Walking Tour**—For a good, quick dose of Rouen's Gothic and half-timbered wonders, begin at the Jeanne d'Arc church and follow the route described below (most sights close 12:00–14:00). The ruins of the old St. Sauveur church near the entry to the Jeanne d'Arc church make a good seat and starting point.

Église Jeanne d'Arc—This modern church is a tribute to Jeanne d'Arc. Nineteen-year-old Jeanne was burned at the stake on this square in 1431. The church, completed in 1979, feels Scandinavian inside and out—reminding us again of Normandy's Nordic roots. Pick up an English pamphlet describing the church (closed 12:30–14:00; public WC 30 yards from church doors). Next door, under a modern roof, is a great outdoor morning market for picnic fixings. It runs until 12:30.

Now turn around. With the town's lacy Gothic skyline and half-timbered buildings solidly on vertical hold, it's hard to imagine the town devastated by WWII bombs. Its restoration attests to the French commitment to their people-friendly city centers (rather than to suburban sprawl).

The striking half-timbered houses (14th–19th centuries) that

Rouen

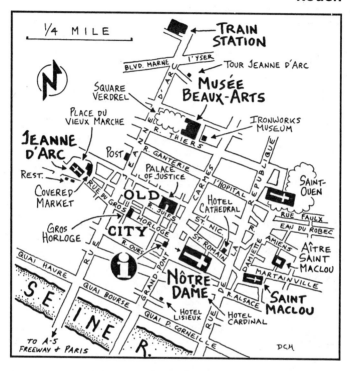

line Rouen's streets remind us that there's more oak than stone in this region. Cantilevered floors were standard until about 1520. These top-heavy designs made sense because city land was limited, property taxes were based on ground-floor square footage, and the cantilevering minimized unsupported spans on upper floors. Rouen's historic wealth was due largely to its advantageous location as the last bridge across the Seine before the Atlantic and its inland river port.

Rue du Gros Horloge—This has been Rouen's main pedestrian and shopping street since Roman times. It links the Église Jeanne d'Arc and the Cathédrale Notre Dame and shows off the impressive Renaissance (1528) public clock, le Gros Horloge. Admire the clock and sculpture in the arch from below. The 10F climb to the top is good only for the exercise.

Palace of Justice—Take the first left after the old clock and in a block you'll see the impressive Flamboyant Gothic Palace of Justice (largely restored after WWII bombing, though the western facade remains littered with pock marks from German guns). Returning to rue du Gros Horloge, turn left and continue to the rue du Bec, where a plaque up on your left commemorates the assassination in Texas of the explorer who named Louisiana, Cavelier de la Salle. Continue to...

Cathédrale Notre Dame—Grab a seat on the shady benches on the right in the square. This is the church Monet painted at various times of day from an apartment he rented solely for this purpose opposite the cathedral. You can (and should) see four of these paintings at the Musée d'Orsay in Paris. This soaring exterior is considered one of France's most beautiful, a fine example of the last overripe stage of Gothic architecture called *"flamboyant"*— flamelike. The ugly concrete buildings across from the cathedral are a fine example of function over form. Enter the cathedral and make a marvel-at-the-Gothic circuit inside, stopping halfway down the nave on the right to see photos showing the severe WWII bomb damage. You'll find helpful English explanations in small plaques near the side chapels. This cathedral is far lighter than it should be; only a few original stained-glass windows— behind the altar—remain after the bombing.

Leave the cathedral via the left (northern) transept, admiring the stone stairway to your left inside the cathedral. Enjoy the Gothic facade behind you as you exit and then turn right to rue St. Romain. This fine old medieval lane leads a few blocks to the St. Maclou Church. A plaque on your right (under the ruined Gothic arch) identifies the site of an old chapel, where Joan of Arc was sentenced to death—and where she was proclaimed innocent 25 years later. Take a look down rue des Chanoines (next left) for a half-timbered fantasy. Rue St. Romain leads to the...

St. Maclou Church—Study the unique bowed facade. Inside, walk to the end of the choir and look back at the stained glass framed by the suspended crucifix.

Leaving the church, turn right and right (giving the boys on the corner a wide berth) and wander past a fine wall of half-timbered buildings fronting rue Martainville. Within a block a passageway on the left leads to...

Aître St. Maclou—Wander all the way into this half-timbered courtyard/graveyard/cloister. Sit at the well in the center. Notice the ghoulish carvings lurking around you. This onetime cemetery for 14th-century plague victims is now an art school. Peek in on the young artists. You can see examples of their art in the new exhibition rooms near the entrance. Can you find the black cat? (Look as you leave the courtyard on your left.)

Return right onto the rue Martainville and stroll toward the leaning towers; take a right on rue Damiette, passing half-timbered antique shops that lead to Rouen's third fine Gothic church, St. Ouen. A thousand-year-old Danish rune stone stands by the church door, reminding locals of their Nordic heritage. The park behind this church is perfect for a picnic and siesta. In front of St. Ouen, rue Hôpital takes you back to rue Jeanne d'Arc and the station or your car.

More Sights—Rouen

(All open Wed–Mon 10:00–13:00, 14:00–18:00, closed Tue).
Musée des Beaux Arts—This beautifully displayed collection features paintings from all periods, including works by Caravaggio, Rubens, Veronese, Steen, Géricault, Ingres, Delacroix, and the Impressionists (22F, 3 blocks from station, 26 bis rue Jean Lecanuet).

Museum of Ironworks (Musee le Seq des Tournelles)—This surprisingly interesting museum contains nothing but iron objects from over 1,500 years ago. Locks, keys, tools—virtually anything made out of iron is on display (15F, behind Musée des Beaux Arts, 2 rue Jacques Villon).

La Tour de Jeanne d'Arc—Originally eight towers such as this formed the fortifications of Rouen. Joan was kept here before being burned at the stake on place du Vieux Marche—where the church of Joan of Arc now stands (12F, rue du Donjon, between Beaux Arts museum and train station).

Sights—Near Rouen

▲**La Route des Anciennes Abbayes**—The route of the ancient abbeys is punctuated with abbeys, apple trees, Seine River views, and pastoral scenery (follow the D-982 west of Rouen if driving or inquire about buses at the TI). Monks are the guides at l'Abbaye de St. Wandrille, and Jumièges has Normandy's most romantic ruined abbey. Get details at Rouen's TI.

Sleeping and Eating in Rouen

(6F = about $1, zip code: 75000)
Sleep Code: **S** = Single, **D** = Double/Twin, **T** = Triple, **Q** = Quad, **b** = bathroom, **t** = toilet only, **s** = shower only, **CC** = Credit Card (Visa, MasterCard, Amex), **SE** = Speaks English, **NSE** = No English, * = Hotel rating (0–4 stars).
All of these hotels are within two blocks of the cathedral; directions are given from the cathedral.

The ideally situated and welcoming **Hotel Cardinal*** is a great value. All of its spotless and comfortable rooms look right onto the cathedral, and a few have private balconies (Db-290–380F, extra bed-55F, CC:VM, elevator, to the right of the cathedral as you face it, 1 place de la Cathedrale, tel. 02 35 70 24 42, fax 02 35 89 75 14).

The central **Hôtel de la Cathédrale*** has a seductive courtyard and generally good rooms (Sb-255–310F, Db-305–360F,

outside the left transept of the cathedral, 12 rue St. Romain, tel.
02 35 71 57 95, fax 02 35 70 15 54). **Hotel de Lisieux**** is very
welcoming, with spacious, colorful rooms and good prices (Db-
260F, Tb-360F, CC:VM, Internet access, 2 blocks from the river
below the cathedral, 4 rue de Savonnerie, tel. 02 35 71 87 73, fax
02 35 89 31 52, e-mail: lisieux@hotel-rouen.com).

Two of Rouen's best moderately priced seafood restaurants
are both on the place du Vieux Marche across from the church
of Joan of Arc: **La Mirabelle** (tel. 02 35 71 58 21) and **Paris
Maraichers** (tel. 02 35 71 57 73). You'll also find many inexpensive alternatives between St. Maclou and St. Ouen churches.

Transportation Connections—Rouen

Rouen is well served by trains from Paris, through Amiens to
other points north, and through Caen to other destinations west
and south.

By train to: Paris' Gare St. Lazare (nearly hrly, 75 min),
Bayeux (3/day, 2.5 hrs, transfer in Caen), **Mont St. Michel** (3/day,
4 hrs, via Caen and Pontorson, short bus ride from Pontorson to
Mont St. Michel or taxi, see Mont St. Michel later in chapter).

By train and bus to: Honfleur (5/day, 1.5 hrs, train to
Le Havre then bus over Pont de Normandie to Honfleur—
Le Havre's bus station is 1 block from the train station, turn left
out of the train station and cross the big boulevard; or in 2 hrs via
Lisieux—train from Rouen to Lisieux then bus to Honfleur).

HONFLEUR

Honfleur (ohn-flur) actually feels as picturesque as it looks.
Gazing at its cozy harbor, surrounded by skinny, soaring houses,
it's easy to overlook the historic importance of this port. For
over a thousand years sailors have enjoyed Honfleur's ideal loca-
tion, where the Seine meets the English Channel. William the
Conqueror received supplies shipped from Honfleur, and
Samuel de Champlain sailed from here in 1608, discovering the
St. Lawrence Waterway and Quebec City. Honfleur was also a
favorite of 19th-century Impressionists: Monet, Dufy, and
Boudin all painted here. Honfleur escaped the bombs of
World War II.

Today's Honfleur, long eclipsed by the gargantuan port of
Le Havre just across the Seine, happily uses its past as a bar stool
and sits on it. All of Honfleur's interesting streets and activities
are packed together within a few minutes' walk of the old port
(Vieux Bassin).

Honfleur is low on sights but high on ambience. (Arriving in
the afternoon and leaving after breakfast works well for most.)
Snoop around the streets behind place Berthelot and Église Ste.
Catherine for some of Normandy's oldest half-timbered homes

and interesting art galleries. For a great view, hike up the Côte de Grace (see below).

Tourist Information: The helpful, English-speaking TI hides a few blocks just off the Vieux Bassin on the Le Havre side of the harbor. Pick up their handy town map and any information you need on Normandy (Easter–Oct daily Mon–Sat 9:00–12:30, 14:00–18:30, no midday closing in summer, Sun 10:00–13:00; Nov–Easter Mon–Sat 9:00–12:00, 14:00–17:30, closed Sun, place Arthur Boudin, tel. 02 31 89 23 30).

Arrival in Honfleur

By Bus: If you're arriving from Lisieux or Deauville, the first stop in Honfleur (Albert Sorel) is closest to most hotels. From this stop, continue along rue de la Republique; in 300 yards you'll hit the old harbor (Vieux Bassin). The other stop is north of the port at the bus station (*gare routière*) and has a useful information counter (see "Transportation Connections," below). From here, walk up rue des Fosses with Hotel Moderne on your left and turn right on rue de la Ville to reach the TI or continue straight to the old port and hotels.

By Car: Follow "*centre-ville*" signs and then park as close to the old port (Vieux Bassin) as possible. Parking lots are just north of the old port. Inquire at your hotel where you can park for free (metered parking is free 19:00–9:00 and 12:00–14:00).

Sights—Honfleur

▲**Eglise Ste. Catherine**—As you step inside this church your first thought is, "If you could turn it over it would float." This unusual church was built in the 15th century—logically, in this ship-building town—by naval architects (replacing a ruined stone church). Rough-hewn wood beams give it a feel-good warmth you don't find in stone churches. In the last months of World War II, a bomb fell through the roof but didn't explode. The exterior is a wonderful conglomeration of wood shingle, brick, and half-timbered construction.

The church's bell tower was built across the square to lighten the load on the roof of the wooden church and to minimize fire hazards. (Tower and church open 9:00–18:30 in summer, other-wise 9:00–12:00, 14:00–18:00.) The church is free. In the tower, the room that has a few church artifacts is not worth the 10F.

▲**Eugène Boudin Museum**—This pleasant museum houses a variety of early Impressionist paintings and Norman costumes (25F, Wed–Mon 10:00–12:00, 14:00–18:00, closed Tue, rue de l'Homme de Bois).

Museums of Old Honfleur—Two museums combine to paint a picture of what daily life has been like in Honfleur since the Middle Ages. The Musée de la Marine, located in an old church

Honfleur

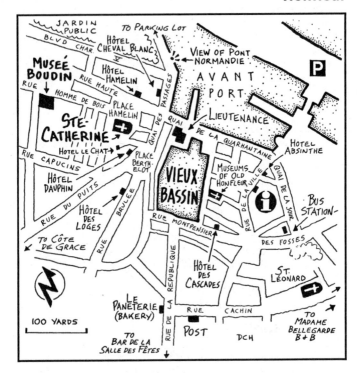

right on the Vieux Bassin near the TI, offers an interesting collection of ship models and marine paraphernalia. The Musée d' Ethnographie et d'Art Populaire, located in the old prison (which you'll visit) behind Musée de la Marine, re-creates typical rooms, cramming them with objects of daily life from various eras (ask for English explanation, 25F for both or 15F each, Tue–Sun 10:00–12:00, 14:00–18:00).

Boat Excursions—Boats to the Pont de Normandie (see below) depart from in front of Hotel Cheval Blanc (Easter–Nov, 40F adult, 30F children, 50 min, tel. 02 31 89 21 10). The 30-minute excursions of Honfleur's harbor on the Calypso are less interesting (25F).

Côte de Grace Walk—For good exercise and a bird's-eye view over Honfleur and the Pont de Normandie, take the short, steep walk up to the Côte de Grace viewpoint (from Église Ste. Catherine, walk past Hotel Dauphin and up rue Brulee, turn right on rue Eugene Boudin, then climb la Rampe de Mont Joli; best early in the morning or at sunset).

Saturday Morning Farmers' Market—The area around the Église Ste. Catherine is transformed into a colorful market each Saturday morning from 9:00 to 12:30.

▲**Normandie Bridge**—The 2.1-kilometer-long Pont de Normandie is the longest cable-stayed bridge in the world (until a Japanese bridge, which will beat it by 40 meters, is completed). This is a key piece of a superfreeway that, in 2000, will link the Atlantic ports from Belgium to Spain. Honfleur's TI has a brochure with all the engineering details. You can view the bridge from Honfleur (best views from an excursion boat or above the town on the Côte de Grace; really impressive when floodlit) or drive over and visit the free Exhibition Hall (under tollbooth on Le Havre side, daily 8:00–19:00). The Seine finishes its winding 500-mile journey here. From its source it drops only 1,500 feet. It flows so slowly that in certain places a stiff breeze can send it flowing upstream.

Sleeping in Honfleur
(6F = about $1, zip code: 14600)
Honfleur is busy on weekends and holidays and in the summer, when many hotels require half-pension. I've listed places that normally don't. English is widely spoken in this town where local merchants appreciate their proximity to England.

Hôtel Dauphin** is a solid and central midrange bet, with a family feel, a homey lounge/breakfast room, an Escher-esque floorplan, great plumbing, and some delightfully funky rooms—some with open-beam ceilings (Db-300–400F, Tb-460–660F, pay-as-you-go breakfast upgrades include cereal-5F, yogurt-5F, fruit-5F, and freshly squeezed juice-12F, CC:VMA, cable TV, all rooms theoretically smoke-free, a stone's throw from the church at 10 place Berthelot, tel. 02 31 89 15 53, fax 02 31 89 92 06, e-mail: hotel.dudauphin@wanadoo.fr).

Hôtel des Loges**, next to the Dauphin, is tranquil and very sharp, with many tastefully renovated rooms and pleasant common areas (Db-325–410F, Tb-350F, CC:VM, 18 rue Brûlée, tel. 02 31 89 38 26).

Hôtel des Cascades* is comfortable and well located a block north of the harbor and has a tangled-fishnet floor plan and laid-back management (Db-200–300F, add 50F for 3rd person, only 10F for a 4th, dinner required during summer weekends, CC:VM, facing rue Montpensier at 17 place Thiers, tel. 02 31 89 05 83, fax 02 31 89 32 13, Melanie SE).

Hôtel Le Cheval Blanc*** is a good three-star splurge right on the water, with port views from every room and the only elevator I saw in town. It's a big, half-timbered place with no restaurant (Db-450–1,100F, most at 630F, add 100F per person for triple and quad, prices include breakfast, CC:VMA, 2 quai de Passagers, tel. 02 31 81 65 00, fax 02 31 89 52 80, e-mail: lecheval.blanc@wa nadoo.fr)

Hotel Le Chat** offers spacious faded-elegant rooms, a bar, and a restaurant in a historic, ivy-covered stone building with a great setting across from the Ste. Catherine church. The gregarious owner will make you smile (Db-420–500F, CC:VMA, place Ste. Catherine, tel. 02 31 14 49 49, fax 02 31 89 28 61, e-mail: hotel.lechat@honfleur.com).

Hotel Absinthe*** is a small, flawlessly restored hotel with seven exceptionally comfortable rooms a half block from the TI behind the restaurant le Bistro du Port. Spacious rooms, Jacuzzi tubs, and exquisite decor make this a good splurge (Db-700F, keys available in restaurant Absinthe across the alley, CC:VM, 1 rue de la Ville, tel. 02 31 89 39 00, fax 02 31 89 53 60).

Chambres d'hôte offer a good option here (the TI has a list), though most are at least one mile from the center of Honfleur. These two are a short walk from the center: Bargain rooms are tucked above the *très* local **Bar de la Salle des Fêtes**, where French is spoken with a shy smile by Monsieur and Madame Leguyon (D-160F, nifty studio with kitchenette-200F, place Albert Sorel, at bus stop Albert Sorel, 300 yards from harbor out rue de la République, tel. 02 31 89 19 69). Gentle **Madame Bellegarde** offers homey and comfortable rooms in her pleasant home (Db-180F, a family-friendly Tb with kitchenette and great bathroom view-300F, 10-minute uphill walk from TI, 3 blocks up from St. Leonard church in nontouristed part of Honfleur, 54 rue St. Leonard, look for sign in window, tel. 02 31 89 06 52).

Eating in Honfleur

Eat seafood here. It's a tough choice between the hard-to-resist waterfront tables of the many look-alike places lining the Vieux Bassin (at least a walk along the port is mandatory after dark) and those with more solid reputations on small side streets.

Several good restaurants lie along rue de l'Homme de Bois, like the unpretentious **La Tortue** (99F *menu*, closed Mon–Tue off-season, 36 rue de l'Homme de Bois, tel. 02 31 89 04 93). Better still, enjoy Honfleur's best affordable seafood in the *charmant* **Au Petit Mareyeur** (120F *menu*, closed Mon, 4 place Hamelin, tel. 02 31 98 84 23 for necessary reservations). The classy and intimate **Auberge du Vieux Clocher** will tempt any romantic (120/170F *menu*, closed Sun and Wed except in summer, 9 rue de l'Homme de Bois, reserve ahead, tel. 02 31 89 12 06). Near the bottom of the street, **La Cidrerie** is a cozy cider bar with freshly made crêpes, Calvados, and ambience (26 place Hamelin).

Near the TI, the moderately priced **Bistro du Port**, with heaters that allow outside dining when others don't, and the Honfleur-elegant and pricey **L'Absinthe** sit side by side, each well respected and offering a wide range of choices (12 and 14 quai de la Quarantine).

The old harbor is ideal for evening picnics, especially as the sun sets. Try the steps in front of the port's bureau (La Lieutenance). **Le Paneterie** is Honfleur's best *boulangerie-pâtisserie* (26 rue de la République) and is nicely complemented by the fine charcuterie, **Au Fin Gourmet**, a few doors down.

Transportation Connections—Honfleur

Buses connect Honfleur with Le Havre, Caen, Deauville, and Lisieux, where you'll catch a train to other points. While train and bus service is usually coordinated, ask at Honfleur's helpful bus station for the best connection for your trip (9:00–12:15, 14:30–17:30, tel. 02 31 89 28 41). If you have a railpass, you'll save money by connecting though the nearest city, as bus fares increase with distance.

By bus and train to: **Bayeux** (5/day, 2.5 hrs, bus to Lisieux or quicker via Caen, then train to Bayeux), **Rouen** (5/day, 90 min, bus over the Pont de Normandie to Le Havre, train to Rouen, or in 2 hrs via Lisieux), **Paris'** Gare St. Lazare (5/day, 3 hrs; bus to Lisieux or Deauville, train to Paris; buses from Honfleur meet most Paris trains).

BAYEUX

Only six miles from the D-day beaches, Bayeux was the first city liberated after the landing and makes an ideal base for visiting the area's sights. Even without its famous tapestry and proximity to the D-day beaches, Bayeux would be worth a visit for its pleasant *centre-ville* and imposing cathedral.

Navigating in Bayeux is a breeze on foot or by car. Look for the church spires and follow the signs to *"centre-ville"* or "tapisserie" to reach the city center (from the train station it's a 15- to 20-minute walk or a 25F taxi to any of the hotels I list). Market days are Wednesday (on pedestrian rue St. Jean) and Saturday (bigger, on place St. Patrice). Both end at noon.

Tourist Information: From the friendly TI on the bridge (Pont St. Jean, leading to pedestrian street rue St. Jean), pick up a town map, the excellent brochure "D-day Landings and the Battle of Normandy," bus schedules, and any regional information you need (Mon–Sat 9:00–12:00, 14:00–18:00, also open Sun Jun–mid-Sept 10:00–12:00, 15:00–18:00, tel. 02 31 51 28 28, fax 02 31 51 28 29).

Bayeux History—The Battle of Hastings

The most memorable date of the Middle Ages is probably 1066 because of this pivotal battle. England's King Edward was about to die without an heir, and the question was who would succeed him: Harold, an English noble, or William, the Duke of Normandy? Harold was captured during a battle in Normandy. To gain his freedom he promised William that, when the ailing King Edward died, he would allow William to ascend the throne. Shortly after that oath was taken, Harold was back in England, Edward died, and Harold grabbed the throne. William, known as William the Bastard, invaded England to claim the throne he figured was rightfully his. Harold met him in southern England at the town of Hastings, where their forces fought a fierce 14-hour battle. Harold was killed, and his Saxon forces were routed. William—now "the Conqueror"—marched on London to claim his throne, becoming King of England as well as Duke of Normandy. The advent of a Norman king of England muddied the political waters, setting in motion 400 years of conflict between England and France not to be resolved until the end of the Hundred Years' War in 1453.

The Norman Conquest of England brought England into the European mainstream. The Normans established a strong central English government. They brought with them the Romanesque style of architecture (e.g., the Tower of London and Durham Cathedral) that the English call "Norman." Historians speculate that, had William not succeeded, England would have remained on the fringe of Europe (like Scandinavia), and French culture (and language) would have prevailed in the New World.

Sights—Bayeux

Note: The 39F ticket for the Bayeux Tapestry gets you into the Baron Gerard Museum and Hotel du Doyon (listed below) but not the WWII museum.

▲▲▲Bayeux Tapestry—Actually woolen embroidery on linen cloth, this document—precious to historians—is a 70-meter cartoon telling the story of William the Conqueror's rise from Duke of Normandy to King of England and his victory over Harold at the Battle of Hastings. Long and skinny, it was designed to hang from the nave of Bayeux's cathedral.

Your visit has three parts (explaining the basic story of the battle three times—which was about right for me): First you'll walk through a "mood-setting images on sails" room into a room with a replica of the tapestry with extensive explanations and a room designed to set the cultural scene for the battle. Next, a 15-minute AV show in the cinema up one flight gives a relaxing dramatization of the event. Finally you'll get to the real McCoy. It's worth the 5F (have exact change) and the wait for the headphones, which give a top-notch, fast-moving, 20-minute, scene-by-scene narration complete with period music. If you lose your place you'll find subtitles in Latin. Remember, this is a piece of Norman propaganda—the English (the bad guys, referred to as *les goddamns*, after a phrase the French kept hearing them say) are shown with mustaches and long hair; the French (*les* good guys) are clean cut and clean shaven (39F, mid-Mar–mid-Oct daily 9:00–18:30, mid-Oct–mid-Mar daily 9:00–12:30, 14:00–18:00, tel. 02 31 92 05 48). When buying your ticket, get the English film showtimes. If you're rushed and the cinema schedule doesn't match yours, skip the film. If you have time, see the film first, exit the way you entered, and backtrack to see the replica (don't follow everyone else; cinemagoers pile into the tapestry room with a crowd).

▲▲**Bayeux Cathedral**—This building dominates the city (which is what Gothic cathedrals were supposed to do). Walk inside. The view of the nave from the top of the steps is as good as Gothic gets. Historians believe the tapestry originally hung here. Imagine it proudly circling the congregation, draped around the nave from the miniarches just below the big and bright upper windows of the clerestory. The nave's huge, round lower arches are Romanesque (11th century) and decorated with the same zigzag pattern that characterizes this "Norman" art in England. But this nave is much brighter because of the later Gothic windows of the top half of the nave. The finest example of 13th-century "Norman" Gothic is in the choir (the fancy area behind the central altar). For maximum 1066 atmosphere, step into the crypt (below the central altar). Study the frescoed angels and the ornately carved 11th-century capitals decorated with Roman-style acanthus leaves and grey meanies (free, daily 9:00–18:00).

Baron Gerard Museum—This museum, located outside the Cathedral's left transept, houses a collection of locally made porcelain and lace and a modest painting gallery (free with ticket to Tapestry, daily 10:00–12:30, 14:00–18:00, in summer until 19:00 with no midday closing).

Hotel du Doyen—Here you can watch lace workers designing and making intricate lace as they did in the 1600s and see a variety of examples of their finest works over the years. You'll get a great view of the cathedral from the front steps (free with ticket to Tapestry, located outside the cathedral's right transept, across the street, same hours as Baron Gerard Museum).

Bayeux Memorial Museum/Battle of Normandy—This museum, providing a good overview of the Battle of Normandy, features tanks, jeeps, uniforms, and countless informative displays (32F, May–mid-Sept daily 9:30–18:30, mid-Sept–Apr closes 12:30–14:00, on Bayeux's ring road, 20 min on foot from center).

Sleeping in Bayeux
(6F = about $1, zip code: 14400)

Hotels are a good value here. **Hôtel Notre Dame***, ideally situated right across from the cathedral, has spacious, funky-comfortable rooms with wall-to-ceiling carpeting (ask for a room with a view of the cathedral) and asks that you dine in its elegant but reasonable restaurant. Annick will take care of your every need (D-160F, Db-270F, Tb-360F, Qb-465F, showers 20F if not in room, CC:VMA, 44 rue des Cuisiniers, tel. 02 31 92 87 24, fax 02 31 92 67 11).

Hôtel de Reine Mathilde**, one block from the cathedral on the street just below it, has modern and comfortable rooms (Db-300F, Tb-340F, CC:VMA, 23 rue Larcher, tel. 02 31 92 08 13, fax 02 31 92 09 93).

For three-plus-star comfort at two-star prices stay at the impeccable **Hotel d'Argouges****. Every room is wood-beamed cozy and meticulously cared for. Named for its builder, Lord d' Argouges, this tranquil retreat has a châteaulike feel and a lovely private garden. It's located just off the huge place St. Patrice, a 10-minute walk from the Tapestry up rue St. Martin; look for an archway leading to its private parking lot (Db-380–450F, several fantastic family suites-540F, extra bed-70F, CC:VM, 21 rue St. Patrice, tel. 02 31 92 88 86, fax 02 31 92 69 16).

Train travelers immune to noise, cat pee odor, and rude owners may appreciate the **Hôtel de la Gare's*** simple rooms (S-95F, D-105F, Db-215F, T-145F, Tb-310F, Q-205–285F, tel. 02 31 92 10 70, fax 02 31 51 95 99).

Chambres d'hôte are a great value around here, and it's worth the effort to find **Andre and Madeleine Sebire**'s wonderful working farmhouse and its four terrific and cheap rooms decorated with family furnishings, a do-it-yourself common kitchen and living room, and a pleasant garden. Located between Bayeux and Arromanches, it's in the tiny village of Ryes at the Ferme du Clos Neuf—look for the faded Chambres signs (Sb-180F, Db-200F, Tb-250F, includes breakfast, zip code: 14400, tel. 02 31 22 32 34, NSE). For more *chambres d'hôte* listings, inquire at the Bayeux or Arromanches TI.

Eating in Bayeux

Bayeux's old city centers around the pedestrian rue St. Jean, which is lined with *crêperies*, cafés, and the best *charcuterie* in town (salads and quiches to go) across from Hotel Churchill. For a traditional meal on grand monastery tables, try the reasonable **La Table du Terroir** (good salads, *menus* from 99F, just off the pedestrian street at 42 rue St. Jean, tel. 02 31 92 05 53). The restaurants at **Hôtel Notre Dame** (95F *menu*, see hotel listing) and **Le Petit Normand** (*menus* start at 80F, 35 rue Larcher) merit their fine reputations.

Transportation Connections—Bayeux

By train to: Paris' St. Lazare (8/day, 2.5 hrs), **Amboise** (8/day, transfers in Caen and Tours or Paris and Tours), **Rouen** (3/day, 3 hrs, transfer in Caen), **Honfleur** (5/day, 2.5 hrs; train to Lisieux or Caen, then bus to Bayeux, bus is cheaper from Lisieux), **Mont St. Michel** (2–3 trains/day, 2 hrs to Pontorson, with a convenient late-afternoon departure; from Pontorson bus to Mont St. Michel—4/day, 2/day Sun, 15 min—or find others to share a taxi—80F, 110F after 19:00 and on weekends, tel. 02 33 60 26 89).

By bus to the D-day beaches: Arromanches is the only accessible destination by bus from Bayeux. **Bus Vert** offers four trips per day (14.5F), one of which works great for day-trippers—leave Bayeux about 12:00 for 90 minutes in Arromanches before returning (4/weekday, 2/Sat, 0/Sun; be careful on Wed; catch the bus at the Bayeux train station or place St. Patrice—a 10-minute walk up rue St. Martin from the center, veer right through the square to bus shelters).

D-DAY BEACHES

Along the 75 miles of Atlantic coast north of Bayeux (from Sainte Marie du Mont to Ouistreham) you'll find museums, monuments, cemeteries, and battle remains left in tribute to the courage of the WWII British, Canadian, and American armies, who successfully carried out the largest military operation in history. It was on these beautiful beaches, at the crack of dawn, June 6, 1944, that the Allies finally gained a foothold in France and Nazi Europe began to crumble.

> *"The first twenty-four hours of the invasion will be decisive...*
> *the fate of Germany depends on the outcome...for the Allies,*
> *as well as Germany, it will be the longest day."*
> —Field Marshall Erwin Rommel to his aide,
> April 22, 1944. From *The Longest Day.*

Getting around the D-Day Beaches

A car is ideal, particularly for three or more persons (figure about 400F per day; the TI lists local rental agencies), though biking is an option for those with time and energy (rent a bike in Bayeux at M. Roue's shop for 80F, boulevard W. Churchill, tel. 02 31 92 27 75). Buses connect Bayeux and Arromanches (see "Transportation Connections—Bayeux," above) to allow you to see the most impressive D-day (*Jour J* in French) sights. Consider a minivan excursion for an even better look. Several companies offer excursions to the D-day beaches from Bayeux for about 180F per adult (160F student). These are not guided tours; you get an English-speaking driver and transportation between key sights. **Bus Fly Excursions** does a good job; they also offer day trips to Mont St. Michel for 300F (tel. 02 31 22 00 08 or 02 33 39 23 52, fax 02 31 92 35 10, e-mail: info@busfly.com). If they're full, try **Jean-Marc Bacon** (tel. 02 31 92 10 70, fax 02 31 51 95 99). Taxis are another good option; figure 95F one way from Bayeux to Arromanches and 150F from Bayeux to the American Cemetery. Ask about "waiting rates" (tel. 02 31 92 92 40). Caen's Museum (see below) offers informative tours of the beaches.

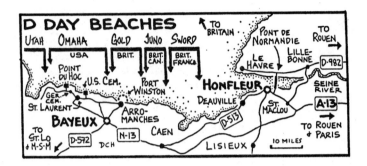

Sights—D-Day Beaches

▲▲▲**Caen's Battle of Normandy Museum**—Caen, the modern capital of lower Normandy, has the best World War II museum in France. Officially named the Memorial for Peace, its intent is to put the Battle of Normandy in a broader context. Your visit has four parts: the lead-up to World War II, the actual Battle of Normandy, the video presentations, and the ongoing fight for peace.

The museum is brilliant. Begin with a downward spiral stroll, tracing (almost psychoanalyzing) the path of Europe from World War I to the rise of fascism to World War II.

The entire lower level gives a thorough look at how World War II was fought—from General de Gaulle's London radio broadcasts to Hitler's early missiles to wartime fashion.

You then see a series of three powerful movies (15 minutes each, for all languages, the cycle starts every 20 minutes—a clock at the end of the lower-level exhibits lets you plan your time). Ninety percent of the incredible D-day footage is real, with a bit taken from the movie *The Longest Day*.

The memorial then takes you beyond World War II to the Gallery of Nobel Prizes. This is a celebration of the courageous work of people like Andrei Sakharov, Elie Wiesel, and Desmond Tutu, who understand that peace is more than an absence of war.

The finale is a walk through the U.S. Armed Forces Memorial Garden. I was a bit bothered by the mindless laughing of light-hearted children unable to appreciate their blessings. Then I read on the pavement, "From the heart of our land flows the blood of our youth, given to you in the name of freedom." And their laughter made me happy.

Memorial Museum entry: 69F, free for World War II veterans, 63F for other veterans, free admission and nursery for kids under 10, daily 9:00–19:00, mid-Jul–mid-Aug until 21:00, ticket office closes 90 minutes before museum. Allow 2.5 hours for your visit, including an hour for the videos (tel. 02 31 06 06 44—as in June 6, 1944—www.unicaen.fr/memorial). Tickets are 8F less if purchased at Caen's TI on place St. Pierre (daily 9:30–19:00, tel. 02 31 27 14 14). The museum offers half- and full-day tours of WWII sights and beaches—call to reserve and pay in advance (340–480F, CC:VM).

The memorial is just off the freeway in Caen (exit: Université, follow signs to Memorial). By train, it's two hours from Paris (14/day) or just 15 minutes from Bayeux (10/day); upon arrival in Caen, take bus #17-Memorial from Caen's train station (exit right out of the station, 2nd shelter, buses every 15 min, or taxi 55F each way).

▲▲▲**Arromanches (Musée du Débarquement)**—The first-ever prefab harbor was created by the British in this town. Churchill's brainchild, it was named Port Winston. Walk along the seafront promenade and imagine 18 old ships and 115 football field–size cement blocks (called Mulberries) being towed across the English Channel and sunk right here to create a seven-mile-long breakwater and harbor for landing 54,000 vehicles and 500,000 troops in six days. You can still see remains of the temporary harbor and visit the beachfront museum, where this incredible undertaking is re-created with models, maps, mementos, and two short audiovisual shows—ask for English (35F, May–Sept daily 9:00–18:30, off-season 9:30–17:30, closed Jan, tel. 02 31 22 34 31). Walk to the top of the bluff behind the museum for a fine view and ponder how, from this makeshift harbor, the liberation of Europe commenced. Here you'll find Arromanches 360's surround theater showing *The Price of Freedom*, a well-produced film that gives you "18 minutes of total emotion" about the Normandy invasion on nine screens with no narration (24F, 2 showings per hour, Jun–Aug 9:40–18:40, otherwise 10:00–17:40, closes at 16:40 in winter, tel. 02 31 22 30 30). For more information on Arromanches, see "Sleeping," below.

Longues Sur Mer—Several German bunkers, guns intact, are left guarding against seaborne attacks on the city of Arromanches. Walk out to the observation post for a territorial view over the Channel (located between Arromanches and Port en Bessin; look for signs).

▲▲▲**American Cemetery at St. Laurent**—Beautifully situated on a bluff just above Omaha Beach, the 9,400 brilliant white-marble crosses and Stars of David glow in memory of Americans who gave their lives to free Europe on the beaches below, where fighting was particularly intense. Notice the names and home states inscribed on the crosses. Behind the monument, surrounded by roses, are the names of 1,557 missing or unidentified soldiers. France has given the United States free permanent use of this 172-acre site. It is immaculately maintained by the American Battle Monuments Commission. Pick up the handout in the small office as you enter. The trail to the beach below is open from 8:00 to 18:00, off-season until 17:00 unless wild boars (*sangliers*) are prowling about.

German Military Cemetery—For an opportunity to ponder German losses, drop by this somber, thought-provoking resting place of 21,000 German soldiers. While the American cemetery is the focus of American visitors, visitors here speak in hushed German. The site is glum, with two graves per simple marker and dark crosses that huddle together in groups of five. It's just south of Point du Hoc (right off N-13 in the village of La Cambe, 22 km west of Bayeux; follow signs to Cimitiere Allemand).

▲▲**Pointe du Hoc**—During the D-day invasion, 225 U.S. Rangers attempted a castle-style siege of the German-occupied cliffs by using grappling hooks and ladders borrowed from London fire departments. Only 90 survived. German bunkers and bomb craters remain as they were found (20 min by car west of American Cemetery in St. Laurent, just past Vierville-sur-Mer).

Sleeping in Arromanches
(6F = about $1)
To really feel the pulse of World War II, sleep in Arromanches. The beach, cliffs, and temporary harbor are mesmerizing early or late in the day. The TI is located across the parking lot from the museum on rue Colonel Rene Michel, behind Hotel de la Marine (daily 10:00–12:00, 14:00–18:00, no midday closing in summer, tel. 02 31 21 47 56, www.arromanches.com). The population of tiny Arromanches just reached 500 persons (about the same as on June 6, 1944). The town has a grocery store (at the bus station), a post office and Laundromat next door, and an ATM near the museum. For Arromanche's only taxi, dial 02 31 92 12 12 or cellular 06 07 61 39 16.

Friendly **Pappagall Hotel d'Arromanches**** is a good value, with a fun bar and cheery restaurant (Db-260–310F, 2 rue Colonel Rene Michel, 14117 Arromanches, tel. 02 31 22 36 26, fax 02 31 22 23 29. **Hotel de la Marine*****, right on the water, offers beach views from most of its cushy rooms and a fine restaurant (Db-300–400F, Tb-380–480F, family room-510–750F, quai du Canada, tel. 02 31 22 34 19, fax 02 31 22 98 80). **Hotel de Normandie***, with bright, clean, and comfortable rooms and peely linoleum bathrooms, is a very good value (Db-150–280F, CC:VM, tel. 02 31 22 34 32, fax 02 31 21 57 56, right on the parking lot near the museum). For evening fun, try the bar at **Pappagall Hotel d'Arromanches** or the **Pub Marie Celeste** (good chili), right around the corner on rue de la Poste.

MONT ST. MICHEL
The distant silhouette of this Gothic island-abbey sends the tired sightseer's spirits soaring. Mont St. Michel, which through the ages has been among the top four pilgrimage sites in Christendom, is one of those rare places that looks as enchanting in reality

as it does in dreams. While it floats like a mirage on the horizon, it does show up on film.

The causeway, built in 1878, stopped the water from flowing around the island, which in turn contributed to the filling in of the bay around Mont St. Michel—so it's no longer an island. A new bridge is being planned that will let the water circulate and turn Mont St. Michel into an island again. Travelers will then be shuttled by bus to the island.

Orientation

Mont St. Michel is connected by a two-mile causeway to the mainland and surrounded by a sandy mud flat. Your visit features a one-street village that winds up to the fortified abbey. Between 10:00 and 16:00, tourists trample the dreamscape (try to remember that this street was just as jammed with ernest pilgrims hundreds of years ago). A ramble on the ramparts offers mud-flat views and an escape from the tourist zone. The only worthwhile entry is the abbey itself, at the summit of the island.

Daytime Mont St. Michel is a touristic gauntlet—worth a stop, but a short one will do. The tourist tide recedes late each afternoon. During nonsummer nights, the island is abbey-quiet, the illumination, beautiful. Poets prefer evenings here. The abbey interior is not an essential visit, and it's open until midnight May through September (off-season until 22:00) as a sound-and-light show anyway, so arriving late and departing early is a good option. If you're spending the night, consider bringing a dinner picnic (see "Eating" below); there are no grocery shops on the island.

Tourist Information: The TI (and WC) is to your left as you enter Mont St. Michel's gates. They have handy brochures listing hotels, *chambres d'hôte*, restaurants, English tour times for the abbey, bus schedules, and the tide table (*Horaires des Marées*), essential if you explore outside Mont St. Michel (daily 9:00–19:00 in summer, off-season 9:00–12:30, 14:00–18:30, tel. 02 33 60 14 30). A post office (PTT) and ATM are 50 yards beyond the TI.

Tides: The tides here (which rise 50 feet) are the largest and most dangerous in Europe. During a flood tide the ocean rushes in at 12 miles per hour. In medieval times it was faster, rushing in "at the speed of a galloping horse." Even today the undertow can sweep a slow horse (or tourist) away. High tides (*grandes marées*) lap against the tourist office door (where you'll find tide hours posted).

Parking: Remember, very high tides rise to the edge of the causeway—leaving the causeway open but any cars parked below it under water. Safe parking is available at the foot of Mont St. Michel; you will be instructed where to park under high-tide conditions. There's plenty of parking, provided you arrive off-season or early or late in high season.

Sights—Mont St. Michel

The Village below the Abbey—Mont St. Michel's main street of shops and hotels leads to the abbey. With only 30 full-time residents, the village lives solely for tourists. After the TI, check the tide warnings posted on the wall. Before the drawbridge, on your left, poke through the door of Restaurant Le Mere Poulard, where a virtual theater-kitchen in action shows the colorful making of the traditional omelet. Don't spend 95F for this edible tourist trap. But watch the show as old-time-costumed cooks beat omelets, daddy, eight to the bar.

As you pass through the old drawbridge, Mont St. Michel welcomes you with the most touristy street this side of Tijuana (remember the pilgrims). You can trudge through this touristic gauntlet uphill past several gimmicky museums and human traffic jams to the abbey (all island hotel receptions are located on this street). Or better, to avoid the tourist deluge, climb the first steps after the drawbridge on your right and then turn right or left at the top; the ramparts lead all the way up and up to the abbey in either direction (quieter if you turn right). Public WCs charge according to altitude: 1F at the entry to Mont St. Michel, 2F halfway up, and 3F at the abbey entrance.

▲▲Abbey of Mont St. Michel—Mont St. Michel has been an important pilgrimage center since A.D. 708, when the Archangel Michael told the bishop of Avranches to "build here and build high." With uncanny foresight he reassured the bishop, "If you build it...they will come." Today's abbey is built on the remains of a Romanesque church, which was built on the remains of a Carolingian church. Saint Michael, whose gilded statue decorates the top of the spire, was the patron saint of many French kings, making this a favored sight for French royalty through the ages. As you enter, imagine the headaches and hassles the monks ran into while building it. They had to ferry the granite from across the bay (then deeper and without the causeway) and make the same hike you just did—with more luggage.

The visit is a one-way route through fine—but barren—Gothic rooms. You'll explore the impressive church, delicate cloisters, and refectory (where the monks ate in austere silence) and then climb down into the dark, damp Romanesque foundations. A highlight is the giant tread-wheel, which six workers would power hamster-style to haul two-ton loads of stones and supplies from the landing below. This was used right up until the 19th century. You'll better appreciate the abbey by renting a Walkman (25F, 35F for 2) or by taking a 75-minute English-language tour (free, tip requested; several tours per day, groups can be large, tour times at TI). For some, the tours make a short story long. Those who go through *sans* tour or Walkman find no English explanations posted—but then, there's not a lot to explain.

(40F, mid-May–mid-Sept daily 9:00–18:30, spring and fall
9:30–17:00, closes at 16:00 in winter, ticket office closes 1 hour
earlier.) Buy your ticket to the abbey and keep climbing. Tours
begin at the very top terrace in front of the church. Allow 20
minutes to climb at a relaxed, steady pace from the TI to the
abbey. For a free near-abbey visit, hike through the ticket room
and gift shop, where you'll find models of the abbey over the ages.
From there you can enter the free abbey gardens.

▲▲**Stroll around Mont St. Michel**—To resurrect that Mont St.
Michel dreamscape and evade all those tacky tourist stalls, walk
out on the mudflats around the island. At low tide it's reasonably
dry and a great memory. This can be extremely dangerous, so be
sure to double-check the tides. Remember the scene from the
Bayeux tapestry where Harold rescues Normans from the quick-
sand? It happened somewhere in this bay. You may notice entire
school groups hiking in from the muddy horizon. Attempting this
popular excursion without a local guide is reckless.

▲▲**Evening on Mont St. Michel**—After dark the island is magi-
cally floodlit. Views from the ramparts are sublime. You must exit
the island and walk out on the causeway a few hundred yards to
best appreciate this magical place. There are plans for a new sound
and light show on Mont St. Michel (to replace the existing one),
but no details are available yet. Inquire at the TI.

Sleeping on or near Mont St. Michel
(6F = about $1, zip code: 50116)

Sleeping on the island, inside the walls, is by far the best way to
experience Mont St. Michel, though you may pay a premium for
your hotel bed. On the island, most hotels are impersonal and pad
their profits by requiring guests to buy dinner from their restaurant. Skip their outrageously priced breakfasts. Several hotels are
closed from November until Easter. To reserve by letter, addresses
are simple: name of hotel, 50116 Mont St. Michel, France. Because
most visitors only day-trip here, you should be able to find a room
at almost any time of the year. However, reserve ahead if possible.

The cozy and comfortable rooms offered at the **Restaurant le
St. Michel** are the best value on the island (Db-210–310F, no dinner requirements but a good restaurant, tel. & fax 02 33 60 14 37).
The rather impersonal **Hôtel du Guesclin**** offers clean rooms at
fair prices (D-190–220F, Db-260–320F, CC:VM, tel. 02 33 60 14
10, fax 02 33 60 45 81). The more congenial **Hotel les Terrasses
Poulard** has several good-value rooms in its main building and too
many overpriced rooms in its annex (Db-300–900F, CC:VMA,
tel. 02 33 60 14 09 fax 02 33 60 37 31). The remaining hotels all
offer a token few inexpensive rooms and many high-priced ones
with similar amenities and prices. The rooms at **Vielle Auberge**,
owned by a moody woman, are among the best for the price in this

crowd; don't let her talk you into more room than you need (Db-320, Db with view-380F, Db with view and terrace-600F, CC:V, tel. 02 33 60 14 34, fax 02 33 70 87 04). You can also try the professionally pleasant **Le Mouton Blanc**'s cozy rooms (Db-330–400F, Tb/Qb-460–600F, CC:VMA, tel. 02 33 60 14 08, fax 02 33 60 05 62) or **Hôtel Croix Blanche***** (fine loft triples, a few superb-view doubles, Sb-390F, Db-450–510F, Tb/Qb-620–900F, CC:VM, tel. 02 33 60 14 04, fax 02 33 48 59 82).

Rooms on the nearby mainland are less atmospheric but cheaper. Among the *chambres d'hôte*, Madame Brault's **La Jacotiere**, with comfortable rooms and views of Mont St. Michel, is a steal (D-200F, in Ardevon, zip code: 50170, tel. 02 33 60 22 94, fax 02 33 60 20 48). **Hôtel de la Digue***** is the best and the closest of the hotels on the approach to Mont St. Michel. Spacious, modern, and cushy rooms and a good restaurant with a view of Mont St. Michel make this hard to beat (Db-330–460F, Tb-490F, Qb-520F, CC:VMA, tel. 02 33 60 14 02, fax 02 33 60 37 59).

Train travelers may prefer sleeping in Pontorson (which for me is like kissing my sister): **Hotel Vauban****, across from the train station, is quiet and comfortable, with a pleasant garden (D-150F, Db-280F, 2 boulevard Clemenceau, 50170 Pontorson, tel. 02 33 60 03 83, fax 02 33 60 35 48). **Hotel de l'Arrivee** has acceptable dirt-cheap rooms (D-150F, 1 rue Docteur Tizon, 50170 Pontorson, tel. & fax 02 33 60 01 57).

Eating on Mont St. Michel

Puffy omelets are the island's specialty. Also look for mussels and seafood platters, locally raised lamb (fed on the saltwater grass), and Muscadet wine (dry, cheap, and white). I let Patricia and Phillipe cook for me at the friendly and reasonable **Le St. Michel** (tel. 02 33 60 14 37), across from Hôtel Mouton Blanc. Or picnic in the small park below the abbey (to the left as you look up at the abbey).

Transportation Connections—Mont St. Michel

The nearest train station is in Pontorson, 15 minutes away by bus (4/day Mon–Fri, 2/day Sun). A Pontorson-MSM taxi will cost about 80F, 110F after 19:00 and on weekends; look for others to share a cab (tel. 02 33 60 26 89). You can rent a bike at the Pontorson train station. All departures below are from Pontorson except where noted:

By train to: Paris (4/day, 4 hrs via Caen or Rennes; there's also a handy bus/TGV train combination right to/from Mont St. Michel via Rennes—2/day, 4 hrs, 1 morning, 1 evening), **Bayeux** (2/day, 2 hrs), **Dinan** (2–3/day, 1 hr via Dol), **Amboise** (4/day via Caen and Tours in 7 hrs, or via Rennes and Paris in 8 hrs, both require a transfer in Tours).

By bus to: St. Malo (2/day, 75 mins direct to Mont St. Michel).

Sights near Normandy—Brittany

The Couesenan River marks the border between Normandy and
Brittany. It hits the sea a few hundred meters west of Mont St.
Michel, leaving the island barely in Normandy. The peninsula of
Brittany is rugged, with an isolated interior, a well-discovered
coast, and strong Celtic ties. This region of independent-minded
locals is distinctly different from Normandy.

Dinan

If you have time for only one stop in Brittany, do Dinan. This
delightful city offers Brittany's best-preserved medieval center
(1 hour from Mont St. Michel). Dinan feels real and untouristy.

Consider this walk: Start at the TI (Jun–Sept 9:00–19:00, closes
off-season at 17:45 and for lunch, 6 rue de l'Horloge, tel. 02 96 39
75 40; the overpriced 15F tourist magazine has more information on
this self-guided tour). Inspect the nearby lookout tower, Tour de
l'Horloge (15F, good view from the top), then continue down rue
de l'Horloge and turn left into Dinan's historic commercial center,
the place des Merciers. The half-timbered arcaded buildings are
Dinan's oldest. They date from the time when property taxes were
based on the square footage of your ground floor. To provide shelter from both the taxes and the rain, owners built out their first
floors. Turn right where the square ends and then rappel partway
down rue Jerzual (for *crêperies*, boutiques, and stiff knees). Crossing
under the medieval gate (Porte Jerzual), turn right and climb to the
only accessible section of the ramparts. Enjoy the view and then
double back down the ramparts. If you're feeling fit, continue down
to the old port; then, to truly get a breath of Brittany, cross the old
bridge, turn right, and follow the river trail 30 minutes to the pristine little village of Lehon, where you'll find a café/*crêperie*. If your
legs disagree, descend no farther but jog right after exiting the gate
of the ramparts above the Porte Jerzual and take the first left uphill
to the Jardins Anglais (English Gardens). Survey Dinan's port and
Rance valley. Then peek inside the very Breton Basilique St.
Sauveur (bordering the park, English explanation inside).

Sleeping and Eating in Dinan
(6F = about $1, zip code: 22100)

Hôtel de la Duchesse Anne*, warmly run by Gilles and Chris-
tine, is a salt-of-the-earth budget home base on a large square at
the edge of the old town (Ss-180F, Sb-220F, Db-260F, 18 place
du Guesclin, tel. 02 96 39 09 43, fax 02 96 87 57 26). Even if
you're not staying here, drop by the hotel bar and have Gilles
draw you a *bolée* of *cidre*. For cozy, spotless, and comfortable
rooms, stay in the well-run **Hotel les Grandes Tours** (S-180F,
Sb-270F, D-200F, Db-290F, Tb-330F, Qb-450F, CC-VM, 6 rue
du Chateau, tel. 02 96 85 16 20, fax 02 96 85 16 04). Nearer the

TI, the small and comfortable **Hotel La Tour de l'Horloge**** is another good value (Db-290–310F, 5 rue de la Chaux, tel. 02 96 39 96 92, fax 02 96 85 06 99). For dinner try any of the cozy *crêperies* in the old city. If you're not in the mood for crêpes, try my favorite restaurant, **Le St. Louis**, just around the corner from Hotel les Grandes Tours. Flames from the fireplace flicker on wood beams and white tablecloths (95F *menu*, great salad bar and desserts, delectable main courses, closed Wed except in summer, 9 rue de Lehon, tel. 02 96 39 89 50).

St. Malo and Fougères

▲**St. Malo**—Come here to experience *the* Breton beach resort. Stroll high up on the impressive ramparts that circle the entire old city, eat seafood, walk as far out on the beaches as the tides allow, then return to Dinan for the night. An easy day trip, St. Malo is a 45-minute drive or a one-hour bus or train ride from Mont St. Michel or Dinan.

▲**Fougères**—This very Breton city is a delightful stop for drivers traveling between the Loire châteaus and Mont St. Michel. Fougères has one of Europe's largest medieval castles, a fine city center, and a panoramic park viewpoint (from St. Leonard church in Jardin Public). Try one of the café/*crêperies* near the castle, such as the tasty **Crêperie des Remparts**, one block uphill from the castle. (Crêpes, called *galettes* in Brittany, are the local fare.) Pick up a city map and castle description in English at the castle entrance. The interior is grass and walls.

THE LOIRE

Named for France's longest river, the Loire Valley is carpeted with fertile fields, crisscrossed by rivers, and studded with hundreds of châteaus in all shapes and sizes. The medieval castles are here because the Loire was strategically important during the Hundred Years' War. The Renaissance palaces replaced medieval castles when the Loire became fashionable among the Parisian rich and royalty during that age.

The valley of a thousand châteaus is also the home to many good wines. As you travel through the Loire, look for *"Dégustation"* (tasting) signs. Inquire at TIs for winery tour and tasting information. Vouvray, several miles west of Amboise, and Chinon, 20 minutes west of Tours, both have many proud and hospitable family wineries.

Planning Your Time

One and a half days is sufficient to sample the best of the Loire châteaus. Amboise and Chenonceaux are ideal springboards for visits to the region's three most interesting ones: Chambord, Chenonceau, and Cheverny. If you have more time, tour Azay le Rideau, Villandry's gardens, and Langeais (using Chinon as a home base).

If arriving by car, try to see one château on your way in (e.g., Chambord if arriving from the north, Langeais from the west, or Azay le Rideau from the south). If arriving by train, go directly to Amboise and try to visit Le Clos Lucé that afternoon.

Don't go overboard on château-hopping. Two châteaus, possibly three (if you're a big person), make up the recommended daily dosage. Famous châteaus are least crowded early, at lunchtime, and late. Most open around 9:00 and close between 18:00 and 19:00. During the off-season many close from 12:00 to 14:00.

The lazy plan for those with low energy, no car, and no money for a day minivan tour is to catch the once-per-day Amboise–Chenonceau bus (from near the TI at 10:54, giving you 90 minutes at the château and departing the château at 12:40). Spend the afternoon enjoying Amboise, its château, and Leonardo's place.

Best Day on the Loire (from Amboise by car)*
9:00–11:00: Chenonceau
11:45–14:00: Chambord and lunch
15:00–16:00: Cheverny or Chaumont
        17:00: Return to Amboise and tour Le Clos Lucé
*Minivan excursions offer a day trip very similar to this plan (see below).

Getting around the Loire Valley
By Train: Amboise is well connected to the city of Tours. The châteaus of Chenonceau, Langeais, Chinon, and Azay le Rideau all have train and or bus service from Tours' main station. (Chenonceau is better done by bus or bike from Amboise, and you should consider sleeping in Chinon if you want to visit Langeais, Chinon, and Azay le Rideau.) Be careful: In Tours, there are two important train stations and a bus station with service to several châteaus; the main train station is referred to as Tours SNCF, and the TGV station is St. Pierre des Corps. Check the schedules carefully, as service is sparse on some lines.

By Bike: Cycling options are endless in this region where the elevation gain is generally manageable (still, many find even the shortest rides described exhausting—evaluate your stamina realistically). Amboise, Blois, and Chinon make the best bike bases. From Amboise allow an hour to Chenonceau and 90 minutes to Chaumont (remember, you've got to return the same distance). Connecting Amboise, Chenonceau, and Chaumont with an all-day 60-kilometer pedal required all the energy I had (see "Loire Valley" map in this chapter for details). From Blois by bike to Chambord and Cheverny is a full-day, 50-kilometer round trip; call the Blois TI for bike-rental information (tel. 02 54 90 41 41). My favorite bike rides are from Chinon to Ussè, Azay le Rideau, Villandry, and/or Langeais (see "Chinon," below, for more information).

By Minibus Tour: Pascal Accolay runs Acco-Dispo, a small and personal minibus company with excellent all-day château tours from Amboise (or other area villages, including Tours, ideal for those day-tripping from Paris). Tour costs vary with itinerary; figure 140F to 180F for a half day, and 240F to 280F for all day. English is the primary language. While you'll get a fun and enthusiastic running commentary on the road, covering each château's background as well as the region's contemporary scene, you're

The Loire Valley

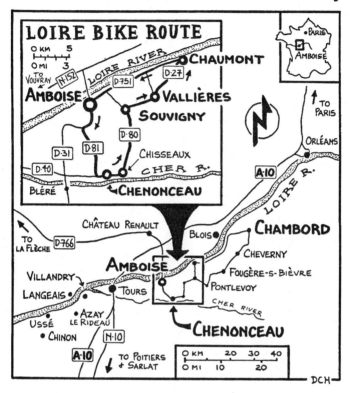

on your own at each château covered (you pay the admission fee). All-day tours depart at about 8:30, afternoon tours depart at about 12:50, and both return to Amboise around 18:30. Several itinerary options are available; most include Chenonceau. Groups range from two to eight château-hoppers (18 rue des Vallees in Amboise, tours go daily, free hotel pickups, reserve by tel. 02 47 57 67 13, fax 02 47 23 15 73, www.accodispo-tours.com). If this doesn't work, any Loire TI can explain your minibus options.

By Taxi: A taxi from Amboise to Chenonceau costs about 100F. Your hotel can call one for you. The meter doesn't start until you do.

By Rental Car: Two reliable car-rental agencies are **Avis** (380F/day unlimited mileage, across from the TI, tel. 02 47 57 01 54, fax 02 47 23 22 47) and **Garage Jourdain** (280F/day, 100 kms free, they'll pick you up at your Amboise hotel, 105 route de Tours,

1.5 kilometers downriver from TI, tel. 02 47 57 17 92, fax 02 47 57 77 50). Both close Monday through Friday from 12:00 to 14:00 and at 18:00, at 17:00 on Saturday, and all day Sunday.

Cuisine Scene—Loire Valley

Here in "the garden of France," anything from the earth is bound to be good. Loire Valley rivers produce fresh trout (*truite*), salmon (*saumon*), and smelt (*éperlau*), which is often served fried (*friture*). *Rillettes*, a stringy pile of whipped pork fat and liver, makes for a cheap, mouthwatering sandwich spread (use lots of mustard and add a baby pickle, called a *cornichon*). The area's fine goat cheeses include Crottin de Chavignol (*crottin* means horse dung, which is what this cheese, when aged, resembles), Saint-Maure Fermier (soft and creamy), and Selles-sur-Cher (mild). The best and most expensive white wines are the Sancerres and Pouilly-Fumés. Less expensive but still tasty are Tourraine Sauvignons and the sweeter Vouvrays. The better reds come from Chinon and Bourgeuil. For dessert try a mouthwatering *tarte Tatin* (upside-down caramel-apple tart).

AMBOISE

Straddling the widest part of the Loire, Amboise slumbers in the shadow of its château. Leonardo da Vinci retired here...just one more fine idea. With or without a car, Amboise is an ideal small-town home base for exploring the best of château country. A castle has overlooked the Loire from Amboise since Roman times. As the royal residence of François I, the town wielded far more importance than you'd imagine from a lazy walk down the pleasant pedestrian-only commercial zone at the base of the palace.

Amboise (am-bwaz, pop. 11,000) covers both sides of the Loire and an island in the middle. The station is on the north side of the river, but everything else of interest is on the south (château) side, including the information-packed TI on the riverbank.

Tourist Information: The TI is on quai du Général de Gaulle in the round building. Their Amboise city map shows restaurants, hotels, and château information, including the time and place of English-language sound-and-light shows (mid-Jun–Sept Mon–Sat 9:00–20:00, Sun 10:00–12:00, 15:00–18:00, Oct–mid-June Mon–Sat 9:00–12:30, 14:00–18:30, Sun 10:00–12:00, tel. 02 47 57 09 28, www.amboise-valloire.com). The Michelin green guide to the Loire provides a good historical and architectural background on the region and each château (sold for about 60F—40 percent off the U.S. price—at all tourist shops).

Arrival in Amboise

By Train: Amboise's train station (tel. 02 47 23 18 23), with a post office and taxi stand, is birds-chirping peaceful. Turn left out of

Amboise

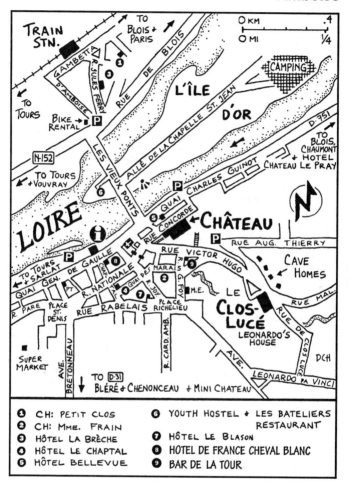

❶ CH: PETIT CLOS
❷ CH: MME. FRAIN
❸ HÔTEL LA BRÈCHE
❹ HÔTEL LE CHAPTAL
❺ HÔTEL BELLEVUE
❻ YOUTH HOSTEL + LES BATELIERS RESTAURANT
❼ HÔTEL LE BLASON
❽ HOTEL DE FRANCE CHEVAL BLANC
❾ BAR DE LA TOUR

the station, make a quick right, and walk down rue de Nazelles five minutes to the bridge that leads you over the Loire and into town. Within three blocks of the station are a recommended hotel, B&B, and bike-rental shop.

By Car: Drivers set their sights on the flag-festooned château capping the hill above downtown Amboise. Most accommodations and restaurants listed in this book cluster just downriver of the château. Street parking near your hotel should be easy.

Helpful Hints

Bike Rental: You'll pay about 70F per half day and 90F per full day, and you'll be asked to leave your passport—or better, a photocopy of it. Two reliable places are **Locacycle** (daily 9:00–19:00, near TI at 2 rue Jean-Jacques Rousseau, tel. 02 47 57 00 28, SE) and **Cycles Richard**, with better bikes (closed 12:00–14:00, on train-station side of river, just past bridge at 2 rue de Nazelles, tel. 02 47 57 01 79, NSE).

Laundromat: The handy coin-op Lav'centre is a block from the rue Chaptal toward the château on 9 allée du Sergent Turpin (daily 7:00–21:00, Oct–May until 20:00, 22F to wash, bring four 10F coins to wash and dry a big load, figure 90 minutes; change machine, 2F detergent dispenser). The door locks at closing time; leave beforehand or you'll trigger the alarm system.

Sights—Amboise

▲**Château d'Amboise**—This one-time royal residence was used in the Middle Ages to greet royal pilgrims en route from Paris to Spain's Santiago de Compostela. Leonardo da Vinci is said to have designed the château's vaulted spiral staircases. Pick up the fine free English tour flier as you enter. The lacy, petite chapel (first stop) is flamboyant Gothic, with two fireplaces "to comfort the king" and a plaque "evoking the final resting place" of Leonardo. Where he's actually buried no local really seems to know. After a fine town and river view, continue into and through the well-furnished château—which, while much larger in the 15th century, feels plenty big. Your last stop is the horsemen's tower, a brick ramp—climbing 40 meters in five spirals—designed to accommodate a mounted soldier in a hurry (39F, Mar–Oct daily 9:00–18:00, until 19:30 in summer, off-season closes 12:00–14:00 and at 17:00, tel. 02 47 57 00 98). The château puts on a sound-and-light spectacle on Wednesday and Saturday evenings in summer; bring your sweater.

▲▲**Le Clos Lucé** (luh clo loo-say)—This "House of Light" is the plush palace where Leonardo spent his last three years. France's Renaissance king François I set Leonardo up just so he could enjoy his intellectual company. There's a touching sketch in Leonardo's bedroom of François comforting his genius pal on his deathbed. The house thoughtfully re-creates (with adequate English descriptions) the everyday atmosphere Leonardo enjoyed as he pursued his passions to the very end. Of all the palaces I've seen on the Loire, I'd live here. The ground floor is filled with sketches recording the storm patterns of Leonardo's brain and models of his remarkable inventions (built by IBM according to his notes). It's hard to imagine that this Roman candle of creativity died nearly 500 years ago (39F, mid-Mar–mid-Nov daily 9:00–19:00, otherwise 9:00–18:00, closes at 17:00 in January and at 20:00 in summer; located a pleasant 10-minute walk from downtown Amboise—you'll pass interesting troglodyte homes on your left).

Caveau des Vignerons—Located under Amboise's château across from the recommended l'Epicerie restaurant, this small cave offers free tastings of regional wines and sells various other products of the Loire (May–Sept 10:00–19:00).

La Maison Enchantée—Your kids will love you for taking them to this automated doll museum. Push the buttons and watch dolls dance in 25 different settings (30F, 22F for children, May–Sept Tue–Sun 10:00–19:00, Oct–Apr 14:00–17:00 only, closed Mon, 7 rue du General Foy, walk down rue de la Tour from château, tel. 02 47 23 24 50).

Mini Château—This five-acre park on the edge of Amboise shows off all the Loire châteaus in 1:25-scale models, forested with 600 bonsai trees and laced together by a model TGV train (59F, kids ages 4–16 39F, Apr–Sept daily 9:00–18:00, until 19:00 in summer, closes at 17:00 in winter, tel. 02 47 23 44 44).

Sound-and-Light Shows—Many Loire Valley châteaus (including Amboise's) offer nighttime sound-and-light shows in the summer. They mix colored floodlights, tape-recorded history, and theater in Renaissance château courtyards. Ask if an English version is offered (they can be impressive even in French) and prepare for a late and probably cool night (bring a sweater or light jacket). The local TI has up-to-date schedules.

Sleeping in Amboise
(6F = about $1, zip code: 37400)

Sleep Code: **S** = Single, **D** = Double/Twin, **T** = Triple, **Q** = Quad, **b** = bathroom, **t** = toilet only, **s** = shower only, **CC** = Credit Card (**V**isa, **M**asterCard, **A**mex), **SE** = Speaks English, **NSE** = No English, * = French hotel rating system (0–4 stars).

Amboise is busy in the summer, but there are lots of hotels and *chambres d'hôte* (CH) in and around the city. Many hotels require half-pension. The TI has photo albums of local hotels and CHs and will reserve either. Except for the first hotel and the first CH, all listings are right in the old-town center.

Hotels

Hôtel La Brèche** is a refuge run by a "we try harder" family (Pierre and Jenny SE) and has spotless rooms and a peaceful garden café (with Ping-Pong). It's 10 minutes from the city center and 100 meters from the train station. Many rooms overlook the garden; those on the street are generally larger. During summer, half-pension is required, and it gets you a prizewinning dinner for an extra 80F per person—I spring 20F more for the *menu du terroir* (S/D-160F, Sb/Db-290F, Tb-320F, Qb-350F, a few good family rooms, CC:VM, 26 rue Jules Ferry, tel. 02 47 57 00 79, fax 02 47 57 65 49).

Hôtel Le Chaptal** is basic, cheap, and central. While less idyllic, it's *très* frumpy, with birds in the lobby and comfortable rooms—quieter off the street—but marginal beds (Db-210–225F, Tb-255F, Qb-295F, CC:VM, 13 rue de Chaptal, tel. 02 47 57 14 46, fax 02 47 57 67 83, NSE). In summer they request that you dine in their cheery, inexpensive dining room.

Hôtel Belle-Vue*** overlooks the river where the bridge hits the town. This spacious hotels has grand public rooms and effective double-paned windows, so traffic is not a serious problem. Half of its pleasant rooms overlook the château, and four rooms come with huge terraces (Sb-270F, Db-300–345F, Tb-360–420F, Qb-460F, CC:VM, elevator, 12 quai Charles-Guinot, tel. 02 47 57 02 26, fax 02 47 30 51 23).

Hotel des Minimes****, a newly renovated 17th-century mansion, is ideal for those seeking luxury in Amboise. It mixes modern comfort with period furniture and affordable four-star prices (Db-600–700F, deluxe Db-830F, 3–4 person suites-1,200–1,400F, extra bed-150F, one block upriver from Hotel Bellevue at 34 quai Charles Guinot, tel. 02 47 30 40 40, fax 02 47 30 40 77, e-mail: manoir-les-minimes@wanadoo.fr).

Hotel Le Blason**, with a friendly, though hard-to-find, staff, is a half-timbered old building sitting on a square five blocks off the river. It offers small, bright, and modern rooms on a noisy street (Sb-270F, Db-300F, Tb-360F, CC:VMA, TV, telephones, easy parking, 11 place Richelieu, tel. 02 47 23 22 41, fax 02 47 57 56 18, Danielle SE). The well-respected restaurant deserves every one of its plaques.

Hotel de France Cheval Blanc* offers big, clean, simple rooms across from the TI (D-160F, Db-200–265F, T-205F, Tb-250–325F, CC:VM, 6 quai du General de Gaulle, tel. 02 47 57 02 44, fax 02 47 57 69 54). *Rue* (street) rooms have double-pane windows but some traffic noise. *Cour* (courtyard) rooms are quieter.

Auberge de Jeunesse is a friendly hostel and a great value (dorm bed-52F, 6 per room max, some 2-person rooms, sheets-17F, 10F 1st-night fee, reception open 15:00–20:00, ideally located on western tip of the island, Centre Charles Péguy, tel. 02 47 57 06 36, fax 02 47 23 15 80).

Chambres d'Hôte in Amboise

The Amboise TI has a long list of private rooms. In summer, if possible, call a day in advance to reserve a room.

Le Petit Clos has three cheery, cottage-type ground-floor rooms on a quiet, picnic-perfect private garden and easy parking. Charming Madame Roullet speaks a leetle English (Db-340F, family room for up to 5 people-700F, includes big, farm-fresh breakfast with homemade everything, three blocks from the station, turn left out of the station and follow the tracks to rue Balzac, 7 rue Balzac, tel. 02 47 57 43 52).

Katia Frain must be the most engaging person in Amboise, and her comfortable *chambres* are cavernous and bright. Stay here for a complete French experience—you'll dive right into French family life. Get ready for a warm reception (Db-280F, huge Tb-320F, extra person-80F, includes breakfast, 14 quai des Marais, tel. 02 47 30 46 51, SE).

Sleeping near Amboise

For a taste of château hotel luxury without going broke, try the grand **Château de Pray*****. You'll feel a hint of the original medieval fortified castle behind the Renaissance elegance of this 750-year-old château that's equipped with a modern swimming pool. The dining room is spendid (160F *menus*). The hotel is only a few minutes upriver from Amboise—toward Chaumont, on the same side of the river as the Amboise château (Db-600–900F, Tb-700–1,000F, Qb-850–1,000F, 37400 Amboise, tel. 02 47 57 23 67, fax 02 47 57 32 50, e-mail: chateau.depray@wanadoo.fr).

One kilometer upriver from Château de Pray are the modern, welcoming *chambres* chez **Madame Clerquin**, complete with vineyards and flowers everywhere and a well-furnished common kitchen (Db-280F, 1 Impasse du Colombier, 37530 Chargé, look for signs and veer right when entering Chargé, tel. 02 47 57 06 33).

For a "Peter Mayle does the Loire" experience 10 minutes from Amboise and Chenonceaux, sleep at Roger and Ann's beautifully renovated 16th-century mill house, **Le Moulin du Fief Gentil**, where you get four acres and a backyard pond (fishing possible), smartly decorated rooms, and an attractive common living room (Db-450–500F, 37150 Blere, tel. 02 47 30 32 51, fax 02 47 57 95 72, e-mail: fiefgentil@wanadoo.fr). It's located on the edge of the pleasant town of Blere (from Blere follow signs toward Luzille), right on the road.

Closer to Amboise, the bargain *chambres* at **La Chevalerie** are family friendly in every way, with total seclusion in a farm setting, a swing set, a tiny fishing pond, great common kitchens, and connecting rooms wrappped in a warm reception (Db-220F, Tb-300F, Qb-380F, 37150 La Croix en Touraine, from Amboise take D-31 toward Blere and look for the sign on your left in about 4 km, tel. 02 47 57 83 64).

Eating in Amboise

Reasonable local eateries abound in Amboise. **Crêperie L'Ecu** is a good spot to sample French crêpes (open daily, indoor and outdoor tables, 7 rue Corneille, just off the pedestrian street). **Hotel Le Blason** offers very fine cuisine in a pleasant setting at affordable prices (see "Hotels," above). In any weather **La Brèche's** restaurant is a good value (see "Hotels"). If you're feeling romantic, try **L'Epicerie** (110F *menu*, off-season closed Mon–Tue, 46 place Michel DeBre, across from château, tel. 02 47 57 08 94). A block uphill, **L'Amboiserie** offers fine value and a friendly staff (7 rue Victor Hugo, tel. 02 47 39 50 40). **Le St. Vincent**, on the island, serves good meals, with an emphasis on wine, at fair prices (7 rue Commire, tel. 02 47 30 49 49). For an after-dinner walk, cross the bridge to the island for a floodlit view of the château. The bar **Le Shaker** offers scenic cocktails and outdoor tables with late-night château views (on the island to the right as you cross from the château).

Transportation Connections—Amboise

Twelve 15-minute trains per day link Amboise to the regional train hub of St. Pierre des Corps (suburban Tours). From there you'll find reasonable connections to distant points (including the TGV to Paris Montparnasse, about hrly, 1 hr). The fastest way to many points, even in the south, may be back through Paris.

By train to: Sarlat (4/day, 6 hrs, via St. Pierre des Corps then TGV to Libourne or Bordeaux St. Jean, then very scenic train through Bordeaux vineyards to Sarlat), **Limoges** (near Oradour sur Glane, 4/day, 4 hrs, then tricky connection to bus to Oradour sur Glane), **Mont St. Michel** (4/day, 7 hrs, via Tours' main train station, Caen, and Pontorson; or 7 hrs via St. Pierre des Corps, Paris Montparnasse, and Rennes), **Bayeux** (6/day, 4 hrs via Tour's main station and Caen), **Paris** (12/day, 90 min, via St. Pierre de Corps/Tours and TGV to Paris' Gare Montparnasse; or by local train, 8/day, 2 hrs, direct from Amboise to Paris' Gare d'Austerlitz).

The Loire's Top Châteaus

▲▲▲**Chenonceau** (shuh-non-so)—The toast of the Loire, this 15th-century Renaissance palace arches gracefully over the Cher River. One look and you know it was designed by women: The original builder's wife designed the part of the château that parallels the river; Diane de Poitiers, mistress of Henry II, added an arched bridge across the river. She enjoyed her lovely retreat until Henry died (pierced in a jousting tournament) and his vengeful wife, Catherine de Médici, unceremoniously kicked her out (and into the château of Chaumont). Catherine added the three-story structure on Diane's bridge. She died before completing her vision of a matching château on the far side of the river but not before turning Chenonceau into the local aristocracy's place to see and be seen. This castle marked the border between free and Nazi France in World War II. Dramatic prisoner swaps took place here. Chenonceau is self-tourable (pick up the English translation), with piped-in classical music and glorious gardens (45F, skip the 10F Musée de Cires—wax museum, mid-Mar–mid-Sept daily 9:00–19:00, early closing off-season, tel. 02 47 23 90 07). There are three trains per day from Tours and one bus per day from Amboise. To beat the crowds, arrive at 8:45. It's a 15-minute walk from the parking lot to the château. The village of Chenonceau welcomes you with a helpful TI, a handy grocery shop, and several cafés.

Sleeping in Chenonceau: If you prefer a quiet village, set up in sleepy little Chenonceau (zip code: 37150). **Hostel du Roy**** is a steal, with better rooms in the annex, spotless bargain rooms in the main building, a quiet garden courtyard, and a cozy but average restaurant (S-130F, Sb-220F, D-130F, Db-225–260F, Tb/Qb-260–310F, CC:VMA, 9 rue Dr. Bretonneau, 5-minute walk to château of Chenonceau, tel. 02 47 23 90 17, fax 02 47 23 89 81). The best three-star value in France might be at **Hotel La Roseraie*****. While English-speaking Laurent spoils you, his delightfully decorated, country-elegant rooms will enchant you (Db-280–480F, a few grand family rooms-480–650F, CC:VMA, free parking, heated pool, a mouthwatering wood-beamed dining room where I dress up and splurge for a great dinner—100F and 150F *menus*, located dead center on the main drag at 7 rue Dr. Bretonneau, tel. 02 47 23 90 09, fax 02 47 23 91 59).

▲▲▲**Chambord** (sham-bor)—More like a city than a château, this place is huge. Surrounded by a lush park full of wild deer and boar, it was originally built as a simple hunting lodge for bored Blois counts. François I, using 1,800 workmen over 15 years, made a few modest additions and created this "weekend retreat" (you'll find his signature salamander everywhere). Highlights are the huge double-spiral staircase designed by Leonardo da Vinci, second-floor vaulted ceilings, enormous towers on all corners, a pin-cushion roof of spires and chimneys, and a 100-foot lantern supported by flying buttresses. To see what happens when you put 365 fireplaces in your house, wander through the forest of spires on the rooftop (fine views). Only 80 of its 440 rooms are open to the public—and that's plenty. If you have limited time or energy, skip the ground floor and second floor (rather bare rooms featuring "the hunt") and focus on the first floor, where you'll find the best royal furnishings. The brochure is useless, so consider the 25F self-guided Walkman tour or the free tours given in English one to three times per day; call ahead to get times (40F, Apr–Sept daily 9:30–18:15, until 19:15 in summer, closes at 17:15 in winter, tel. 02 54 50 40 00). Chambord's TI, next to the souvenir shops, will show you where to rent bikes (25F/hr, 50F/half day, 80F/day) and has a good list of nearby *chambres d'hôte*. Four daily 40-minute buses connect Chambord with Blois' train station on weekdays (2 on Saturday, 1 on Sunday). To wake up with Chambord out your window, **Hotel du Grand St-Michel**** comes with Old World hunting-lodge charm, an elegant dining room (100F *menu*), and a chance to roam the château grounds after the peasants leave

(Db-300–450F, extra person 70F, CC:VM, 41250 Chambord, tel. 02 54 20 31 31, fax 02 54 20 36 40).

▲▲**Chaumont-sur-Loire** (show-mon-sur-lwahr)—Chaumont's first priority was defense—you can't even see it from the town below. As you approach the château (an interesting mix of Gothic and Renaissance architecture), veer left along the path for a better view. Originally there was another wing on the riverside that completely encircled the courtyard. Catherine de Médici force-swapped this place for Diane de Poitier's Chenonceau, so you'll see tidbits about both women inside. Don't miss the the royal horse house (*écuries*); they took this hobby seriously. From June to September, enjoy the Festival des Jardins (Garden Festival)—a new display of gorgeous flowers makes this the Loire's best flower-garden stop. There's a guide during summer; otherwise, pick up the English brochure (32F, 45F during garden festival, mid-Mar–Sept daily 9:30–18:00, off-season 10:00–16:30, tel. 02 54 20 98 03).

▲▲▲**Cheverny** (sheh-vayr-nee)—The most lavish furnishings of all the Loire châteaus decorate this very stately hunting palace. Those who complain that the Loire châteaus have stark and barren interiors missed Cheverny. This château was built in 1634, and it's been in the same family for nearly seven centuries. Family pride shows in its flawless preservation and intimate feel. The viscount's family still lives on the third floor—you'll see some family photos. Cheverny was spared by the French Revolution; the owners were popular then, as today, even among the poorer farmers. Barking dogs remind visitors that the viscount still loves to hunt. The kennel (200 yards in front of the château) is especially interesting at dinnertime (17:00), when the 70 hounds are fed. (The dogs—half English foxhound and half French bloodhound or Poitevin—are a hunter's dream come true.) The trophy room next door bristles with 2,000 stag antlers (35F, pick up the English self-guided tour brochure at the château, not where you buy your ticket; June–mid-Sept daily 9:15–18:30, otherwise 9:30–12:00, 14:15–17:00, tel. 02 54 79 96 29). Cheverny village, in front of the château, has a grocery shop and a few cafés.

▲**Azay le Rideau** (ah-zay luh ree-doh)—Most famous for its romantic reflecting pond setting, Azay le Rideau features glorious gardens and a skippable interior (35F, daily 9:30–18:00, until 19:00 in summer, closes 12:30–14:00 and at 17:30 off-season, imaginative 60F sound-and-light show, tel. 02 47 45 42 04). If you're staying the night in the pleasant town of Azay, try the comfortable rooms at the ideally located and beautiful **Hôtel Biencourt**** (Ds-220F, Db-280–340F, CC:VM, on pedestrian street near château at 7 rue de Balzac, zip code: 37190, tel. 02 47 45 20 75, fax 02 47 45 91 73).

▲▲**Chinon** (shee-non)—This pleasing medieval town hides its ancient cobbles under a historic castle filled with Joan of Arc memories (28F, 9:00–18:00). Don't underestimate this interesting château, especially if you're looking for a stark medieval contrast to those of the lavish hunting-lodge variety.

Chinon makes the best home base for seeing châteaus to the west of Tours (Azay le Rideau, Villandry, Langeais, Ussè). The TI (Mon–Sat 9:00–12:15, 13:30–18:00, Sun 10:–12:00, in the village center on place Hofhein, tel. 02 47 93 17 85) can tell you about bike rental, *chambres d'hôte*, and wine tasting. **Hôtel Diderot****, which has fine rooms in a centrally located 18th-century manor house (Sb-260–320F, Db-310–420F, CC:VMA, 4 rue Buffon, zip code: 37500, tel. 02 47 93 18 87, fax 02 47 93 37 10). **Les Années 30** is my favorite restaurant in town (78 rue Voltaire).

▲▲**Langeais** (lahn-zhay)—This epitome of a medieval castle, complete with a moat, a drawbridge, lavish defenses, and turrets, is elegantly furnished and has English descriptions in each room. Langeais, which provides a good feudal contrast to the other, more playful châteaus, is the area's fourth most interesting castle after Chenonceau, Chambord, and Cheverny (40F, Apr–Oct daily 9:00–18:30, until 21:00 in summer, Nov–Mar closes 12:00–14:00 and at 17:00, tel. 02 47 96 72 60, frequent train service from Tours).

▲**Villandry** (vee-lahn-dree)—This otherwise mediocre castle has elaborate geometric gardens and a fine *Four Seasons of Villandry* slide show. Skip the château interior. Come here for the Loire's most complete gardens. Don't miss the overview behind the château, above the gardens (45F, 32F for gardens, Easter–Sept daily 9:00–19:00, until 20:00 in summer, Oct–Easter closes at 17:00, tel. 02 47 50 02 09).

Ussè (oos-seh)—This château, famous as the *"Sleeping Beauty* castle," is worth a quick photo stop for its fairy-tale turrets and gardens, but don't bother touring it. The best view, with reflections and a golden-slipper picnic spot, is from just across the bridge.

DORDOGNE

The Dordogne River Valley is a dreamy blend of natural and man-made beauty. Hundreds of fortified castles line the sublime Dordogne, a testament to its strategic importance in the Middle Ages. During the brutal Hundred Years' War, this river separated Britain and France. Today the sleepy Dordogne carries more tourists than goods and struggles to manage its popularity with British and Dutch tourists.

The joys of the region include rock-sculpted villages, fertile farms surrounding I-could-retire-there cottages, film-gobbling vistas, lazy canoe rides, and a local cuisine worth loosening your belt for. The Dordogne's most thrilling sights are its caves decorated with prehistoric artwork. The cave of Font-de-Gaume has the greatest ancient (15,000-year-old) cave paintings still open to the public.

To explore this beautiful river valley, sleep in or near Beynac if you have a car and in Sarlat if you don't.

Planning Your Time

You'll need a minimum of a day and a half to explore this magnificent region. Your sightseeing obligations in order of priority are prehistoric cave art, the Dordogne River Valley and its villages and castles, and the well-restored town of Sarlat. The Dordogne riverfront villages offer exciting canoe-trip possibilities and an ideal break from your sightseeing. If possible, call well in advance to reserve a ticket to the cave art at Grotte de Font-de-Gaume or ask your hotel to do this.

A good (and exhausting) driving day might go something like this: Morning and lunch in Sarlat (Wed and Sat are market days), 13:00–Cave tour, 15:00–Two-hour canoe trip, 18:00–Tour Beynac castle with river view, 19:00–Walk behind the castle to the goose farm, 20:00–Dine. This plan can also work well with a cave tour as the first or last stop of the day. For part or most of a second day, explore the twisting alleys in Beynac, tour the castle at Castlenaud, and consider visiting Lascaux II caves.

A good day for train travelers based in Sarlat: Morning train to Les Eyzies, see Font-de-Gaume caves, taxi back to Sarlat (150F) and arrange an afternoon canoe trip (pick-up possible in Sarlat) or hire a taxi for an all- or part-day excursion (see below for details on both).

As you drive in or out the day before or after (connecting the Dordogne with the Loire and Carcassonne), break the long drives with stops in Oradour-sur-Glane (to the north) and Cahors/Albi (to the south). With good preparation, train travelers can manage these stops as well (see "Transportation Connections—Sarlat").

Getting around the Dordogne

This region is a joy with a car but tough without. You could rent a car or a bike (in Sarlat, Les Eyzies, or Beynac), hire an all-day taxi service (see below), or get to Beynac and toss your itinerary into the Dordogne.

By Bike or Moped: Bikers find the Dordogne scenic but hilly, with crowded roads. Consider a moped. In Sarlat you can rent mopeds (200F/day) or mountain bikes (100F/day) at Peugeot Cycles (36 avenue Thiers, tel. 05 53 28 51 87, fax 05 53 30 23 90). In Beynac rent a bike at the TI. A scenic Dordogne Valley loop ride is described below.

By Train: Train service in this region is limited to important cities and still is sparse. You can train from Sarlat to the Font-de-Gaume caves in Les Eyzies (transfer in Le Buisson), but service is limited, leaving you with about five hours in Les Eyzies. Consider taking a train to Les Eyzies (good early morning connection in Le Buisson) and a taxi home (see below) if you want to canoe that day or use your time in Les Eyzies to rent a bike and ride to Abri du Cap-Blanc (rent bikes at Les Eyzies TI, tel. 05 53 06 97 05, fax 05 53 06 90 79).

Car Rental in Sarlat: Remember, most rental agencies close between 12:00 and 14:00 and all day Sunday. The cheapest in town is **ADA Locations** (Garages St. Michel on route de Brive, tel. 05 53 29 97 95, fax 05 53 30 25 38); another is **Europcar** (le Pontet, place de la Lattre de Tassigny, tel. 05 53 30 30 40, fax 05 53 31 10 39).

By Taxi: These taxis offer customized taxi tours (split the cost with up to six travelers, find partners at your hotel, figure 600F/half day, 1,200F/day, but call and compare): **Allo Sarlat Taxi** at tel. 05 53 59 02 43 or 06 08 97 87 37; **Allo Taxi Bernard** at tel. 05 53 59 39 65; or **Taxis Tardieu** at tel. 05 53 29 28 74. For taxi service from Sarlat to Beynac or La Roque-Gageac, allow 90F (130F at night); from Sarlat to Les Eyzies allow 150F (230F at night and on Sun).

Cuisine Scene—Dordogne River Valley

Gourmets flock to this area for its geese, ducks, and wild mushrooms. The geese produce (involuntarily) the region's famous foie gras (they're force-fed, denied exercise, and slaughtered for their livers). Foie gras tastes like butter and costs like gold. The duck specialty is *confit de canard* (duck meat preserved in its own fat—sounds terrible but tastes great). *Pommes Sarladaise* are mouthwatering, thinly-sliced potatoes fried in duck fat and commonly served with *confit de canard*. Wild truffles are dirty black mushrooms. Farmers traditionally locate the mushrooms with sniffing pigs and then charge a fortune for them (3,000F per kilo, $250 per pound). Native cheeses are Cabécou (a silver-dollar-sized, pungent, nutty-flavored goat cheese) and Echourgnac (made by local Trappist monks). You'll find walnuts (*noix*) in salads, cakes, and liqueurs. Wines to sample are Bergerac (red and white) and Cahors (a full-bodied red). The *vin de noix* is a sweet walnut liqueur.

Dordogne Market Days

Market day is a major event in this cuisine-rich area and should be high among your priorities. Try to visit at least one of these markets (they end at 12:00):

Sunday:	St. Cyprien (5 miles west of Beynac)
Monday:	Les Eyzies
Tuesday:	Cenac (canoe float begins here)
Wednesday:	Sarlat
Thursday:	Domme
Friday:	Le Buisson (transfer point to Les Eyzies), Souillac (transfer point to Cahors, Carcassonne)
Saturday:	Sarlat, Cahors

SARLAT

Sarlat (sar-lah) is a pedestrian-friendly banquet of a town scenically set amid forested hills. The bustling old city overflows with historical monuments and, in the summer, tourists. Sarlat is just the right size: large enough to have a theater with four screens (as the locals boast) and small enough so that everything is an easy stroll from the town center. One-time capital of Périgord and current capital of foie gras, Sarlat has been a haven for writers and artists throughout the centuries and remains so today. Geese hate Sarlat.

Orientation

Like Italy's Siena, Sarlat is a museum city: no blockbuster sights, just a seductive tangle of cobblestone alleys peppered with medieval and Renaissance buildings and foie gras stores. Rue de la République slices like an arrow through the circular old town. Sarlat's smaller half has no important sights but many quiet lanes. Get lost.

Sarlat

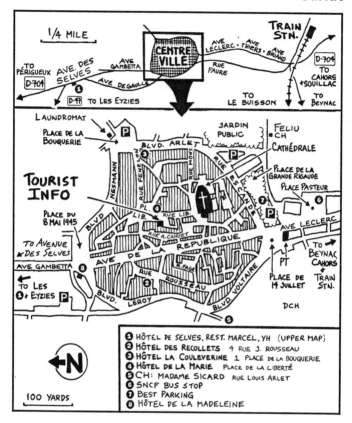

① HÔTEL DE SELVES, REST. MARCEL, YH (UPPER MAP)
② HÔTEL DES RECOLLETS   4 RUE J. ROUSSEAU
③ HÔTEL LA COULEVERINE 1 PLACE DE LA BOUQUERIE
④ HÔTEL DE LA MARIE   PLACE DE LA LIBERTÉ
⑤ CH: MADAME SICARD RUE LOUIS ARLET
⑥ SNCF BUS STOP
⑦ BEST PARKING
⑧ HÔTEL DE LA MADELEINE

Tourist Information: The helpful but cramped English-speaking TI, in the center on place de la Liberté, has free maps of the city and region; *chambres d'hôte* listings; a list of market days in the region; and the useful *Guide Practique* booklet, which lists bus and train schedules as well as car, bike, and canoe rentals; and so on (Jul–Sept Mon–Sat 9:00–20:00, Sun 10:00–12:00, 14:00–18:00; Oct–Jun Mon–Sat 9:00–12:00, 14:00–18:00, tel. 05 53 31 45 45). Some English-language walking tours are offered June through September and leave from the TI (25F, 90 min, ask TI for times).

Laundromats: One is across from the recommended Hôtel Couleverine (self-serve or leave and pick up); another is at 74 avenue de Selves, near the recommended Hotel de Selves. Both are open daily from 6:00 to 22:00.

Sights—Sarlat

▲▲**Stroll through Sarlat**—The well-done three-panel "City of Sarlat" brochure (26F, on sale at many shops and the TI) describes a good walking tour of the city. Start by exploring the musty cathedral. Exit out the right transept. Snoop around through a few quiet courtyards and then turn left, making your way toward the rear of the cathedral. Climb up the steps to that medieval space capsule called the Lanterne des Morts (Lantern of the Dead). Big shots were buried here in the Middle Ages. Exit right (with your back to the Lantern) toward my favorite house in Sarlat. Turn right and climb to the top of this lane for a good look back over Sarlat and then meander back down to the place de la Liberte, ground zero for market days. Save time to prowl the quiet side of town (the other side of the rue de la République). An automobile museum is just west of the old town (rue Thiers).

▲**Open-Air Markets**—Outdoor markets thrive on Wednesday morning and all day Saturday. Saturday's market is best in the morning (produce and food vendors leave at noon) and seems to swallow the entire town. Ask at the TI for markets in nearby towns if you miss Sarlat's (the best after Sarlat's is in St. Cyprien on Sunday).

Sleeping in Sarlat
(6F = about $1, zip code: 24200)

Sleep Code: **S** = Single, **D** = Double/Twin, **T** = Triple, **Q** = Quad, **b** = bathroom, **t** = toilet only, **s** = shower only, **CC** = Credit Card (Visa, MasterCard, Amex), **SE** = Speaks English, **NSE** = No English, * = French hotel rating system (0–4 stars).

Even with summer crowds, Sarlat is the train traveler's best home base. In July and August many hotels require half-pension. These hotels are listed in about the order you would find them, starting at the upper, north end of the city on the rue de Selves. The first four hotels are in the town center.

Hotel de la Madeleine*** is grand in every way, with Old World lounges, hotelesque service, and cavernous, polished rooms (Sb-330–395F, Db-350–590F, Tb-515F, Qb-490–580F, CC:VMA, elevator, air-con, at the north end of ring road at 1 place de la Petite Rigaudie, tel. 05 53 59 10 41, fax 05 53 31 03 62, e-mail: hotel.madeleine@wanadoo.fr, SE).

Hôtel des Recollets** offers modern comfort under heavy stone arches, with smartly decorated rooms, big beds, and a mellow courtyard on Sarlat's quiet side, three blocks down from Hotel Madeleine (Db-250–350F, Tb-350F, Qb-400–450F, obligatory breakfast-35F, no half-pension, CC:VM, 4 rue Jean-Jacques Rousseau, tel. 05 53 31 36 00, fax 05 53 30 32 62, e-mail: otelrecol@aol.com, Christophe SE).

Hôtel La Couleverine** has stiff management but plenty of medieval character in its well appointed rooms. Families enjoy *les châmbre familles*, particularly the tower room (Db-270–360F, Tb-380F, Qb-420F, CC:VMA, elevator, on the eastern edge of ring road at 1 place de la Bouquerie, tel. 05 53 59 27 80, fax 05 53 31 26 83). Half-pension (fine cuisine in an elegant restaurant, about 560F for 2) is encouraged at busy periods and in summer.

Hôtel de la Marie** is run haphazardly from the busy café but has big rooms and is as central as can be (Ds-220F, Db-260–290F, Ts-270–330F, Qb-420F, CC:VM, on place de la Liberté, tel. 05 53 59 05 71, NSE).

The next four listings are a five-minute walk down Avenue Gambetta from Hotel de la Madeleine.

Hotel Marcel* is a souvenir of old Sarlat with dark, wood-beamed lobby and flowery wallpaper (Db-250–300F, 50 rue de Selves, tel. 05 53 59 21 98, fax 05 53 30 27 77). A few blocks farther up the street, the poorly marked **Auberge de Jeunesse** (hostel) is a casual and very basic, do-it-yourself place (bunks-48F, sheets-16F, opens at 18:00, no curfew, small kitchen, 77 rue de Selves, call ahead for a bed, tel. 05 53 59 47 59 or 05 53 30 21 27). Closer to the city center, **Hotel de Selves***** is sleek and modern, with pastel French decor surrounding a swimming pool and quiet garden (Db-410–570F, CC:VMA, elevator, cable TV, air-con, all the hotel extras, 93 avenue de Selves, tel. 05 53 31 50 00, fax 05 53 31 23 52, e-mail: hotel@selves-sarlat.com). Across the street, the modern but less snazzy **Hotel de Compostelle**** has spacious rooms and a few excellent family suites (Db-290–320F, Tb/Qb-450F, CC:VMA, elevator, 64 avenue de Selves, tel. 05 53 59 08 53, fax 05 53 30 31 65).

Chambres d'Hôtes in Sarlat

The **Sicards** rent two fine rooms on the southeastern edge of the old town a five-minute walk below the ring road (Sb-170F, Db-180–210F, Tb-230F, Le Pignol, rue Louis Arlet, tel. 05 53 59 14 28). **Madame Feliu's** three rooms, just off the ring road below the park, are more central but less homey (Db-220–260F, tel. 05 53 59 03 21). **Madame Delibie** has four rooms right on the main square, dead center in Sarlat (Db-250F, Tb/Qb-360F, 11 place de la Liberte, inquire in the shop, tel. 05 53 59 35 27).

Eating in Sarlat

Sarlat is packed with moderately priced restaurants, most of which serve local specialties. Opposite the cathedral, **La Rapiere** provides wood-beam coziness and fine regional cuisine, with *menus* from 105F (daily Jun–Sept, off-season closed Sun, tel. 05 53 59 03 13). On the quieter side, just off rue de la Republique, **Les 4 Saisons** offers a good 95F *menu* (daily Jun–Sept, closed Wed off-season, 2 Cote de Toulouse, tel. 05 53 29 48 59). If you have a car, drive to Beynac or La Roque Gageac for a beautiful setting and excellent value (see below).

Transportation Connections—Sarlat

The Sarlat TI has schedules for all modes of transport to and from Sarlat. Soulliac and Perigueux are the train hubs for points within the greater region. The train traveler's gateways to distant points are Souillac to the east and Bordeaux St. Jean or Libourne to the west. For all destinations below you have the choice of traveling via Libourne/Bordeaux St. Jean or Souillac (the bus connecting Souillac and Sarlat is covered by railpasses). I've listed the fastest path in each case. Sarlat train station: tel. 05 53 59 00 21.

By train to: Paris (4/day, 6 hrs, via Libourne or Bordeaux St. Jean, then TGV), **Amboise** (4/day, 6 hrs, via scenic train to Bordeaux/Libourne, then TGV to St. Pierre des Corps, then local train to Amboise), **Oradour sur Glane** (difficult, 3/day, 3–4 hrs via bus to Souillac, train to Limoges and bus to Oradour; return to Limoges to continue to Amboise), **Cahors** (4/day, 2–3 hrs, SNCF bus to Souillac, then train to Cahors), **Albi** or **Carcassonne** (6/day, 6 hrs, bus to Souillac then train with transfer in Toulouse, or train to Bordeaux and Toulouse in same time).

To Beynac: Beynac is accessible only by taxi (90F) or bike, though the folks at Hôtel du Château will pick you up at the Sarlat station for no charge (see "Sleeping in Beynac," below).

BEYNAC

The cliff-hanging village of Beynac (bay-nak) sees far fewer tourists than its big brother, Sarlat, and feels more welcoming. You'll have the Dordogne River at your doorstep and a perfectly preserved medieval village winding like a sepia film set from the place where you beach your canoe to the hill-capping castle above. The floodlit village is always open for evening strollers.

The **Beynac TI** (Apr–Sept daily 9:30–12:30, 14:30–18:00, closed Sun off-season, tel. & fax 05 53 29 43 08), post office (with ATM), and grocery shop cluster around the village riverside parking lot. Beynac's scenic cafés are right on the river below the TI and high above, near the castle entry. You can park at pay lots on the river (take everything out of your car), way up at the castle (follow signs to Château de Beynac), or partway up to the castle. A pleasant trail follows the river toward Castlenaud (it begins across from Hotel Bonnet), offering great views back toward Beynac, a good restaurant (see "Eating," below), and, for able route finders, a nifty hike to Castlenaud (1 hr). You can rent bikes at Canoe Copeyre, below the TI (60F/half day, 90F/day, tel. 05 53 28 95 01, fax 05 53 31 24 22).

Sights—Beynac

▲**Château de Beynac**—This cliff-clinging castle soars like a trapeze artist 500 feet straight up above the Dordogne River. During the Hundred Years' War, the castle of Beynac housed the French, while

Heart of the Dordogne

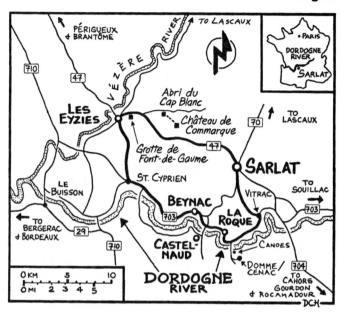

the British headquarters was across the river at Castelnaud. From the condition of the castles, it appears that France won. The sparsely furnished castle is most interesting for the valley views. From 12:15 to 13:45 you can walk through on your own; otherwise you will be required to tour with a French-speaking guide. Pick up the English translation. (40F, Mar 15–Nov 15, tours 10:00–18:30 except for lunch break, usually starting on the half hour, in summer last visit is 18:00, tel. 05 53 29 50 40.)

River Cruise Trips—Boats leave from Beynac's parking lot. Providing a mildly interesting, but relaxed and scenic, view of the Dordogne with English explanations of the battles that raged here during the Hundred Years' War (35F, daily Easter–Oct, 1 hr).

Sleeping in Beynac
(6F = about $1, zip code: 24220)

Those with a car should sleep in or near Beynac. With hotel pickup services, taxis, and bike-rental possibilities, even those without a car may find Beynac worth the trouble. To write any Beynac hotel, simply use the 24220 postal code. The tiny Beynac TI posts a listing on its door of all accommodations with prices and current availability. Leave nothing in your car at night; the riverfront lot is a thief's dream.

The central **Hôtel du Château****, at ground zero in Beynac, is reasonable and has many amenities, including a new pool, a bar, a terrace café, and a gourmet shop selling local products (ask for a tasting). The rooms are generally comfortable, but those on the river can be loud—ask for one in the back. Charming Patricia (NSE) and *le beeg boss* Phillipe (a *leetle* SE) will welcome you and feed you very well (Db-260–330F, extra person-60F, CC:VM, free pickup at Sarlat train station upon request, they're happy to reserve cave visits, tel. 05 53 29 50 13, fax 05 53 28 53 05, e-mail: Hotel_du_Chateau @Perigord.com). Right next door the less personal **Hostellerie Malleville**** offers quieter, cozier rooms in an annex up the street at their **Hotel Pontet** (check in at Hostelerie Malleville, Db-240–300F, includes use of pool at their other hotel in nearby Vézac, CC:VMA, tel. 05 53 29 50 06, fax 05 53 28 28 52). For truly basic and nearly clean rooms with a romantic view of the river, hike up to **Hôtel de la Poste***, run by gregarious Madame Montestier and her mother-in-law (NSE). Relaxed cleaning standards, no TVs, no credit cards, fax . . . what's that?, but a cool garden and pleasant sitting room (D-175F, Db-215–245F, Tb/Qb-310F, walk a short distance past Hotel du Château and then turn right up pedestrian street 75 yards, tel. 05 53 29 50 22).

Hotel Bonnet**, on the eastern edge of town, offers classy Old World comfort, river views from many of its rooms (noise can be a problem for some), a peaceful backyard garden, and a fine restaurant (Db-300–360F, Tb-350F–380F, CC:VMA, tel. 05 53 29 50 01, fax 05 53 29 83 74).

Sleeping near Beynac
Chambres d'Hôtes: Less than two kilometers toward Castelnaud is **M. Rubio** (D-160F, tel. 05 53 29 53 32). In Bezenac, six kilometers from Beynac toward St. Cyprien, friendly British expats **Doug and Jenny Cree** have three very pleasant rooms with river views (D-200F, tel. 05 53 59 32 69).

Hotels: For motellike comfort and a pool, drive two kilometers east from Beynac to Vézac and try either the more elegant **Relais des 5 Châteaux**** (Db-270–290F, good restaurant, CC:VM, tel. 05 53 30 30 72, fax 05 53 31 19 39) or the quieter and kid-ideal **Hotel l'Oustal**, with a pool, Ping-Pong, volleyball, and grass to burn (Db-290F, Tb-340F, CC:VMA, 24220 Vézac, tel. 05 53 29 50 06, fax 05 53 28 28 52).

Eating in and near Beynac
You'll dine well in air-conditioned comfort at **Hôtel du Château** and for a bit more at the classier **Hotel Bonnet**. If you can manage the hike up to the castle or have a car, **Taverne des**

Remparts is another good value (across from castle, CC:VM, tel. 05 53 29 57 76, Jerome SE). I can't imagine leaving Beynac *sans* relaxing at their view-perfect café, which is best at night (try the *salade gourmande* for lunch). Beynac also offers the Dordogne's dreamy dinner-picnic site. Walk up the hill, pass the château, continue out of the village, and turn right at the cemetery. I also enjoy walking one mile along the river toward Castlenaud to the reasonable **Auberge du Point de Vue** (open daily in summer, otherwise closed Mon and Wed, turn left at rail bridge and follow the road, great views of Beynac, tel. 05 53 30 49 90).

In nearby La Roque-Gageac, the restaurant **Hôtel Belle Étoile** serves top regional cuisine in elegant surroundings (*menus* from 120F, reserve ahead, tel. 05 53 29 51 44).

Sleeping in the Middle of Nowhere

The perfect getaway for hungry travelers tired of crowded villages and noisy rooms awaits a few minutes from Les Eyzies at **Ferme Veyret**. This 14-room renovated farm (with a pool) situated on the route to Abri du Cap-Blanc (below; look for yellow signs) is as friendly as it gets. You'll be expected to dine here, and you'd be a fool not to, as dinner includes everything from apéritif to *digestif*, with five courses in between and wine throughout (Db-250F per person, includes breakfast and dinner, 24620 Les Eyzies de Tayac-Sireuil, tel. 05 53 29 68 44, fax 05 53 31 58 28).

Sights—Dordogne Valley Region

Cro-Magnon Caves—There are four caves in this region with original cave paintings that tourist can still admire: the top-quality Grotte de Font-de-Gaume (tours in English offered only in summer), the immense Grotte de Rouffignac, the less spectacular but friendly Grotte de Cougnac (some tours in English), and the sprawling Grotte de Peche Merle (some English tours). The latter two are listed under "Sights—Southeast of the Dordogne," below. Whichever caves you visit, dress warmly, even if it's hot outside.
Les Eyzies—The town of Les Eyzies-de-Tayac is the touristic hub of this cluster of historic caves, castles, and rivers. Except for its interesting museum of prehistory (22F, Wed–Mon 9:30–12:00, 14:00–18:00, closed Tue and at 17:00 Nov–Mar) next to the big statue of Mr. Cro-Magnon, there's little reason to stop here. The ambitious construction next to the museum is the new museum, which will be a showcase for this region's prehistoric artifacts when completed. The Les Eyzies TI rents bikes (daily 10:00–12:00, 14:00–18:00, tel. 05 53 06 97 05, fax 05 53 06 90 79).
▲▲▲**Grotte de Font-de-Gaume**—Even if you're not a connoisseur of Cro-Magnon art, you'll dig this cave. It's the last cave in Europe with prehistoric (polychrome) painting still open to the public, and its turnstile days are numbered. On a carefully guided

The Dordogne Region

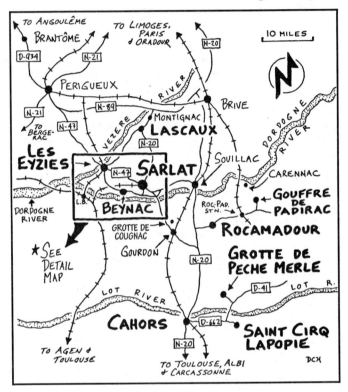

and controlled 100-yard walk, you'll see about 20 red and black bison—often in elegant motion—painted with a moving sensitivity. Your guide—with a laser pointer and great reverence—will trace the faded outline of the bison and explain how, 15,000 years ago, cave dwellers used local minerals and the rock's natural contour to give the paintings dimension. The paintings were discovered by the village schoolteacher in 1901. Now, since heavy-breathing tourist hordes damage the art by raising and lowering the temperature and humidity levels, tickets are limited to 200 a day.

Visits are by appointment only. Reserve in advance by phone; your hotel can make the call. Summertime spots are booked two weeks in advance. Even during the off-season, it's smart to call ahead and get a time. Request an English tour (usually summers only) and be on time or lose your spot. You'll find it interesting even in French but ask for the English brochure and read through the books in the gift shop before you go (35F, Thu–Tue 9:00–12:00, 14:00–17:30, closed Wed and at 17:00 Nov–Feb, no photography or large bags, tel. 05 53 06 90 80). Drivers who can't get a spot here can try the caves at Rouffignac (see below) or aim for the more remote Grotte de Peche Merle, an hour east of Cahors (see below, "Sights—Southeast of the Dordogne").

▲**Abri du Cap-Blanc**—Just up the road from Font de Gaume, in this prehistoric cave sculpture, early artists used the rock's natural contours to add dimension to their sculpting. The small museum, with English explanations, will prepare you, and the handy English handout will guide you. Look for places where the artists smoothed or roughed the surfaces to add depth. In this single stone room, your French-speaking guide will spend 30 minutes explaining 14,000-year-old carvings. Impressive as these carvings are, their subtle majesty bypasses some. Tours leave on the half hour. No lines (30F, Wed–Mon 9:30–19:00 in summer, off-season 10:00–12:00, 14:00–18:00, closed on Tue and Nov–Apr, tel. 05 53 29 21 74). The sight is well signed, two miles after Grotte de Font-de-Gaume on the road to Sarlat, and is the trailhead for the hike to Commarque castle (see below).

▲▲**Grotte de Rouffignac**—This is the second-best cave after Font de Gaume. Dress warmly; the visit lasts 70 minutes and extends one kilometer into the hillside. In this massive cave, a French-speaking guide escorts you on a small train, stopping to point out engravings of mammoths (done with wood sticks—many of those vertical lines are bearclaw scratches) and brilliant black paintings of rhinos, bison, horses, mammoths, and reindeer. The most interesting stop is at the end as you descend the train into a vault of ceiling paintings (notice the original level of the floor through the end of this cave; the artists had to crawl to this place and draw while lying on their backs). The horse is amazingly realistic. The helpful guides make time to answer questions in English but lead the tour in French (31F, daily 10:00–11:30, 14:00–17:30, opens at 9:30 in summer, closed Nov–Mar, no reservations, tours leave about every 30 min, best strategy is to arrive before opening time and take the first tour—afternoons are busier, and the summertime 14:00 lineup can be ugly, tel. 05 53 05 41 71). It's well signed from the route between Les Eyzies and Perigueux; allow 20 minutes from Les Eyzies.

▲**Grotte de Cougnac**—Thirty-five kilometers south of Sarlat, near Gourdon in Payrignac, this far less touristed cave offers a more intimate look at Cro-Magnon cave art and stalagmites (32F, daily 9:00–18:00 in summer, otherwise 9:30–11:00, 14:00–17:00; 70-min tours, some in English; call to reserve, tel. 05 65 41 47 54).

Château de Commarque and Château de Laussel—These castles' heydays passed 400 years ago with the Hundred Years' War. You can see (and reach) Château de Commarque from Abri du Cap-Blanc. Indiana Jones would appreciate the 30-minute hike (best in summer and fall, impossible if it's been raining) down the unmarked, unmaintained, and often marshy path past Laussel Castle (privately owned) to the crumbled orange walls of Commarque (to the right across the field). The castles are soon to be "officially" open to the public (with an entry fee). Rugged hikers find it worth the scratches and soaked feet to get here. Ask at Abri du Cap-Blanc about the condition of the path.

Sights—Along the Dordogne River

▲▲▲**Dordogne Valley Scenic Loop Ride or Drive**—The most scenic stretch of the Dordogne lies between Carsac and Beynac. From Sarlat, follow signs toward Cahors and Carsac and then veer right to the Église de Carsac (wander into this tiny Romanesque church if it's open). From Carsac, follow the river via Montfort, La Roque-Gageac, and Beynac. The town of Domme, snuggling a hilltop in the distance, is overrun. For bikers, the round trip from Sarlat totals about 45 kilometers (28 miles). Less-ambitious bikers will find the 30-kilometer (18-mile) loop ride from Sarlat to La Roque-Gageac to Beynac and back to Sarlat sufficient. This trip works just as well from Beynac.

Foie Gras in the Making—You can witness (evenings only) the force-feeding of geese (*la gavage*) at many places. Look for *gavage* signs but beware: You are expected to buy. Friendly Madame Gauthier's farm offers a peek at the *gavage* and is just down the road from Château de Beynac (park right there or walk 10 minutes from the château away from river through parking lot—you'll see the signs, demonstrations 18:00–19:30, tel. 05 53 29 51 45).

▲▲**Castelnaud**—Château de Beynac's crumbling rival looks a little less mighty, but the inside packs a medieval punch. Several rooms display weaponry and artifacts from the Hundred Years' War. The courtyard comes with a 46-meter-deep well (drop a pebble) and an entertaining video showing the catapults, which litter the grounds, in action. The rampart views are unbeatable, and the siege tools outside the walls are formidable. Borrow the English explanations from the ticket lady for the room-by-room story (35F, May–Jun daily 10:00–19:00, 9:00–20:00 in summer, otherwise 10:00–18:00; it's a steep hike through a pleasant peasant village, the car park gets you a bit closer, tel. 05 53 31 30 00). You can stop here halfway through your canoe trip or take a one-hour hike from Beynac along a difficult-to-follow riverside path (it hugs the river as it passes though campgrounds and farms).

▲▲▲**Dordogne Canoe Trips**—For a refreshing break from the car or train, explore the riverside castles and villages of the Dordogne by rented canoe. Several outfits rent plastic two-person canoes (and one-person kayaks) and will pick you up at an agreed-upon spot. If Beynac is home, make sure the outfit allows you to get out in Beynac. For 130F, two can paddle the best two-hour stretch from Cénac to Beynac (shuttle included, call ahead to arrange if you don't have a car, in summer the usual pickup time in Beynac is 9:00). In Cénac, look for **Dordogne Randonées** (coming from Sarlat or Beynac, take the first left after crossing the bridge to Cénac, tel. 05 53 28 22 01). In La Roque Gageac, **Canoe-Dordogne** rents canoes for the pleasant two-hour float to Château Milandes (130F, tel. 05 53 29 58 50). While you need to be in good shape for the longer trips, it's OK if you're a complete novice—the only white water you'll encounter will be your partner frothing at the views. You'll get a life vest and, for a few extra francs, a watertight bucket. Beach your boat wherever you want to take a break. The best two stops are the village of La Roque-Gageac and the castle at Castelnaud.

▲**La Roque-Gageac**—La Roque (the rock), as the locals call this village, is sculpted into the cliffs rising from the Dordogne River (small TI in parking lot open summers 10:00–12:00, 14:00–18:00). As you walk along the main street, look for the markers showing the water levels of three floods and ask someone about the occasional rock avalanches from above. La Roque was once a thriving port, exporting Limousin oak to Bordeaux for making wine barrels. Find the old ramp leading down to the river. For great views, wander up the narrow tangle of back streets that seem to disappear into the cliffs. The sky-high Fort Troglodyte is a good energy burner but offers little more than views (25F, get English explanation, open 10:00–19:00). For a small splurge, have a romantic dinner; better yet, sleep at the remarkably reasonable **Hôtel Belle Étoile****, with classic decor and a cozy bar, river views from most rooms, some squishy beds, and a dreamy restaurant (Ds-210F, Db-280–310F, Tb/Qb-350F, no half-pension requirement, zip code: 24250, tel. 05 53 29 51 44, fax 05 53 29 45 63). **Hotel Gardette**** has well-kept rooms at bargain rates and pleasant terraces and is right above the main village parking lot (D-180F, Ds-200F, Db-250F, CC:VM, zip code: 24250, tel. 05 53 29 51 58).

Sights—North of the Dordogne

▲▲**Lascaux**—The region's most vivid and famous cave paintings are at Lascaux, 30 minutes north of Sarlat. In the interest of preservation, these caves are closed to tourists. But the adjacent Lascaux II copy caves are impressive in everything but authenticity. At Lascaux II, the reindeer, horses, and bulls of Lascaux I are painstakingly reproduced by top artists using the same dyes, tools, and techniques their predecessors did 15,000 years ago. Anyone into caveman art will appreciate the thoughtful explanations. It's worth working your schedule around English tour times (Call ahead for English tour times, 5 times daily in summer, on demand in off-season; 50F; Jul–Aug daily 9:30–19:00; Sept–Jun Tue–Sun 10:00–12:00, 14:00–17:30; 2.5 kilometers south of Montignac; in July and August tickets are sold only at Montignac TI, tel. 05 53 51 95 03).

▲▲▲**Oradour-sur-Glane**—Located two hours north of Sarlat and 25 kilometers west of Limoges, this is one of the most powerful sights in France. French schoolchildren know this town well. Most make a pilgrimage here. "La Ville Martyr," as it is known, was machine-gunned and burned on June 10, 1944, by Nazi troops. The Nazis were either seeking revenge for the killing of one of their officers (by French resistance fighters in a neighboring village) or simply terrorizing the populace in preparation for the upcoming Allied invasion (this was four days after D day). With cool German attention to detail, the Nazis methodically rounded up the entire population of 642 townspeople. The women and children were herded into the town church, where they were tear-gassed and machine-gunned. Plaques mark the place where the town's men were grouped and executed. The town was then set on fire, its victims left under a blanket of ashes. Today the ghost town, left untouched for 50 years, greets every pilgrim who enters with only one English word: Remember.

The new underground museum at the entry provides a helpful introduction. Hushed visitors walk the length of Oradour's main street, past gutted, charred buildings in the shade of lush trees, to the underground memorial on the market square (rusted toys, broken crucifixes, town mementos under glass). Visit the cemetery where most lives ended on June 10, 1944, and finish with the church with its bullet-pocked altar (free, daily, long hours, helpful 10F English booklet).

You'll have to be dedicated to get here by public transport. Four daily buses connect Limoges with Oradour in 20 minutes (10-min walk to bus stop from train station to place Winston Churchill). Consider a taxi. Limoges is a stop on an alternative train route between Amboise and Sarlat.

With a car and extra time, visit the lovely, untouristed village of Mortemart (15 min northwest of Oradour on D-675), where you'll find a medieval market hall, a few cafés, and a cute château (good picnic benches behind). **Hotel Relais**** offers five comfortable rooms over a superb restaurant (Sb-280F, Db-300F, Tb-320F, CC:VM, *menus* from 95F, 87330 Mortemart, tel. 05 55 68 12 09).

Sights—Southeast of the Dordogne
▲**Rocamadour**—Ninety minutes east of Sarlat, this historic pilgrimmage town's spectacular setting and medieval charm can be trampled by daily hordes of tourists and pilgrims. But most find it worth the risk. Those who spend the night enjoy fewer crowds and a floodlit fantasy. **Hotel Sainte Marie****, ideally situated in the Cité Medievale, is comfortable enough and welcoming (D-180F, Db-260F, tel. 05 65 33 63 07, fax 05 65 33 69 08.) Trains (via Brive-la-Gaillarde) leave you five kilometers from the village (taxi, rent a bike from the station, hitch, or hike).

▲▲**Gouffre de Padirac**—Ten kilometers from Rocamadour is a fascinating cave (lots of stalagmites but no cave art). Follow the 90-minute French-language tour through this huge system of caverns. You'll ride elevators, hike along a buried stream, and even take a subterranean boat ride (47F, Apr–Oct daily 9:00–12:00, 14:00–18:00; longer hours, crowds, and delays in summer; closed off-season; day trips organized from Rocamadour TI, tel. 01 65 33 47 17). The nearest train station is in Rocamadour.

Idyllic Carennac makes a good home base. Stay in the simple, friendly **Hotel des Touristes*** (Db-210F, tel. & fax 05 65 10 94 31) or the upscale **Hotel Fenelon**** (Db-260–340F, CC:VM, pool, tel. 05 65 10 96 46, fax 05 65 10 94 86). Or sleep peacefully five miles from Rocamadour in the exceptionally comfortable and beautifully situated *chambre d'hôte* **Moulin de Fresquet** (Db-400F, 46500 Gramat, tel. & fax. 05 65 38 70 60, cellular 06 08 85 09 21, SE).

Lot River and Cahors—The Lot is one of France's most beautiful river valleys. The prehistoric cave paintings at Grotte de Peche Merle, the fortified bridge at Cahors (Pont Valentré), and the rock-top village of St. Cirq Lapopie are remarkable sights in this valley and are within a half hour of each other and within a 90-minute drive of Sarlat. These sights are worthwhile for drivers connecting the Dordogne (Sarlat) with Albi or Carcassonne or as a long day trip from Sarlat. Without a car, skip 'em.

▲▲**Pont Valentré at Cahors**—One of Europe's finest medieval monuments, this fortified bridge was built in 1308 to keep the English out of Cahors. It worked. Find out the reason for the devil on the center tower. The steep trail on the noncity side leads to great views (keep climbing, avoid branch trails, be careful if trail is wet). Just past the city-side end of the bridge is Le Cedre, a wine shop/café/souvenir stand with delightful owners. Taste Cahors' black wine and foie gras (duck is cheaper than goose and just as tasty).

▲▲**Grotte de Peche Merle**—About 30 minutes east of Cahors lies this relatively obscure cave with prehistoric paintings rivaling the better-known ones at Grotte de Font-de-Gaume. The cave is filled with stalactites and stalagmites, and you can even see a Cro-Magnon footprint preserved in the mud. Call to reserve a time. If you arrive early, start at the museum, with a film subtitled in English, and then descend to the caves. If you can't join an English tour, ask for the English translation booklet (46F, 38F during off-season, Easter–Oct daily 9:30–12:00, 14:00–18:00, closes earlier off-season, tel. 05 65 31 27 05, fax 05 65 31 20 47).

▲**St. Cirq Lapopie**—Soaring high above the Lot River, this is one of southern France's most spectacularly situated hill towns. Be careful of summer crowds. Wander the rambling footpaths and stay for lunch. You'll find ideal picnic perches and several reasonable restaurants. Sleep at **Auberge du Sombral**** (Db-300–400F, good 100F *menu*, CC:VM, tel. 05 65 31 26 08, fax 05 65 30 26 37).

LANGUEDOC

From the 10th to the 13th centuries, this powerful, open-minded, and independent region ruled an area reaching from the Rhône River to the Pyrénées. The Albigensian (Cathar) Crusades started here in 1208 and ultimately led to Languedoc's demise and incorporation into the state of France. The word *languedoc* comes from the language its people spoke at that time: *Langue d'oc* ("language of Oc," *Oc* for the way they said "yes") was the dialect of southern France, as opposed to *langue d'oil*, the dialect of northern France (where *oil*, later to become *oui*, was the way of saying "yes"). As Languedoc's power faded, so did its language.

The Moors, Charlemagne, and the Spanish have all called this home. You'll see, hear, and feel the strong Spanish influence on this dry, hilly region. We're lumping Albi in with the Languedoc region, though locals don't think of it as true Languedoc.

Planning Your Time

Key sights in this region are Albi, Carcassonne, Minerve, the Cathar castle ruins, and Collioure. Albi makes a good day or overnight stop between the Dordogne region and Carcassonne. Plan your arrival at Carcassonne carefully: Arrive late in the afternoon, spend the night, and leave by noon the next day and you'll miss the day-trippers. Collioure is your Mediterranean beach town vacation-from-your-vacation. You'll need wheels of your own and a good map to find the Cathar castle ruins and Minerve. If you're driving, the most exciting Cathar castles—Peyrepertuse and Queribus—work well as stops between Carcassonne and Collioure. No matter what method of transport you use, Languedoc is a logical stop between the Dordogne and Provence or on the way to Barcelona, which is just over the border.

Languedoc

Getting around Languedoc

Albi, Carcassonne, and Collioure are a snap by train, but a car is essential for seeing the remote sights in this area. You can rent a car near the train stations in Albi or Carcassonne or in downtown Collioure. Buy the local Michelin map #83. The roads can be tiny and the traffic very slow.

Cuisine Scene—Languedoc

Hearty peasant cooking and full-bodied red wines are Languedoc's tasty trademarks. Be adventurous—treat your taste buds well. Cassoulet, an old Roman concoction of goose, duck, pork, mutton, sausage, and white beans, is the main-course specialty. You'll also see *cargolade*, a stew of snail, lamb, and sausage. Local cheeses are Roquefort and Pelardon (a nutty-tasting goat cheese). Corbières, Minervois, and Côtes du Roussillon are the area's good-value red wines. The locals distill a fine brandy, Armagnac, that tastes just like cognac and costs less.

The Cathars

The Cathars, a heretical group of Christians based in Languedoc from the 11th through the 13th centuries, saw life as a battle between good (the spiritual) and bad (the material). They considered material things evil and of the devil. While others called them "Cathars" (from the Greek word for "pure") or "Albigenses" (for their main city, Albi), they called themselves simply "friends of God."

Cathars focused on the teachings of St. John and recognized only baptism as a sacrament. Because they believed in reincarnation, they were vegetarians.

Travelers encounter the Cathars in their Languedoc sightseeing because of the Albigensian Crusades (1209–1240s). The king of France wanted to consolidate his grip on southern France. The pope needed to make a strong point that the only acceptable Christianity was Roman style. Both found self-serving reasons to wage a genocidal war against these people—who never amounted to more than 10 percent of the local population and who coexisted happily with their non-Cathar neighbors. After a terrible generation of torture and mass burnings, the Cathars were wiped out. The last Cathar was burnt in 1321.

Today tourists find haunting castle ruins (once Cathar strongholds) high in the Pyrénées and eat hearty *salade Cathar*.

ALBI

Those coming to see the basilica and the Toulouse-Lautrec Museum will be pleasantly surprised by Albi's enchanting city center. The Albigensian Crusades were born here, as was Toulouse-Lautrec. The visitor's Albi (TI, Toulouse-Lautrec Museum, and cobbled pedestrian zone) clusters around its fortress basilica. Consider spending a night.

Tourist Information: Albi's information-packed TI is between the basilica and the Toulouse-Lautrec Museum (Jul–Aug Mon–Sat 9:00–19:30, Sun 10:30–12:30, 15:30–18:30; Sept–Jun Mon–Sat 9:00–12:00, 14:00–18:00, Sun 10:30–12:30, 15:30–17:30, tel. 05 63 49 48 80).

Arrival in Albi

By Train: Take a left onto avenue Marechal Joffre and then another left on avenue General de Gaulle; follow the signs to *cathédrale* and to Albi's old city.

By Car: Follow signs to *centre-ville* and *cathédrale* and park in front of the cathedral.

Sights—Albi

Pick up a map of the city center at the TI (get the purple *circuit poupre* walking tour in English) and follow its suggested walking tour, reading the English information posted at key points along the way. On this walk you'll see...

▲▲▲**Basilique Ste. Cécile**—This 13th-century fortress/basilica was the nail in the Albigensian coffin. Both the imposing exterior and the stunning interior of this cathedral drive home the message of the Catholic (read "universal") Church. The extravagant porch seems like an afterthought. Inside, be prepared for an explosion of colors and geometric shapes and a vivid *Last Judgment*. Even with the gaping hole that was cut from it to make room for a newer pipe organ, the *Last Judgment* makes its point in a way that would stick with any medieval worshiper (Jun–Sept 8:30–19:00, otherwise closes 12:00–14:00 and at 17:45). The choir is worth the small admission, and the S*on et Lumière Spectacle*, offered in summer, is worth staying up for (30F, 22:00, ask at TI).

▲▲**Musée Toulouse-Lautrec**—The Palais de la Berbie (once the fortified home of the archbishop) has the world's best collection of Lautrec's paintings, posters, and sketches. The artist, crippled from youth and therefore on the fringe of society, had an affinity for people who didn't quite fit in. He painted the dregs of Parisian society because that was his world. His famous Parisian-nightlife posters are here. The top floor houses a skipable collection of contemporary art (25F, Apr–May daily 10:00–12:00, 14:00–18:00; Jun–Sept daily 9:00–12:00, 14:00–18:00; Oct–Mar Wed–Mon 10:00–12:00, 14:00–17:00; tel. 05 63 49 48 70). Even if you decide against this museum, walk underneath it to the palace's gardens for the great views.

Église St. Salvy and Clôitre—This is an OK church with fine cloisters. Delicate arches surround an enclosed courtyard, providing a peaceful interlude from the maniacal shoppers that fill the pedestrian streets (open all day).

Market Hall—This quiet Art Nouveau market is good for picnic-gathering and people watching (open daily except Monday until 13:00, two blocks from the basilica).

Sleeping and Eating in Albi
(6F = about $1 zip code: 81000)
Sleep Code: **S** = Single, **D** = Double/Twin, **T** = Triple, **Q** = Quad, **b** = bathroom, **t** = toilet only, **s** = shower only, **CC** = Credit Card (Visa, MasterCard, Amex), **SE** = Speaks English, **NSE** = No English, * = French hotel rating system (0–4 stars).

Hôtel St. Clair**, offering steep stairs and elegant rooms, is decorated with a loving touch (Db-240–300F, Tb-350–420F, CC:VM, easy parking, 20-min walk from station, two blocks from cathedral in pedestrian zone on rue St. Clair, tel. 05 63 54 25 66, fax 05 63 47 27 58). **Le Vieil Alby Hotel****, located in the heart of Albi's pedestrian area, offers an excellent restaurant and good rooms in a pleasant atmosphere (Sb-250F, Db-250–300F,

Tb-330F, garage-40F, 25 rue Toulouse Lautrec, tel. 05 63 54 14
69, fax 05 63 54 96 75). **Hotel Laperouse**** has a pool and is a
great value (Db-280–300F, 21 place Laperouse, tel. 05 63 54 69
22, fax 05 63 38 03 69). Albi's **hostel** is cheap, clean, and basic
(hostel card mandatory, check-in 18:00–21:00, 13 rue de la
République, tel. 05 63 54 53 65).

Albi is filled with inexpensive restaurants. Rue Toulouse-
Lautrec (two blocks from Hotel St. Clair) is home to many good
places: For exceptional couscous in a "Little Morocco," try **Le
Marrakesh** at #11 (hearty, even splitable 60F couscous, closed
Mon and Jul–Aug). **Le Vieil Alby** at #25 is one of Albi's more
respected restaurants. For a real treat, find **Le Robinson**, where
Lices Georges Pompidou meets the river—a path leads down to
the river to this vine-strewn paradise (reasonable *menus*, 142 rue
Eurand Branly, tel. 03 63 46 15 69). Just off place Vigan, the
locally popular and cheap **Lou Sicret** is filled with atmosphere
and local specialties . . . such as pig's feet (through the small
passage at #1 rue Trimbal).

Transportation Connections—Albi

You'll connect to just about any destination through Toulouse.

By train to: Toulouse (12/day, 75 min; no trains
14:00–17:00 from Toulouse or 18:45–21:00 from Albi), **Carcassonne** (12/day, 2.5 hrs, transfer in Toulouse), **Sarlat** (6/day, 6 hrs;
train to Toulouse, then either transfer to Souillac and catch bus to
Sarlat or train to Bordeaux St. Jean and take scenic train to Sarlat),
Paris (7.5 hrs via Toulouse, then TGV).

CARCASSONNE

Medieval Carcassonne is a 13th-century world of towers, turrets,
and cobblestone alleys. It's a walled city and Camelot's castle rolled
into one, frosted with too many tourists. At 10:00 the salespeople
stand at the doors of their main-street shops, their gauntlet of tacky
temptations poised and ready for their daily ration of customers. A
quieter Carcassonne rattles in the early morning or evening breeze.
Enjoy the town early or late by spending the night. If you're here
from June through September and are sensitive to crowds, consider
sleeping in nearby Caunes-Minervois (see below).

Locals like to believe that Carcassonne got its name this way:
1,200 years ago Charlemagne stood before this fortress/town
with his troops and besieged it for several years. A cunning towns-
person named Madame Carcas saved La Cité. Just as food was
running out, she fed the last bits of grain to the last pig and tossed
him over the wall. Splat. Charlemagne's bored and frustrated
forces, amazed that the town still had enough food to throw fat
party pigs over the wall, decided they would never succeed in
starving the people out. They ended the siege, and the city was

Carcassonne

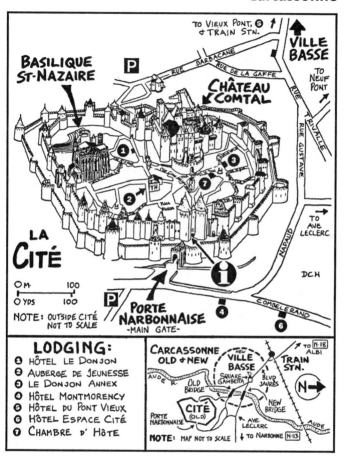

TO VIEUX PONT, ⊕ & TRAIN STN.

VILLE BASSE

BASILIQUE ST-NAZAIRE

RUE BARBACANE

RUE DE LA GAFFE

TO NEUF PONT

CHÂTEAU COMTAL

RUE GUSTAVE

RUE TRIVALLE

LA CITÉ

TO AVE LECLERC

O M 100
O YDS 100
NOTE: OUTSIDE CITÉ NOT TO SCALE

DCH

PORTE NARBONNAISE
-MAIN GATE-

COMBELERAND

NAPAUD

LODGING:
- ❶ HÔTEL LE DONJON
- ❷ AUBERGE DE JEUNESSE
- ❸ LE DONJON ANNEX
- ❹ HÔTEL MONTMORENCY
- ❺ HÔTEL DU PONT VIEUX
- ❻ HÔTEL ESPACE CITÉ
- ❼ CHAMBRE D' HÔTE

CARCASSONNE OLD & NEW

TO ALBI N-118

VILLE BASSE

TRAIN STN.

AUDE R.

OLD BRIDGE

SQUARE GAMBETTA

BLVD JAURÈS

N →

NEW BRIDGE

PORTE NARBONNAISE

CITÉ (OLD)

AVE. LECLERC

AUDE

NOTE: MAP NOT TO SCALE

↓ TO NARBONNE N-113

saved. Madame Carcas *sonne*-d (sounded) the long-awaited victory bells, and La Cité had a name, "Carcas-sonne." Historians, however, suspect that Carcassonne is a Frenchified version of the town's original name (Carcas).

From Rick's journal on his first visit to Carcassonne: "Before me lives Carcassonne, the perfect medieval city. Like a fish that everyone thought was extinct, somehow Europe's greatest Romanesque fortress city has survived the centuries. I was supposed to be gone yesterday, but here I sit imprisoned by choice—curled in a cranny on top of the wall. The wind blows away the sounds of today, and my imagination 'medievals' me. The moat is one foot over and 100 feet down. Small plants and moss upholster my throne."

Orientation

Contemporary Carcassonne is neatly divided into two cities: the magnificent Cité (medieval city) and the lively *ville basse* (modern downtown).

Tourist Information: Carcassonne has two TIs, one in the Cité and one in the *ville basse*. The handy Cité TI is just to your right as you enter the main gate called Narbonnaise (Jul–Sept daily 9:00–19:00, Oct–Jun 9:00–13:00, 14:00–18:00). The *ville basse* TI is on place Gambetta, near the huge French flags, at 15 boulevard Camille Pelletan (Mon–Sat 9:00–12:15, 14:00–18:30, closed Sun, tel. 04 68 10 24 30 or 04 68 25 68 81). Pick up the map of La Cité with English explanations, get English tour times for Château Comtal, and ask about festivals.

Arrival in Carcassonne

By Train: The train station is located in the *ville basse*. A shuttle bus signed La Cité connects the station with La Cité except on Sunday and during winter months (2/hrly, 5.F, pay driver, in the winter take bus #2 or #8 to place Gambetta, as close as you can get). Or you can walk 30 minutes across Canal du Midi, across the traffic circle, and up the pedestrian street to the heart of the *ville basse*. From there a left on rue de Verdun takes you to place Gambetta and across Pont Vieux to La Cité. Figure 55F for a taxi to La Cité from the train station.

By Car: Following signs to La Cité, you'll come to a large parking lot (20F) and a drawbridge (Porte Narbonnaise) at the walled city's entrance. If you're staying inside the walls, show your reservation (verbal assurances won't do) and you can park free in the outside lot and drive into the city after 18:00. Theft is common—leave nothing in your car overnight.

Sights—Carcassonne

▲▲▲**Medieval Wall Walk**—La Cité is a medieval fortress first constructed during the time of the Roman Empire. It was completely reconstructed in 1844 as part of a program to restore France's important monuments. Walk the entire outer wall (no charge; in town, follow signs to *lices*). The higher inner walls are mostly inaccessible, except for those in Château Comtal. Savor every step and view.

▲**Carcassonne Terre d'Histoire**—A busy medieval fair fills up most of the first three weeks of August. Don't miss the jousting tournament (*spectacle équestre*), usually at 18:00.

▲▲▲**Walk to Pont Vieux**—For the best view back onto

the floodlit city, hike down to the old bridge. As you exit the Narbonnaise Gate, go left on rue Nadaud to rue Gustave and then turn left onto rue Trivalle. Ask, *"Où est le Pont Vieux?"* (oo ay la pohn vee-uh). Return via the back-door entry to La Cité near Basilique St. Nazaire.

▲**Basilique St. Nazaire**—Enter this church and slowly walk down the aisle. Enjoy the colors of the 14th-century stained glass sparkling all around you and find the delicately vaulted Gothic ceiling behind the altar. This is one of the best examples of Gothic architecture in southern France.

Château Comtal—Carcassonne's third layer of defense was originally built in 1125 but was completely redesigned in later reconstructions. Peek into the inner courtyard and admire the towers but skip the French tour (no English translation) and ask about English tours (free with admission, generally 2–4 times per day May–Sept, 34F, Jun–Sept daily 9:00–19:00, Oct–May 9:30–12:30, 14:00–18:00).

Wine Cooperative—In the tower next to La Cité TI you can sample a fine selection of local wines under Gothic arches. You are expected to buy a bottle if you taste, but it's cheap.

Exposition Torture—You'll have even more sympathy for the Cathars after touring Carcassonne's torture chamber, worth a look only if you've got the time and money to burn (40F, children 20F, Jun–Nov daily 10:00–20:00, 9 rue St. Jean, to the right of the main drag as you enter La Cité, ticket gets you free entry to The Middle Ages in La Cité).

The Middle Ages in La Cité—This is another entrepreneurial "museum," with five rooms of costumes trying to re-create life in old Carcassonne (40F, children 20F, free with ticket from Exposition Torture, daily 10:00–18:00, decent English explanations). It's worthwhile only for kids.

Canal du Midi—Completed in 1681, this sleepy, 150-mile canal connects France's Mediterranean and Atlantic coasts. Before railways, Canal du Midi was jammed with commercial traffic. Today it's busy with pleasure craft. Look for the slow-moving hotel barges strewn with tanned, well-fed, and well-watered vacationers. The towpath that spans the length of the canal makes for ideal biking. The canal runs right in front of the train station in Carcassonne.

Sleeping in Carcassonne
(6F = about $1, zip code: 11000)

Sleeping in Carcassonne's La Cité
Ideally, sleep inside the old walls in La Cité. In the summer, when La Cité is jammed with tourists, consider sleeping in quieter Caunes-Minervois (see below). Three hotels and a great hostel offer rooms inside the walls. The obligatory half-pension doesn't

seem to exist in Carcassonne, and except for the mid-July to mid-August peak of high season, there are plenty of rooms.

Best Western's **Hotel Le Donjon*** offers small, pricey, but well-appointed rooms, a comfortable lobby, and a great location inside the walls (Sb-325–400F, Db-400–500F, Tb-410–580F, CC:VMA, tel. 04 68 11 23 00, fax 04 68 25 06 60, e-mail: hotel .donjon.best.western@wanadoo.fr).

Best Western recently acquired an annex, formerly known as Hôtel des Ramparts. Right by the castle, it has a 12th-century staircase leading to modern rooms with saggy beds (Db-475F, Tb-530F, parking-25F, CC:VM, 5 place de Grands-Puits, to book rooms at the annex, call or drop by the Hotel Le Donjon, above).

The *chambre d'hôte* across from Hôtel des Remparts (inquire in Brocante shop) rents two huge apartment-like rooms that could sleep five and have a kitchenette and private *terasse* (Db/Tb-290F, 360F family deals, stocked fridge and self-serve breakfast included, tel. & fax 04 68 25 16 67).

The **Auberge de Jeunesse** (youth hostel) is clean and well run and has an outdoor garden courtyard, a self-service kitchen, a TV room, a bar, video games, and a welcoming ambience. If you ever wanted to bunk down in a hostel, do it here. Only July is tight. Nonmembers pay 20F extra (74F per bed with breakfast, 17F for a sheet, 2 doubles, a few quads, otherwise 6 to a room, open all day, closes at 01:00, rue de Vicomte Trencavel, tel. 04 68 25 23 16, fax 04 68 71 14 84).

Sleeping near La Cité

Hôtel Montmorency**, 100 yards away from La Cité's draw-bridge, is a Santa Fe–style place sporting a pool with a fortress view (Sb-225F, Db with shower-265–310F, Db with tub-360–460F, Tb-480F, Qb-510F, CC:VMA, free parking, 2 rue Camille St. Saens, tel. 04 68 25 19 92, fax 04 68 25 43 15, SE).

Hôtel Espace Cité**, two blocks downhill from Hotel Montmorency, is sterile and modern but handy for drivers (Db-300F, Tb-350F, Qb-400F, small rooms, CC:VMA, 132 rue Trivalle, tel. 04 68 25 24 24, fax 04 68 25 17 17).

Hôtel du Pont Vieux** is a 10-minute downhill walk from La Cité. This Old World hotel offers spacious rooms around a garden courtyard, 30F garage parking, and a third-floor three-person suite (#19) that opens out onto a private terrace with a five-star view of La Cité (Db-250–320F, Tb-360F, Qb-400F, CC:VM, 32 rue Trivalle, tel. 04 68 25 24 99, fax 04 68 47 62 71).

Train travelers will appreciate the spotless, dirt-cheap **Hôtel Astoria*** (S-110F, D-130F, Db-190F, Ts-190–210F, Tb-240F, Qs-250F, near station at 18 rue Tourtel, tel. 04 68 25 31 38, fax 04 68 71 34 14, e-mail: hotelastoria@wanadoo.fr).

Sleeping near Carcassonne in Caunes-Minervois
If too many tourists make you antsy, sleep 15 minutes from
Carcassonne in the unspoiled wine village of Caunes-Minervois
(zip code: 11600). These two great places sit side by side in the
heart of the village. Expat Americans Terry and Lois Link take care
of your every need at **L'Ancienne Boulangerie** (D-225F, Db-350F,
extra bed-100F, includes breakfast, tel. 04 68 78 01 32, e-mail:
ancienneboulangerie@compuserve.com). **Hotel d'Alibert****, a
wonderful Old World place, is run by Frederic with relaxed panache
(large Db-250F, Tb-300F, tel. 04 68 78 00 54). Don't skip a meal
in his terrific restaurant (*menus* from 75F).

Eating in La Cité
Other than in the touristy joints lining the main drag, prices and
quality seem about the same everywhere. Dine with Jacques Brel at
L'Auberge du Grand Puits (75F for a hearty *salade Cathar* and
cassoulet with dessert, next to Hôtel des Remparts, tel. 04 68 71 27
88). For above-average cassoulet, try **La Table Ronde** (80F *menu*,
30 rue du Plô, tel. 04 68 47 38 21). For a bit more money, enjoy
the fine regional cuisine in an elegant setting at **l'Ecu d'Or** (*menus*
from 125F, tel. 04 68 25 49 03), across from Hôtel Donjon. True
gourmets enjoy a splurge at the country-posh **Auberge du Pont
Levi** (off main parking lot just outside walls, tel. 04 68 25 55 23).

Picnics can be gathered at the small *alimentation* on the main
drag (generally open until 20:30). For your beggar's banquet, picnic on the city walls. For fast, cheap, hot food, look for places on
the main drag with quiche and pizza to go.

Transportation Connections—Carcassonne
By train to: Sarlat (both of these routes may require a transfer in
Toulouse, 6/day, 6 hrs, transfer at Bordeaux's St. Jean station or
via Souillac, then bus from Souillac), **Arles** (8/day, 3 hrs, a few are
direct, but most require a transfer in Narbonne), **Nice** (6/day,
6.5 hrs, a few are direct, most transfer in Narbonne and/or
Marseille), **Paris'** Gare Montparnasse (8/day, a few direct in 10 hrs
or in 6.5 hrs by TGV via Toulouse, additional transfer possible
in Bordeaux), **Toulouse** (hrly, 1 hr), **Barcelona** (3/day, 5 hrs,
transfer in Narbonne and Port Bou, the border town).

Sights—Languedoc
These sights are worth a visit only if you're driving. Peyrepertuse
and Queribus make ideal stops between Carcassonne and
Collioure (allow two hours from Carcassonne on narrow,
winding roads).
▲▲▲**Chateaus of Hautes Corbières**—Two hours south of
Carcassonne toward the boring little country of Andorra, in the
scenic foothills of the Pyrénées, lies a series of surreal, mountain-

capping castle ruins. The Maginot Line of the 13th century, these sky-high castles were strategically located between France and the Spanish kingdom of Roussillon. As you can see by flipping through the picture books in Carcassonne tourist shops, these castles' crumpled ruins are an impressive contrast to the restored walls of Carcassonne. Bring a good map (lots of tiny roads) and sturdy walking shoes—prepare for a climb.

The most spectacular is the château of **Peyrepertuse**. The ruins seem to grow right out of a narrow splinter of cliff. The views are so sensational you can almost reach out and touch Spain. Let your imagination soar, but watch your step as you try to reconstruct this eagle's nest (20F, 10:00–sunset all year, tel. 04 68 45 40 55).

Nearby, **Queribus** (20F) is also impressive and is famous as the last Cathar castle to fall. It was left useless when the border between France and Spain was moved (in 1659) farther south into the high Pyrénées.

▲**Châteaus of Lastours**—Ten miles north of Carcassonne (forget public transportation), these five side-by-side ruined hilltop castles offer drivers the most accessible look at the region's Cathar castles and an ideal picnic site. From Carcassonne follow signs to Conques and then Lastours. In Lastours follow signs to the Bellevedere for a panorama overlooking the five castles. The small fee also allows you to hike up to the castles (park back down the hill). It's steep but worthwhile if it's not too hot.

▲**Minerve**—A onetime Cathar hideout, Minerve is remarkably situated in the middle of a deep canyon that provided a natural defense. Strong as it was, it didn't keep out the pope's army. The entire village was destroyed and all residents were killed during the Albigensian Crusades. An interesting path leads down to the river and around the village. There are two pleasant cafés, one hotel, an interesting museum of prehistory—and not much more—in Minerve.

Minerve, between Carcassonne and Beziers, is 15 kilometers northeast of Olonzac (40 min by car from Carcassonne). It makes an ideal stop between Provence and Carcassonne. In the mood for wine tasting? The friendly (and French-only) Remaurys offer a good selection and an exquiste setting from which to sample the local product. Just over the hill from Minerve toward Carcassonne and past Azillanet, you'll see the signs to **Domaine de Pech d'Andre** (tel. 04 68 91 22 66).

Sleeping and eating in Minerve: If you're tired of competing with tourists, stay here and melt into southern France. Sleep and eat at the friendly and cozy **Relais Chantovent** (Sb-180F, Db-225–260F, Tb-260F, Qb-290F, ask for the new rooms, CC:VM, zip code: 34210, tel. 04 68 91 14 18, fax 04 68 91 81 99). People travel great distances to dine at their moderately priced restaurant (closed Sun–Mon), so reserve early.

COLLIOURE

Collioure, while surrounded by less appealing resorts, is blessed with an ideal climate (the temperature has not dropped below 55 degrees in three years) and a romantic setting. By Mediterranean standards this seaside village should be overrun—it has everything. Like an ice-cream shop, Collioure offers 31 flavors of pastel houses and six petite, scooped-out, and pebbled beaches sprinkled lightly with beachgoers. This sweet scene, capped by a winking lighthouse, sits under a once-mighty castle in the shade of the Pyrénées.

Come here to unwind and do nothing. Even with its crowds of French vacationers in peak season, Collioure is what many are looking for when heading to the Riviera—a sunny, peaceful vacation from their vacation.

Tourist Information: The TI is just behind the main beachfront cafés at 5 place du 18 Juin (Mon–Sat 9:00–19:00, Sun 10:00–12:00, 15:00–18:00 in summer only, otherwise Mon–Fri 9:30–12:00, 14:00–18:00, tel. 04 68 82 15 47).

Laundromat: Laverie 3L will do your laundry while you do your relaxing (daily 9:00–19:00 in summer, otherwise daily 9:00–12:00, 15:00–18:00, 1 block up from the post office at 28 rue de la Republique, tel. 04 68 98 04 17).

Car Rental: Garage Renault, opposite the Laundromat on rue de la Republique, is the only game in town (tel. 04 68 82 08 34).

Taxi: Tel. 04 68 82 27 80 or 04 68 82 05 30.

Arrival in Collioure

By Train: Walk straight out of the station, turn right, and follow the road down until you see Hotel Fregate (hotels are listed from this point).

By Car: Follow Collioure, "*centre-ville*" signs. Look for a parking spot on the street or, if you have no luck, follow Gare SNCF signs (pay lot at the train station until you find better). Ask your hotel for ideas and take absolutely everything out of the car.

Sights—Collioure

Check your ambition at the station. Enjoy a slow coffee, snuggle into the pebble-sand beach, and lose yourself in the old city's narrow, hilly streets. The 800-year-old **Château Royal** (great ramparts and views, a mildly interesting exhibit on the local history, and contemporary art exhibits) and the waterfront **Notre Dame des Anges** church are worth exploring. The **Chemin de Fauvism** (path of fauvism) displays copies of Derain's and Matisse's works inspired by Collioure on walls along the waterfront (TI has details). Consider relaxing on a paddleboat or taking a **Promenade sur Mer** motorboat or sailboat excursion (1 or 3 hours, the longer trip is better, all boats depart from the breakwater near the château). For those who can't slow down, the TI has information on hikes into the hills (the ruined castle of St. Elme, one mile in one hour straight up, offers the best views).

The TI also has a list of wine shops offering relaxed tastings of the locally produced sweet Banyuls and Collioure reds and rosés. Evenings are best in Collioure—make sure to inspect every foot of the waterfront you can find. As the sky darkens, yellow lamps reflect warm pastels and deep blues.

Sights—Near Collioure

The picturesque village of Castelnou and its 10th-century castle make an easy day trip for drivers (20 km from Collioure, ask at TI). Trainers can day-trip to Spain, to either Barcelona (3.5 hours one way) or, closer, Figures and its Dalí museum (get schedules at the station). The modern-art museum in nearby Ceret is accessible to everyone.

Sleeping and Eating in Collioure
(6F = about $1, zip code: 66190)

You have two good choices for hotel location: in the old city, tucked behind the castle (closer to train station); or in a quieter area across the bay, with views of the old city (10-min walk from castle). The first four hotels are in the old city; directions are given from the big Hotel Fregate, at the entrance to the old city.

The cheapest rooms in the old city are the clean and comfortable rooms at Monsieur and Madame Peroneille's **Chambres** on the pedestrian street two blocks past the Hotel Fregate at 20 rue Pasteur (Ds-230F, Db-270F, Tb-370F, Qb-420F, rooms in the main building are pricier but far better than those in annex, ask to see rooftop terrace, tel. 04 68 82 15 31, fax 04 68 82 35 94). One block from the Fregate, the artsy and eternally hip **Hôtel Templiers**** has a complacent staff but rents delightfully decorated rooms, some with views (Db-340–400F, Tb-460F, 12 avenue l'Amiraute, tel. 04 68 98 31 10, fax 04 68 98 01 24). Opposite Hotel Fregate, Collioure's best splurge is the Mediterranean-elegant **Casa Pairal*****, with a cozy lounge and fine air-conditioned rooms surrounding a garden courtyard and pool (small Db-360–410F, pleasant Db-480–550F, big Db-540–760F, Tb-810–960F, extra bed-130F, CC:VMA, impasse Palmiers, tel. 04 68 82 05 81, fax 04 68 82 52 10, e-mail: roussillhotel@wanadoo.fr, SE).

For American style and efficiency, try the modern **Princes de Catalogne's***** spacious, comfortable, and air-conditioned rooms (Db- 380–420F, Tb/Qb-550–700F, next to Casa Pairal, rue des Palmiers, tel. 04 68 98 30 00, fax 04 68 98 30 31).

On the view side of the bay, your best bet is the ideal **Hotel Boramar****. Get a room with a terrace facing the sea or sleep elsewhere (no view Db-260F, Db with view-320F, Tb with view-360F, rue Jean Bart, tel. 04 68 82 07 06). Next door, the neon-pink

Hôtel Triton** is less personal but has good enough roo
rates, many with fine views (Ds-190F, Db-260–300F, ver
first, rue Jean Bart, tel. 04 68 98 39 39, fax 04 68 82 11 32).

Eating in Collioure

In the old city, **El Capillo** is a good value (2 rue Pasteur), but **La Marinade** is where you should go for fine seafood (120F *menu*, near TI at 14 place du 18 Juin, tel. 04 68 82 09 76). For a lively, local, and smoky tapas bar experience, find **La Cave Arago** (18 rue Pasteur, open Thu–Sun, tourists tolerated). I love buying something to go (*a emporter*) and finding a romantic spot somewhere on the water.

Transportation Connections—Collioure

By train to: Carcassonne (8/day, a few direct in 2 hrs, via Narbonne in 2.5 hrs), **Paris** (1/day direct to Gare d'Austerlitz, 10 hrs; or, even better, transfer at Narbonne and Toulouse to TGV and zip into Gare Montparnasse, 7 hrs), **Barcelona** (5/day, 3.5 hrs), **Avignon/Arles** (12/day, 3 hrs, transfer in Narbonne). The train station ticket office closes at 17:45 (tel. 04 68 82 05 89). Consider handy night trains to Paris, key Italy destinations, and Geneva.

PROVENCE

This magnificent region is shaped like a wedge of quiche. From its sunburnt crust fanning out along the Mediterranean coast from Nîmes to Nice, it stretches north along the Rhône Valley to Orange. The Romans were here in force and left many ruins—some of the best anywhere. Seven popes; great artists, such as van Gogh, Cézanne, and Picasso; and author Peter Mayle all enjoyed their years in Provence. Provence offers a splendid recipe of arid climate (but brutal winds known as the mistral), captivating cities, exciting hill towns, and remarkably varied landscapes.

Wander through the ghost town of ancient Les Baux and under France's greatest Roman ruin, Pont du Gard. Spend your starry, starry nights where van Gogh did, in Arles. Explore its Roman past then find the linger-longer squares and café corners that inspired Vincent. Some may prefer Avignon's more elegant feel and softer edge as a home base. Youthful but classy Avignon bustles in the shadow of its brooding popes' palace. It's a short hop from Arles or Avignon into the splendid scenery and villages of the Côtes du Rhône and Luberon regions that make Provence so popular today.

Planning Your Time

Make Arles or Avignon your base (hotels are a better value in Arles). Italophiles prefer Arles, while poodles pick Avignon. If you're driving, consider basing in a town nearby and leave absolutely nothing in your car at any stop. Avignon (well connected to Arles by train) is the regional transportation hub for destinations north of Arles: Pont du Gard, Uzès, Orange, Vaison la Romaine, and Isle sur la Sorgue. You'll want a full day for sightseeing in Arles (ideally on Wed or Sat, when the morning market

rages), a half day for Avignon, and a day or two for the villages and sights in the countryside. To best feel the pulse of Provence, get out of the city and spend a night in a Provençale village (as described below).

Getting around Provence

The yellow Michelin map to this region is essential for drivers. Public transit is fairly good: Frequent trains link Avignon, Arles, and Nîmes (about 30 mins between each). Les Baux is accessible by bus from Arles. Pont du Gard, St. Rémy, Vaison la Romaine, and some Luberon villages are all accessible by bus from Avignon. While a tour of the villages of Luberon is worthwhile only by car, Isle sur la Sorgue is an easy hop by train from Avignon. The TIs in Arles and Avignon have information on bus excursions to regional sights that are hard to reach *sans* car (95F/half day, 150F/day).

Cuisine Scene—Provence

The almost extravagant use of garlic, olive oil, herbs, and tomatoes makes Provence's cuisine France's liveliest. To sample it, order anything *à la Provençale*. Among the area's spicy specialties are ratatouille (a thick mixture of vegetables in an herb-flavored tomato sauce), *brandade* (a salt cod, garlic, and cream mousse), aioli (a garlicky mayonnaise often served atop fresh vegetables), *tapenade* (a paste of puréed olives, capers, anchovies, herbs, and sometimes tuna), *soupe au pistou* (vegetable soup with basil, garlic, and cheese), and *soupe à l'ail* (garlic soup). Look also for *riz Camarguaise* (rice from the Camargue) and *taureau* (bull meat). Banon (wrapped in chestnut leaves) and Picodon (nutty taste) are the native cheeses. Provence also produces some of France's great wines at relatively reasonable prices. Look for Gigondas, Sablet, Côtes du Rhône, and Côte de Provence. If you like rosé, try the Tavel. This is the place to splurge for a bottle of Châteauneuf-du-Pape.

Provence Market Days

Provençal market days offer France's most colorful and tantalizing outdoor shopping. Here's a list to help plan your excursions. The best markets are Wednesday in St. Rémy, Thursday in Nyons, Saturday in Arles, and, best of all, Sunday in Isle sur la Sorgue. Crowds and parking problems abound at these popular events—arrive by 9:00 or, better, sleep in the town the night before.

Monday: Cadenet (near Vaison la Romaine), Cavaillon
Tuesday: Avignon, Tarascon, Gordes, Vaison la Romaine, Beaumes de Venise
Wednesday: Arles, Avignon, St. Rémy, Violes (near Vaison la Romaine)
Thursday: Carianne (near Vaison la Romaine), Nyons, Orange, Avignon, Beaucaire, Vacqueyras, Isle sur la Sorgue
Friday: Remoulins (Pont du Gard), Carpentras, Bonnieux, Visan, Châteauneuf-du-Pape
Saturday: Arles, Avignon, Oppède, Valreas
Sunday: Avignon, Isle sur la Sorgue, Uzès, Coustelet, Beaucaire

ARLES

By helping Julius Caesar defeat Marseille, Arles earned the imperial nod and was made an important port city. With the first bridge over the Rhône, Arles was a key stop on the Roman road from Italy to Spain, the Via Domitia. After reigning as a political center of the early Christian church (the seat of an archbishopric for centuries) and thriving as a trading city on and off until the 18th century, Arles all but disappeared from the map. Van Gogh settled here a hundred years ago but left only memories. American bombers destroyed much of Arles in World War II, but today Arles thrives again. This compact city is alive with great Roman ruins, some fine early Christian art, an eclectic assortment of museums, made-for-ice-cream pedestrian zones, and squares that play hide-and-seek with visitors.

Tourist Information: The small TI at the train station will likely be closed in 2000, but check anyway. The main TI, on the ring road esplanade Charles de Gaulle, is a high-powered mega-information site (daily 9:00–19:00, in winter Mon–Sat 9:00–19:00, Sun 9:00–13:00, tel. 04 90 18 41 20). Pick up the "Arles et Vincent Van Gogh" walking tour brochure (5F) and the free *Guide Touristique 2000* and ask about bullfights and bus excursions to regional sights.

Arrival in Arles

By Train and Bus: Both stations sit side by side on the river a 10-minute walk from the city center. Lockers are available at the train station. Pick up (or note) the bus schedule to Les Baux on your way into Arles. To reach the old town, walk to the river and turn left.

By Car: Follow signs to *centre-ville* then follow signs toward the *gare SNCF* (train station). You'll come to a huge roundabout (place Lamartine) with a Monoprix department store to the right. There is parking on the left, along the city wall (pay attention to no-parking signs on Wed and Sat until 13:00—they mean it). Theft is a problem; park at your hotel if possible. Take everything out of your car for safety. From place Lamartine, walk into the city through the two stumpy towers.

Helpful Hints

Supermarket: Place Lamartine has a big, handy Monoprix supermarket/department store (Mon–Sat 8:30–19:25, closed Sun).

Banks: Several banks on place de la République across from St. Trophime change money.

Laundry: A Laundromat is at 12 rue Portagnel (Mon–Sat 8:00–12:00, 14:00–19:00). Another, nearby at 6 rue Cavalarie, near place Voltaire (daily 7:00–21:00, later once you're in), has a confusing central-command panel: 20F for wash (push machine number on top row), 10F for 25 minutes of dryer (push dryer number on third row five times slowly), 2F for flakes (button #11). Dine at the recommended L'Arlatan restaurant, across the street, while you clean.

Getting around Arles

Arles faces the Mediterranean more than Paris. Its spaghetti street plan disorients the first-time visitor. Landmarks hide in the medieval tangle of narrow, winding streets. Everything is deceptively close. While Arles sits on the Rhône, it completely ignores the river. The elevated riverside walk does provide a direct route to the excellent Ancient History Museum and an easy return to the station. Hotels have free city maps, but Arles works best if you simply follow the numerous street-corner signs pointing you toward the sights and hotels of the town center. Racing cars seem to enjoy Arles' medieval lanes, turning sidewalks into tightropes and pedestrians into leaping targets.

By Minibus: The free "Starlette" shuttle minibus, which circles the town's major sights twice an hour, is worthwhile only to get to or from the distant Ancient History Museum (just wave at the driver and hop in; Mon–Sat 7:30–19:30, never on Sun), though I prefer the 20-minute walk along the river.

By Bike: While Isle sur la Sorgue makes a better biking base (see below), rides to Les Baux or into the Camargue work well from Arles. The Peugeot store rents bikes (15 rue du Pont, tel. 04 90 96 03 77), as does the newsstand next to the main TI (tel. 04 90 96 44 20).

By Taxi: Arles' taxis charge a minimum flat 50F fee. Nothing in town is worth a taxi ride (figure 100F to Les Baux, tel. 04 90 96 90 03).

Car Rental: You can rent cars at ADA (cheapest, 22 avenue Stalingrad, tel. 04 90 52 93 69), Avis (at train station, tel. 04 90 96 82 42), and Europcar (downtown at 15 boulevard Victor Hugo, tel. 04 90 93 23 24).

Sights—Arles' Museums

Arles' Global Billet covers all of the following sights (60F, sold at each sight). Otherwise, it's 15F per sight and museum (35F for the ancient history museum). While any sight is worth a few minutes of your time, many aren't worth the individual admission. For the small price of a Global Billet, the city is yours. (All sights except the Ancient History Museum and Arlatan folk museum are open Jun–mid-Sept 9:00–19:00; Apr–May and latter half of Sept 9:00–12:30, 14:00–19:00; otherwise 10:00–12:30, 14:00–17:30; closes 1 hour earlier in winter.) See Ancient History Museum and Musée Arlatan listings, below, for their hours.

▲▲▲**Ancient History Museum (Musée de L'Arles Antique)**— The sights of Roman Arles make maximum sense if you start your visit in this superb, air-conditioned museum. Models and original sculpture (with the help of the free English handout) re-create the Roman city of Arles, making workaday life and culture easier to imagine. Notice what a radical improvement the Roman buildings were over the simple mud-brick homes of pre-Roman peoples. Models of Arles' arena even illustrate the moveable stadium cover, good for shade and rain. While virtually nothing is left of Arles' chariot racecourse, the model shows how it must have rivaled Rome's Circus Maximus. Jewelry, fine metal and glass artifacts, and fine mosaic floors make it clear that Roman Arles was a city of art and culture. The finale is an impressive row of pagan and early

Arles

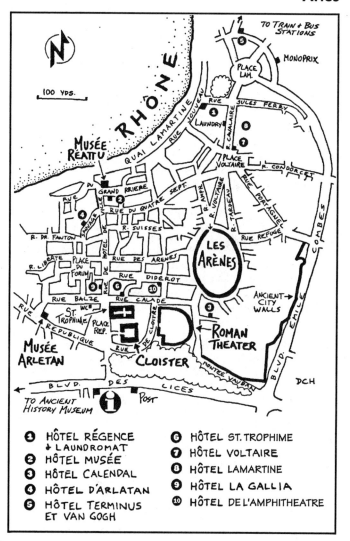

N

100 YDS.

TO TRAIN & BUS STATIONS

MONOPRIX

PLACE LAM.

RHÔNE

QUAI LAMARTINE

RUE JOUVEN

RUE JULES FERRY

RUE AMPH

Laundry

PLACE VOLTAIRE

R. CONDORCET

R. CANALAIRE

MUSÉE RÉATTU

DU GRAND PRIERE

RUE DU QUATRE SEPT.

RUE PORTAGNEL

RUE TARDEAU

RUE DE VOLTAIRE

RUE DE VILLE

R. SUISSES

RUE REFUGE

R. DR. FANTON

RUE DES ARENES

LES ARÈNES

COMBES

PLACE DU FORUM

R. LIBERTE

RUE DE

RUE DIDEROT

ANCIENT CITY WALLS

RUE BALZE

RUE CALADE

WC

ST. TROPHIME

PLACE REP.

ROMAN THEATER

RUE DE CLOISTRE

BLVD. EMILE

RUE REPUBLIQUE

RUE

MUSÉE ARLETAN

RUE DE CLOISTRE

CLOISTER

MONTÉE VAUBAN

BLVD.

DCH

BLVD. DES LICES

TO ANCIENT HISTORY MUSEUM

Post

1 HÔTEL RÉGENCE & LAUNDROMAT
2 HÔTEL MUSÉE
3 HÔTEL CALENDAL
4 HÔTEL D'ARLATAN
5 HÔTEL TERMINUS ET VAN GOGH
6 HÔTEL ST. TROPHIME
7 HÔTEL VOLTAIRE
8 HÔTEL LAMARTINE
9 HÔTEL LA GALLIA
10 HÔTEL DE L'AMPHITHEATRE

Christian sarcophagi (second to fifth centuries). In the early days of the Church, Jesus was often portrayed beardless and as the good shepherd—with a lamb over his shoulder.

Built at the site of the chariot racecourse, this museum is a

20-minute walk from Arles along the river. Turn left at the river and follow it to the big modern building just past the new bridge—or ride the free Starlette shuttle bus. (35F, daily 9:00–19:00 Apr–Sept, otherwise Wed–Mon 10:00–18:00, closed Tue, tel. 04 90 18 88 88.)

▲▲**Roman Arena (Amphithéâtre)**—Nearly 2,000 years ago, gladiators fought wild animals here to the delight of 20,000 screaming fans—cruel. Today matadors fight wild bulls to the delight of local fans—still cruel. While the ancient third row of arches is long gone, three towers survive from medieval times, when the arena was used as a fortress. In the 1800s it corralled 200 humble homes and functioned as a town within the town. Climb the tower. Walk through the inner corridors of this 440-by-350-foot oval and notice the similarity to 20th-century stadium floor plans. And if you don't mind the gore, a bullfight is an exciting show.

Classical Theater (Théâtre Antique)—Precious little survives from this Roman theater, which served as a handy town quarry throughout the Middle Ages. Two lonely Corinthian columns look from the stage out over the audience. The 10,000 mostly modern seats are still used for concerts and festivals. Take a stroll backstage through broken bits of Rome.

Musée Réattu—Highlights of this mildly interesting museum are a fun collection of 70 Picasso drawings (some two-sided and all done in a flurry of creativity) and a room of Henri Rousseau's Camargue watercolors.

▲**Musée Arlatan**—This cluttered folklore museum, given to Arles by Monsieur Mistral, is filled with interesting odds and ends of Provence life. The employees wear the native costumes. It's like a failed turn-of-the-century garage sale: You'll find shoes, hats, wigs, old photos, bread cupboards, and the beetle-dragon monster. If you're into folklore, this museum is for you (Apr–Sept daily 9:00–12:00, 14:00–19:00, otherwise closes at 17:00).

▲▲**St. Trophime Cloisters and Church**—This church, named after a third-century bishop of Arles, sports the finest Romanesque west portal (main doorway) I've seen anywhere.

But first enjoy the place de la République. Sit on the steps opposite the church. The Egyptian obelisk used to be the center-piece of Arles' Roman Circus. Watch the peasants—pilgrims, locals, buskers. There's nothing new about this scene. Like a Roman triumphal arch, the church trumpets the promise of Judgment Day. The tympanum is filled with Christian symbolism. Christ sits in majesty, surrounded by symbols of the four evangelists (Matthew—the winged man, Mark—the winged lion, Luke—the ox, and John—the eagle). The Twelve Apostles are lined up below Jesus. Move up closer. This is it. Some are saved and others aren't. Notice the condemned—a chain gang on the right bunny-hopping over the fires of hell. For them the tune trumpeted by the three angels on the very top isn't a happy one. Ride the exquisite detail back to a simpler age. In an illiterate medieval world long before the vivid images of our Technicolor age, this message was a neon billboard over this town's square. A chart just inside the church (on the right) helps explain the carvings. On the right side of the nave, a fourth-century early-Christian sarcophagus is used as an altar.

The adjacent cloisters are the best in Provence (15F, enter from the square, 20 meters to right of church). Enjoy the sculpted capitals of the rounded Romanesque columns (12th century) and the pointed Gothic columns (14th century). The second floor offers only a view of the cloisters from above.

More Sights—Arles

▲▲**Place du Forum**—This café-crammed square, while always lively, is best at night. Named for the Roman Forum that stood here, only two columns from a second-century temple survive. They are incorporated into the wall of Hotel Nord Pinus. (After a few drinks at Café van Gogh, the corner of that hotel actually starts to look phallic.) Van Gogh hung out here under these same plane trees. In fact, his *Le Café de Nuit* was painted from this square. The bistros on the square, while no place for a fine dinner, put together a good salad, and when you sprinkle in the ambience, that's 45F well spent. The guy on the pedestal is Frederic Mistral; in 1904 he received the Nobel Prize for literature. He used his prize money to preserve and display the folk identity of Provence at a time when France was rapidly centralizing. (He founded the Arlatan folk museum—see above.)

▲▲**Wednesday and Saturday Markets**—On these days until around noon, Arles' ring road (boulevard Emile Combes on Wednesday, boulevard Lices on Saturday) erupts into an outdoor market of fish, flowers, produce, and you-name-it. Join in, buy flowers, try the olives, sample some wine, and slap a pickpocket. On the first Wednesday of the month it's a grand flea market.

Fondation Van Gogh—A two-star sight for his fans, this small gallery features works by several well-known contemporary artists who pay homage to Vincent through their thought-provoking interpretations of his art (30F, not covered by Global Billet, Apr–Sept daily 10:00–19:00, otherwise 10:00–12:30, 14:00–17:00, facing the Roman arena at #24).

The 5F "Arles et Vincent Van Gogh" brochure (available at TI) takes you on several interesting walks through Arles using pavement markers as guides; by far the most interesting walk follows the footsteps of Vincent van Gogh.

▲▲**Bullfights (Courses Camarguaise)**—Occupy the same seats fans have been sitting in for 1,900 years and take in one of Arles' most memorable treats—a bullfight *à la Provençale*. Three classes of bullfights take place here. The *course protection* is for aspiring matadors; it's a daring dodge-bull game of scraping hair off the angry bull's nose for prize money offered by local businesses (no blood). The *trophée de l'avenir* is the next class, with amateur matadors. The *trophée des as excellence* is the real thing à la Spain: outfits, swords, spikes, and the whole gory shebang (tickets 30–50F; Apr–Oct Sat, Sun, and holidays; skip the "rodeo" spectacle, tel. 04 90 96 03 70 or ask at TI). There are nearby village bullfights in small wooden bullrings nearly every weekend (TI has schedule).

Sleeping in Arles
(6F = about $1, zip code: 13200)
Sleep Code: **S** = Single, **D** = Double/Twin, **T** = Triple, **Q** = Quad, **b** = bathroom, **t** = toilet only, **s** = shower only, **CC** = Credit Card (Visa, MasterCard, Amex), **SE** = Speaks English, **NSE** = No English, * = French hotel rating system (0–4 stars).

Hôtel Régence** sits right on the river and has immaculate and comfortable rooms, good beds, and easy access to the train station and safe parking. Helpful and gentle Sylvie speaks English (Db-200–290F, Tb-260–350F, Qb-360F; choose riverview or quiet, air-con courtyard rooms; CC:VM, 5 rue Marius Jouveau, from place Lamartine turn right immediately after passing through the towers, tel. 04 90 96 39 85, fax 04 90 96 67 64).

Hotel de l'Amphithéâtre**, a boutique hotel, is small, friendly, and *très* cozy, with thoughtfully decorated and air-conditioned rooms and a pleasant atrium breakfast room. It's located one block from the arena toward place du Forum (Db-290–350F, Tb-450–490F, parking-25F, CC:VMA, 5 rue Diderot, tel. 04 90 96 10 30, fax 04 90 93 98 69, SE).

Hôtel du Musée** is a quiet, delightful manor house hideaway with air-conditioned rooms and a terrific courtyard terrace. M. and Mme. Dubreuil speak some English (Sb-230F, Db-290–360F, Tb-370–410F, Qb-480F, parking-40F, CC:VMA, 11 rue de la Grande Prieure, follow signs to Musée Réattu, tel. 04 90 93 88 88, fax 04 90 49 98 15).

Hotel St. Trophime** is another fine, very central place with a grand entry, large rooms, and helpful owners (Sb-210F, Db-290F, spacious Db-340F, Tb-385F, huge Qb-430F, CC:VM, 16 rue de la Calade, near place de la République, tel. 04 90 96 88 38, fax 04 90 96 92 19).

Hôtel Calendal** is Provençal chic, with a tranquil outdoor garden, smartly decorated rooms, and a seductive ambience (Db-380–430F, Tb-470F, Qb-510F, extra bed-115F, parking-60F, air-con, strong beds, modern bathrooms, CC:VMA, located above arena at 22 place Dr. Pomme, tel. 04 90 96 11 89, fax 04 90 96 05 84, www.lecalendal.com, SE).

Hôtel d'Arlatan***, one of France's more affordable classy hotels, has a beautiful lobby; a courtyard terrace; and air-conditioned, antique-filled rooms. In the lobby of this 15th-century building, a glass floor looks down into Roman ruins (Db-500–800F, Db/suites-1,000–1,400F, parking-80F, CC:VMA, elevator, very central, a block off place du Forum at 26 rue du Sauvage, tel. 04 90 93 56 66, fax 04 90 49 68 45, e-mail: hotel-arlatan@provnet.fr, SE).

Hotel Terminus et Van Gogh* has bright, cheery rooms facing a busy square at the gate of the old town, a block from the train station. This building is in the painting of van Gogh's house, which was bombed in World War II (D-150F with no shower available, Ds-185F, Db-225F, CC:VM, 5 place Lamartine, tel. & fax 04 90 96 12 32).

Starving artists can afford these two clean but spartan places: **Hôtel Voltaire*** rents 12 small rooms with great balconies overlooking a caffeine-stained square a block below the arena (D-160F, Ds-180F, Db-200F, add 50F per person for 3 or 4, CC:VM, 1 place Voltaire, tel. 04 90 96 49 18). **Hôtel La Gallia** has small but clean rooms and is a steal (Ds-125–150F, above friendly café, 22 rue de l'Hôtel de Ville, tel. 04 90 96 00 63, fax 04 90 96 45 49).

Sleeping near Arles

In Fontvielle: Many drivers, particularly those with families, prefer setting up in the peaceful countryside with good access to the area's sights. Just 10 minutes from Arles and Les Baux (20 minutes to Avignon) you'll find the Provençal farmhouse/resort **Le Domaine de la Forêt**, which has modern apartments for five to six people (kitchen, 2 bedrooms, private terrace). Surrounded by vineyards and rice fields, this retreat offers a pool, swings, and a volleyball court. While most spend a full week here, shorter stays are possible (nightly-600F, weekly in summer only-3,450F, 2,750F in shoulder season, 2,250F in low season, from Arles take the D-17 toward Fontvieille, veer right in 6 km onto D-82, follow the Gites Ruraux signs, route de L'Aqueduc Romain, 13990 Fontvielle, tel. 04 90 54 70 25, fax 04 90 54 60 50).

Near Les Baux: Easier for short stays is the very welcoming **Mas de L'Esparou**, with three-star *chambre d'hôte* rooms, a swimming pool, and views of Les Baux (Db-380F, extra person-80F, just below Les Baux on the D-5, look for their sign, route de St. Rémy de Provence, 13520 Les Baux, tel. & fax 04 90 54 41 32).

Eating in Arles

You can eat basic food with great atmosphere on place du Forum or, better, have a drink there and then try one of these places for dinner. Near Hotel Regence, **L'Arlatan** is unpretentious and friendly and serves a fine meal and great desserts (95F *menu*, opposite Laundromat on rue Cavalarie, closed Wed). Just up the street on the place Voltaire, **La Giraudiere** offers excellent regional cooking (110F *menu*, closed Tue, tel. 04 90 93 27 52). Near Hotel du Musée, **L'Olivier** is my Arles splurge, offering exquisite *Provençale* cuisine (160F *menu*, 1 bis rue Reattu, reserve ahead, tel. 04 90 49 64 88). Vegetarians love **La Vitamine**'s salads and pastas (closed Sat–Sun, just below place du Forum on 16 rue Dr. Fanton, tel. 04 90 93 77 36). Almost next door, **La Paillotte** specializes in tradional *Provençale* cuisine (95F *menu*, 28 rue Dr. Fanton). **Le Criquet** is cheap, fun, and good (1 block from Hôtel Calendal at 12 Porte de Laure).

Transportation Connections—Arles
By bus to: Les Baux (4/day, 30 min; none on Sun, ideal departure about 8:30 with a return from Les Baux about 11:20 or 12:40, departs Arles bus station and 16 boulevard Clemenceau downtown; service reduced Nov–Mar; tel. 04 90 93 74 90).

By train to: Paris (2 direct TGVs, 4.5 hrs; otherwise transfer in Avignon, 8/day, 5.5 hrs), **Avignon** (8/day, 20 min, check for afternoon gaps), **Carcassonne** (8/day, 3 hrs, a few direct, most require a painless transfer in Narbonne), **Beaune** (3/day, 5 hrs, transfer in Lyon), **Nice** (8/day, 3.5 hrs, likely transfer in Marseille), **Barcelona** (3/day, 7 hrs, at least 1 transfer), **Italy** (3/day, via Marseille and Nice; from Arles it's 5 hrs to Ventimiglia on the border, 9 hrs to the Cinque Terre, 9 hrs to Milan, 11 hrs to Florence, 13 hrs to Venice or Rome). Train info: tel. 04 90 96 43 94.

AVIGNON
Famous for its nursery rhyme, medieval bridge, and brooding Palace of the Popes, contemporary Avignon bustles and prospers behind its walls. During the 68 years (1309–1377) that Avignon played Franco Vaticano, it grew from a quiet village to the thriving city it still is. Today this city combines a youthful student population with a white-collar, sophisticated city feel. Street mimes play to crowds enjoying Avignon's slick cafés and chic boutiques. If you're here any time in July, save evening time for Avignon's rollicking theater festival and reserve your hotel early. The streets throng with jugglers, skits, and singing, as visitors from around the world converge on Avignon.

Orientation
The cours Jean Jaurés (which turns into the rue de la République) leads from the train station to place de l'Horloge and the Palace of the Popes, forming Avignon's spine. Climb to the parc de Rochers des Doms for a fine view, enjoy the people scene on place de l'Horloge, and meander the back streets (see below). Avignon's shopping district fills the pedestrian streets where rue de la République meets place de l'Horloge (great gelato just off

place de l'Horloge, where St. Agricol meets Joseph-Vernet). Walk across Pont Daladier (bridge) for a great view of Avignon and the Rhône River.

Tourist Information: The main TI is between the train station and the old town at 41 cours Jean Juarés (Mon–Fri 9:00–13:00, 14:00–18:00, Sat–Sun until 17:00, closed Sun in winter, tel. 04 90 82 65 11, e-mail: information@avignon.fr), while a smaller branch is just inside the city wall at the entrance to Pont St. Bénezet (same hours as main TI). Pick up their Avignon discovery guide, which has a good, but long, walking tour, "Strolling along the Old Streets" (consider shortcutting the route after place St. Pierre and continuing from there to the Palace of the Popes). The TI offers English-language walking tours of Avignon (50F, Tue and Thu at 10:00). They also have regional bus and train schedules to all destinations described in this chapter and information on bus excursions to popular regional sights.

Arrival in Avignon

By Train: Cross the big street and walk through the city walls onto the cours Jean Juarés (TI 3 blocks down at #41). The bus station (*halte routière*) and car rentals are 100 yards to the right as you exit the train station, near the IBIS hotel.

By Car: Drivers enter Avignon following *centre-ville* signs. Park along the wall close to Pont St. Bénezet (ruined old bridge) and use that TI. Hotels have advice for smart overnight parking.

Sights—Avignon

▲**Palace of the Popes (Palais des Papes)**—In 1309 a French pope was elected (Pope Clement V). At the urging of the French king, His Holiness decided he'd had enough of unholy Italy. So he loaded up his carts and moved out of the chaos north to Avignon for a steady rule under a friendly, supportive king. The Catholic Church literally bought Avignon, then a two-bit town, and popes resided here until 1403. From 1378 on, there were twin popes, one in Rome and one in Avignon, causing a split in the Catholic Church that wasn't fully resolved until 1417.

The pope's palace is two distinct buildings, one old and one older. Along with lots of big, barren rooms, you'll see frescoes, tapestries, and remarkable floor tiles. The new audiophone self-guided tours do a good job overcoming the lack of furnishings and give a great history lesson while allowing you to tour this vast place at your own pace (don't miss the view and windswept café from the tower, 45–55F, occasional supplements for special exhibits, Apr–Oct daily 9:00–19:00, until 20:00 in summer, off-season 9:00–17:45, ticket office closes 1 hour earlier, tours in English twice daily Mar–Oct, call 04 90 27 50 74 to confirm.)

▲**Musée du Petit Palais**—This palace superbly displays collections of 14th- and 15th-century Italian painting and sculpture. Since the Catholic Church was the patron of the arts in those days, all 350 paintings deal with Christian themes. Visiting this museum before going to the Palace of the Popes gives you a sense of art and life during the Avignon papacy. Notice the improvement in perspective in the later paintings (30F, Wed–Mon 9:30–18:00 in summer, otherwise 9:30–12:00, 14:00–18:00, closed Tue).

▲**Parc de Rochers des Doms and Pont St. Bénezet**—Hike above the Palace of the Popes for a panoramic view over Avignon and the Rhône valley. At the far end, drop down a few steps for a good view of Pont St. Bénezet. This is the famous "sur le Pont d'Avignon," whose construction and location were inspired by a shepherd's religious vision. Imagine a 22-arch, 3,000-foot-long bridge extending across two rivers to that lonely Tower of Philippe the Fair (the bridge's former tollgate on the distant side). The island the bridge spanned is now filled with campgrounds. You can pay 15F to walk along a section of the ramparts and do your own jig on the bridge (good view), but it's best appreciated from where you are. The castle on the right, the St. André Fortress, was once another island in the Rhône. Cross Daladier Bridge for the best view of the old bridge and Avignon's skyline.

Fondation Angladon Dubrujeaud—This newly opened museum displays an engaging collection of art from Postimpressionists to contemporary artists (30F, Wed–Sun 13:00–18:00, closed Tue, 5 rue Laboureur).

Avignon 2000—Avignon has been selected as one of several European Capitals of Culture for the millennium. Many projects and events are under consideration to celebrate this event (including rebuilding Pont St. Benezet). Check at the TI for year 2000 events that might coincide with your visit.

Sleeping in Avignon
(6F = about $1, zip code: 84000)
These hotels are listed in the order you would pass them from the train station.

Hôtel Splendid* rents firm beds in good rooms for a fair price near the station, on the small park near the TI (S-165F, Ds-170–220F, Db-180F–270F, 17 rue Agricol Perdiguier, tel. 04 90 86 14 46, fax 04 90 85 38 55). Across the street at #18, **Hotel du Parc***'s sharply renovated rooms are a better value but have small beds (D-165F, Ds-215F, Db-230–260F, tel. 04 90 82 71 55, fax 04 90 85 64 86).

Hotel Colbert**, one block down, is a one-star hotel masquerading as a two-star hotel, but it does have air-conditioning and cheap rates (Sb-180–250F, Db-210–290F, Tb-260-350F, 7 rue Agricol Perdiguier, tel. 04 90 86 20 20 , fax 04 90 85 97 00).

Hôtel Blauvac** offers cozy rooms with stone walls in an old manor home near the pedestrian zone (Sb-350F, Db-370–450F, Tb/Qb-400–525F, CC:VMA, 1 block off rue de la République, 11 rue de La Bancasse, tel. 04 90 86 34 11, fax 04 90 86 27 41, M. Surcouf SE). Right on the loud rue de la République at #17, the bright and cheery **Hotel Danieli**** offers modern and comfortable rooms in shiny surroundings at Parisian prices (Db-330–475F, Tb-570F, CC:VM, tel. 04 90 86 46 82, fax 04 90 27 09 24).

Hotel Medieval** is a fine value in an old mansion with friendly owners and kitchenettes in all of its unimaginative, but comfortable and fairly spacious, rooms (Db-240–350F, Tb-380F, extra bed-50F, 15 rue Petite Saunerie, 5 blocks east of place de l'Horloge, behind Eglise St. Pierre, tel. 04 90 86 11 06, fax 04 90 82 08 64).

For reliable, ultramodern comfort and a great location, try one of two **Hotel Mercures***** (Db-550–650F). One is just inside the walls near Pont St. Bénezet (Quartier de la Balance, tel. 04 90 85 91 23, fax 04 90 85 32 40); the other is near the Palace of the Popes (Cité des Papes, 1 rue Jean Vilar, tel. 04 90 86 22 45, fax 04 90 27 39 21).

You'll find good cheap beds across Pont Daladier on the Island (Ile de la) Barthelasse at the **Auberge Bagatelle's hostel/campground,** which has a pool, laundry, a cheap café, and campers for neighbors (dorm bed-61F, Ile de la Barthelasse, tel. 04 90 86 30 39).

Eating in Avignon
L'Epicerie is charmingly located on a tiny square a few blocks east of place de l'Horloge, and offers a good selection of à la carte items (10 place St. Pierre, tel. 04 90 82 74 22).

Transportation Connections—Avignon
By train to: Arles (8/day, 20 min), **Orange** (hrly, 15 min), **Nîmes** (hrly, 20 min), **Nice** (10/day, 4 hrs; a few direct, most require transfer in Marseille), **Carcassonne** (8/day, 3 hrs, possible transfer in Narbonne), **Lyon** (14/day, 2.5 hrs), **Paris'** Gare du Lyon (10 TGVs/day, 4 hrs), **Barcelona** (2/day, 5 hrs, possible transfer in Narbonne; direct night train is convenient).

By bus to Pont du Gard: Bus service can leave you stranded for hours (3/day, 45 min, to Auberge Blanche stop, a 15-min walk to Pont du Gard). Consider visiting Pont du Gard, continuing on to Nîmes or Uzès (both merit exploration), and returning to Avignon from there (try these plans: Take the noon bus from Avignon, arriving at Pont du Gard at 12:45; then take either the 14:45 bus from there to Nîmes, where trains run hourly back to Avignon, or a 16:00 bus, Mon–Fri, on to Uzès, arriving at 16:30, with a return bus to Avignon at 18:30). Make sure you're waiting for the bus on the right side of the road at the Pont du Gard Auberge Blanche stop (ask at

the small inn: "*Nîmes? Uzès? Avignon? Par ici?*"). The
Avignon TI has all schedules. Service is reduced or nonexistent on
Sunday and holidays. In Avignon, the bus station (tel. 04 90 82 07
35) is adjacent to the train station (tel. 08 36 35 35 35).

By bus to other regional destinations: St. Rémy (6/day,
45 min, handy way to visit its Wed market), **Isle sur la Sorgue**
(5/day, 45 min), **Vaison la Romaine** (2/day, 75 min), **Gordes** (via
Cavaillon, 1/day, very early, 2 hrs, you must spend the night or
taxi back to Cavaillon), **Nyons** (2/day, 2 hrs).

Sights—Provence

▲▲▲**Les Baux**—This rock-top ghost town is worth visiting for the
lunar landscape alone. Arrive by 9:00 or after 17:00 to avoid the
crowds. A 12th-century regional powerhouse with 6,000 fierce residents, Les Baux was razed in 1632 by a paranoid Louis XIII, afraid
of these troublemaking upstarts. What remains are a reconstructed
"live city" of tourist shops and snack stands and the "dead city" ruins
carved into, out of, and on top of a 600-foot-high rock. Spend most
of your time in the dead city—it's most dramatic and enjoyable in
the morning or early-evening light. Don't miss the slideshow on
van Gogh, Gaugin, and Cézanne in the small chapel near the entry.
Spend some time in the small museum as you enter (good exhibits)
and pick up the English explanations before exploring the dead city.
In the tourist-trampled live city, you'll find artsy shops, several
interesting Renaissance homes, and a fine exhibit of paintings by
Yves Brayer (20F), who spent his final years here (entrance to dead
city costs 36F, includes entry to all the town's sights; Easter–Oct
9:00–19:00, until 20:00 in summer, otherwise 9:30–17:00; pick up
the excellent brochure, "A Sense of Place," at TI, tel. 04 90 54 34
39). To best experience the bauxite rock quarries and enjoy a great
view of Les Baux, drive or hike one kilometer up D-27 and sample
wines with atmosphere at **Caves de Sarragnan** (tel. 04 90 54 33
58). Nearby, the **Cathedrale d'Images** uses 48 projectors showing
3,000 images inside a rock quarry to immerse its visitors in themes
from the region (43F, daily 10:00–18:00, on D-27 as you leave Les
Baux toward St. Rémy). If you're tempted to spend the night, try
the enchanting **Hotel Reine Jeanne****, 50 yards on your right after
the main entry (Db-270–360F, great family suite-520F, ask for a
chambre avec terasse, menus from 110F, CC:VM, 13520 Les Baux, tel.
04 90 54 32 06, fax 04 90 54 32 33).

Four daily buses serve Les Baux from the Arles train station,
and two daily buses (summers only) leave from Avignon. Les Baux
is 15 kilometers northeast of Arles, just past Fontvielle.

St. Rémy—This chic Provençal town is a scenic ride just over the
hill from Les Baux. Here you'll find a thriving Wednesday market
(until noon); the crumbled ruins of **Glanum**, a once-thriving
Roman city located at the crossroads of two ancient trade routes

between Italy and Spain; and the mental ward where Vincent van Gogh was sent after cutting off his ear. Glanum is just outside St. Rémy on the road to Les Baux (D-5). Walk to the gate and peek in to get a feel for its scale. The ruins are worth the effort if you have the time and haven't been to Pompeii or Ephesus (33F, Apr–Sept daily 9:00–12:00, 14:00–19:00, otherwise 9:30–12:00, 14:00–17:00). Across the street, opposite the entrance, is a Roman arch and tower. The arch marked the entry into Glanum. The tower is a memorial to the grandsons of Emperor Augustus.

Across the street from Glanum is the still-functioning mental hospital that housed van Gogh (Clinique St. Paul). Wander into the small chapel and intimate cloisters. Vincent's favorite walks outside the hospital are clearly signposted. If St. Rémy charms you into a longer visit, sleep dead center at the comfortable **Hotel du Cheval Blanc**** (Db-280–300F, CC:VM, 6 avenue Fauconnet, tel. 04 90 92 09 28, fax 04 90 92 69 05) or just outside town at the tranquil **Canto Cigalo** (Db-280–340F, chemin Canto Cigalo, tel. 04 90 92 14 28, fax 04 90 92 24 48).

▲▲▲**Pont du Gard**—One of Europe's great treats, this remarkably well preserved Roman aqueduct was built before the time of Christ. It was the missing link of a 35-mile canal that, by dropping one foot for every 300, supplied 44 million gallons of water to Nîmes daily. While the top is now closed to daredevils, just walking under it is a marvel. Study it up close. There's no mortar—just expertly cut stones. Signs direct you to "panaromas" above the bridge on either side. The best view of the aqueduct is from the cool of the river below, floating flat on your back—bring a swimsuit and sandals for the rocks (always open and free). Consider renting a canoe from Collas to Remoulins, ending at the Pont du Gard (2-hour trip, 175F per 2-person canoe; shuttle to bus stop, car park, or Remoulins included; Collas Canoes, tel. 04 66 22 85 54).

Buses run to Pont du Gard from Nîmes, Uzès, and Avignon. Combine Uzès (see below) and Pont du Gard for an ideal day excursion from Avignon (see "Transportation Connections—Avignon," above). By car, Pont du Gard is an easy 30-minute drive due west of Avignon (follow signs to Nîmes) and 45 minutes northwest of Arles (via Tarascon). Park on the *rive gauche* side (you'll see signs) and leave nothing in your car.

Uzès—An intriguing, less-trampled town near Pont du Gard, Uzès is best seen slowly on foot, with a long coffee break in its mellow main square, the place aux Herbes (not so mellow during the colorful Sunday morning market). Check out the round Tour Fenestrelle (all that remains of a 12th-century cathedral) and the Duché de Uzès. Uzès is a short hop west (by bus) of Pont du Gard and is well served from Nîmes (9/day) and Avignon (3/day).

The Camargue—This is one of the few truly "wild areas" of France, where pink flamingos, wild bulls, and the famous white horses wander freely amid rice fields and lagoons. Skip it. The Camargue's biggest town is Aigue Mortes. That means "dead town," and it should stay that way.

▲▲**Orange**—This most northern town in Provence is notable for its Roman arch and theater. Its 60-foot-tall Roman arch (from 25 B.C.) shows off Julius Caesar's defeat of the Gauls in 49 B.C. Its best-preserved Roman theater in existence still seats 10,000; the 120-foot-high stage wall is awesome (30F, Apr–early Oct daily 9:00–18:30, off-season 9:00–12:00, 13:30–17:00; ticket includes entrance to city museum across street, which has more Roman art; Orange TI tel. 04 90 34 70 88). Trains run hourly between Avignon and Orange (15-min ride; bus #2 takes you the mile from Orange station to the old town center). From Orange drivers can tour the adjacent wine region, described below.

Villages of the Côtes du Rhône: A Loop Trip for Wine Lovers

If you have a car (or a bike, best rented in Vaison la Romaine— ideal riding from here) and a fondness for fine wine or beautiful countryside, take a loop trip through Provence's Côtes du Rhône wine country. You'll find countless *dégustation* (tasting) opportunities well signed, the easiest of which are the cave cooperatives (wine-maker cooperatives). If possible, spend a night in one of the villages listed below. From Avignon, head to Carpentras and then connect the wine villages of Vaqueryas, Gigondas, Rasteau, Sablet, Vaison la Romaine, and adorable, if overrestored, Seguret (figure on a 100-kilometer round trip from Avignon). This is a hospitable and relaxed wine-tasting region, with generous samples and little pres-sure to buy. Near Rasteau village, at Le Domaine des Girasols, friendly Francoise (SE) will take your palate on a tour of some of the area's best wine. It's well marked and worth a stop, and while you aren't pressured to buy, their wine is a good value.

If you have extra time, consider exploring the less-traveled Dromme region just north of Vaison la Romaine. It's laced with vineyards (producing less-expensive yet fine wines), lavender fields (blooms late Jun–mid-Jul), and postcard-perfect villages. From Vaison take the loop north to Visan, Valreas, Taulignan, and Nyons, and then back to Vaison. Each of these villages is a detour waiting to happen. Picturesque Nyons is France's olive capital and a pleasant place to stroll, particularly on Thursday mornings (market day).

Sleeping and Eating in the Wine Country

Gigondas: Ideally, have lunch in the trendy town of Gigondas at an outdoor restaurant on the small town square. The comfortable **Hostellerie les Florets***, one kilometer above the village, is most famous for its truly exceptional restaurant (*menus* from 130F, Db-430F, 84190 Gigondas, tel. 04 90 65 85 01, fax 04 90 65 83 80).

Sablet: This nearby wine village, which makes a good base for budget travelers, is chock-full of *chambres d'hôte* (try **Madame Fert's Chambres,** Db-300–330F, includes breakfast, follow the signs, tel. & fax 04 90 46 94 77).

Vaison la Romaine: If you're *sans* car or need a larger town, stay in Vaison la Romaine, where you get two villages for the price of one (2 buses/day, 90 mins from Avignon; 3/day, 45 mins from Orange; tel. 04 90 36 09 90). Vaison's "modern" lower city is like a mini Arles, with impressive Roman ruins and a *Provençale* pedestrian street. The medieval hill town (Ville-Haute), with its meandering cobbled lanes, art galleries, tranquil cafés, and a ruined castle, overlooks the lower city from across the river.

The excellent TI is in the lower city, across from the Roman ruins and the main parking lot at place de Chanoine Sautel (tel. 04 90 36 02 11, ask about bike rentals). **Hotel Burrhus****, easily the best value in the lower city, is right in the thick of things on the raucous place Montfort (ask for a room off the square if you want to sleep, Db-280–320F, tel. 04 90 36 00 11, fax 04 90 36 39 05; if they're full ask about their other hotel, **Hotel des Lis*****, next door). The Ville-Haute offers Vaison's quieter and more costly accommodations. You'll sleep and dine like royalty at **Hotel Beffroi***** (Db-470–660F; I enjoy their cheaper garden *menu*, great setting; rue de l'Eveche, tel. 04 90 36 04 71, fax 04 90 36 24 78). **La Bartavelle** is the place to savor a slow meal in the lower town (145F *menu*, 12 place sus-Auze). The Ville-Haute has a *crêperie* and pizzeria with fair prices. Surrounded by vineyards just outside town, **Château Taulignan**'s *chambres d'hôte* offer a welcoming and dreamy setting from which to contemplate this beautiful region (Db-450–550F, 84110 St. Marcellin, tel. 04 90 28 71 16, fax 04 90 28 75 04, e-mail: chateau@pacwan.fr).

The best view in Provence might well be from **Restaurant Le Panorama** in tiny Crestet, a five-minute drive from Vaison la Romaine (98F *menu* or simple à la carte, call ahead, tel. 04 90 28 86 62).

NOT QUITE A YEAR IN PROVENCE: THE HILL TOWNS OF LUBERON

The Luberon region, stretching 30 miles along a ridge of rugged hills east of Avignon, hides some of France's most appealing hill towns. Bonnieux, Lacoste, Oppède le Vieux, Roussillon, and the very-discovered (and overpriced) Gordes, to mention a few, are quintessential Provençal hill towns.

Those intrigued by Peter Mayle's *A Year in Provence* will enjoy a day joyriding through the region. Mayle's best-selling book describes the ruddy local culture from an Englishman's perspective as he buys an old home, fixes it up, and adopts the region as his new home.

The Luberon terrain in general (much of which is a French

regional natural park) is as appealing as its hill towns. Gnarled vineyards and wind-sculpted trees separate tidy stone structures from abandoned buildings—little more than rock piles—that seem to challenge city slickers to fix them up.

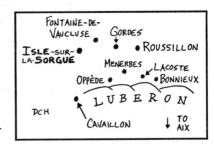

The wind is an integral part of life here. The infamous mistral, finishing its long ride in from Siberia, hits like a hammer—hard enough, it's said, to blow the ears off a donkey. Throughout the region you'll see houses designed with windowless walls facing the mistral. Walking from village to village is a popular pastime here—local TIs have trail information.

Planning Your Time

To enjoy the windblown ambience of the Luberon, plan a leisurely day trip visiting three or four of the characteristic towns. While the area is tough without a car, Isle sur la Sorgue is handy to Avignon by train and offers a good introduction to this sunny slice of France and makes an ideal biking base (Isle sur la Sorgue's train station is called l'Isle Fontaine de Vaucluse).

Getting around the Luberon

By Bus: To reach the hill towns such as Roussillon by bus, you must go to Cavaillon or Apt and then taxi (1 bus/day from Avignon to Gordes, 2 buses/day from Cavaillon to Gordes, tel. 04 90 71 03 00).

By Car: Town-hop for a day, side-tripping from Arles or as a detour en route to the French Riviera. Of course, tumbling in for an hour from the car park, you'll be just another flash-in-the-pan, camera-toting Provence fan. Spend a night and you'll feel more a part of the scene. By car, get on the N-100 toward Apt, east of Avignon. Veer left onto the D-2, where you'll see signs to Gordes. Roussillon is signed from Gordes.

Isle sur la Sorgue

This sturdy market town, literally, "Island on the Sorgue River," sits within a split in its happy little river. (Do not confuse it with the nearby plain town of Sorgue.) While Isle sur la Sorgue is renowned for its Sunday market, it is otherwise a pleasantly average town with no important sights and a steady trickle of tourism.

With clear water babbling under pedestrian bridges decorated with flower boxes and its old-time carousel always spinning, Isle sur la Sorgue erupts into a market frenzy, with hearty crafts and local produce each Sunday and Thursday (the Sunday market is more impressive and more crowded).

Navigate the town by its mossy waterwheels, which, while still turning, power only memories of the town's wool and silk industries. The shopping streets are rue de la République and rue Carnot. The 12th-century church with a festive Baroque interior seems too big for its town. Next to it is the antique green **Café de France**—the place to sip a pastis with locals and ponder the action on place de la Liberté. Find the old waterwheels on rue Dr. Jean Roux and stroll the shady riverside park one kilometer upstream. Isle sur la Sorgue is dead on Mondays. The pretty nearby village of Velleron (ideal by bike) is a tiny version of Isle sur la Sorgue, complete with waterwheels, fountains, a château, and a not-to-miss evening farmer's market every night but Sunday from 18:00 to 20:00.

Isle sur la Sorgue's **TI**, next to the cathedral, has information on handy Avignon train and bus connections and a line on rooms in private homes (Tue–Sat 9:00–12:30, 14:00–18:00, Sun 9:00–12:30, closed Mon, tel. 04 90 38 04 78). There's a Laundromat just off rue de la République on l'impasse de la République (open 8:00–20:00). You can rent mountain bikes at Plein Air Location, 30 yards in front of the train station (60F/half day, 100F/day, tel. 04 90 38 25 80, cellular 06 83 37 04 90).

Sleeping in Isle sur la Sorgue
(6F = about $1, zip code: 84800)

Arrive the night before market day to best experience Isle sur la Sorgue. Drivers may prefer sleeping in a quieter Luberon village listed below.

Hotel Restaurant La Gueulardiere**, while at a busy intersection, has good rooms away from the street that open onto a garden courtyard and an artsy, reasonably priced restaurant (Db-300F, 1 rue de l'Apt, tel. 04 90 38 10 52, fax 04 90 20 83 70). **Hotel les Nevons****, two blocks from the center, is motel-modern but seems to do everything right, with large, comfortable, and air-conditioned rooms (a few family suites), a rooftop pool, and eager-to-please owners, Mireille and Jean-Philipe (Sb-265F, Db-280–300F, Tb-360F, Qb-460F, easy and secure parking, 205 Chemin des Nevons, tel. 04 90 20 72 00, fax 04 90 20 56 20). The best bargain beds in town are sufficiently clean and quiet and above a local bar at **Hotel Le Cours** (D-120F, Db-180F, place Gambetta, tel. 04 90 38 01 18). A mile from the center toward Apt along the Sorgue River sits the peaceful and reasonable **Hotel Le Pescador*** (Db-200–290F, Le Partage des Eaux, tel. 04 90 38 09 69, fax 04 90 38 27 80).

Eating in Isle sur la Sorgue

Begin any meal with a glass of wine at the incredibly cool **Le Caveau de la Tour de l'Isle**—part wine bar, part wine shop (12 rue de la République). If you want to dine well, **l'Oustau de l'Isle** is the place (*menus* from 130F, closed Wed–Thu off-season, on the ring road near the post office, 21 avenue des 4 Otages, tel. 04 90 38 54 83). For a cheaper meal, **Bella Vita**, next to Café de France on place de l'Eglise, has good Italian food (closed Mon), and **Bistrot de l'Industrie** is a cozy café serving salads, pizza, crêpes, and steak *frites* right on the river (open daily, near Total station at 2 quai de la Charité).

Transportation Connections— Isle sur la Sorgue

Isle sur la Sorgue's train station is called l'Isle Fontaine de Vaucluse.

By train to: Avignon (6/day, 30 min), **Nice** (4/day, 3 hrs, transfer in Marseille).

By bus to: Avignon (5/day, 45 min).

Roussillon

With all the trendy charm of Santa Fe on a hilltop, this town will cost you at least a roll of film (and 15F for parking). Climb a few minutes from either car park, past the picture-perfect square and under the church to the summit of the town (signs to *castum*), where a dramatic view, complete with a howling mistral and an interesting *table d'orientation*, awaits. Then, back under the church, see how local (or artsy) you can look over a cup of coffee on what must be the most scenic village square in the Luberon. On the south end of town, beyond the upper parking lot, a brilliant ochre canyon (10F)—formerly a quarry—stands ready for those who wish they were in Bryce Canyon. You could paint the entire town without ever leaving the red and orange corner of your palette. Many do.

Sleeping in or near Roussillon
(6F = about $1, zip code: 84220)

The **TI**, across from the David restaurant, posts a list of hotels and *chambres d'hôte* (tel. 04 90 05 60 25). Just below the charm, near the north-side lower parking, is the ideal **Hôtel Reves d'Ocres**** with helpful owners (Db-320–380F, Tb-500F, Qb-600F, CC:VM, air-con, tel. 04 90 05 60 50, fax 04 90 05 79 74). **Madame Cherel** rents simple but clean rooms with firm mattresses (D-200F, inexpensive dinners available, 3 blocks from upper parking lot, between gas station and school, tel. 04 90 05 68 47). Cherel is well traveled, speaks English, is a wealth of regional travel tips, and rents mountain bikes (100F/day). The *chambre d'hôte* **Les Huguets**, on the D-108, 1.5 kilometers outside the village toward Apt, is another good and comfortable value (Db-

270–300F, includes breakfast, les Passiflors, tel. and fax 04 90 05 69 61, friendly Chantal).

Mas Garrigon*** takes elaborate care of upscale travelers in a beautiful setting, with a pool, fine rooms, and an elegant restaurant where they kindly request that you have dinner (300F *menu*, Db-690–850F, CC:VMA, 1 mile below Roussillon, tel. 04 90 05 63 22, fax 04 90 05 70 01).

Gordes and Oppède le Vieux

Gordes—This is the most touristy and trendy town in the Luberon. Parisian big shots love it. Once a virtual ghost town of derelict buildings, it's now completely fixed up and filled by people who live in a world without callouses. See it from a distance.

Oppède le Vieux—This is a windy barnacle of a town with a few boutiques and a dusty main square at the base of a short, ankle-twisting climb to an evocative ruined church and castle. The Luberon views justify the effort. This way-off-the-beaten-path fixer-upper of a village must be how Gordes looked before it became chic. It's ideal for those looking to perish in Provence. The cozy **Restaurant L'Oppidum** rents two classy rooms and dorm beds in a larger room (Db-300F, dorm bed-120F, place de la Croix, tel. 04 90 76 74 01 or 04 90 76 84 15, NSE).

THE FRENCH RIVIERA

A hundred years ago, celebrities from London to Moscow flocked here to escape the drab, dreary weather at home. The belle époque is today the tourist *époque*, as this most sought after fun-in-the-sun destination now caters to more than Europe's aristocracy. Some of the Continent's most stunning scenery and intriguing museums lie along this strip of land—as do millions of sun-worshiping tourists.

Nice is this region's capital and your best home base, with excellent public transportation to most regional sights, world-class museums, plenty of hotels in all price ranges, and a marvelous beachfront promenade. Nearby Antibes or Villefranche offer sandy beaches, small-town warmth, good public transport, and much easier parking. I've focused my accommodations listings on these three cities. If you choose Nice, remember that it's France's fifth-biggest city. And if you plan to visit three or more Riviera museums, the new regional Carte Musées is a steal (see "Nice," below).

Day trips are easy. Monte Carlo welcomes all with open cash registers, and the hill towns offer a breezy and photogenic alternative to the beach scene. Evenings on the Riviera, a.k.a. the Côte d'Azur, were made for the promenade and outdoor dining.

Planning Your Time
Once situated, spend a day in Nice and then consider half-day trips to Monaco, Antibes, St. Paul/Vence, Villefranche, and Eze—in that order.

Getting around the Riviera
Getting around the Côte d'Azur by train or bus is easy (drivers should seriously consider parking their cars and leaving the driving to others).

Nice is perfectly located for exploring the region. Like prostitutes on bar stools, the resort towns of the Riviera await your visit. Monaco, Eze, Villefranche, Antibes, St. Paul, and Cannes are all a 15- to 60-minute bus or train ride apart from each other.

While rail travelers have a tough time breaking away from the tracks, bus service can be cheaper and more frequent and scenic—plus it often drops you closer to where you want to be. At Nice's efficient bus station (*gare routière*, on boulevard J. Jaures—see map of Nice), competing companies vie for your business, offering free return trips (keep your ticket). Get schedules and prices at the helpful information desk in the bus station.

Here's an overview of public transport options to key Riviera destinations from Nice (rt = round-trip):

Destination	Bus	Train
Monaco	4/hrly, 40 min, 20F rt	2/hrly, 20 min, 20F 1 way
Villefranche	4/hrly, 15 min, 7.5F rt	2/hrly, 10 min, 8F 1 way
Antibes	3/hrly, 50 min, 25F, 1 way	2/hrly, 15 min, 22F 1 way
Cannes	way too long	2/hrly, 30 min, 40F 1 way
St. Paul	2/hrly, 30 min, 20F, 1 way	none
Eze Village	every 2 hrs, 25 min, 15F, rt	none

Two bus companies, RCA and Cars Broch, provide service between Nice, Villefranche, and Monaco; RCA's buses run far more frequently, giving you more flexibility on your return (tel. 04 93 85 61 81 for info on both).

Cuisine Scene—Côte d'Azur

The Côte d'Azur (technically a part of Provence) gives Provence's cuisine a Mediterranean flair. Local specialties are bouillabaisse (the spicy seafood stew-soup that seems worth the cost only for those with a seafood fetish), bourride (a creamy fish soup thickened with aioli, a garlic sauce), and *salade niçoise* (neeswaz; a tasty tomato, potato, olive, anchovy, and tuna salad). You'll also find these tasty bread treats: *pissaladière* (bread dough topped with onions, olives, and anchovies), *fougasse* (a spindly, lacelike bread), *socca* (a thin chickpea crêpe), and *pan bagnat* (a bread shell stuffed with tomatoes, anchovies, olives, onions, and tuna). If you need a break from French cooking, excellent Italian cuisine is readily available in this region. White and rosé Bellet and the rich reds and rosés of Bandol are the local wines.

The French Riviera

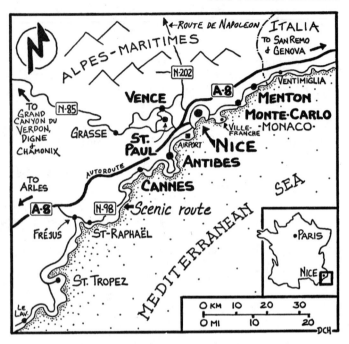

NICE

Nice is a melting pot of thousands of tanning tourists and 340,000 already-tanned residents. Here you'll rub shoulders with the chicest of the chic, the cheapest of the cheap, and everyone else in this scramble to be where the mountains meet the water. Nice's spectacular Alps-to-Mediterranean scenery, thriving Old City, eternally entertaining seafront promenade, and superb museums make settling into this city exciting. Nice is nice—but hot and jammed in July and August. Get a room with air-conditioning.

Take only a piece of Nice and leave the rest to the residents. Outside of a few museums, everything you want is within a small area—near the Old City and along the seafront.

Orientation

Tourist Information: Nice has four helpful TIs (inside the airport; next to the train station; on the RN-7 as you drive into town, on the right just after the airport; and downtown at 5 promenade des Anglais). All are open daily from 8:00 to 19:00—until 20:00 in summer (tel. 04 93 87 07 07 or 04 93 87 60 60). Pick up the excellent free Nice map (which lists all the sights and hours), the museums booklet, and the extensive *Practical Guide to Nice*. TIs make hotel reservations for a small fee.

Arrival in Nice

By Train: Nice has one main station with luggage lockers (Nice-Ville) where all trains stop and you get off. Avoid the suburban station (Gare Riquier). The TI is next door to the left as you exit the train station; Avis car rental is to the right. To reach my recommended hotels, turn left out of the station then right on avenue Jean Médecin. To get to the beach and the promenade des Anglais from the station, continue on foot for 20 minutes down avenue Jean Médecin or take bus #12 (catch it across the street from the station). To get to the Old City and the bus station (*gare routière*), catch bus #5 from avenue Jean Médecin (one block left out of the station, then right on Jean Médecin).

By Car: For some of the Riviera's best scenery, follow the coast road between Cannes and Fréjus (when arriving in or leaving the Côte d'Azur) and take the short drive along *Moyenne Corniche* from Nice to Eze Village. Use the roadside TI just past the airport and park at the lot at Nice Étoile on avenue Jean Médecin (about 80F/day). Most Nice street parking is metered, and garages cost from 60F to 90F per day.

By Plane: Nice's mellow and TI-equipped airport (tel. 04 93 21 30 30) is right on the Mediterranean. The TI and international flights use terminal 1; domestic flights use terminal 2. The airport is about 25 minutes from the city center. To get downtown, take bus #23 (direction: St. Maurice, 4/hrly, 8.5F) to the *gare* SNCF (train station). This station is near most of my hotel listings and is where you catch the train to Antibes. To get to Villefranche from the airport, take the yellow bus signed "Nice" (3/hrly, 21F) to the *gare routière* (bus station) and then transfer to the Villefranche bus (4/hrly, 7.5F). Taxis to Nice will cost about 150F; to Villefranche pay no more than 250F.

Helpful Hints

Think safety first. Have nothing important on or around your waist, unless it's a moneybelt tucked out of sight (no fanny packs, please), and stick to main streets in old Nice after dark.

The new regional museum pass, Carte Musées, is a great deal for those planning to visit three or more museums in the area (70F for 3 consecutive days, 140F for 7 consecutive days, valid at all museums described in this chapter except the Foundation Maeght). You can buy it at any museum or TI.

The American Express office faces the beach at 11 promenade des Anglais (tel. 04 93 16 53 53). For new and used English-language books and guidebooks, try The Cat's Whiskers (closed

Sun, 26 rue Lamartine, near Hôtel Star). Cycles Arnaud rents mountain bikes (100F/day, 4 place Grimaldi, just off avenue Jean Médecin, tel. 04 93 87 88 55). Self-serve Laundromats abound in Nice; ask your hotelier and guard your load.

Sights—Nice

▲▲Promenade des Anglais—There's something for everyone along this seafront circus. Watch the Europeans at play, admire the azure Mediterranean, anchor yourself in a blue chair, and prop your feet up on the made-to-order guardrail. Join the evening parade of tans along the promenade. Start at the pink-domed Hotel Negresco and, like the belle époque English aristocrats for whom the promenade was built, stroll to the Old City and Castle Hill.

Hotel Negresco, Nice's finest hotel and a historic monument, offers the city's most costly beds and a free "museum" interior (reasonable attire is necessary to enter). March through the lobby into the exquisite Salon Royal. The tsar's chandelier hangs from an Eiffel-built dome. Read the explanation, check out the room photos, and stroll the circle. On your way out, pop into the Salon Louis XIV.

The next block to your left as you exit has a lush park and the Masséna Museum. The TI is just beyond that. Cross over to the promenade.

Pull up a chair and admire the scene (come back after dark for a real treat). To your right is the airport (built on a landfill) and, on that tip of land way out there, Cap d'Antibes (good hiking trail there, see "Sights—Antibes"). Until the late 1800s, Antibes and Nice were in different countries; the Italians gave Nice to the French in thanks for their help during the reunification of Italy in 1870. To the left lies Villefranche (after the second tip of land), Monaco, then Italy. Behind you are the pre-Alps (les Alpes Maritimes), which gather threatening clouds and leave the Côte d'Azur in sunshine over 300 days per year. Get down to that beach.

Beaches—The beaches of Nice are where the jet set lays on rocks. After settling into the smooth pebbles, you can play beach volleyball, Ping-Pong, or *boules*; rent paddleboats, Jet Skis, or Windsurfers; explore ways to use your zoom lens as a telescope; or snooze on comfy beach beds with end tables (55F for a mattress, 65F for a mattress and chaise lounge, 25F for an umbrella). Before you head off in search of sandy beaches, try it on the rocks.

▲▲Old City (Vieux Nice)—This thriving Old City is characteristic Nice in the buff. Here Italian and French flavors mix to create a spicy Mediterranean dressing. The 20th century has driven old Nice into a triangle of spindly streets filling a corner between the castle hill and beach. A broad, park-lined boulevard seals it off. The streets, while straight, are anything but predictable. Stealth pigeons fly under tall, pastel, domestic cliffs, while tattoo shops show their

Nice

Map legend:

1. HÔTEL LES CAMELIAS
2. HÔTEL VENDOME
3. STAR HÔTEL
4. HÔTEL DU PETIT LOUVRE
5. HÔTEL CLEMENCEAU & ST. GEORGE
6. Rest. LOU NISSART
7. HÔTEL LORRAINE
8. HÔTEL WINDSOR
9. HOTEL MASSENA

work. The Naples-like rue Droite plays host to simple bars, chic art shops, and shady walking; stop by Le Four à Bois bakery (at #38) and watch them make *fougasse*. Cours Saleya, a long broad square, collects people and produce like a trough between all this and the sea. Restaurant tables tangle with market stalls here. The daily flower and fish market becomes a flea market on Monday. Place Rosetti is simply charming at night (but avoid the restaurants here); you'll find great gelato at several nearby locations (I like Gelateria Azzurro, just off place Rosetti on rue Reparate).

Castle Hill—Climb or elevator up this saddle horn in the otherwise flat city center only for exercise or the view. Walk up rue Rossetti or catch the elevator from the beach side. The 360-degree view of Nice, the Alps foothills, and the Mediterranean is a decent reward. You'll find a waterfall, tacky souvenirs, a playground, and a cemetery but no castle on Castle Hill.

Shopping Streets—The pedestrian street rue Masséna is packed with tourists, run-of-the-mill cafés, and boutiques. Window shop the expensive boutiques and sift through the international crowds.

▲**Russian Cathedral**—Even if you've been to Russia, this Russian Orthodox church, which claims to be the finest outside Russia, is interesting. Its one-room interior is filled with icons and candles. Tsar Nicholas II gave his aristocratic countryfolk—who wintered on the Riviera—this church in 1912. (A few years later, Russian comrades who didn't winter on the Riviera shot him.) Here in the land of olives and anchovies, these proud onion domes seem odd. But so did, I imagine, those old Russians (12F, daily 9:00–12:00, 14:30–18:00, services Sat at 18:00, Sun at 10:00, no shorts, 10-minute walk behind station at 17 boulevard du Tsarevitch, tel. 04 93 96 88 02).

Nightlife—Nice's bars play host to a lively late-night scene full of jazz and rock 'n' roll. Most activity focuses on Old Nice, near place Rossetti. If you're out very late, avoid walking alone. Plan on a cover charge or expensive drinks.

Museums—Nice

▲▲▲**Musée National Marc Chagall**—Even if you're suspicious of modern art, this museum—with the largest collection of Chagall's work anywhere—is a delight. After World War II, Chagall returned from the United States to settle in Vence, a hill town above Nice. Between 1954 and 1967 he painted a cycle of 17 large murals designed for and donated to this museum. These paintings, inspired by the books of Genesis, Exodus, and the Song of Songs, make up the "nave," or core, of what Chagall called the "House of Brotherhood."

Each painting is a lighter-than-air collage of images drawing from Chagall's Russian-folk-village youth, his Jewish heritage, Biblical themes, and his feeling that he existed somewhere between heaven and earth. He felt the Bible was a synonym for nature, and color and Biblical themes were key ingredients for understanding God's love for his creation. Chagall's brilliant blues and reds celebrate nature, as do his spiritual and folk themes. Notice the focus on couples. To Chagall, humans loving each other mirrored God's love of creation.

Don't miss the stained-glass windows of the auditorium (enter through the garden), early family photos of the artist, and a room full of Chagall lithographs. The small 20F guidebook begins with a philosophical introduction by Chagall himself (30F, Jul–Sept

Wed–Mon 10:00–17:40, Oct–Jun 10:00–16:40, closed Tue, 30F English tours often available on request, tel. 04 93 53 87 20). An idyllic café awaits in the pleasant garden.

Getting to Chagall and Matisse Museums: The Chagall Museum is a confusing 15-minute walk from the top of avenue Jean Médecin and the train station; the Matisse Museum is a 30-minute uphill walk from there. Walk to the Chagall and then take bus #15 to Matisse (6/hrly, 8.5F). The walk down from the Matisse is far easier.

To walk to the Chagall Museum, get to the train station end of avenue Jean Médecin and turn right onto rue Raimbaldi along the overpasses, then turn left under the overpasses onto avenue Comboul. Once under the overpass, angle right up rue Olivetto to the alley with the big wall on your right. A pedestrian path soon emerges, leading up and up to signs for Chagall and Matisse. The bus to Matisse is on avenue Cimiez, two blocks up from Chagall (ask for Musée Matisse and get off when you see the Roman ruins).

▲**Matisse Museum**—This is a three-star sight for his fans. The art is beautifully displayed in this brilliant orange mansion and represents the single largest collection of Matisse paintings. While many (including one of your authors) don't get Matisse, this museum offers a painless introduction to this very influential artist; watch as his style becomes progressively more simple with age. A room on the top floor has models of his famous Chapelle du Rosaire in Vence and illustrates the beauty of his simple design (25F, Apr–Sept Wed–Mon 10:00–18:00, Oct–Mar 10:00–17:00, closed Tue; take bus #15, #17, or #22 to Arènes stop, also see directions under Chagall listing above, tel. 04 93 81 08 08.)

Nice City Museum (Musée Masséna)—The city-history museum, housed in a beautiful mansion, is packed with historical—but forgettable—paraphernalia (25F, May–Sept Tue–Sun 10:00–12:00, 14:00–18:00, Oct–Apr 10:00–12:00, 14:00–17:00, closed Mon; in a fine garden facing the beach next to Hotel Negresco at 65 rue de France, tel. 04 93 88 11 34).

Modern Art Museum—This ultramodern museum features a fine collection of art from the 1960s and 1970s (25F, Wed–Mon 11:00–18:00, Fri evening until 22:00, closed Tue, on promenade des Arts near bus station).

Sleeping in Nice
(6F = about $1, zip code: 06000)
Sleep Code: **S** = Single, **D** = Double/Twin, **T** = Triple, **Q** = Quad, **b** = bathroom, **t** = toilet only, **s** = shower only, **CC** = Credit Card (Visa, MasterCard, Amex), **SE** = Speaks English, **NSE** = No English, * = Hotel rating (0–4 stars).

Don't look for charm in Nice. Go for modern and clean with a central location. Reserve early for summer visits. Prices go down from October to April. There are few hotels in the Old City, and the hotels near the station are overrun, overpriced, and loud. I sleep halfway between the Old City (Vieux Nice) and the train station, near avenue Jean Médecin. From the train station, turn left onto avenue Thiers and then right onto avenue Jean Médecin. Drivers can park under the Nice Étoile shopping center (at avenue Jean Médecin and boulevard Dubouchage/Victor Hugo), midway between the Old City, the train station, the bus station, and the seafront.

Hôtel du Petit Louvre* has art-festooned walls, lighthearted owners, and close-to-clean rooms (Ds-205F, Db-230F, Tb-250–290F, CC:VM, elevator, 10 rue Emma Tiranty, tel. 04 93 80 15 54, fax 04 93 62 45 08).

Hôtel Clemenceau** comes with generally spacious and comfortable rooms (S-150–165F, Db-200–310F, Tb-250–360F, Qb-400–520F, plus 50F for a kitchenette, CC:VM, 1 block west of avenue Jean Médecin, 3 avenue Clemenceau, tel. 04 93 88 61 19, fax 04 93 16 88 96, daughter Marianne SE).

Hôtel St. Georges**, a block away, is bigger and more modern and has a bit less personality, but it's still a good value. It has a peaceful garden courtyard and reasonably spacious and comfortable rooms (Sb-300F, Db-360F, 3-bed Tb-450F, CC: VMA, TVs with CNN, air-con, elevator, 7 avenue Clemenceau, tel. 04 93 88 79 21, fax 04 93 16 22 85).

Hôtel Star**, located a few blocks east of avenue Jean Médecin, is utterly immaculate, air-conditoned, comfortable, and a great value. Unfortunately, the owners seem deluged with my readers and are losing patience with imperfect behavior. It's earnestly run by Françoise and Georges, who work very hard and expect you to respect their standards and toe the line—don't use your towels for anything but drying your body (Sb-200–250F, Db-280–350F, Tb-370–450F, CC:VMA, fine beds, beach towels, no elevator, 14 rue Biscarra, tel. 04 93 85 19 03, fax 04 93 13 04 23, SE).

For a taste of faded belle époque, pink pastels, and high ceilings, waltz into **Hotel Vendome*****, well located in an old manor house with off-street parking. Some rooms are just average, but the best have balconies—request *avec balcon*. The best rooms are 105, 102, or any on the fifth floor (Sb-380–480F, Db-480–590F, Tb-500–670F, Qb-570–770F, 26 rue Pastorelli, tel. 04 93 62 00 77, fax 04 93 13 40 78).

Hôtel Lorrain* is my best bargain listing, with clean rooms with kitchenettes. It's ideally located near the bus station and Old Nice. Delightful Patricia Scoffier tries her best to speak English (S-165F, Ds-200F, Db-220–260F, Tb-280F, CC:VM, 6 rue Gubernatis, push the top buzzer to release the door, tel. 04 93 85 42 90, fax 04 93 85 55 54). This simple hotel may request longer stays in the high season and a two-night minimum off-season.

Hôtel les Camelias** reminds me of the Old World places
I stayed in as a kid traveling with my parents. An ideally located,
dark and floral place burrowed in a garden, it has simple rooms
(some lumpy beds) and a loyal clientele who give the TV lounge
a retirement-home-after-dinner feeling. Some basic rooms have
balconies—request a *chambre avec balcon* (S-180F, Ss-220F, Sb-300F,
Db-360–400F, Tb-400–450F, includes breakfast, parking-30F,
CC:VM, elevator, 3 rue Spitaleri, tel. 04 93 62 15 54, fax 04 93 80
42 96. Formal Madame Vimont and her son Jean Claude SE).
Guests here will gum their 70F four-course dinner—simple, hearty,
and stressless.

Hotel Massena***, well located a few blocks from place
Massena, offers 100 rooms with all the modern comforts (for a
price), including air-conditioned rooms, spacious lounges, and a
parking garage (Sb-610–810F, Db-650–890F, parking-80F,
CC:VMA, 58 rue Giofreddo, tel. 04 93 85 49 25, fax 04 93 62 43
27, e-mail: info@hotel-massena-nice.com, SE).

Hôtel Windsor***, is a snazzy, airy garden retreat with many
contemporary rooms designed by modern artists and the only
swimming pool I saw in Nice (Sb-550F, Db-550–750F, extra bed-
100, sauna 60F, free gym, rooms over the garden are worth the
higher price, CC:VMA, elevator, 10 blocks west of avenue J.
Medecin and 5 blocks from the sea, 11 rue Dalpozzo, tel. 04 93 88
59 35, fax 04 93 88 94 57, e-mail: windsor@webstore.fr, SE).

Eating in Nice

Nice's Old City overflows with cheap, moderate, and expensive
restaurants, pizza stands, and taverns.

Charcuterie Julien is a good deli that sells an impressive array
of local dishes by weight. Buy 200 grams of your choice plopped
into a plastic carton to go (Thu–Tue 11:00–19:30, closed Wed, rue
de la Poissonnerie, at the Castle Hill end of cours Saleya).

For maximum ambience at fair prices, **Spaghetissimo** serves
mostly Italian (3 cours Saleya). On the same side of cours Saleya at
#5, locally popular **La Cambuse** serves more traditional cuisine.

Nissa Socca café offers the best cheap Italian cuisine in town
in a lively atmosphere (opens at 19:00, arrive early, a block off
place Rossetti on rue Reparate). If they're full, try the mirror
image across the alley, **Nissa la Bella Socca**.

Just below place Massena, **Lou Nissart** serves excellent regional
specialities to appreciative locals in nonair-conditioned rooms (moderate, across place Masséna at 1 rue de l'Opéra, tel. 04 93 85 34 49).

Near most hotels recommended in this book: **L'Authentic**
offers good pastas and seafood in a relaxed setting (65F daily special, 80F *menus*, 18 rue Biscarra, tel. 04 93 62 48 88). **Le Chantilly**,
a 10-minute walk west of my hotels, is friendly and serves local
specialties at very reasonable prices in air-conditioned comfort

(12 rue Grimaldi, tel. 04 93 87 50 08). For a splurge, try the bouillabaisse or other à la carte dishes at **Les Viviers** (5-minute walk west of avenue Jean Médecin at 22 rue Alphonse Karr, tel. 04 93 16 00 48; they also run the elegant restaurant next door).

Transportation Connections—Nice

By train to: Arles (8/day, 3.5 hrs, transfer in Marseille), **Paris'** Gare de Lyon (3 direct TGVs/day, 6.5 hrs; 6/day via Marseille then TGV, 8 hrs; 1 direct night train), **Dijon** (8/day, 8 hrs, 4 are direct, others via Lyon), **Chamonix** (2/day, 10–12 hrs, 1 morning train and 1 night train at about 21:30), **Digne/Grenoble** (consider the scenic little trains that run from Nice to Digne then on to Grenoble; see "Travel Notes for La Route de Napoleon" at the end of this chapter), **Munich** (2/day, 12 hrs, night train with transfer in Verona), **Interlaken** (1/day, 12 hrs), **Florence** (2/day, 7 hrs, transfer in Pisa and/or Genoa, 1 morning departure, 1 night train), **Milan** (4/day 6 hrs), **Venice** (3/day, 8 hrs, direct night train), **Barcelona** (3/day, 10 hrs, direct night train or day trips with at least one transfer). Train info: tel. 04 36 35 35 35.

By plane to: Paris (hrly, 1 hr, about the same price as a train ticket).

VILLEFRANCHE-SUR-MER

Come here for upscale, small-town Mediterranean atmosphere. Villefranche (between Nice and Monte Carlo, with frequent 15-minute buses and trains to both) is quieter and more exotic than Nice. Narrow, cobbled streets tumble into the mellow waterfront; a scenic walkway below the castle leads to the hidden port; and luxury yachts glisten in the harbor below. More-or-less sandy beaches and a handful of interesting sights keep visitors just busy enough.

The **TI** is in the park Francois Binon just below the main bus stop (daily 8:30–12:30, 14:00–19:00, 20-minute walk or a 40F taxi from the train station, tel. 04 93 01 73 68). They have a brochure with a nifty self-guided walking tour of Villefranche (don't miss the tiny 18th-century Church of St. Pierre, decorated by Jean Cocteau, at the entry to the small port) and information on the Rothschild Villa Ephrussi's beautiful gardens (a scenic 40-minute walk around the bay past the train station or a 10-minute bus ride away—even if you don't visit the gardens, walk beyond the train station for views and a quieter beach).

Boat rides (*promenades en mer*) are offered in the summer below the Welcome hotel (80F, 2 hrs). Even if you're sleeping elsewhere, consider a beachfront dinner or an ice cream–licking village stroll. The last bus leaves Nice for Villefranche at about 19:45; the last bus from Villefranche to Nice leaves at about 21:00; and trains run later. Beware of taxi drivers who overcharge—the normal weekday daytime rate to central Nice is 100F; to the airport, 200F.

Sleeping in Villefranche-sur-Mer
(6F = about $1, zip code: 06230)
The first two hotels listed are the fanciest in this entire chapter.

If your idea of sightseeing is to enjoy the view from your bedroom deck, the dining room, or the pool, stay at the welcoming **Hôtel La Flore*** (Db-550–800F, Tb-900F, Qb-1,100F, less Nov–Mar, no half-pension required but a superb restaurant, smartly designed family rooms, CC:VMA, elevator, private pool, just off the main road high above the harbor, most rooms with unbeatable views, 2 blocks from TI toward Nice on boulevard Princess Grace de Monaco, tel. 04 93 76 30 30, fax 04 93 76 99 99, e-mail: Hotel-La-Flore@wanadoo.fr, SE).

Hotel Welcome* is buried in the heart of the Old City, right on the water, with most rooms overlooking the harbor. You'll pay top dollar for all the comforts in a formal hotel that seems to do everything right and couldn't be better located (Db-690–950F, extra person-200F, 1 quai Courbet, tel. 04 93 76 27 62, fax 04 93 76 27 66, e-mail: usa@welcomehotel.com, SE). The rooms at both Hôtel La Flore and Hotel Welcome, while different in cost, are about the same in comfort. La Flore is on a road; Welcome is on the harbor.

The hotelesque **Hôtel Provençal** ** offers fine views from well-worn rooms, some with air-conditioning (skip the no-view rooms, Db-310–560F, Tb-480F–560F, extra bed-60F, CC:VMA, a block from TI at 4 avenue Maréchal Joffre, tel. 04 93 76 53 53, fax 04 93 76 96 00, e-mail: provencal@riviera.fr).

Hôtel la Darse **, a simple hotel sitting in the shadow of its highbrow brothers, offers a low-key and fine alternative right on the water in Villefranche's Port de la Darse. Quiet, cheery, and plain rooms with linoleum floors and incredible view balconies on the sea side (easily worth the extra cost) greet the weary traveler. Pleasant Madame Guillou speaks English (Db-240–360F, extra person-60F; from TI walk across park then down steps and down avenue General de Gaulle; Port de la Darse, tel. 04 93 01 72 54, fax 04 93 01 84 37).

At **Le Home**, Madame Repellin-Villard rents the town's best budget beds in 10 simple rooms around a lovely garden with a welcoming terrace (Db-240F; from main road near TI, walk between cafés Riche and Regence and then climb the steps and turn left; avenue de Grande Bretagne, tel. 04 93 76 79 88).

Eating in Villefranche sur Mer
If you want to eat well, spring for dinner at **Hôtel la Flore** (see "Sleeping in Villefranche," above) or, for a cool view and good-enough food at reasonable prices, try **Restaurant Le Marinieres** on the beach, below the train station (good salads, open daily, tel. 04 93 01 76 06). The many places on the harbor all look the same to me.

ANTIBES

Antibes is larger than Villefranche but far smaller than Nice. Come here for sandy beaches, an enjoyable old town, and a great Picasso collection. A quick 15 minutes from Nice by train (skip the 50-minute bus), Antibes' glamorous port glistens below its fortifications, with luxurious yachts and colorful fishing boats. Boat lovers are welcome to browse. The Fort Carré that dominates the port was the last fortification before Italy in the 1500s. The festive Old City is charming in a sandy-sophisticated way and sits atop the ruins of the fourth-century B.C. Greek city of Antipolis. The daily market (Marche Provençal) under a 19th-century canopy brings out the locals (behind Picasso Museum on cours Masséna, daily until 13:00 except Mon off-season). Make sure to stroll along the sea between the Picasso Museum and place Albert 1er (where boulevard Albert 1er meets the sea). Place Audiberti becomes a flea market on Thursdays and Saturdays (7:00–18:00, in the Old City a block from the port). Kids like the terrific play areas on place des Martyrs de la Resistance (near recommended Hotel Relais du Postillon). All of this compact town's attractions and worthwhile hotels lie between rue Robert Soleau and boulevard Albert 1er (the grand shopping streets of modern Antibes) and the water.

Tourist Information: The sultry Maison de Tourisme has an interesting "Discovering Old Antibes" walking-tour brochure, good city maps, and plenty of information on area sights (Mon–Sat 9:00–20:00, Sun 9:00–13:00, off-season lunch breaks, downtown at 11 place de Gaulle, tel. 04 92 90 53 00). The Nice TI has Antibes maps; plan ahead.

Arrival in Antibes

By Train: From the train station, the port is five minutes straight ahead. The TI is a 10-minute walk to the right down avenue Soleau (veer a bit left at the first major intersection to stay on avenue Soleau and then look for the TI on the right on the green place de Gaulle). The Old City center lies between the port and avenue Soleau. A free minibus circulates around Antibes from the train station and serves place Albert 1er, the Old City, and the port. The Nice–Antibes train (20 min, 23F) beats the Nice–Antibes bus (1 hr, 25F). Train info: tel. 04 93 99 50 50.

By Bus: The bus station is a block from the TI on place Guynemer.

By Car: Park near the Old City walls on the port.

Sights—Antibes

▲▲**Musée Picasso**—Sitting serenely where the Old City meets the sea (look for signs from the Old City) in Château Grimaldi, this museum offers a remarkable collection of Picasso's work—paintings, sketches, and ceramics. Picasso, who lived and worked here in 1946, said if you want to see work from his Antibes period, you'll have to do it in Antibes. You'll understand why Picasso liked working here. Several photos of the artist make this already-intimate museum more so. In his famous *Joie de Vivre* (the museum's highlight), there's a new love in Picasso's life, and he's feelin' groovy (30F, Jun–Sept Tue–Sun 10:00–18:00, closed Mon and off-season 12:00–14:00, tel. 04 92 90 54 20).

Musee d'Histoire et d'Archeologie—Featuring Greek, Roman, and Etruscan odds and ends, this is the only place to get a sense of this city's ancient roots. I liked the 2,000-year-old lead anchors (10F, no English explanations, Tue–Sun 10:00–12:00, 14:00–18:00, closed Mon, on the water between Picasso Museum and place Albert 1er).

Beaches—The best beaches stretch between Antibes' port and Cap d'Antibes. The main beaches (near Cap d'Antibes) are jammed on weekends and in the summer, though the smaller Plage de la Gravette at the port remains relatively calm in any season.

Cap d'Antibes Hike (Sentier Touristique de Tirepoll)—At the end of the peninsula (Cap d'Antibes) is a nature trail that will delight those in need of a walk through the woods to a beautiful coastline. Take a city bus or drive to Plage de la Garoupe and begin the trail there. Allow about two hours round-trip to Villa Eden Roc and get details at the TI or your hotel.

Day Trips—Antibes is halfway between Nice and Cannes (fast train service to both) and close to the artsy pottery and glass-blowing village of Biot, home of the Fernand Léger Museum (frequent buses, ask at TI).

Sleeping in Antibes
(6F = about $1, zip code: 06600)

Relais du Postillon** offers good rooms on a thriving square, accordion bathrooms, and helpful owners who take more pride in their well-respected restaurant (*menus* from 155F, Db-260–450F, extra bed-60F, CC:VM, elevator, 8 rue Championnet, tel. 04 93 34 20 77, fax 04 93 34 61 24, e-mail: postillon@atsat.com, SE).

Hotel Le Cameo** is a big, rambling, refreshingly unaggressive old place. It faces Antibes' main square above a bar filled with smoky locals. The public areas are dark and disorienting, but its nine *bon petit* rooms are almost huggable (Ss-230F, Ds-280F, Db-350F, Ts-350F, Tb-450F, 5 place Nationale, tel. 04 93 34 24 17, fax 04 93 34 35 80, NSE).

Auberge Provençale*, on the same square, has seven fine rooms, mysterious management, and a popular restaurant (reception in the restaurant, Sb-250–400F, Db-300–450F, Tb-350–500F, Qb-550F, CC:VMA, 61 place Nationale, tel. 04 93 34 13 24, fax 04 93 34 89 88). Their loft room, named Celine, is huge. It comes with a royal canopy bed and a dramatic open-timbered ceiling, and, if it's available, it costs no more than the other rooms.

Hotel Mediterranee** is Old World simple with quiet rooms around a garden courtyard and louder rooms on the street (Sb-260F, Db-320–350F, Tb-390F, Qb-430F, CC:VM, 6 avenue Maréchal Reille, tel. 04 93 34 14 84, fax 04 93 34 43 31, NSE).

These last two unique listings are located near place Albert 1er in a classy neighborhood and make most sense for drivers (free and safe private parking). Both expect you to join them for dinner in summer and give priority to those who book dinner in other seasons.

Hôtel Ponteil's** gregarious owners offer bungalow-style rooms in and around a breezy manor house, a garden terrace, quick beach access, and attract a loyal clientele willing to pay their prices (S-292F, D-284–394F, Db-444–494F, bunky family deals, includes breakfast, add about 100F per person for dinner, CC:VM, 11 impasse Jean-Mesnier, tel. 04 93 34 67 92, fax 04 93 34 49 47).

A few blocks uphill, **Mas Djoliba***** is my best splurge in Antibes but is a 10-minute walk to the beach. Reserve early for this tranquil, bird-chirping, flowers-everywhere manor house that has cushy rooms, a nifty pool, and pleasant staff (Sb-390F, Db-430–590F, Tb-650–690F, Qb-750–980F, add about 130F per person for dinner and 50F for breakfast when figuring half-pension, 29 avenue de Provence, tel. 04 93 34 02 48, fax 04 93 34 05 81, e-mail: info @hotel-pcastel-djoliba.com).

MONACO

Still impressive despite overdevelopment, crass commercialization, and wall-to-wall tourists, Monaco will disappoint those who look for something below the surface. This is the kind of place you visit once and don't need to see again. This two-square-kilometer country is a tax haven for its tiny full-time population.

The **TI** is near the casino (Mon–Sat 9:00–19:00, Sun 9:00–12:00, 2 boulevard des Moulins, tel. 00-377/92 16 61 66). To call Monaco from France, dial 00, 377 (Monaco's country code), and the eight-digit number. Within Monaco simply dial the eight-digit number.

Monaco (the principality) is best understood when separated into its two key areas: Monaco Ville, the Old City housing Prince Rainier's palace; and Monte Carlo, the area around the casino. The harbor divides the two. A short bus ride on routes #1 or #2 link these sights (6/hrly, 8.5F, 20F for four tickets). It's a 20-minute uphill walk from the train station or bus stop to Prince Rainier's palace and a 40-minute hilly walk between Monaco Ville and the casino.

Arrival in Monaco

By Bus from Nice and Villefranche: Remember to keep your receipt for the return ride and that RCA buses run twice as often as Cars Broch. There are three stops in Monaco, in order from Nice: in front of a tunnel at the base of Monaco

Ville (place d'Armes), on the port, and near the first stop is the best starting point. To walk up t Ville or catch a local bus there (lines #1 or #2), street right in front of the tunnel and turn right rock on your right—the bus stop and steps up to Monaco Ville are in 70 yards. The bus stop back to Nice is across the major road from your arrival point at the light. The last bus leaves Monaco for Nice at about 19:00; the last train leaves about 23:30 (confirm at the station or TI).

By Train from Nice: A new train station may be completed sometime in 2000; this information applies to Monaco's old train station. Walk out of the station downhill, curving left and passing the first bus shelter. Across the big intersection you'll see steps leading up to Monaco Ville and bus stops for lines #1 and #2.

Sights—Monaco

Start with a look at Monaco Ville for a *magnifique* view (particularly at night) over the harbor and the casino. If you arrive in the morning you can watch the charming changing of the guard (11:55); wander over to the beautiful **Cathédrale de Monaco,** where Princess Grace is buried; and picnic in the immaculate and scenic gardens overlooking the blue Mediterranean (pick up a *pan bagna* sandwich in the Old City).

The nearby and costly **Musée de l'Océanographique** (Cousteau Aquarium, 60F, CC:VM) is the largest of its kind. It can be jammed and disappoints some, though aquarium lovers leave impressed. The *Monte Carlo Story* film gives an interesting account in English of this city's history, mostly about Prince Rainier's family (40F, in parking garage next to aquarium, take escalator down to elevator and then another escalator down 1 more level).

Leave Monaco Ville and ride the shuttle bus or stroll the harborfront up to the **casino.** Count the counts and Rolls Royces in front of Hôtel de Paris. Strut inside the lavish casino (opens at 12:00)—anyone can get as far as the one-armed bandits, but only adults (21 and older) are allowed to pay the 50F or 100F charge to enter the private game rooms and rub elbows with high rollers (some rooms open at 15:00, others at 21:00). Entrance is free to all games in the new, plebeian, American-style Loews Casino, adjacent to the main casino. If you must spend the night, try **Hôtel de France** (Db-350–390F, 6 rue de la Turbie, near train station, tel. 00-377/93 30 24 64, fax 00-377/92 16 13 34).

MORE FRENCH RIVIERA TOWNS

Menton—Just a few minutes by train (8/day) from Monte Carlo or 40 minutes from Nice, beautiful and overlooked Menton is a peaceful and relaxing spa/beach town with a fine beachfront promenade and a sandy-cobbled old town (TI tel. 04 93 57 57 00).

ιnnes—Its sister city is Beverly Hills, but its beaches and the
ιeachfront promenade are beautiful.

St. Paul-de-Vence and Vence—If you prefer hill towns to
beaches, head for St. Paul and Vence (the same bus from Nice's
bus station serves both towns, 20F one way, 2/hrly, 45 min).
Unless you go early, you'll escape only some of the heat and none
of the crowds. **St. Paul** is part cozy medieval hill town and part
local artist shopping mall. It's charmingly artsy but gets swamped
with tour buses. Meander into St. Paul's quieter streets and
wander far to enjoy the panoramic views (TI tel. 04 93 32 86 95).

The prestigious, far-out, and high-priced **Fondation Maeght**
art gallery is a steep, uphill 10-minute walk from St. Paul. If ever
modern art could appeal to you, it would be here. Its world-class
contemporary-art collection is arranged between pleasant gardens
and well-lit rooms (45F, Jul–Sept daily 10:00–19:00, Oct–Jun
10:00–12:30, 14:30–18:00, tel. 04 93 32 81 63).

The enjoyable hill town of Vence (10 min from St. Paul
by bus) disperses St. Paul's crowds over a larger and more engaging city. Vence bubbles with workaday and tourist activity.
Catch the daily market (ends at 12:30) and don't miss the small
cathedral in the town center, with its Chagall mosaic and moving Chapelle St. Sacrament. The Vence TI is on place du Grand
Jardin (tel. 04 93 58 06 38). Matisse's much-raved-about **Chapelle du Rosaire** may disappoint all but Matisse fans, for whom
this is a necessary pilgrimage (1 mile from Vence toward St.
Jeannet; taxi or walk). The yellow-, blue-, and green-filtered
sunlight does a cheery dance in stark contrast to the brooding
tile sketches (donation, open only Tue and Thu 10:00–11:30,
14:30–17:30; in summer the chapel is also open on Wed and
Fri afternoons and on Sat 10:00–11:30, 14:30–17:30; closed
Nov–mid-Dec, tel. 04 93 58 03 26).

Eze Village—Floating high above the sea, Eze Village (don't
confuse it with the average seafront town of Eze-Bord de la
Mer), is a spectacularly set medieval hill town mixing perfume
outlets, upscale boutiques, outrageously priced hotels, steep
cobbled lanes, and jaw-numbing views. About 15 minutes east of
Villefranche on the Moyenne Corniche (6 buses/day from Nice,
25 min), Eze Village makes a handy stop between Nice and
Monaco. You can drop in on the Fragonard or Gallimard perfume outlets to understand the interesting fabrication process
and shop the impressive collections (both open daily 8:30–18:00,
Gallimard breaks for lunch 12:00–14:00); you can also enjoy
the charming church (Eglise Paroissial), but skip the Jardins
Exotiques (exotic gardens). For a panoramic view and ideal
picnic perch (they say on a clear day you can see Corsica), walk
up to the hill town from the parking lot, take a left at the top of
the first hill, and walk 20 yards down a dirt path.

Travel Notes on Connecting Nice and the Alps—La Route de Napoleon

After getting bored in his toy Elba empire, Napoleon gathered his entourage, landed on the Riviera, bared his breast, and told his fellow Frenchmen, "Strike me down or follow me." France followed. But just in case, he took the high road, returning to Paris along the route today's holiday-goers call La Route de Napoleon. (Waterloo followed shortly afterward.)

By Car: When driving between the Riviera and the Alps, take the scenic route (from south to north follow Digne, Sisteron, and Grenoble). You'll join the route Napoleon followed when returning from his exile. An assortment of pleasant villages with inexpensive hotels and restaurants lies on this route, making an ovenight easy. Idyllic little Entrevaux feels forgotten and still stuck in its medieval shell. Cross the bridge, meet someone friendly, and consider the steep hike up to the citadel (10F). **Hotel Vauban** provides overnight refuge (tel. 04 93 05 42 40, fax 04 93 05 48 38). Sisteron's Romanesque church alone makes it worth a quick leg stretch. If a night in this area appeals, stay farther north, surrounded by mountains near the tiny hamlet of Clelles at **Hôtel Ferrat****. This family-run mountain hacienda at the base of Mont Aiguille (after which Gibraltar was modeled) is the place to break this long drive. Enjoy your own *boules* court, a swimming pool, lovely rooms, a fine restaurant, and a warm welcome (Db-280–380F, zip code: 38930, tel. 04 76 34 42 70, fax 04 76 34 47 47).

By Train: Leave the tourists far behind and take the scenic train-bus-train combination (free with railpass) that runs between Nice, Digne, and Grenoble through canyons, along whitewater rivers, between snow-capped peaks, and through many tempting villages. Start with a 9:00 departure on the little Chemins de Fer de Provence train to Digne (4/day, 3 hrs, Chemins de Fer de Provence departs from a different train station about 10 blocks behind Nice's main station, 4 rue Alfred Binet, tel. 04 93 82 10 17). In Digne you can catch a main line to other destinations or, better, catch the bus (quick transfer, free with railpass) to Veynes (6/day, 90 min) and in Veynes catch the most scenic two-car train to Grenoble (5/day, 2 hrs). From Grenoble connections are available to many destinations. If you want to do the entire trip from Nice to Grenoble in one day, you must start with the 9:00 departure from Nice (arrives Grenoble about 18:00), but I'd spend the night in one of the tiny villages en route: Clelles has the best hotel (listed above), Sisteron and Entrevaux (hotel listed above) are interesting villages, and Thoranne-Haute and Barreme are also appealing, with small hotels.

THE FRENCH ALPS
(ALPES-SAVOIE)

Savoie is the northern and highest tier of the French Alps (the
Alpes-Dauphiné lie to the south). In the 11th century, Savoie was
a powerful region with borders stretching down to the Riviera and
out to the Rhône. Today it is France's mountain-sports capital,
with Europe's highest point, Mont Blanc, as its centerpiece.
Savoie, which didn't become part of France until 1860, feels more
Swiss than French.

The scenery is spectacular. Serene yet thriving Annecy is
a picture-perfect blend of natural and manmade beauty. In
Chamonix, it's just you and Madame Nature—there's not a
museum or important building in sight. If the weather's right,
take Europe's ultimate cable-car ride to the 12,600-foot Aiguille
du Midi in Chamonix.

Lyon is the southern gateway to the Alps, easily accessible
by train or car. This captivating city is France's most interesting
major city after Paris. If you need a city fix, linger in Lyon.

Planning Your Time

Annecy is charmingly elegant, and enjoyable for an evening. But
if you've got Alps on your mind, go directly to Chamonix (most
trains to Chamonix pass through Annecy, making it a convenient
stopover). Here you can skip along high ridges or stroll the tranquil Arve River Valley paths. You can zip down the mountain on a
wheeled bobsled or rent a mountain bike. Ride the gondolas early
(crowds and clouds roll in later in the morning) and save your
afternoons for lower altitudes. Plan a minimum of two nights and
one day in Chamonix. (Note: If you're driving or training from
here to the Riviera, see "La Route de Napoleon" tips at the end
of the previous chapter.) Lyon is France's best-kept urban secret.

The French Alps

Strategically situated at the foot of the Alps where the Saone and Rhone Rivers meet, this very manageable city merits at least one night and a full day.

Getting around the Alps

Lyon, Annecy, and Chamonix are well connected by trains. Buses run from Chamonix to nearby villages (though no longer through the Mont Blanc tunnel to Aosta), and the Aiguille du Midi lift takes travelers from Chamonix to Italy over Europe's most scenic border crossing.

Cuisine Scene—Savoie and Lyon

The Savoie offers mountain-country cuisine. Robust and hearty, it shares much with the Swiss. Specialities include *fondue savoyarde* (melted Beaufort and Comté cheeses and local white wine, sometimes with a dash of cognac), raclette (chunks of semi-melted cheese served with potatoes, pickles, sausage, and bread), *tartiflettes* (hearty scalloped potatoes with melted cheese), *poulet de Bresse* (the best chicken in France), *morteau* (smoked pork sausage), *gratin savoyarde* (a potato dish using cream, cheese, and garlic), and freshly caught fish. Local cheeses are Morbier (look for a charcoal streak down the middle), Comté (like Gruyère), Beaufort (aged for two years; hard and strong), Reblochon (mild and creamy), and Tomme de Savoie (semihard and mild). Evian water comes from Savoie, as does Chartreuse liqueur. Aprémont and Crépy are two of the area's surprisingly good white wines.

Lyon is French cuisine at its best. Surprisingly affordable, this is an intense palate experience—try the *salad lyonnaise* (croutons, ham, and a poached egg on a bed of lettuce), andouillettes (pork sausages), and quenelles (large dumplings, sometimes flavored with fish).

ANNECY

There's something for everyone in this lakefront resort city: mountain views, flowery cobbled lanes and canals, a château, and swimming or boating in the lake. Annecy (ahn-see) is France's answer to Switzerland's Luzern. You may not have the mountains in your lap as in nearby Chamonix, but the distant peaks make a beautiful picture, with Annecy's lakefront setting.

Tourist Information: The TI is a few blocks from the old center in the modern Bonlieu shopping center (daily in summer 9:00–18:30, otherwise 9:00–12:00, 13:45–18:30, 1 rue Jean Jaures, tel. 04 50 45 00 33).

Sights—Annecy

Strolling—Amble along the canals and famous arcaded streets of the handsome old city. Saunter by the Palais de l'Île, where you'll find the Museum of Annecy (30F). The views from the château alone make it worth the entry price. Luscious ice-cream shops line the pedestrian streets (scout out the impressive display at Glaces l'Arlequin, across from Hotel du Palais de l'Isle, listed below).

Boating—Rent a paddleboat (60F/hr) and tool around the lake or let a one-hour cruise do the work for you (60F, several departures/day, Compagnie des Bateaux du Lac Annecy, tel. 04 50 51 08 40). Or consider a one-way cruise to the quiet village of Talloires (about 30F, 60F round-trip) and return by bus. Schedules and prices are at the TI or at the boat dock right on the lake where the canal meets the old city.

Open-Air Market—A thriving outdoor market occupies most of the old-city center on Tuesday, Friday, and Sunday mornings.

Sleeping and Eating in Annecy
(6F = about $1, zip code: 74000)
Sleep Code: **S** = Single, **D** = Double/Twin, **T** = Triple, **Q** = Quad, **b** = bathroom, **t** = toilet only, **s** = shower only, **CC** = Credit Card (Visa, MasterCard, Amex), **SE** = Speaks English, **NSE** = No English, * = French hotel rating system (0–4 stars).

Hike (or drive) up to the spotless and just-renovated rooms at the **Hôtel du Château**** and enjoy its view terrace (Sb-260F, Db-290–330F, Tb-340F, Qb-430F, several rooms with views, on the way up to the château at 16 rampe du Château, reserve early in the summer, tel. 04 50 45 27 66, fax 04 50 52 75 26). Right on the canal near the lake, the cozy and louder **Hôtel de Savoie**** has a few view rooms (S-150F, D-210F, Db-290–360F, Tb-400–430F, Qb-440–490F, CC:VM, place St. François, tel. 04 50 45 15 45, fax 04 50 45 11 99, e-mail: hotel.savoie@mail.dotcom.fr). **Hotel du Palais de l'Isle***** is in the heart of the old city and offers very modern, almost sterile three-star comfort (Db-385–535F, extra bed-100F, 13 rue Perriere, tel. 04 50 45 86 87, fax 04 50 51 87 15). The American-esque **Hotel Ibis**** is a good last resort, well situated on a modern square in the old city with modern, tight, and tidy rooms (Sb-335F, Db-350–400F, extra person-55F, CC:VMA, 12 rue de la Gare, tel. 04 50 45 43 21, fax 04 50 52 81 08). Basic budget rooms can be found near Hotel Ibis above the **Auberge du Lyonnais** restaurant right on the canal (S-165F, Sb-265F, D-205F, Db-265–315F, tel. 04 50 51 26 10, fax 04 50 51 05 04).

Restaurant John specializes in tasty regional cusine (10 rue Perriére, at the foot of rampe du Château, tel. 04 50 51 36 15). **Restaurant Vivaldi** offers reasonably priced Italian food (where the old city meets the lake at 12 Faubourg des Annociades, tel. 04 50 51 08 41). **Le Lilas Rose** is a fine place for fondue (passage de l'Eveche).

Transportation Connections—Annecy
By train to: Chamonix (5/day, 2.5 hrs, transfer in St. Gervais), **Beaune** (6/day, 6.5 hrs, transfer in Lyon), **Nice** (8/day, 10 hrs, transfer in Lyon), **Paris'** Gare de Lyon (6 TGVs/day, 4 hrs).

CHAMONIX
Hemmed in by snow-capped peaks, churning with mountain lifts, and crisscrossed with hikes of all levels of difficulty, the resort of Chamonix is France's best base for Alpine exploration. Chamonix is the largest of five villages at the base of Mont Blanc and is served by several mountain lifts. Chamonix's purpose in life has always been to accommodate those coming here for some of Europe's top Alpine thrills. To the east is the Mont Blanc range; to the west, the Aiguilles Rouges chain.

Chamonix 3–D

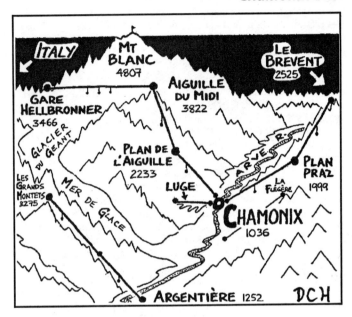

Planning Your Time

If you have one sunny day, spend it this way: Start with the
Aiguille du Midi lift (go as early as you can), take it all the way to
Hellbronner (hang around the needle longer if you can't get
to Hellbronner), double back to Plan de l'Aiguille, hike to
Montenvers (Mer de Glace—snow level permitting), and train
(or hike) down from there. If the weather disappoints or the snow
line's too low, hike the Petit Balcon Sud trail.

Orientation

The small pedestrian zone is the center of Chamonix, though
you'll find most activity along the rue du Docteur Paccard. The
TI is on the le Brevent–side lift of town while the train station is
on the Aiguille du Midi side.

Tourist Information: The TI provides hotel and hut reservations, a map of the town and valley (listing restaurants and
hotels), and an essential 25F hiking mountain map called Carte
des Sentiers. It's located one block west of rue du Docteur
Paccard and the pedestrian zone, on place de l'Église (Jul–Aug
daily 8:30–19:30, Sept–Jun daily 8:30–12:30, 14:00–19:00, tel. 04
50 53 00 24, fax 04 50 53 58 90). Ask for the weather forecast.

    Laundromats: One is off rue Joseph Vallot, three blocks north of the Hotel Touring at 40 impasse Primaviere (daily 8:00–20:00), and another is near Aiguille du Midi at 174 avenue du Aiguille du Midi (daily 9:00–20:00).

Chamonix Quick History

1786—Mssrs. Balmot and Paccard are the first to climb Mont Blanc
1818—First ascent of Aiguille du Midi
1860—After a visit by Louis Napoleon, the trickle of nature-loving
      visitors to Chamonix turns to a gush
1924—First winter Olympics held in Chamonix
1955—Aiguille du Midi *téléphérique* open to tourists
2000—Your visit

Arrival in Chamonix

By Train: Walk straight out of the station and up avenue Michel Croz. In three blocks you'll hit the center and TI.

    By Car: Take the second Chamonix turnoff (coming from the Annecy direction) and park in the huge lot adjacent to the large traffic circle near Hôtel Alpina or at your hotel.

Getting around Chamonix

By Lifts: Gondolas (*téléphériques*) climb mountains all along the valley, but the best two leave from Chamonix (explained below). Sightseeing is optimal from the Aiguille du Midi gondola, but hiking is better from the Le Brévent gondola. Those buying tickets at the hostel, or those over 59, get a 10 to 20 percent reduction on the area's lifts. Kids ages 4 to 12 ride for half price. While the lift to Aiguille du Midi stays open year-round, the *télécabines* to the Panoramic du Mont Blanc in Hellbronner (Italy) close from early October to May or June and in bad weather (call the TI to confirm). Other area lifts close around mid-April through June and in late October through December.

    By Hiking: For all your options, visit the Office de Haute Montagne (Office of the High Mountains, a block uphill from the TI on 3rd floor of building marked Maison de la Montagne). Review maps and get opinions on the best hikes and up-to-date weather and trail-condition reports from the English-speaking staff (daily 8:30–12:00, 14:30–18:00, tel. 04 50 23 22 08). Remember to bring rain gear, warm clothes, water, sunglasses, good shoes, and picnic food on your hike.

    By Bike: Mountain bikes are rented by the hour and day. The TI has a brochure proposing the best bike rides. The peaceful river-valley trail is ideal for bikes and pedestrians. Chamonix Mountain Bike has good bikes and English-speaking staff (opposite Hôtel Alpina, tel. 04 50 53 54 76).

    By Bus or Train: One road and one rail line lace together

Chamonix Town

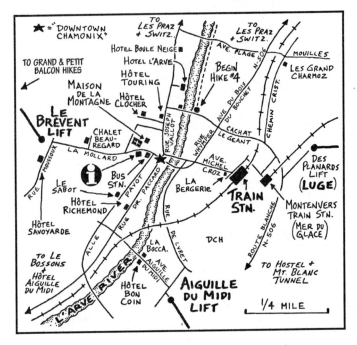

the towns and lifts of the valley. Local buses run twice an hour from in front of the TI for local destinations.

Sights—Chamonix

▲▲▲**Aiguille du Midi**—This is easily the valley's (and arguably, Europe's) most spectacular and popular lift. If the weather's clear, the price doesn't matter. Pile into the *téléphérique* (gondola) and soar to the tip of a rock needle 12,600 feet above sea level. Chamonix shrinks as trees fly by, soon replaced by whizzing rocks, ice, and snow until you reach the top. No matter how sunny it is, it's cold. The air is thin. People are giddy. Fun things can happen at Aiguille du Midi if you're not too winded to join the locals in the halfway-to-heaven tango.

From the top of the lift, cross the bridge and ride the elevator through the rock to the summit of this pinnacle. Missing the elevator is a kind of Alpus-Interruptus I'd rather not experience. The Alps spread before you. In the distance is the bent little Matterhorn (a tall, shady pyramid behind a broader mountain, listed on the observation table in French as "Cervin—4,505 meters").

Over the Alps—France to Italy

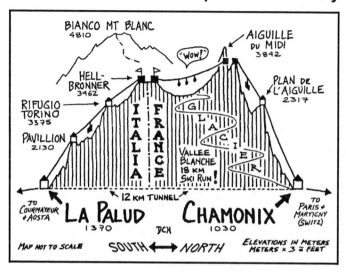

And looming just over there is Mont Blanc, at 15,781 feet, Europe's highest point. Use the free telescope to spot mountain climbers; over 2,000 climb this mountain each year. Dial English and let the info box take you on a visual tour. Check the temperature next to the elevator.

Explore Europe's tallest lift station. More than 150 meters of tunnels lead to a cafeteria, a restaurant, a gift shop, and the icicle-covered gateway to the glacial world. This "ice tunnel" is where summer skiers and mountain climbers depart. Just observing is exhilarating. Peek down the icy cliff and ponder the value of an ice axe.

Next, for your own private glacial dream world, get into the little red *télécabine* and head south to the Panoramic du Mont Blanc at Hellbronner Point, the Italian border station. This line stretches five kilometers with no solid pylon. (It's propped by a "suspended pylon," a line stretched between two peaks 400 meters from the Italian end.) In a gondola for four, you'll dangle silently for 40 minutes as you glide over the glacier to Italy. Hang your head out the window; explore every corner of your view. From Hellbronner Point you can continue into Italy (see "Transportation Connections," below), but there's really no point unless you're traveling that way.

From Aiguille du Midi you can ride all the way back to Chamonix or get off halfway down (Plan de l'Aiguille) and hike three to four hours from 7,500 feet to the valley floor at 3,400 feet. Or better yet, hike the scenic, undulating two-hour trail to Montenvers (the Mer de Glace glacier, 6,000 feet). From there you can hike or ride the train (56F) back into Chamonix.

To beat the clouds and crowds, ride the lifts (up and down) as early as you can. To beat major delays in August, leave by 7:00. If the weather's good, don't dillydally. Lift hours are weather dependent, but generally it runs daily from 7:00 to 17:00 in summer; 8:00 to 16:45 in May, June, and September; and 8:00 to 15:45 in winter. The last *télécabine* departure to Panoramic du Mont Blanc (Hellbronner) is at around 14:00. Summertime travelers can call to reserve up to 10 days in advance (toll-free tel. 08 36 68 00 67; you must retrieve your reservation at the lift station at least 30 minutes before your departure).

Approximate ticket costs for summer (slightly less in off-season) from Chamonix to: Plan de l'Aiguille—83F round-trip (65F one way); Aiguille du Midi—196F round-trip (164F one way, not including parachute); the Panoramic du Mont Blanc at Hellbronner—292F round-trip (222F one way).

Tickets from Aiguille du Midi to Hellbronner/Panoramic du Mont Blanc are sold at the base or on top (98F or 60F one way). It's L38,000 (about $22, sold there, many currencies accepted) to drop down into Italy. (Yes, you can bring your luggage on board.)

Time to allow: Chamonix to Aiguille du Midi—20 minutes, two hours round-trip, three to four hours in peak season; Chamonix to Hellbronner: 90 minutes one-way, three to four hours round-trip, longer in peak season. Plan on 32 degrees Fahrenheit even on a sunny day. Sunglasses are essential. On busy days, minimize delays by getting your return lift time upon arrival at the top (tel. 04 50 53 30 80).

Mer de Glace—From the little station over the tracks from Chamonix's main train station, a two-car cogwheel train (look for the red trains, 75F round-trip, 58F one way) toots you up to a rapidly moving and very dirty glacier called the Mer de Glace, or Sea of Ice. The glacier—France's largest, at six miles long—is interesting, as are its funky ice caves (17F entry) filled with ice sculpture (take the small lift, 13F round-trip to the caves, or a short uphill hike). The view is glorious, but if you've already seen a glacier up close, you might skip this one. One good option is to get off the Chamonix–Aiguille du Midi lift (on the way down) at Plan de l'Aiguille and hike the pleasant two-hour trail to Montenvers/Mer de Glace. From there you can hike or ride the train into Chamonix.

▲**Luge**—Here's something new for the thrill seeker in you. You can ride a chairlift up the mountain and scream down a windy, banked concrete slalom course on a wheeled sled. Chamonix has two roughly parallel luge courses. While each course is a kilometer long and about the same speed, one is marked for slower bobsledders, the other for the speed demons. Young or old, hare or tortoise, any fit person can manage a luge. Don't take your hands off your stick. The course is fast and slippery. (34F/1 ride, 135F/5 rides, 240F/10 rides, splitable with companions, Jul–Aug daily 10:00–19:30, otherwise weekends only 13:30–about 18:00; 10-min walk from the center, just beyond train station, tel. 04 50 53 08 97.)

▲▲▲*Téléphérique* **to Le Brévent**—While the Aiguille de Midi offers a more spectacular ride, hiking options are better on this lower side of the valley, with views of the Mont Blanc range to the east and the Aiguilles Rouges peaks to the west.

From Chamonix, walk up the road past the TI and keep going to the Le Brévent station. Take the *téléphérique* to Planpraz (57F round-trip, 47F one way, good views and hiking, particularly the 2-hour hike along the Grand Balcon Sud to La Flégère lift, see "Hike #3," below) and then catch the *téléphérique* up to Brévent (great views and hikes, 82F round-trip, 56F one way from Chamonix, daily 8:00–18:00, closed April–mid-June and Nov).

Chamonix-Area Hikes

Four fine hikes give nature lovers of almost any ability in just about any weather a good opportunity to enjoy the valley. You'll find the region's hiking map extremely helpful; pick it up at the TI (25F).

Hike #1: Plan de l'Aiguille to Montenvers (Grand Balcon Nord): This is the easiest way to incorporate a two-hour high-country walk into your ride down from the valley's greatest lift and check out a glacier to boot. From Aiguille du Midi, get off halfway down (Plan de l'Aiguille) and hike the scenic up-and-down two-hour trail to Montenvers and the Mer de Glace. From there, hike or ride the train (56F) into Chamonix. Snow covers this trail generally until June.

Hike #2: Chamonix to les Praz (Grand Balcon Sud): For a moderately easy and scenic high-country hike, walk 40 minutes along the Arve River or take the Chamonix bus (five-minute ride, every 30 minutes from the TI) to the tiny village of Les Praz. Ride the lift from Les Praz to La Flégère (43F one way, 56F round-trip) and then hike the scenic Grand Balcon Sud two hours back to Chamonix, take the lift down to Chamonix at Plan Praz (46F one way, 55F round-trip), or hike down a very steep trail. Of course, this can be reversed by hiking from Chamonix, taking the Le Brévent lift to Plan Praz, and hiking the Grand Balcon Sud to Les Praz.

Hike #3: Petit Balcon Sud: This hike parallels the Grand Balcon Sud at a lower elevation and is ideal when snow or poor weather make the Grand Balcon Sud inaccessible. No lifts are required—just firm thighs to climb to the trail. From Chamonix, walk up to Le Brévent lift station. Follow the asphalt road to the left of the lift leading uphill; it turns into a dirt road that signs mark as the Petit

Chamonix Valley

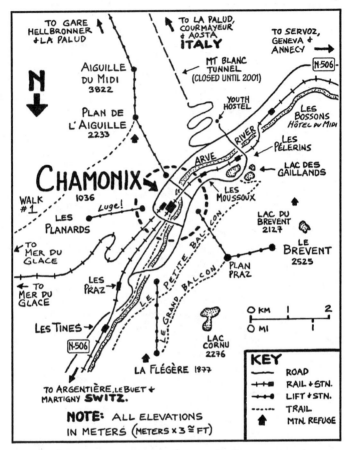

TO GARE HELLBRONNER + LA PALUD

TO LA PALUD, COURMAYEUR + AOSTA ITALY

TO SERVOZ, GENEVA + ANNECY

N-506

AIGUILLE DU MIDI 3822

MT BLANC TUNNEL (CLOSED UNTIL 2001)

YOUTH HOSTEL

LES BOSSONS Hôtel du Midi

PLAN DE L'AIGUILLE 2233

RIVER

ARVE

LES PÉLERINS

LAC DES GAILLANDS

CHAMONIX 1036

LES MOUSSOUX

WALK #1

Luge!

LES PLANARDS

LAC DU BREVENT 2127

LE BREVENT 2525

TO MER DU GLACE

LE PETITE BALCON

LE GRAND BALCON

PLAN PRAZ

LES PRAZ

TO MER DU GLACE

LES TINES →

N-506

0 KM   1   2
0 MI

LAC CORNU 2276

LA FLÉGÈRE 1877

TO ARGENTIÈRE, LE BUET + MARTIGNY SWITZ.

NOTE: ALL ELEVATIONS IN METERS (METERS × 3 ≅ FT)

KEY
— ROAD
+++■ RAIL + STN.
•—•● LIFT + STN.
----- TRAIL
▲ MTN. REFUGE

Balcon Sud trail. Walk north about two hours on the trail to Les Praz village (follow the lift wires leading down to La Flégère lift to reach Les Praz). Return by Chamonix bus or by walking the level Arve River trail (40 minutes), or walk only as far as your legs take you and turn around. This hike works just as well in reverse.

Hike #4: Arve riverbank stroll: For an easy forested-valley stroll, follow the sleepy Arve River out of Chamonix toward Les Praz (the path starts across the river from Chamonix's Hôtel Alpina). Les Praz makes a pleasant destination. Several cafés, restaurants, and a charming village green lend a tranquil air to this alpine hamlet.

Other good hiking destinations: The trail to Lac Blanc (from La Flégère lift in Les Praz) and the trail to La Pierre à Berard refuge (leaves from Le Buet lift) are each ideal, moderate day hikes and offer refuges with overnight accommodations. Get details at the Office de la Haute Montagne.

Sleeping in Chamonix
(6F = about $1, zip code: 74400)
Reasonable hotels and dormlike chalets abound. With the helpful TI, you can find budget accommodations anytime. July 20 to August 16 is most difficult, though you may find some last-minute cancellations at the better hotels. Prices tumble off-season.

Hotels
Hôtel de l'Arve** has a slick, modern, Alpine feel, with nice view rooms right on the Arve River overlooking Mont Blanc or cheaper rooms without the view (Sb-260–440F, Db-308–476F, extra bed-68F, ask for the few cheaper rooms *sans* bathroom, CC:VMA, elevator, fireplace lounge, pleasant garden, across the river from the Olympic complex, 60 impasse des Anémones, tel. 04 50 53 02 31, fax 04 50 53 56 92, e-mail: contact@hotelarve-chamonix.com, Isabelle and Bertrice SE).

Hotel Savoyarde***, a steep but rewarding walk above Chamonix, has good views from the outdoor café tables, elegant chalet ambience, and a fine restaurant. The owner's attention to detail is evident. This is a worthwhile splurge (Db-682–840F, Tb-843–1,080F, Qb-984–1,300F, includes breakfast, add only 80F per person for dinner, CC:VMA, a 15-min walk above TI, over-looking Chamonix at 28 rue des Moussoux, tel. 04 50 53 00 77, fax 04 50 55 86 82, e-mail: savoyarde@mail.silicone.fr).

Hôtel de Clocher**, a small family-run place, offers eight small but cozy rooms, private parking, a backyard garden, and a smokers' lobby (Sb-265–295F, Db-285–335F, extra bed-50F, CC:VMA, a block to the right of the church as you face it on l'impasse de l'Androsace, tel. 04 50 53 30 27, fax 04 50 53 73 19).

Hôtel Au Bon Coin** is an Old World place with great views, private balconies, and thin walls in most of its spotless rooms; the cheaper rooms are wood-panel cozy but lack the views (Ds-235F, Db-350–380F, Tb-400F, Qb-450F, closed mid-Apr–Jun and Oct–mid-Dec, 80 avenue L'Aiguille du Midi, tel. 04 50 53 15 67, fax 04 50 53 51 51, friendly Nadine SE).

Boule de Niege* ("Snowball") hotel is a fun, simple and central budget option with a backyard view terrace (Ss-160–220F, Ds-205–245F, Ts-285–345F, add 40F for a room with bath, 362 rue Joseph Vallot, tel. 04 50 53 04 48, fax 04 50 55 91 09).

Hôtel Touring**, with basic but cavernous rooms (many with 4 beds) and a friendly British staff, is ideal for families

(Ds-235–300F, Db-285–375F, add 60F for 3 and 40F more for 4, 95 rue Joseph Vallot, tel. 04 50 53 59 18, fax 04 50 53 67 25, e-mail: n.gulliford@aol.com). They also run the nearby **Hotel di Midi****, which has a pleasant courtyard café. The Midi often has rooms when other hotels don't (small rooms with view Db-260–300F, same tel. & fax as Hotel Touring).

Chamonix's most classy *chambre d'hôte*, **Chalet Beauregard**, is friendly and peaceful, with a private garden. Five of its seven sharp rooms have a glorious view balcony (Sb-200F, Db-330–600F, Tb-460–600F, includes breakfast, free parking, 5-minute walk above the TI toward Le Brévent lift, 182 montée La Mollard, tel. & fax 04 50 55 86 30, www.chalet-beauregard.com, Manuel and Laurence SE). **La Girandole** is another fine *chambre d'hôte* near the Le Brévent lift (Db-320F, includes breakfast, 46 Chemin de la Perserverance, tel. 04 50 53 37 58, fax 04 50 55 81 77).

Hôtel le Chamonix** is tall, old, and skinny and has no elevator. Its rooms are clean and simple (some with balconies), above a café, and across from the TI (Db-300–390F, Tb/Qb-400–470F, CC:VM, 58 place de l'Eglise, tel. 04 50 53 11 07, fax 04 50 53 64 78).

Richemond Hôtel** offers Old World alpine elegance, spacious lobbies, overstuffed chairs, a private terrace, serious management, and terrific rooms (Sb-310F, Db-380–470F, Tb-530F, Qb-580F, CC:VMA, 228 rue du Docteur Paccard, tel. 04 50 53 08 85, fax 04 50 55 91 69, e-mail: richemond@wanadoo.fr).

Sleeping near Chamonix

If nature beckons or summer crowds heckle, spend the night in one of the valley's overlooked lower-profile villages. The small village of Les Praz (lay prah), while just up the valley from Chamonix (5 minutes by car, 30 minutes on foot), is a world away. The town is home to the Flégère lift, which allows access to the recommended le Grand Balcon Sud and Lac Blanc hikes.

Hotel Rhodendron** sits right on the village green (Db-300–330F, Tb-340–380F, half-pension required in summer, CC:VM, 100 route des Tines, tel. 04 50 53 06 39, fax 04 50 53 55 76). The simple, tranquil and idyllic **La Bagna Auberge-Gîte** is surrounded by trees and has a relaxing patio and common room and well-maintained rooms at fair prices (80F dorm beds, 120F per bed in 2–3-person rooms, half-pension required in summer, 220F per person, 337 route des Gaudenays, tel. 04 50 53 62 90, fax 04 50 53 64 88, e-mail: montblan@cyberaccess.fr).

Three miles away down the valley (toward Annecy), in the village of Les Bossons, is the almost luxurious **Hôtel l'Aiguille du Midi****. The friendly owner offers polished service, gorgeous gardens, a swimming pool, tennis courts, comfortable rooms, and a restaurant where Chamonix locals go for their Sunday meal

(Db-350–460F, add 30 percent each for 3 and 4 persons, half-pension required in summer, Les Bossons, tel. 04 50 53 00 65, fax 04 50 55 93 69, www.hotel-aiguilledumidi.com, SE).

Dormlike Accommodations

For cheaper, dormlike accommodations in a quiet neighborhood a 10-minute walk to Chamonix, try **Les Grands Charmoz.** Seventy-five francs buys a bunk and sheet, showers, and a kitchen. They also have a few clean doubles (200F) with kitchen privileges as well as apartments upstairs (468 chemin des Cristalliers; turn right out of the station, walk under the bridge and into Hotel Albert's driveway, veer right, cross the tracks, then turn left; tel. & fax 04 50 53 45 57). **Chalet Ski Station** also has bunks but no doubles (dorm bed-65F, showers-5F, reductions on area lifts for clients, next to Brévent *téléphérique*, a 10-min hike up from TI, 6 rue des Moussoux, tel. 04 50 53 20 25).

Chamonix's classy **hostel** was formerly the barracks for the diggers of the Mont Blanc tunnel. Well run, cheap, and as comfortable as hostels get, it sells substantially discounted lift tickets for the most expensive lifts in the valley. Hostel members are welcome to drop in and buy these discounted tickets even if they sleep elsewhere (dorm bed-76F, S-135F, D-210F, office open daily 8:00–12:00, 17:00–22:00, 30-min walk from base of Aiguille du Midi lift or 15-min walk from Les Pèlerins Station, 2 kilometers below Chamonix in Les Pèlerins, tel. 04 50 53 14 52).

Refuges

The French have the perfect answer for hikers who don't want to pack tents, sleeping bags, stoves, and food: refuges. For about 60F per person you can sleep on bunks high in the peaceful mountains. Bring your own food or let the guardian cook your dinner and breakfast (80–100F for dinner, about 40F for breakfast). The Office de Haute Montagne in Chamonix can explain your options and make reservations. Some refuges are located an easy walk from a lift station, and most are open from mid-June to mid-September. Comfort ranges from very basic to downright luxurious. Try **La Pierre à Berard** refuge, a beautiful hike from Le Buet (50F per bed, 155F half-pension, tel. 04 50 54 62 08).

Eating in Chamonix

While Chamonix, like any mountain resort, has its share of bad food and badly priced restaurants, there are several good values to be found.

Bistrot des Sports is a rare souvenir of old Chamonix, with wood tables, old photos, good food, and smoky locals (50–100F, 182 rue Joseph Vallot, tel. 04 50 53 00 46). **La Bergerie** is where I go for alpine ambience, fondue, wood-fired raclette, and other regional dishes (232 avenue Michel Croz, near train station, tel. 04 50 53 45 04). **La Boccalatte** is an excellent value and offers a large selection of local specialties (across from Hotel au Bon Coin at 59 avenue de l'Aiguille du Midi, tel. 04 50 53 52 14).

If dipping bread into hot, gurgling cheese isn't your idea of haute cuisine, try **Le Sabot** for crêpes and Italian food on allée Recteur Payot (above the intersection of avenue Aguille du Midi and rue du Docteur Paccard). **La Caboulé**, next to the Brévent *téléphérique*, is a hip eatery with great omelets and an unbeatable view from its outdoor tables. **L'Impossible** is a characteristic place a five-minute walk beyond the Aiguille du Midi lift; it's named for a local ski champ who could do *"l'impossible"* (100F *menus*, daily in summer, route des Pelerins, tel. 04 50 53 20 36).

After dinner, hang out with the local hikers at **Bar Choucas** (206 rue du Docteur Paccard) or **Bistrot des Sports** (182 rue Joseph Vallot).

Picnic assembly: A good *boulangerie* and a vegetable market are adjacent to the TI. The best grocery is Codec, below Hôtel Alpina. The more central Super U is next to Hotel Touring at #117 (open even Sun morning), and there's a long-hours grocery a block in front of the train station. The park next to the church is picnic-pretty.

Transportation Connections—Chamonix

Bus and train service to Chamonix are surprisingly good. Both the bus and train stations (on the same square) have helpful information desks.

By train to: Annecy (5/day, 2.5 hrs, transfer in St. Gervais), **Beaune** and **Dijon** (3/day, 8 hrs, transfers in St. Gervais and Lyon), **Nice** (4/day, 10 hrs, transfer in St. Gervais and Lyon, night train possible), **Arles** (5/day, 8 hrs, transfer in St. Gervais and Lyon), **Paris'** Gare de Lyon (4/day, 7 hrs, longer at night, transfers in St. Gervais and Annecy; take the handy night train), **Martigny, Switzerland** (2 hrs, a very scenic trip), **Geneva** (3/day, 2.5 hrs, quick transfers in St. Gervais, La Roche-sur-Foron, and Annemasse).

By bus: Buses provide service to destinations not served by train and also to some cities that are served by train—but at a lower cost and higher speed. Get information at the bus station (*gare routière*) in the SNCF train station (tel. 04 50 53 01 15). To reach Italy while the Mt. Blanc tunnel is closed (until 2000) train to Martigny and bus from there to Courmayeur (2/day, 1 hr, Italian side of Aiguille du Midi gondola) and Aosta (2/day, 2 hrs).

Itinerary Options from Chamonix

A Day in French-Speaking Switzerland—There are plenty of tempting Alpine and cultural thrills just an hour or two away in Switzerland. A road and train line sneak you scenically from

Chamonix to the Swiss town of Martigny. Remember, while train travelers cross without formalities, drivers are charged the $32 Swiss annual highway tax just to cross the border.

A Little Italy—The remote Valle d'Aosta and its historic capital city of Aosta are a spectacular gondola ride over the Mont Blanc range. The side trip is worthwhile if you'd like to taste Italy (spaghetti, gelato, and cappuccino), enjoy the town's great evening ambience, or look at the ancient ruins in Aosta, often called the "Rome of the North."

From Hellbronner (see "Aiguille du Midi lift," above), catch the 38,000L lift down to Entreves and take the bus to Aosta (hrly, change in Courmayeur); or, if you have exceptional social skill, try to talk a gondola mate with a car in Entreves into a ride down the valley. From Aosta, trains or buses will take you to Milan and the rest of Italy.

Sleeping in Aosta, Italy (L1,700 = $1, zip code: 11100): **Hotel Ponte Romano** is on the Roman bridge. With a warm, woody interior, it's one of Aosta's better hotels (Sb-L100,000, Db-L140,000, Via Ponte Romano 27, tel. 0165-45262, fax 0165-31736). **La Belle Epoque** offers clean and simple rooms and a grumpy staff (Sb-L50,000–65,000, Db-L70,000–85,000, Via D'Avise 18, off Via E. Aubert, tel. 0165-262-276). Cheaper beds are found in a less charming, more industrial area at the **Barrano** family (S-L40,000, D-L80,000, Via Voison 9, tel. 0165/43224) and Senora Mancuso's **Albergo Mancuso** (Sb-L60,000, Db-L70,000, Via Voison 32, tel. 0165/34526).

LYON

Comfortably nestled at the base of the Alps between Burgundy and Provence, overlooked Lyon is one of France's delightful surprises. Its strategic and impressive location, straddling the Rhône and Saone Rivers, has made Lyon important since pre-Roman times. After Paris, Lyon is the most historic and culturally important city in France. Here you get two distinctly different feeling cities: the *molto* Italian café–crammed cobbled alleys, Renaissance mansions, and colorful facades of Vieux Lyon; and the more staid but classy, Parisian-feeling shopping streets of Presqu'ile. On a three-week tour of France, Lyon merits two nights and a day for its enchanting old city (Vieux Lyon), superb Gallo-Roman museum, one-of-a-kind museum on the French resistance, thriving pedestrian streets, and France's undisputedly best cuisine at digestible prices. Lyon makes a handy day visit for train travelers, as many trains pass through Lyon and both stations have baggage lockers.

Orientation

Lyon is France's second-largest city, but inside it feels small. Most of your sightseeing is near the Saone River and can be done on foot. If you stick to the sights listed below, you probably won't need more than the funicular to help you get around, though the subway is a joy to use. Your area of focus is from west to east between the hill of Fourvière and the Rhône River and from south to north from Perrache station to the place Terreaux. Place Bellecour is ground zero.

Lyon's sights are concentrated in three areas: Fourvière hill, Vieux Lyon, and the Presqu'ile. Start your day on Fourvière hill (take the funicular near St. Jean Cathedral in Vieux Lyon to Fourvière) and visit the Gallo-Roman Museum (lunch closing at 11:40), Roman Theater, and Basilique Notre Dame before catching the funicular or walking down to Vieux Lyon. In Vieux Lyon, take the *traboule* walk outlined below and then finish your day on the Presqu'ile. Beware: Most of Lyon's important sights close Monday and Tuesday.

Tourist Information: The well-equipped and central TI, in the middle of place Bellecour, will get you oriented (Mon–Fri 9:00–18:00, until 17:00 on weekends and in winter, until 19:00 mid-Jun–mid-Sept). Pay 4F for the helpful English map of Lyon, which has museum hours and descriptions, or get it free at your hotel. Pick up the free map of Vieux Lyon, the list of open *traboules* (passageways, see below), and a schedule of events and concerts. The TI sells a museum pass that should interest serious sightseers (1 day-90F, 2 day-160F, 3 day-200F, includes all museums, a day pass on the bus or Métro, and Walkman or guided walking tours of Lyon). They sell useful guidebooks on Lyon (50F) and rent handy Walkman casettes (40F) with good walking tours of Lyon (see below). Summer concerts in the Roman Theater and any event in the new opera house keep Lyon's music scene lively.

Arrival in Lyon

By Train: Two train stations serve Lyon (Perrache and Part-Dieu); many trains stop at both, and through trains connect the two stations every 10 minutes. Both have lockers and baggage-checking services, making Lyon an easy stopover visit for train travelers. It doesn't matter which station you choose, as both are well served by métro, bus, and taxi. Perrache is more central and within a 20-minute walk of place Bellecour (cross place Carnot and walk straight up rue Victor Hugo). Or take the Métro (direction Laurent Bonnevay) two stops to Bellecour and follow "*sortie rue République*" signs (see Métro lesson below).

Leave the Part Dieu station, following sortie Vivier Merle signs to the Métro; take it in the direction Jean Mace; transfer at Saxe Gambetta; take direction Gare de Vaise; get off at Bellecour; and follow sortie rue République (see Métro lesson below). Figure 60F to 80F to taxi from either train station to the hotels listed near place Bellecour.

By Car: The city center is easy to navigate, though you'll likely encounter traffic on the surrounding freeways. From the freeways, follow signs to *centre-ville* and Presqu'ile and then follow place Bellecour signs. Park in the lots under place Bellecour or place des Celestins or get advice from your hotel. The TI's map has all public car parks well identified.

Getting around Lyon

Lyon's Métro, with only four lines (A, B, C and D), is a breeze. While similar to Paris' Métro in many ways (e.g., routes are signed by direction for the last stop on the line), Lyon's Métro is highly automated, cleaner, and far less crowded. There are no turnstyles and no obvious ticket windows. Efficient ticket machines (coins only) are located just before the platforms and give change (1 ride-8F, 10 rides-68F). Buy your ticket (firmly push the top button for one ticket and then put your coins in) then punch your ticket in the nearby orange box and you're in business. Study the wall maps to be sure of your direction; ask a local if you're not certain. Your ticket is good until you complete your one-way trip. Métro tickets can be used on the two funiculars, but you cannot transfer from subway to funicular with the same ticket.

Walking Tours of Lyon

Self-guided: The TI rents Walkman casettes (40F, in English, covered by museum pass) that take you on a three-hour walking tour (at your own pace) that connects most of the sights described below and provide good explanations. The simple map is easy to follow, and while the information may be overkill for some, I enjoyed it. Clip the Walkman to your pocket or belt. If pressed for time, end your tour in Vieux Lyon, skipping the last segment covering the Presqu'ile.

With Guide: Most days of the week the TI offers interesting walking tours covering different aspects of Lyon (50F, covered by museum pass). The principal language is French, though they will translate (schedule available at the TI).

Sights—Fourvière Hill

▲▲▲**Gallo-Roman Museum (Musée de la Civilisation Gallo-romaine)**—Constructed in the hillside with views of the Roman Theater, this museum makes Lyon's importance in Roman times clear. Lyon was the military base that Julius Caesar used to conquer Gaul (much of modern-day France). Admire the bronze chariot from the seventh century B.C. and then orient yourself with the model of Roman Lyon. As the museum cascades downhill you'll pass Gallo-Roman artifacts that allow you to piece together life in Lyon during the Roman occupation, including 2,000-year-old lead pipes, a speech by Claudius (translated into English),

Roman coins, models of Roman theaters complete with moving stage curtains, and haunting funeral masks (20F, Wed–Sun 9:00–12:00, 14:00–18:00, rooms begin closing 20 min early, helpful English explanations).

Basilique Notre Dame de Fourvière—In the late 1800s the Bishop of Lyon vowed to build a magnificent tribute to God if the Prussians left his city alone (the same reason and vow that built the Sacré-Coeur in Paris). The whipped-cream exterior is neo-everything, and the interior screams overdone with mosaics. Don't miss the chapel below or the panoramic views from behind the church.

Sights—Vieux Lyon (Old Lyon)

▲*Traboules* (covered passageways)—Lyon is the Florence of France, offering the best concentration of well-preserved Renaissance buildings in the country. From the 16th to the 19th century Lyon was king of Europe's silk industry; at one point it hummed with more than 18,000 looms. The fine buildings of the old center were designed by Italians and financed by the silk industry. Pastel courtyards, beautiful loggias, and delicate arches line the passageways (*traboules*) connecting these buildings. The serpentine *traboules* provided shelter when the silk was being moved from one stage to the next and would provide ideal cover for the French resistance in World War II. Several of Lyon's 315 *traboules* are open to the public (press the top button next to the streetfront door to release the door when entering; push the light buttons to illuminate the dark walkways; pull the lever sideways at the door handle when leaving; please respect the residents' peace when wandering through). The TI's map of Vieux Lyon proposes an interesting route connecting some of the most interesting *traboules*. Try this quick introductory route: cross the pedestrian bridge, Passerelle du Palais du Justice, over the Saone, angle right across the busy street and find the quai Roman Rolland, enter #17, and cross to rue des Trois-Maries. Find #8, cross to rue St. Jean, and turn left then right onto the café-popular place Neuve-St. Jean. Now find the rue de Boeuf, go left, and enter Lyon's longest *traboule* at #27 (push buttons as you go for mood lights). cross back to rue St. Jean; turn right here to reach the cathedral.

Cathedral of St. Jean—Stand as far back as you can in the square for the best view. This took 300 years to build and transcends Romanesque and Gothic styles. This cathedral does not soar like northern French cathedrals from the same period (churches in southern France are typically less vertical than those in the north). Inside you'll find a few beautiful stained-glass windows and a remarkable astrological clock with a performance at noon, 14:00, 15:00, and 16:00 (Mon–Fri 8:00–12:00, 14:00–19:30, Sat–Sun 14:00–17:00). Check out the ruins predating the cathedral outside the left transept.

Sights—On or near Lyon's Presqu'ile

From Perrache station to place des Terreaux, the Presqu'ile is Lyon's shopping spine, with thriving pedestrian streets and chic boutiques. Cruise the shops of rue de la République and the *bouchons* (characteristic bistros) of rue Merciere and relax at a café on place des Terreaux. You'll also find these interesting museums.

▲**Musee des Beaux Arts**—Located in a former abbey, this fine-arts museum has an impressive collection ranging from Egyptian antiquities to medieval armor to Impressionist paintings. Still, if you're short on time and going to Paris, it's skippable (25F, Wed–Sun 10:30–18:00, closed Mon–Tue, pick up a museum layout on entering, great café-terrace, 20 place des Terreaux, Mo: Hôtel de Ville).

Museums of Fabrics and Decorative Arts (Musées des Tissus et des Arts Decoratifs)—Here you get two museums for the price of one. The beautifully organized Musée des Tissus takes you on a historical tour of Lyon's silk industry. The less-engaging Musée des Arts Decoratif is a large manor home decorated with period furniture and art objects (28F covers both museums, Tue–Sun 10:00–17:30, closed Mon, 34 rue de la Charite, Mo: Bellecour).

▲▲**Resistance and Deportation Center (Centre d'Histoire de la Resistance et de la Déportation)**—Located near Vichy, the capital of the French puppet state, Lyon was the center of French resistance from 1942 to 1945. This well-organized museum, once used as a Nazi torture chamber, uses headsets, videos, reconstructed rooms, and, it seems, anything they can get their hands on to help you understand how the resistance came to be and what life was like for its members. English explanations and headsets help, but you need to move slowly with your headset and stand near the remote signal boxes or you'll feel like you're decoding your own enemy messages (25F, Wed–Sun 9:00–17:30, 15-min walk from Perrache station, cross pont Gallieni, and walk 3 blocks to 14 avenue Berthelot; or, easier, take the Métro to Jean Mace and walk back 3 blocks toward the river).

Sleeping in Lyon
(6F = about $1, zip code: 69002)

Hotels in Lyon are a steal compared to those in Paris. Weekends are discounted. Skip the hotels near either train station. All hotels listed below are on the Presqu'ile; the first three are on or very near the intimate place des Celestins (two blocks from place Bellecour, Mo: Bellecour).

Hotel des Artistes*, ideally located right on place des Celestins, is plush, comfortable, central, and the best value in its price range (Sb-350–470F, Db-400–510F, CC:VMA, SE, 8 rue Gaspard-Andre, tel. 04 78 42 04 88, fax 04 78 42 93 76, email: hartiste@clubinternet.fr).

Hotel du Theatre**, across the small square from Hotel des

Artistes, is a fun place with breezy rooms in all sizes and shapes, many wonderfully funky, some with sliver showers. Those overlooking the place Celestins tend to be larger and are worth the extra cost. Expect friendly owners and plenty of stairs (S-180F, Sb-275–310F, Db-275–350F, extra bed-50F, 10 rue de Savoie, entrance on the back side of place des Celestins, tel. 04 78 42 33 32, fax 04 72 40 00 61).

Hotel Colbert**, just off the place des Celestins, is ideal, warmly run, spotless, and charming. Rooms on the street side are larger but come with street noise (Sb-300F, Db-320F–350F, elevator, TV, good buffet breakfast, 4 rue des Archers, CC: VMA, elevator, tel. 04 72 56 08 98, fax 04 72 56 08 65).

The last three hotels are located closer to place des Terreaux, about 10 to 15 blocks north of place Bellecour.

Hotel Moderne** is a pretty good value, with comfortable rooms and a cheery lobby, in the heart of the shopping area (Db-315–335F, 15 rue Dubois, Mo: Cordeliers, tel. 04 78 42 21 83, fax 04 72 41 04 40).

Hotel de Bretagne* is the best one-star value I could find. It has sincere owners, tight and tidy rooms, and good beds but needs new carpeting (Sb-200F, DB-240F, Tb-275F, 10 rue Dubois, tel. 04 78 37 79 33, fax 04 72 77 99 92, CC:VM, Mo: Cordeliers,

Grand Hotel des Terreaux*** is very well situated and a good value and has a slightly faded Old World elegance (Sb-370F, Db-405, Tb or Qb-445F, just below place Terreaux, a block off the Saone River at 16 rue Lanterne, Mo: Hôtel de Ville, tel. 04 78 27 04 10, fax 04 78 27 97 75).

Eating in Vieux Lyon

With an abundance of excellent restaurants in all price ranges, it's hard to go wrong—unless you order *tripes* (cow stomach). Look instead for these classics: quenelles (large dumplings), roasted chicken from Bresse, and *salade lyonnaise* (lettuce, ham, and poached eggs).

Bouchons are small bistros evolving from the days when mama would feed the silk workers. I can't imagine a better area to restaurant shop than in Vieux Lyon, though the rue Merciere on the Presqu'ile offers many good places. Here are a few *bouchons* to get you started:

The epicenter of restaurant activity in Vieux Lyon is the place Neuve St. Jean—compare the crowds and sift through their menus. **Le Comptoir de Boeuf** is worth the reservations you may need (90F and 120F *menus*, outdoor terrace, 3 place Neuve-St. Jean, tel. 04 78 82 35). Around the corner at 38 rue de Boeuf, **Les Retrouvailles** offers an excellent 120F *menu*, a charming dining room, and a terrific overall experience (38 rue de Boeuf). A block south, **Les Lyonnais** is cheaper, lighthearted, and locally popular, with photo portraits of loyal customers lining the walls (95F *menu*, 1 rue Tramssac, tel. 04 78 37 64 82).

Eating on the Presqu'ile

At #8 place des Celestins the classic, cozy bistro **la Francotte** is good for a relaxing drink or a meal and is handy to many hotels (closed Sun). Vegetarians and nondrinkers will appreciate the fair-priced fine cuisine at **Le Patisson** (2 blocks north of place des Celestin at 17 rue du Port du Temple, closed Fri, Sat, and Sun, tel. 04 72 41 81 71). Near the Hotel des Terreaux are two establishments worth the detour, both on the short rue Major-Martin: The **Café des Federations** at #8 is a venerable institution worth a stop for the traditional Lyonnais ambience and good wine selection (150F *menu*, closed Sun and in Aug). Next door at #12, **La Table des Echevins** serves up authentic medieval cuisine in a lively wood-beamed setting, (90F *menu*, tel. 04 78 39 98 33, closed Sun, tel. 04 78 39 98 33).

Transportation Connections—Lyon

After Paris, Lyon is France's most important rail hub. The first TGV train built connects Paris and Lyon. Rail travelers will find this gateway to the Alps, Provence, the Riviera, and Burgundy a convenient stopover. To **Paris** (20/day, 2 hrs), **Dijon** (14/day, 2 hrs), **Beaune** (9/day, 2 hrs), **Avignon** (14/day, 2.5 hrs), **Nice** (14/day, 6 hrs), **Annecy** (8/day, 90 min), **Venice** (3/day, 10 hrs), **Rome** (3/day, 11 hrs), **Florence** (3/day, 10 hrs), **Geneva** (6/day, 2 hrs), **Barcelona** (2/day, 9 hrs).

    Drivers: If you're heading south to Provence, consider a three-hour detour through the spectacular Ardeches Gorges (exit the A-6 autoroute at Privas and follow Aubenas, Vallon Pont d'Arc, and Pont St. Esprit.) All-day canoe/kayak floats through the gorges are easy to find in Vallon Pont d'Arc.

BURGUNDY

The soft rolling hills of Burgundy gave birth to superior wine, fine cuisine, and sublime countryside crisscrossed with canals and dotted with untouristed hill towns. Bucolic Burgundy is the transportation funnel for eastern France and makes a convenient stopover for travelers (car or train), with quick access north to Paris or the Alsace, east to the Alps, and south to Provence. Only a small part of Burgundy's land is covered by vineyards, but wine making is what they do best. The white cows you see everywhere are Charolais. They make France's best beef and end up in *boeuf bourguignonne*. The Romanesque churches dotting the countryside owe their origins to the once-powerful influence of the Abbey of Cluny in southern Burgundy.

Planning Your Time

Dijon, the capital of Burgundy, is worth a look but is skippable if time's limited. Stay in cozier Beaune. It's better located for touring the vineyards and countryside. You'll need at least one day for Beaune and its environs and a half day for Dijon.

Getting around Burgundy

Trains link Beaune and Dijon with ease; less-frequent buses cruise the wine route between Beaune and Dijon. Bikes and mini-van tours get nondrivers into the countryside from Beaune. Buses serve Semur-en-Auxois from Dijon and Montbard.

Cuisine Scene—Burgundy

Your taste buds are going to thank you for bringing them here. Considered by many to be France's best, Burgundian cuisine is peasant cooking elevated to an art. Several classic dishes were born

Burgundy

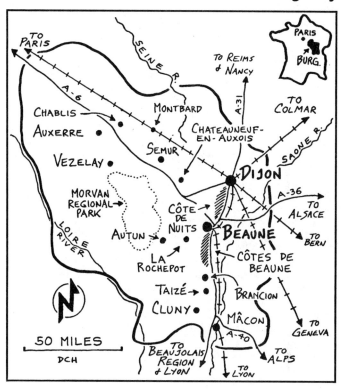

here—escargots *bourguignonne* (snails served sizzling hot in garlic butter), *boeuf bourguignonne* (beef simmered for hours in red wine with onions and mushrooms), coq au vin (chicken stewed in red wine), and *oeufs en meurette* (poached eggs on a large crouton in red wine)—as were the famous Dijon mustards. Look also for *jambon persillé* (cold ham layered in a garlic-parsley gelatin), *pain d'épices* (spice bread), and *gougère* (light, puffy cheese pastries). Native cheeses are Epoisses and Langres (both mushy and great) and, my favorite, Montrachet (a tasty goat cheese). *Crème de cassis* (a black currant liqueur) is another Burgundian specialty; look for it in desserts and snazzy drinks (try a *kir*).

With Bordeaux, Burgundy is why France is famous for wine. From Chablis to the Beaujolais, you'll find it all here—great, fruity reds; dry whites; and crisp rosés. The three key grapes are Chardonnay (dry white wines), Pinot Noir (medium-bodied red wines), and Gamay (light, fruity wines like Beaujolais). Every village produces its own distinctive wine—like Chablis and Meursault; road maps read like fine wine lists. If the wine village has a hyphenated name (most do), the latter half of its name comes from the town's most important vineyard (e.g., Gevery-Chamberin, Ladoix-Serrigny). Look for the *"Dégustation Gratuite"* (free tasting) signs and prepare for serious tasting and steep prices if you're not careful. For more-relaxed tastings, head for the hills; the less prestigious Hautes-Côtes (upper slopes) produce some terrific and overlooked wines. Look for village cooperatives or see my suggestions for Beaune tastings. The least expensive (but still tasty) wines are the Bourgogne Aligoté (white), Bourgogne Ordinaire and Passetoutgrain (both red), and those from the Macon, Chalon, and Beaujolais areas. If you like rosé, try the Marsannay, considered France's best.

BEAUNE

You'll feel comfortable right away in this polished but fun-loving wine capital, where life centers around the production and consumption of the prestigious, expensive Côte d'Or wines. *Côte d'Or* means "golden hillsides," and they are a spectacle to enjoy in late October, as the leaves of the vineyards turn colors.

Beaune is a compact, thriving little city (pop. 25,000) with vineyards on its doorstep. Limit your Beaune ramblings to the town center, contained within its medieval walls and circled by a one-way ring road. All roads and activities converge on the perfectly French place Carnot.

Tourist Information: The TI, across the street from Hôtel Dieu on place de la Halle, has city maps, a room-finding service, *chambre d'hôte* pamphlets, bus schedules, and information on wine-tasting tours (Apr–Sept daily 9:00–19:00, summers until 20:00, closes at 18:00 in winter; from place Carnot, walk toward thin spire; tel. 03 80 26 21 30, e-mail: OT.beaune@wanadoo.fr).

Arrival in Beaune

By Train: To reach the city center from the train station (lockers available), walk straight out of the station up avenue du Huit (8) Septembre, cross the busy ring road, and continue up rue du Château.

By Bus: Beaune has no bus station—only several stops in the center. Ask the driver for un *arret dans le centre ville* (a central stop)—the Jules Ferry stop is central and closest to the train station.

By Car: Follow *"centre-ville"* signs to the ring road. Once on the ring road, turn right at the first signal after the new post office (rue d'Alsace) and park (free) in the place Madeleine.

Helpful Hints

Laundromat: Just off place Madeleine in the Casino supermarket's courtyard.

Internet Access: Not available in Beaune.
Best Souvenir Shopping: The **Athenaeum** has a great variety of souvenirs and many books in English (daily 10:00–19:00, across from Hôtel Dieu at 7 rue de l'Hôtel Dieu).
Best Wine Store: Dennis Perret has a great selection from a variety of producers in all price ranges and a helpful, English-speaking staff (they can chill a white for your dinner picnic). If you've tasted a wine you like elsewhere, they can usually find a less costly bottle with similar qualities (Mon–Sat 10:00–19:00, closed Sun, 40 place Carnot).

Sights—Beaune

▲▲▲**Hôtel Dieu**—The Hundred Years' War and the Black Death devastated Beaune, leaving more than 90 percent of its population destitute. Nicholas Rolin, Chancellor of Burgundy and a peasant by birth, had to do something for "his people." So, in 1443, he paid to build this flamboyant Flemish/Gothic charity hospital. It was completed in only eight years. Tour it on your own; you'll find (for once) good English explanations. Pick up a tour brochure at the ticket desk. Start in the oldest part of the hospital, the churchlike room of the paupers. At busy times there were twice as many beds filling this room, with two patients per bed! Notice the inverted ship-hull ceiling and sea-monster beams. The extraordinary five-paneled polyptych by Roger Van der Weyden (which you'll see later) was hung behind the altar in the chapel at the end of the room. Next, shuffle through the St. Hughes room (wealthier clients stayed here) and study the images of blood-letting operations. The infirmary (now the hospital museum) is next—how about those medical instruments? Yeow! The nearby pharmacy once provided slug-slime cures for sore throats and cockroach powders for constipation. In the St. Louis wing (where patients replaced winepresses that occupied this space) you'll find Van der Weyden's dramatic *Last Judgment* polyptych, commissioned by Rolin to give the dying something to ponder. Ask the attendant to let the giant roaming monocle give you a closer look. Your visit ends with a look at Flemish tapestries. *The Story of Jacob*, woven by one person in 17 years, is magnificent (32F, Apr–Nov daily 9:00–18:30, otherwise 9:00–11:30, 14:00–17:30).
▲**Collégiale Notre Dame**—Built in the 12th and 13th centuries, this is a good example of Cluny-style architecture (except for the front porch). Enter to see the 15th-century tapestries (behind the altar, drop in a franc for lights), a variety of stained glass, and what's left of frescoes depicting the life of Lazarus (daily 8:30–19:00). To find the Musée du Vin from here, walk 30 steps straight out of the cathedral, turn left down a cobbled alley, keep left, and enter the courtyard of the Hotel des Ducs, today's Musée du Vin, located in the old residence of the dukes of Burgundy.

Beaune

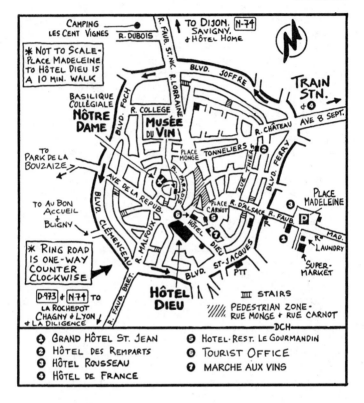

① GRAND HÔTEL ST. JEAN
② HÔTEL DES REMPARTS
③ HÔTEL ROUSSEAU
④ HÔTEL DE FRANCE
⑤ HOTEL·REST. LE GOURMANDIN
⑥ TOURIST OFFICE
⑦ MARCHE AUX VINS

Musée du Vin—You don't have to like wine to appreciate this folk-wine museum. The history and culture of Burgundy and wine were fermented in the same bottle. Even if you opt against the museum, wander into the courtyard for a look at the duke's palace, antique winepresses (in the barn), and a nifty model of 15th-century Beaune. Inside the museum you'll find a great model of the regions, tools, costumes, and scenes of Burgundian wine history—but no tasting. English explanations are promised in each room for 2000 (25F, ticket good for other Beaune museums, daily 9:30–18:00, closed Tue in winter).

Parc de la Bouzaise and vineyards—Walk toward the ring road on avenue de la République, cross it, and follow the stream for three blocks; the park and vineyards are straight ahead. Stroll through the peaceful park and then enter the vineyards just beyond, climbing high on dirt paths for the best views.

Wine Tasting in and near Beaune

Countless opportunities exist (for a price) for you to learn the fine points of Burgundy's wine. Many small wine shops offer free tastings (with the expectation that you'll buy), and several large cellars (caves) charge an entry fee and allow you to taste from a variety of wines (with less expectation that you'll buy). Most caves offer some form of introduction or self-guided tours and are open daily, generally 9:30 to 11:30 and 14:00 to 17:30. (Also see "Minibus Tours," below.)

Start or end your tour at **Athenaeum**, a bookstore (with many titles in English), wine bar, and Burgundian wine chamber of commerce all in one (across from the Hôtel Dieu, next to TI). ▲▲▲**Marché aux Vins**—This is Beaune's wine smorgasbord and the best way to sample its impressive wines. You pay 50F for a wine-tasting cup (you keep it) and get 45 minutes to sip. Plunge into the labyrinth of candlelit caves dotted with tables, each offering a new tasting experience. You're on your own. Relax; this is world-class stuff. The $70 reds are upstairs in the chapel, at the end of the tasting. (Hint: Taste better by sneaking in a hunk of bread or crackers.) If you grab an empty wine basket at the beginning and at least pretend you're going to buy, the occasional time checker will leave you alone. (Daily 9:00–12:00, 14:30–18:30, last entry at 18:00, closes at 17:00 in winter, tel. 03 80 25 08 20.)

More Self-Guided Tours in Beaune—While the Marché aux Vins is the ultimate wine-tasting experience, you may want to sample other cellars. If you have less time for wine, **Caves des Cordeliers** offers good self-guided tours (with English explanations) and six wines to taste for just 20F (6 rue de l'Hôtel Dieu, tel. 03 80 24 53 79). **Cave Patriache Père et Fils** also has self-guided tours, Beaune's largest underground cellars, and 13 different wines to sample (50F, tasting cup included, 7 rue du Collège, tel. 03 80 24 53 78). The TI has a complete list of area vintners for those who want to venture into the countryside; remember, you're expected to buy. (Also see "The Hautes-Côtes to Châteauneuf-en-Auxois," below, for tastings in the less prestigious, more relaxed Hautes-Côtes.)

Minibus Tours of Vineyards near Beaune—Wine Safari minibus wine-tasting tours offer three two-hour itineraries (190F, tour #2 is best for beginners, departs from TI, call TI for information, tel. 03 80 26 21 30). These tours are well run, in English, and will get you through the countryside and to the wineries you couldn't get into otherwise. Transco buses run from Beaune through all the great wine villages for those who want to explore the wine road on their own (see "Getting around the Beaune Region," below).

Sleeping in Beaune
(6F = about $1, zip code: 21200)
Sleep Code: **S** = Single, **D** = Double/Twin, **T** = Triple, **Q** = Quad, **b** = bathroom, **t** = toilet only, **s** = shower only, **CC** = Credit Card

(Visa, MasterCard, Amex), **SE** = Speaks English, **NSE** = No English, * = French hotel rating system (0–4 stars).

Hôtel des Remparts*** offers affordable luxury, with fine rooms in a manor house complete with beamed ceilings, period furniture, a quiet courtyard, and great rooms for families (Db-300–450F, Db suites-620F, Tb-490–520F, Qb-520–690F, attic rooms are cozy, parking-45F, CC:VM; between the train station and the main square, just inside the ring road at 48 rue Thiers; tel. 03 80 24 94 94, fax 03 80 24 97 08, e-mail: hotel.des .remparts@wanadoo.fr, SE).

Hotel Tulip Inn-Athanor*** mixes modern comfort with a touch of old Beaune and is very central (Sb-290–450F, Db-375–550F, most at 450F, Tb/Qb-750F, CC:VMA, elevator, 9 avenue de la République, tel. 03 80 24 09 20, fax 03 80 24 09 15, e-mail: Hotel.Athanor@wanadoo.fr, SE).

Abbaye de Mazieres is ideally located and has four quiet, colorful, and spacious rooms in a 15th-century building over a restaurant near the basilica (Db-390–450F, Tb-550F, 19 rue Mazieres, tel. 03 80 24 74 64, fax 03 80 22 49 49, if no response contact Hotel Tulip, above).

The **Le Gourmandin** restaurant rents three central, comfortable rooms (Db-350F, big Db/Tb or Qb-450F, many stairs, 8 place Carnot, tel. 03 80 24 07 88, fax 03 80 22 27 42).

Train travelers will appreciate the friendly and well-run **Hôtel de France****, across from the train station (Sb-200F, Db-270–290F, Tb/Qb-330–350F, 35 avenue du 8 Septembre, tel. 03 80 24 10 34, fax 03 80 24 96 78).

Hotel Arcade**, modern and comfortable, is located right at the ring road and avenue Charles de Gaulle, (Db-300–350F, tel. 03 80 22 75 67, fax 03 80 22 77 17).

Sleeping on Place Madeleine

These hotels are a few blocks from the city center and train station and offer easy parking.

What **Hôtel au Grand St. Jean**** lacks in character it makes up for in value and location (Db-265F, Tb/Qb-315F, CC:VM, on place Madeleine, tel. 03 80 24 12 22, fax 03 80 24 15 43). Like a sprawling motel with ample and safe parking, it's simple, practical, and, with its helpful, English-speaking owner, M. Neaux, plenty French. Color-blind travelers will love the TV lounge.

Across the square, the no-frills **Hôtel Rousseau** will make you smile, with cheerful and quirky owners, pet birds, and a pleasant enclosed garden. The cheapest rooms are simple but fine; those with showers are like grandma's, though maintenance can be spotty (S-135F, D-180F, Db-300F, Tt-245F, Tb-350F, Q-290F, Qb-350F, includes breakfast, 20F showers down the hall, free private parking, 11 place Madeleine, tel. 03 80 22 13 59).

Hotel de la Paix***, just off place de la Madeleine, is a great value and Beaune's cheapest three stars in a flawlessly renovated building (Sb-280F, Db-350F, Tb-450F, loft Tb-550F, Qb-600F, CC:VM, 45 rue du Faubourg Madeleine, tel. 03 80 24 78 08, fax 03 80 24 10 18, SE).

Sleeping near Beaune

Hotels: Hôtel Le Home** is Beaune's most elegant value, with cushy rooms in an old mansion. It's a half mile out of town on N-74 toward Dijon. The less expensive rooms are fine, but the rooms on the parking courtyard (400F) have a nice terrace (Db-330–460F, Tb/Qb-500F, CC:VM, free parking, 138 route de Dijon, tel. 03 80 22 16 43, fax 03 80 24 90 74). Call ahead—it's popular.

Hotel Parc**, three kilometers from Beaune in Levernois, is a delightful vine-covered manor house with fine rooms and a welcoming staff (Db-200–500F, CC:VM, 21200 Levernois, tel. 03 80 24 63 00, fax 03 80 24 21 19).

Drivers can park below their room window at one of their many modern chain hotels on the way into Beaune from the autoroute. The simple, sterile **Villages Hotel*** is dirt cheap (Db/Tb-165F, CC:VM, rue Burgalat, tel. 03 80 24 14 50, fax 03 80 24 14 45). For twice the price, **Hotel IBIS**** offers more comfort, a pool, a play area, and a reasonable restaurant (Db-300–375F, avenue Charles de Gaulle, tel. 03 80 22 46 75, fax 03 80 22 21 16).

Chambres d'Hôte: The Côte d'Or has many *chambres d'hôte*; get a pamphlet at the TI and reserve ahead in the summer. Most can be found only in small wine villages, and many are only a short drive from Beaune. In Magny le Villers, the friendly **Dumays** have two attached rooms in a restored farmhouse, ideal for three or more (Ss-185F, Db-225F, Tb-285F, Qb-350F; from Beaune go north on N-74 then west at Ladoix; in Magny look behind the church; tel. 03 80 62 91 16). There are scads of *chambres d'hôtes* in the cliff-dwelling villages of Baubigny and Orches, just under La Rochepot (zip code for both: 21340). In Baubigny, **M. Fussi** has 4 comfortable rooms in a modern home over a sweeping lawn (Db-250F, Tb-300F, tel. & fax 03 80 21 84 66). A few kilometers away in Orches, **M. Muhlenbaumer** has two cozy rooms and a pleasant courtyard terrace (Db-250F, Tb/Qb suite-450F, Baubigny-Orches, tel. 03 80 21 81 13), and **M. Raby** offers one double room and a good room for families in her newly renovated home with a cute pool and a nice yard (Db-290F, extra person-50F, 5 maximum, big breakfast, tel. 03 80 21 78 45).

Eating in Beaune

For a traditional Burgundian setting, step down to the wine-soaked cellar atmosphere of the 12th-century **Abbaye de Mazieres** (98F *menu*, closed Tue, see "Sleeping in Beaune," above) or the similar **Caveau des Arches** (good 85F *menu*, 10 boulevard Perpreuil, on the ring road at rue d'Alsace, tel. 03 80 22 10 37). For good steaks, salads, and *oeufs en meurette*, cross the ring road and try **Le Picboeuf** (closed Thu, 2 rue Faubourg Madeleine). Almost next door, at #8, step down into the relaxed ambience and friendly surroundings of **Les Caves Madeleine** and dine surrounded by shelves of wine (good wines by the glass, reasonable *plats du jour* and *menus*, closed Sun). For fine traditional Burgundian cuisine at digestible prices, consider **La Grilladine** (75F, 105F, and 135F *menus*, fine escargot, hot goat-cheese salad, and *oeufs en meurette*, closed Mon, 17 rue Maufoux, tel. 03 80 22 22 36) or the nearby **Rotisserie Fleury** (15 place Fleury, tel. 03 80 2 35 50). Beaune's best budget restaurant is **Relais de la Madeleine**, run by the entertaining M. Neaux Problem, pronounced "no problem" (44 place Madeleine, tel. 03 80 22 07 47).

Beaune's most interesting wine bar is the relaxed **Bistrot Bourgignon** (excellent but costly wines by the glass and a good but limited *menu*; 8 rue Monge, a pedestrian-only street, closed Sun). If you've had enough wine, drop by **Café Hallebarde** for a grand selection of draft beer (24 rue d'Alsace); and if you're tired of speaking French, pop into the late-night-lively **Pickwicks Pub** (behind the church at 2 rue Notre Dame).

Eating near Beaune

You'll find many fine restaurants just outside Beaune. Five minutes away is **Le Relais de la Diligence**, where you can dine surrounded by vineyards and taste the area's best budget Burgundian cuisine with many *menu* options (inexpensive/moderate, closed Tue evening and all day Wed, take N-74 toward Chagny/Chalon and make a left at L'Hôpital Meursault on D-23, tel. 03 80 21 21 32). **Au Bon Accueil** is relaxed and ideal, on a hill above Beaune, with great outdoor tables, a cozy interior, and five-course *menus* for 105F (closed Mon–Wed, leave Beaune's ring road and take the Bligny-sur-Ouche turnoff, a few minutes outside Beaune you'll see signs to Au Bon Accueil, tel. 03 80 22 08 80). If you're willing to drive 45 minutes, consider a late afternoon and evening in Châteauneuf-en-Auxois (see below).

Transportation Connections—Beaune

By train to: Dijon (9/day, 30 min), **Colmar** (5/day, 4.5 hrs, transfers in Dijon and Belfort), **Arles** (7/day, 5 hrs, transfer in Lyon), **Nice** (7/day, 8 hrs, transfer in Lyon), **Chamonix** (3/day, 8.5 hrs, transfers in Lyon and St. Gervais), **Paris'** Gare de Lyon (3 TGVs/day, 2 hrs; otherwise transfer to the TGV in Dijon, 3 hrs).

Getting around the Beaune Region

By Bus: Transco buses run from Beaune through the vineyards and villages north to Dijon south to Chalon-sur-Saône, and west to La Rochepot. Ask at the TI for schedules and stops or call for information (tel. 03 80 42 11 00).

By Bike: The well-organized, English-speaking, and helpful Bourgogne Randonnées has good bikes, bike racks, maps, and good countryside itineraries; they can deliver your bike to your hotel anywhere in France (bikes 20F/hr, 90F/day, Mon–Sat 9:00–12:00, 13:30–19:00, Sun 10:00–12:00, 14:00–17:00, near train station at 7 avenue Huit Septembre, tel. 03 80 22 06 03, fax 03 80 22 15 58).

Sights—Beaune Region

Bike Routes—Get the local Michelin map and suggestions from Bourgogne Randonnées (see above) and consider the long scenic loop ride through vineyards and over hills to La Rochepot. Take the D-17 from Pommard through St. Romain and Orches (it adds time but is more scenic and has fewer cars compared to the D-973). From La Rochepot return to Beaune or continue to St. Aubin and Gamay via the D-33 (it runs behind Hôtel Relais du Château in La Rochepot), follow the tiny road to Puligny-Montrachet and Meursault, and head back to Beaune via the D-973 (all day, 35 kilometers round-trip). To give your legs a break, ride instead along D-18 to Savigny-les-Beaune and Pernand Vergelesses. (Check out Savigny's unusual château.)

▲▲Château La Rochepot—This very Burgundian castle rises above the trees 12 kilometers from Beaune. It's accessible by car, bike (hilly), or infrequent bus. Cross the drawbridge and knock three times with the ancient knocker to enter. This pint-size castle is splendid inside and out. You'll tour half on your own and the other half with a French guide (get the English explanations). The kitchen will bowl you over. Look for the 15th-century high chair in the dining room. Climb the tower and see the Chinese room, sing chants in the resonant chapel, and make ripples in the well. (Can you spit a bull's-eye? It's 72 meters down!) And don't leave without driving, walking, or pedaling up the D-33 a few hundred meters toward St. Aubin (behind Hôtel Relais du Château) for a romantic view of this classically Burgundian castle. (32F, Jun–Aug Wed–Mon 10:00–18:00, closed Tue, closes 11:30–14:00 and at 16:30 in winter, tel. 03 80 21 71 37.)

▲▲Brancion and Chapaize—An hour south of Beaune by car (20 kilometers west of Tournus on the D-14) are two must-see churches that owe their existence and architectural design to the nearby once-powerful Cluny Abbey. Brancion's nine-building hamlet floats on a hill above Chapaize and offers the purest example of Romanesque architecture I've seen—a 12th-century church (with faint frescoes inside), a cute château (climb the tower for views), and a 15th-century market hall. **Auberge du Vieux Brancion** offers fine Burgundian cuisine at fair prices. For a peaceful break, spend a night in one of the Auberge's cozy rooms (D-220F, Db-310F, tel. & fax 03 85 51 03 83). If you're really on vacation, a night here is ideal. One mile downhill from Brancion, Chapaize's

Beaune Region

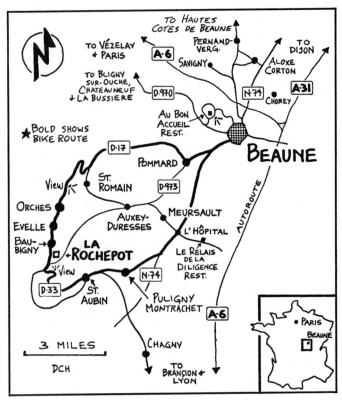

beautifully restored church is famous for its 11th-century belfry and its listing interior. Wander around the back for a great view of the belfry and check out the friendly café across the street.

Cluny and Taizé—Twenty kilometers southwest of Brancion lies the historic town of Cluny. The center of a rich and powerful monastic movement in the Middle Ages is today a pleasant town with very sparse and crumbled remains of its once-powerful abbey. For a new trend in monasticism, consider visiting the booming Christian community of Taizé (teh-zay), just north of Cluny. Brother Roger and his community welcome visitors who'd like to spend a few days getting close to God through meditation, singing, and simple living. Call or write first if you plan to stay overnight. There are dorm beds only. (Taizé Community, 71250 Cluny, tel. 03 85 50 14 14.)

The Hautes-Côtes to Châteauneuf-en-Auxois

This half-day loop trip takes you through untouristed vineyards and pastoral landscapes, along the Burgundy canal, past abbeys, and through medieval villages. (If you're heading to Paris, Châteauneuf-en-Auxois can be done en route or as an overnight stop). It requires a car, the local Michelin map, and navigational patience. From Beaune's ring road, head toward Dijon on N-74. In a few minutes take the Savigny les Beaune turnoff then connect Pernand Vergelesses with the Hautes-Côtes villages of Echevronne, Magny-les Villiers, Villers la Faye, and Marey-les-Fussey. Wineries in these villages offer stress-free tastings. Remember, you should plan on buying when tasting. (More serious tasters should consider these wineries: Lucien Jacob in Echevronne, tel. 03 80 21 91 50, SE; Domaine Thevenot Le Brun in Marey-les-Fussey, tel. 03 80 62 91 64, NSE; and Marcel Fribourg in Villers la Faye, tel. 03 80 62 91 74, NSE.) Then head west over the hills to Pont d'Ouche. At Pont d'Ouche follow the canal toward Châteauneuf-en-Auxois. In about 10 minutes you'll see a stunning view of the towns brooding castle; follow the signs.

Châteauneuf's medieval château towers over the valleys below. The village huddles securely in the shadow of the castle and merits close inspection. Park at the lot in the upper end of the village and stroll down into the village. Don't miss the panoramic viewpoint near the parking lot or the small church at the opposite end of town. Walk into the château's courtyard (the interior is skippable, 25F, daily 10:00–12:00, 14:00–19:00, pick up the English handout).

Following the signs behind Châteauneuf, take the tiny roads to La Bussière and wander into its abbey grounds. The abbey was founded in the 1200s by Cistercian monks but goes largely unnoticed by tourists today. Stroll the lovely gardens, check out the refectory (look for the door in the rear of the main building marked *"Accueil"*; enter and walk upstairs), and consider the cheap 90F dinner (includes wine, must call to reserve, tel. 03 80 49 02 29). Ask for the key to the *vieux pressoir* (old press).

To return to Beaune in scenic fashion, go back to Pont d'Ouche, turn left, and head uphill through Bouilland then downhill through Savigny-les Beaune.

Sleeping and Eating in or near Châteauneuf-en-Auxois
(6F = about $1, zip code: 21320)

Hostellerie du Château**, in Châteauneuf, offers rooms in two locations. Its main building is a better-value "Hotel," and its annex up the street is called "La Residence." Many rooms in the "Hotel" are half-timbered and have views of the château next door; the tiny top-floor doubles will melt a romantic's heart (Db-280–380F, T/QB-430F). "La Residence" has larger, pricier, but very comfortable rooms (D-430F, Tb-480F). The excellent restaurant serves *menus* from 140F (tel. 03 80 49 22 00, fax 03 80 49 21 27).

Annie Bagatelle, at the upper end of the village, has four charming rooms (two with lofts); look for the green plaque (Db-270–330F, tel. 03 80 49 21 00, fax 03 80 49 21 49, SE).

To sleep floating on a luxury hotel barge at two-star hotel prices with views up to Châteauneuf's brooding castle, find the canal-front village of Vandenesse-en-Auxois. Here the *Lady A* barge offers tight yet surprisingly comfortable rooms (Sb-250F, Db-300F, includes breakfast, tel. 03 80 49 26 96, fax 03 80 49 27 00, call way ahead for summer, friendly Lisa SE and cooks an elaborate dinner upon request for 130F, including wine). The *ecluse* (lockhouse) at the bridge offers drinks, snacks, wine tastings, and the good-value *chambre d'hôte* of **chez Monique et Pascal** (Sb/Db-250F, Tb-300F, tel. 03 80 49 27 12, fax 03 80 49 26 05).

Three restaurants offer Burgundian cuisine at fair prices. Try **La Grill du Castel** (meal-sized salads, great escargots, fine *boeuf bourguignonne*, CC:VM, tel. 03 80 49 26 82) and **L'Oree du Bois Creperie** (friendly owner, many inexpensive dishes and a *chambre d'hôte* room, tel. 03 80 49 25 32). **Hostellerie du Château** (see accommodations above) is where I splurge for dinner.

SEMUR-EN-AUXOIS

If you have time for one more night in Burgundy, spend it here. This overlooked town is a delight—particularly at night. There are no important sights to digest—just a seductive jumble of perfectly Burgundian alleys and courtyards perched above the meandering Armancon River, all of this beautifully illuminated after dark. Just 20 minutes by car from the impresssive Abbey of Fontenay, 40 minutes from the famous church in Vezelay, and two hours from Paris, Semur makes an ideal first- or last- night stop on your trip.

The brilliant TI across from Hotel Côte d'Or, at Semur's medieval entry, has information on everything you'll need (Mon–Sat 9:00–19:00, Sun 10:00–12:00, 15:00–18:00, off-season closes earlier and on Sun, 2 place Gaveau, tel. 03 80 97 05 96). Pick up their city- walks brochure, bike routes, and information on the many area sights. The town has two sights: the Church of Notre Dame, which dominates its small square, and the small Municipal Museum. But Semur is best experienced by following the TI's walking tours. The longer yellow route gets you down to the river and up to good views over Semur. Buses connect with every TGV train from nearby Montbard and serve Dijon (3/day, 1 hr).

Sleeping and Eating in Semur-en-Auxois
(6F = about $1, zip code: 21140)

Hotels and restaurants are a good value here. The ideal **Hotel les Cymaises**** surrounds a quiet courtyard, has private parking, and gives three-star comfort for the price of two (Sb-310F, Db-340F, Tb-410F, CC:VM, 7 rue du Renaudot, tel. 03 80 97 21 44, fax 03 80 97 18 23). The simple, quiet, and unspoiled **Hotel des Gourmets*** is equally ideal for those on a budget and has a good restaurant (D-130–160F, Db-210F, T/Q-180F, room for up to 6-320F, CC:VMA, 4 rue Varenne, tel. 03 80 97 09 41, fax 03 80 97 17 95). Semur is surrounded by *chambres d'hôte*; friendly British ex-pat **Roger Collins** has four fine rooms in nearby Villars-Villenotte (Db-300F, tel. 03 80 96 65 11, fax 03 80 97 32 28).

Franco-American-owned **Le Calibressan** offers fine *menus* and coziness from 80F (closed Sun–Mon, 16 rue Fevret, tel. 03 80 97 32 40), and **Les Minimes** is reasonable and adorably French (closed Sun–Mon, 39 rue des Vaux, tel. 03 80 97 26 86). The historic *charcuterie* across from the church is ready for your dinner picnic.

DIJON

Beaune may be Burgundy's wine capital, but prosperous and sprawling Dijon is its undisputed economic powerhouse and cultural capital. This is an untouristed and enjoyable city (pop. 150,000) offering half-timbered houses, bustling pedestrian streets, and interesting churches. Allow half a day for it.

Tourist Information: Dijon has two helpful TIs—one on place Darcy, between the train station and city center (May–Oct daily 9:00–21:00, Nov–Apr 9:00–13:00, 14:00–19:00), and another in the pedestrian-street thick of things (Mon–Fri 9:00–12:00, 13:00–18:00, 34 rue des Forges, tel. 03 80 44 11 44). Pick up the English map (2F) illustrating a walking tour through the nicely restored old-town center and consider the Dijon museum package deal with a self-guided Walkman tour of Dijon (40F, worthwhile only if you have at least a full day for Dijon).

Arrival in Dijon

By Train: Walk out of the station and up avenue Marechal Foch. Stop at the main TI; continue to the arch to enter Dijon's center.

By Car: Enter Dijon following signs to *"centre-ville"* then follow the blue "P" (parking) for place Darcy and park in the underground structure.

Sights—Dijon

▲▲**Dijon Walking Tour**—Use the TI's maps and English explanations and follow an extensive walking tour of old Dijon or save time and focus on the heart of Dijon with an abbreviated walk connecting the sights described below. From the TI (on place Darcy), walk through the arch at the other end of place Darcy and down rue de la Liberté (passing the famous Grey Poupon store on the right, #32) to place Rude, ground zero in Dijon. From here Dijon's sights radiate in all directions.

▲**Église de Notre Dame**—Gushing with three tiers of gargoyles (look up before you enter), this is a fine example of 13th-century Burgundian design. Notice the clock Jacquemart above the right tower; for 600 years it has rung out the time in three-part harmony. Inside you'll find beautiful 13th-century stained glass and a curious, almost haunting, 11th-century *vierge noir* (black virgin) whose hands and feet were sawed off during the Revolution.

Église St. Michel and Musee Rude— Admire the jumble of 16th-century Gothic and Renaissance styles and don't miss the free Musée Rude (next to the church) for a great look at Napoleonic (neoclassical) sculpture—you'll come face-to-face with an overpowering study for the Arc de Triomphe.

▲▲**Musée des Beaux Arts**—This impressive museum occupies one wing of the once-powerful Palace of the Dukes of Burgundy and has a little something for everyone. Besides its fine collection of European paintings from all periods are the Salle des Gardes (home to 2 incredibly ornate tombs; climb the stairs to the balcony for the best angle), the sculptures of Carpeaux and Rude near the Salles des Gardes, a 3-D modern-art room, and the huge model of the Palais des Ducs de Bourgogne (22F, free on Sun; Mon and Wed–Sat 10:00–18:00, Sun 10:00–12:30, 14:00–18:00, closed Tue). The Musée des Beaux Arts occupies part of what was once the Palace of the Dukes of Burgundy. The only interesting vestige that remains is the Tour (tower) Phillipe Bon; you can climb it for fine views over Dijon (15F for 320 steps, escorted trips up the tower leave every 30 min 9:00–17:30, frequently closed).

Sleeping in Dijon
(6F = about $1, zip code 21000)
Stay at **Hotel le Jaquemart** (D-180F, Db-280–350F, 32 rue Verrerie, Dijon 21000, tel. 03 80 60 09 60, fax 03 80 60 09 69).

Transportation Connections—Dijon
Dijon is Burgundy's hub, with excellent bus and rail service.

By train to: Colmar (5/day, 4 hrs, transfer in Belfort), **Beaune** (9/day, 30 min), **Paris'** Gare de Lyon (10 TGVs/day, 95 min), **Arles** (5/day, 5 hrs; other departures possible, with a transfer in Lyon), **Nice** (8/day, 8 hrs, most are direct), **Chamonix** (3/day, 8 hrs, transfer in Lyon and St. Gervais).

By bus: Buses leave from the train station for villages along the wine route and many Burgundian cities; to **Beaune** (3/day, 1 hr), **Semur-en-Auxois** (3/day, 1 hr); tel. 03 80 42 11 00.

ALSACE AND NORTHERN FRANCE

The French province of Alsace stands like a flower-child referee between Germany and France. Bounded by the Rhine on the east and the softly rolling Vosges Mountains on the west, this is a lush land of villages, vineyards, ruined castles, and almost naive cheeriness. Wine is the primary industry, topic of conversation, dominant mouthwash, and perfect excuse for countless festivals.

Because of its location, natural wealth, naked vulnerability, and the fact that Germany thinks the mountains are the natural border while France thinks the Rhine is, Alsace has changed hands several times. Having been a political pawn between Germany and France for 1,000 years, Alsace has a hybrid culture—locals who swear do so bilingually, and the local cuisine features sauerkraut and fine wine. And if you're traveling in December, come here for France's most celebrated Christmas markets and festivals.

The humbling battlefields of Verdun and the bubbly vigor of Reims in northern France are closer to Paris than the Alsace and follow logically only if your next destination is Paris.

Planning Your Time

Set up in or near Colmar. Allow most of a day for Colmar and a full afternoon for the Route du Vin. If you have one day, wander Colmar's sights until after lunch and then set out for the Route du Vin. Strasbourg has a big, impressive church but is otherwise only a bloated version of Colmar. With limited time, I'd skip it. Reims and Verdun are doable by car as stops between Paris and Colmar—if you're speedy. Train travelers with only one day between Colmar and Paris must choose Reims or Verdun.

Reims, Verdun, and Colmar

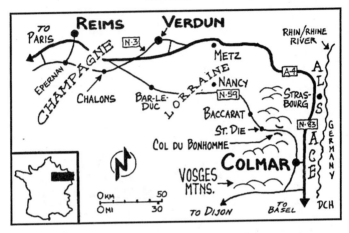

Getting around the Alsace

Trains link Colmar and Strasbourg hourly in 50 minutes. Buses and minivan excursions radiate from Colmar to villages along the Route du Vin, and you can rent bikes in Colmar and Turckheim if you want to pedal the wine route (for details on all of these options, see "Route du Vin," below).

Cuisine Scene—Alsace

Alsatian cuisine is a major tourist attraction in itself. You can't miss the German influence—sausages, potatoes, onions, and sauerkraut are everywhere. For dinner, look for *choucroute garni* (sauerkraut and sausage—although it seems a shame to eat it in a fancy restaurant), the more traditionally Alsatian *baeckeanoffe* (potato, meat, and onion stew), *rösti* (an oven-baked potato and cheese dish), fresh trout, and foie gras. At lunch, or for a lighter dinner, try a *tarte à l'oignon* (like an onion quiche but better) or *tarte flambée* (like a thin-crust pizza with onion and bacon bits). If you're picnicking, buy some smelly Münster cheese. Dessert specialties are *glace Kugelhopf* (a light cake mixed with raisins, almonds, dried fruit, and cherry liqueur) and *tarte Alsacienne* (fruit tart).

Alsatian Wines

Alsatian wines are named for their grapes, unlike in Burgundy or Provence, where wines are commonly named after villages, or in Bordeaux, where wines are commonly named after châteaus. White wines dominate in the Alsace; the following wines are made entirely of that grape variety: Sylvaner (fairly light, fruity, and inexpensive), Riesling (more robust than Sylvaner but drier than the German style you're probably used to), Gerwürtztraminer (spicy, with a powerful bouquet; good with pâtés and local cheeses), Muscat (very dry, with a distinctive bouquet and taste; best as a before-dinner wine), Tokay/Pinot Gris (more full-bodied than Riesling but fine with many local main courses), Pinot Noir (the local red is overpriced; very light and fruity and generally served chilled), and the tasty Crèmant d'Alsace (the region's good and inexpensive champagne). You'll also see eaux-de-vie, powerful fruit-flavored brandies; try the *framboise* (raspberry) flavor.

COLMAR

There isn't a straight street in Colmar. Thankfully, it's a lovely town to be lost in. Navigate by the high church steeples and the helpful signs directing visitors to the various sights.

Colmar is a well-pickled old place of 70,000 residents offering heavyweight sights in a warm small-town package. Historic beauty was usually a poor excuse to be spared the ravages of World War II, but it worked for Colmar. The American and British military were careful not to bomb the half-timbered old burghers' houses characteristic red- and green-tiled roofs, and cobbled lanes of Alsace's most beautiful city.

Today Colmar thrives with colorful buildings, impressive art treasures, and popular Alsatian cuisine. Schoolgirls park their rickety horse carriages in front of the city hall, ready to give visitors a clip-clop tour of Old Town. Antique shops welcome browsers, and hotel managers run down the sleepy streets to pick up fresh croissants in time for breakfast.

Orientation

For tourists, the town center is place Unterlinden (a 15-min walk from the train station), where you'll find the TI, a major museum, and a huge and handy Monoprix department store and supermarket (Mon–Sat 8:30–20:30, closed Sun). Every city bus starts or finishes on place Unterlinden.

Colmar is most crowded from May through September. The impressive music festival crowds hotels the first two weeks of July, the local wine festival rages for 10 days in early August, and Sauerkraut Days are celebrated in October. Open-air markets bustle next to the Dominican and St. Martin Churches on Thursdays and Saturdays.

Tourist Information: The TI is next to the Unterlinden Museum on place Unterlinden. Pick up a city map, a Route du Vin map, and *Colmar Actualités*, a booklet with bus schedules. Ask about concerts, wine festivals, and Colmar's Folklore Tuesdays (with folk dancing at 20:30 every Tue mid-May–mid-Sept on place de l'Ancienne). The TI reserves hotel rooms and has *chambre* *d'hôte* listings for the region and Colmar (Apr–Oct Mon–Sat 9:00–18:00, Sun 10:00–14:00; Nov–Mar Mon–Sat 9:00–12:00, 14:00–18:00, Sun 10:00–14:00, tel. 03 89 20 68 92). A public WC is 20 yards to the left of the TI.

Arrival in Colmar

By Train or Bus: To reach Colmar's city center from the train station (buses stop here for Route du Vin villages; lockers available at train station), walk straight out, turn left on avenue de la République, and keep walking. Allow 15 minutes. Buses #1, #2, and #3 each go from the station to the TI (about 5.60F, pay the driver). Allow 50F for a taxi to a hotel in central Colmar.

    By Car: Follow signs to *centre-ville* then place Rapp. There are several handy pay lots (under place Rapp) and (for now) a huge free lot at parking du Musée Unterlinden (across from Primo 99 hotel).

Helpful Hints

Tours: The TI organizes walking tours of Old Town for 25F and of the Unterlinden Museum for 20F (daily in summer, weekends only in other months). You can hire a private guide for a walking tour (470F, ask at TI). A minibus tour company, Les Circuits d'Alsace, organizes day trips around the Alsace (across from train station at 6 place de la Gare, tel. 03 89 41 90 88).

    Laundromat: The only central Laundromat is near Maison Jund (see "Sleeping in Colmar," below) at 1 rue Ruest, just off the pedestrian street rue Vauban (usually open daily 8:00–21:00).

    Internet Access: Cafe de Haut Rhin (15-min walk from TI, 76 route d'Ingersheim, tel. 03 89 79 17 47).

Self-Guided Tour of Colmar's Old Town

This walk is ideal after dark, when many of Colmar's pedestrian streets and important monuments are beautifully illuminated by mood-setting colored lights. Look for handy information plaques with English explanations at various points throughout this walk.

    The importance of 15th- to 17th-century Colmar is clear as you wander its pedestrian-friendly old center, which is decorated with 45 buildings classified as historic monuments. Back in feudal times, most of Europe was fragmented into chaotic little princedoms and dukedoms. Merchant-dominated cities, which were natural proponents of the formation of large nation-states, banded together to form "trading leagues." The Hanseatic League was the super-league of northern Europe. Prosperous Colmar was a member of a smaller league of 10 Alsatian cities called the Decapolis (founded 1354). Delegates of this group met in Colmar's Old Custom House.

    Start your tour at the **Old Custom's House** (Koifhus). Walk under it and you'll find yourself facing the place de l'Ancienne Douane and a Bertholdi statue—arm raised, à la *Statue of Liberty*.

Colmar

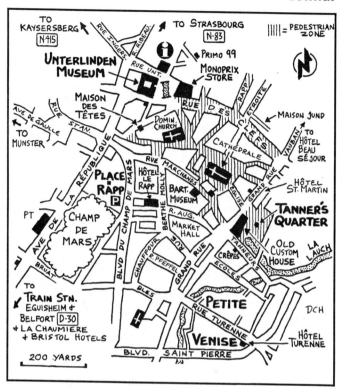

The place de l'Ancienne Douane is the festive site of outdoor wine tasting many summer evenings. The soaring, half-timbered commotion of higgledy-piggledy rooftops just beyond marks the **Tanners' Quarters**. These 17th- and 18th-century rooftops competed to get space in the sun to dry their freshly tanned hides. Wander down to the end of rue des Tanneurs, turn right, and take the first left along the stream and you'll come to the old market hall (fish, produce, and other products were brought here by flat-bottomed boat). Cross the canal and turn right and you'll enter "la Petite Venise" quarter, a bundle of Colmar's most colorful houses lining the small canal. This area is well lit and even cuter at night.

Double back to the Old Custom House via rue des Écoles. From the Custom House, walk up rue des Marchands (Merchant's Street). Those overhanging roofs you're walking under were a medieval tax dodge. Since houses were taxed on square footage at street level, owners would expand tax-free up and over the street. In two blocks you'll come face to face with the Pfister House, a richly decorated merchant's house from 1537 with an external spiral staircase turret and painted walls showing the city folk's taste for Renaissance humanism (the wine shop on the ground floor is Colmar's best). The man carved into the side of the building next door (to the left) was a sheet maker; he's shown holding a bar, Colmar's measure of about one meter. (In the Middle Ages it was common for cities to have their own length for a meter.) One more block on the left is the Bartholdi Museum (described below). A passage to the right leads to Colmar's Cathedral St. Martin. Compare this beautiful soaring structure with the typically sober Dominican Church (housing Schongauer's *Virgin in the Rosebush*, described below), a few blocks toward the TI. The House of Heads on rue des Têtes near the TI is Colmar's other famous merchant's house; it was built in 1609 and is decorated with 105 faces and masks. From here it's a short walk to the TI and the Unterlinden Museum.

Sights—Colmar

▲▲▲**Unterlinden Museum**—Colmar's touristic claim to fame, this is one of my favorite museums in Europe. Its extensive yet manageable collection ranges from Roman Colmar to medieval wine-making exhibits and from traditional wedding dresses to paintings that give vivid insight into the High Middle Ages.

The highlight of the museum (and, for me, the city) is Grünewald's gripping *Isenheim Altarpiece*, actually a series of three different paintings on hinges that pivot like shutters (study the little model on the wall, explained in English). Designed to help people in a medieval hospital endure horrible skin diseases (such as St. Anthony's Fire, later called rye ergotism) long before the age of painkillers, it's one of the most powerful paintings ever produced.

Stand like medieval peasant in front of the centerpiece and let the agony and suffering of the Crucifixion drag its fingers down your face. The point—Jesus' suffering—is drilled home: the weight of his body bending the crossbar, his elbows pulled from their sockets by the weight of his dead body, his mangled feet, the grief on Mary's face. In hopes that the intended viewers—the hospital's patients—would know that Jesus understands their suffering, he was even painted looking like he, too, had a skin disease. Study the faces and the Christian symbolism.

The three scenes of the painting changed with the seasons of the church year. The happy ending—a psychedelic explosion of Resurrection joy—is the spiritual equivalent of jumping from the dentist's chair directly into a Jacuzzi. The last two panels, showing the meeting of St. Paul the hermit and St. Anthony, are the product of a fertile imagination and the stuff nightmares are made of.

There's more to the museum. Ringing the peaceful cloister is a fine series of medieval church paintings and sculpture and a room filled with old wine presses. Downstairs you'll find Roman and prehistoric artifacts. The upstairs contains local and folk history, with everything from medieval armor to old-time toys (35F, Apr–Oct daily 9:00–18:00, Nov–Mar Wed–Mon 9:00–17:00, closed Tue, tel. 03 89 41 89 23).

▲▲**Dominican Church**—Here is another medieval mind blower. In Colmar's Église des Dominicains, you'll find Martin Schongauer's angelically beautiful *Virgin in the Rosebush* (from 1473 but looking like it was painted yesterday) holding court centerstage. Here, Mary is shown as a welcoming mother. Jesus clings to her, reminding the viewer of the possibility of an intimate relationship with Mary. The Latin on her halo reads: "Pick me also for your child, O very Holy Virgin." Rather than telling a particular Bible story, this is a general scene...designed to meet the personal devotional needs of any worshiper. Here, nature is not a backdrop. Mary and Jesus are encircled by it. Schongauer's robins, sparrows, and goldfinches bring extra life to an already impressively natural rosebush. The contrast provided by the simple Dominican setting heightens the flamboyance of this late-Gothic masterpiece. Dominican churches were particularly austere, as the 13th-century Catholic Church was combating a wave of heretical movements, such as the Cathars, whose message was a simpler faith (8F, daily 10:00–18:00). This Dominican austerity is more apparent after a visit to Colmar's fancier—and Franciscan—St. Martin's cathedral.

Bartholdi Museum—This little museum recalls the life and work of the local boy who gained fame by sculpting the *Statue of Liberty*. Several of his statues grace Colmar's squares (20F, Wed–Mon 10:00–12:00, 14:00–18:00, closed Tue and Jan–Feb, in the heart of the Old Town at 30 rue des Marchands).

Sleeping in Colmar
(6F = about $1, zip code: 68000)

Sleep Code: **S** = Single, **D** = Double/Twin, **T** = Triple, **Q** = Quad, **b** = bathroom, **t** = toilet only, **s** = shower only, **CC** = Credit Card (Visa, MasterCard, Amex), **SE** = Speaks English, **NSE** = No English, * = French hotel rating system (0–4 stars).

Hotels are more expensive here than in other areas of France and are jammed on weekends in May, June, September, and October. July and August are busy, but there are always rooms—somewhere. Should you have trouble finding a room in Colmar, look in a nearby village where small hotels and bed-and-breakfasts are plentiful and see my recommendations for "Sleeping in Eguisheim" (under "Route du Vin," below).

Maison Jund offers my favorite budget beds in Colmar. This easygoing B&B is the home of a wine maker. This ramshackle yet magnificent half-timbered home feels like a medieval treehouse soaked in wine and filled with flowers. The simple but comfortable rooms are spacious and equipped with kitchenettes. Rooms are generally available only from April to mid-September, with the cheapest rooms available only in summer (D-170F, Db/Tb-210–250F, 12 rue de l'Ange, tel. 03 89 41 58 72, fax 03 89 23 15 83, e-mail: mjund@terre-net.fr). Leave your car at the lot across from the Primo 99 hotel and walk from Unterlinden Museum past Monoprix and veer left on rue des Clefs. This is not a hotel, so there is no real reception, though friendly Myriam (SE) seems to be around, somewhere, most of the time. You can enjoy a friendly wine tasting here without leaving sight of your bedroom door.

Hôtel Le Rapp**, just off place Rapp, with 40 modern and slightly tight rooms, a small basement pool, a sauna, a hamman, and a cozy indoor/outdoor bar-café, is the best-located two-star hotel in Colmar. It's well run and family friendly, with a park one block away (Sb-305–335F, Db-395F, extra person-80F, good buffet breakfasts, CC:VMA, 1 rue Berthe-Molley, tel. 03 89 41 62 10, fax 03 89 24 13 58, www.rapp-hotel.com, SE). Its restaurant serves a classy Alsatian *menu* with impeccable service (closed Fri).

Hôtel Turenne** is a fine value and has 83 rooms in a historic building a 10-minute walk from the city center. It's on a busy street with easy parking. Rooms are bright, pastel, and comfortable (Sb-260–400F, street-side Db-280F, quiet-side Db-400F, Tb-400, family-friendly studios-620F, parking-20F, CC:VMA, from the train station walk up avenue Raymond Poincaré and turn left on rue des Americains, 10 route du Bale, tel. 03 89 41 12 26, fax 03 89 41 27 64, www.turenne.com, SE). A third of its rooms are nonsmoking.

Hotel St. Martin***, next to the Custom House, is a classy family-run place with a history as a coaching inn (since 1361). It's small and has Old World-yet-modern rooms woven into its antique frame. Half of its 24 rooms are in the annex, opposite a peaceful courtyard. While just as comfortable, these cheaper rooms have showers instead of tubs and no elevator or air-conditioning (Sb-320–550F, Db-360–750F, Tb-570–830F, CC:VMA, free public parking nearby, 38 Grand Rue, tel. 03 89 24 11 51, fax 03 89 23 47 78, www.hotel-saint-martin.com, the Winterstein family SE). For about the same money without a hint of the Old World or a family, you can sleep comfortably and park easily in one of two central and modern **Hotel Mercures***** (Sb-505F, Db-550F, extra person-100F, CC:VMA, air-con), one in Colmar's central park just off place Rapp on 2 avenue de la Marne (tel. 03 89 41 54 54, fax 03 89 23 93 76), the other near Unterlinden Museum on 5 rue Golbery (tel. 03 89 41 71 71, fax 03 89 23 82 71, SE).

Primo 99**, near Unterlinden Museum, is a French prefab hotel—a modern, cheap, efficient, bright, nothing-but-the-plastic-and-concrete-basics place to sleep for those to whom ambience is a four-letter word. It's one of Colmar's few budget deals (S/D/T-160F, Sb-270F, Db-300F, 3rd person-50F, CC:VM, 5 rue des Ancêtres, free parking in the big square in front, rooms held until 18:30 if you call, friendly staff, tel. 03 89 24 22 24, fax 03 89 24 55 96, e-mail: hotel-primo-99@rmcnet.fr, SE). Half the beds have footboards—a problem if you're taller than 6'2".

Hotel Hagueneck** is the cheapest two-star place in Colmar, with comfortable rooms in a small manor home. It's a few minutes' drive from the station over the tracks on the road to Epinal and a 20-minute walk from the city center (Db-230F, Tb-300F, Qb-350F, CC:M, 83 avenue du General-de-Gaulle, tel. 03 89 80 68 98, fax 03 89 79 55 29).

Hôtel Beau Séjour** is upscale and cushy, with easy parking and a well-respected restaurant (Db-320–520F, extra person-100F, a 15-min walk from center, 27 rue du Ladhof, tel. 03 89 41 37 16, fax 03 89 41 43 07).

Sleeping near the Train Station

Hotel Bristol*** couldn't be closer to the station and, in spite of its Best Western plaque, is Old World with grand public spaces and comfortable rooms (Sb-360–560F, Db-400–750F, most about 450F, CC:VMA, 7 place de la Gare, tel. 03 89 23 59 59, fax 03 89 23 92 26).

La Chaumière*, on a big street two blocks from the station, is above a truly French café. The simple, sleepable rooms surround a courtyard and are much quieter off the street (S-170F, Sb-240F, D-180F, Db-220–240F, CC:VM, walk straight out of the station and turn left on avenue de la République, 74 avenue de la République, tel. 03 89 41 08 99).

The best cheap beds in Colmar are located in a fine mansion at **Maison des Jeunes** (46F beds in large dorms, sheets-20F, meals-60F; office open 7:00–12:00, 14:00–23:00; walk straight out of station, take the 2nd right after the light, 17 rue Schlumberger, tel. 03 89 41 26 87, fax 03 89 23 20 16, SE). The **hostel** is less central (dorm bed-68F, sheets-20F, includes breakfast, cheap dinners, office open 7:00–9:00, 17:00–23:00, 15-min walk from station, turn left out of the station and cross over the tracks or take bus #4, 2 rue Pasteur, tel. 03 89 80 57 39, fax 03 89 80 76 16).

Eating in Colmar

For reasonably priced, good, traditional Alsatian cuisine, try **La Maison Rouge** (78F and 95F *menus*, closed Sun, 9 rue des Écoles, tel. 03 89 23 53 22). Nearby, **La Taverne** serves fine *tartes flambées* and other regional specialities (closed Sun, 2 impasse de la Maison Rouge, tel. 03 89 41 70 33). Join the fun in wood-cozy ambience at **Winstub Schwendi**; try one of their robust 50F Swiss *rösti* plates (facing the Old Custom House at 3 Grand Rue). For crêpes and salads with atmosphere, eat at **Crêperie Tom Pouce** (daily, 10 rue des Tanneurs). For canal-front dining, head into La Petite Venise to the bridge on rue Turenne, where you'll find a pizzeria, a *winstub*/café (both cheap), and a fine but somewhat pricey canal-level restaurant, **Les Bateliers.**

Hôtel Restaurant Le Rapp is my dress-up, high-cuisine splurge. I comb my hair, spit out my gum, and savor a slow, elegant meal served with grace and fine Alsatian wine (*menus* start at 100F, the *baeckeanoffe* is great, good salads, closed Fri, air-con, 1 rue Berthe-Molley, tel. 03 89 41 62 10, SE).

Patisserie Salon de Thé Kuhn, just across the photo-perfect bridge in La Petite Venise on place des Six Montagnes Noires, serves good quiche and salads (open until 19:00, closed Mon).

Transportation Connections—Colmar

By train to: Strasbourg (hrly, 50 min), **Reims** (3/day, 5–7 hrs, with probable transfers in Strasbourg, Nancy, and Chalons-sur-Marne or Epernay), **Dijon/Beaune** (5/day to Dijon, 4 hrs, transfer in Besançon; add 30 min to Beaune), **Paris'** Gare de l'Est (10/day, 5.5 hrs, transfer in Strasbourg or Mulhouse), **Amboise** (8/day, 9 hrs, transfer in Paris), **Basel,** Switzerland (8/day, 1 hr), **Karlsruhe,** Germany (3/day, 90 min, via Strasbourg; from Karlsruhe it's 90 min to Frankfurt, 3 hrs to Munich).

Route du Vin (The Wine Road)

Alsace's Route du Vin is an asphalt ribbon tying 90 miles of vineyards, villages, and feudal fortresses into an understandably popular tourist package. The generally dry, sunny climate has made for good wine and happy tourists since Roman days. Colmar and Eguisheim are ideally located for exploring the 30,000 acres of vineyards blanketing the hills from Marlenheim to Thann. If you have only a day, focus on towns within easy striking range of Colmar. Top ones are Eguisheim, Kaysersberg, too-popular Riquewihr, Hunawhir, and Turckheim. Get a map of the Route du Vin from any TI.

Throughout Alsace you'll see "Dégustation" signs. *Dégustation* means "come on in and taste," and *gratuit* means "free;" though many charge a small fee. Most towns have wineries that give tours; those in Eguisheim and Riquewihr are good. The modern cooperatives at Bennwhir, Hunawhir, and Ribbeauville, created after the destruction of World War II, provide a good look at a more-modern and efficient method of production. Most villages have many smaller, family-owned wineries eager to impress you with their wines. The Colmar TI can give you information or even telephone a winery for you to confirm tour times. You may have to wait for a group and tag along for a tour and free tasting at the big places. Be sure to try the local spicy specialty, Gewürztraminer. Crèmant,

Alsace's Wine Road

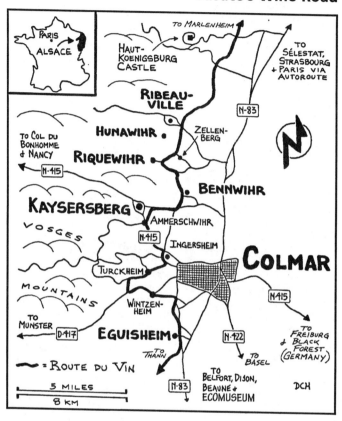

the Alsatian "champagne," is very good—and much cheaper. The French term for headache, if you really get "Alsaced," is *mal à la tête*.

Getting around the Wine Road

Pick up a Michelin regional map before heading out.

By Bus: Public buses connect Colmar's train station with most of the villages along the Route du Vin. The schedules are fairly convenient, less so on Sunday (from Colmar to Eguisheim: 6/day, 5 min; Kaysersberg: hrly, 30 min; Riquewihr, Bennwhir, Hunawhir, and Ribeauville: 6/day, 30–45 min), Turckheim: 6/day, 20 min). Get schedules from the TI and buy tickets from the driver.

By Bike: The Wine Road's level terrain makes biking a good option. You can rent a bike in Colmar at Cycles Geiswiller

(6 blvd. du Champs du Mars, tel. 03 89 41 30 59), at Cyclotheque (31 route d'Igersheim, tel. 03 89 79 14 18), or on the Route du Vin in Turckheim (84 Grand Rue, tel. 03 89 27 06 36), saving you the ride out of Colmar. Turckheim, Kaysersberg, Riquewihr and Hunawhir make good biking destinations (get advice from a bike shop; pick up a good map and leave Colmar on the bike path following directions under "By Car," below).

By Car: To reach the Wine Road, leave Colmar from the station following signs to Epinal; in Ingersheim turn right (north) on D-10 for Riquewihr, Hunwihr, and Ribbeauville or follow N-415 to Kayserberg. You'll soon see signs to the Route du Vin. For Eguisheim, leave Colmar on N-83 to Belfort.

By Foot: A few well-signed walking trails connect Route du Vin villages through the vineyards (get info at local TI), and hikers can climb to the higher ruined castles of the Vosges Mountains (Eguisheim and Ribbeauville are good bases). Kayserberg to Riquewihr is a pleasant one- to two-hour walk (return by bus).

Eguisheim

Just a few kilometers (a flat and easy bike ride) from Colmar, this flowery scenic town is ideal for a relaxing lunch and makes a good small-town base for exploring the Alsace. It's ideal by car (easy parking) and accessible by bus (6/day, 5 min, departs from Colmar's train station). The **TI** on the street that bisects the town has information on accommodations, festivals, walks in the vineyards, and hikes into the Vosges (Apr–Sept daily 9:00–12:00, 14:00–18:00; Oct–Mar closed Sun–Mon, 22 Grand Rue, tel. 03 89 23 40 33). Eguisheim is best explored by walking around its narrow circular road (rue des Remparts) and then cutting through the middle. Visit the newly renovated church and one of Eguisheim's countless cozy wineries or the big and modern Wine Cooperative (Wolfberger, Cave Vinicole d'Eguisheim, daily 10:00–12:00, 14:00–19:00, folklore and tastings in summer on Wed 17:00–19:00, 6 Grand Rue, tel. 03 89 22 20 20). If you have a car, follow signs up to Les Husseren and Les 5 Châteaux for a pleasant walk to the ruined castle towers and a good view of the Vosges above and vineyards below. Without wheels, stroll into the vineyards above Eguisheim for good views.

Sleeping and Eating in Eguisheim
(6F = about $1, zip code: 68420)

Chambres d'Hôte: While none of the owners speak English, they're creative at communicating. Please remember to cancel if you reserved and can't make it.

Your Alsatian grandmother **Madame Hertz-Meyers** welcomes you with big rooms in a mansion surrounded by vineyards only 75 yards from the village center. Rooms in the main house are ideal for families and are better than her two modern apartments (Sb-235F, Db-290–320F, Tb-375F, includes breakfast, 3 rue Riesling, no sign, tel. 03 89 23 67 74, fax 03 89 23 99 23). **Madame Dirringer's** five spacious rooms surround a traditional courtyard (Db-165–185F, breakfast-30F, 11 rue Riesling, tel. 03 89 41 71 87). It's hard to imagine a better location, more comfortable rooms, or a more charming owner than **Monique Freudenreich** (Db-245F, includes breakfast, 4 cour Unterlinden, one block from TI, tel. & fax 03 89 23 16 44). Gentle **Madame Bombenger's** modern home has nice views into the vineyards and over Eguisheim (D-160F, Db-240F, 3 rue de Trois Pierres, tel. 03 89 23 71 19). The **Stockys** offer comfortable rooms (Db-155–175F, 24 rue de Colmar, tel. 03 89 41 68 04).

Hotels: Eguisheim also has hotels for every taste and budget. The simple, funky, and fun **Auberge de Trois Chateaux** is creaky, wood-beamed, and unpolished and has sleepable rooms, each with a kitchenette and shower; WCs are down the hall (Ds-160–210F, 26 Grand Rue, tel. 03 89 23 11 22). At the other extreme, snazzy **Hostellerie du Chateau***** is ideally located in front of the church and provides stylish, contemporary luxury (Sb-410F, Db-500–580F, 2 rue du Château St. Leon IX, tel. 03 89 23 72 00, fax 03 89 23 79 99). The picturesque **Auberge Alsacienne***** gives three stars for the price of two (Db-300–420F, 12 Grand Rue, tel. 03 89 41 50 20, fax 03 89 23 89 32). Overlooking the village, the modern yet cozy **Hotel St. Hubert***** offers polished comfort, an indoor pool and sauna, vineyards out your window, and a free pickup at Colmar's train station (Db-450–580F, extra bed-100F, 6 rue des Trois Pierres, tel. 03 89 41 40 50, fax 03 89 41 46 88, www.alsanet.com).

Eating in Eguisheim: Auberge de Trois Chateaux is cozy and ideal for an inexpensive dinner (off-season closed Tue–Wed) and **Auberge Alsacienne** serves fine local specialities for moderate prices (see above, for both). **Auberge du Rempart** has good *tarte flambée* and outdoor tables surrounding a fountain with monster fish (near TI, 3 rue du Rempart Sud).

More Sights—The Wine Road

Kaysersberg—Albert Schweitzer's hometown is cute but feels overrun much of the year. Climb to the castle (under long-term renovation), browse the boutiques, and enjoy the colorful jumble of 15th-century houses and the stork's nest near the fortified town bridge. Drop by Dr. Schweitzer's house (10F, closed 12:00–14:00), check out the church and its notable 400-year-old altarpiece, taste some wine, and wander into nearby vineyards. Kaysersberg's TI is inside the Hôtel de Ville (tel. 03 89 78 22 78). Walking trails through the vineyards to Riquewhir (1.5–2.5 hrs) and other Route du Vin towns are well marked; walk under the arch (10 yards to the right of the TI as you face it) and you'll see signs.

Turckheim—This pleasant town, with a small castle, is just enough off the beaten path to be overlooked.

Riquewihr—Overly picturesque, this walled village is crammed with tourists shops, cafés, galleries, cobblestones, and flowers. Try the excellent tasting and tour at Caves Dopff et Irion (Cour du Château, tel. 03 89 47 92 51, TI tel. 03 89 47 80 80).

Zellenburg—This town has an impressive setting and is worth a quick stop for the views from either side of its narrow perch.

Hunawhir—This bit of wine-soaked Alsatian cuteness is far less visited than its more famous neighbors and comes complete with a 16th-century fortified church that today is shared by Catholics and Protestants (the Catholics are buried next to the church; the Protestants are buried outside the church wall). Park below the church at the small lot with picnic tables and follow the trail up to the church then loop back through the village. Your kids will enjoy Hunawhir's small stork park (Parc des Cygognes, 35F, Apr–Nov daily 10:00–12:00, 14:00–18:00, other animals take part in the afternoon shows). If you spend the night, try the charming and creaky **Relais du Poete** (Db-230F, fun restaurant and outdoor terrace, 6 rue du Nord, tel. 03 89 73 60 14, fax 03 89 73 36 86,). You'll also find a few *chambres d'hôte* and a good wine cooperative in Hunawhir.

▲▲**Eco Musée**—In 1971 a group of private citizens got together to oppose any further destruction of traditional architecture and created this impressive, outdoor, open-air museum. Every building at the museum was originally slated for demolition; each was moved here piece by piece. You'll stroll through an entire Alsatian town of buildings from the 1500s to the 1800s and witness about 20 different demonstrations of everything from barrel making and bread making to blacksmiths, steam tractors, and a puppet theater. While the demonstrations and virtually all posted information are in French, you'll get a good English handout explaining the buildings and a great map with demonstration/show (*animation/spectacle*) times, which are generally easy to follow (adults-78F, kids 6–16-48F, under 6-free, Apr–Sept daily 9:30–18:00, 9:00–19:00 in summer, Oct 10:00–17:00, closed in winter, about 20 min south of Colmar in Ungersheim, well-signed off the N-83, tel. 03 89 74 44 74).

STRASBOURG

Sitting right on the Rhine River, Strasbourg provides an urban blend of Franco-Germanic culture, architecture, and ambience. It's home to the European Parliament and a fascinating *vielle ville* (old city) of pedestrian streets, canals, and half-timbered homes.

Arrival in Strasbourg: The TI (daly 9:00–18:00, tel. 03 88 52 28 28) is in front of the train station (park there). Pick up a city map and walk 15 minutes straight up rue Marie Kuss to rue Gutenberg to find the center.

Sights—Strasbourg

▲▲**Strasbourg Cathedral**—This uniquely Alsatian cathedral, with its tall, slender spire; multicolored tile; and red stone roof is well worth a side trip. Approach the cathedral on foot from place Gutenberg and rue Mercière. It's particularly stunning in the late-afternoon light. Don't miss the Doomsday pillar, 15th-century astronomical clock inside, or climb up the tower. (10F, 8:30–18:30). When you're done, take a stroll through Strasbourg's enchanting La Petite France (follow signs from place Gutenberg).

Transportation Connections—Strasbourg

Side trip from Colmar or stop on the way to or from Paris.

By train to: Colmar (hrly, 50 min), **Paris'** Gare de l'Est (10/day, 4.5 hrs), **Karlsruhe,** Germany (3/day, 50 min), **Basel,** Switzerland (hrly, 2 hrs).

VERDUN

Little remains in Europe today to remind us of World War I, but Verdun provides a fine tribute to the million-plus lives lost in the battles fought here. While the lunar landscape of World War I is now forested over, countless craters and trenches are visible (look into the woods as you drive)—along with millions of undetonated bombs in vast cordoned-off areas. Drive through the eerie moguls surrounding Verdun, stopping at melted-sugar-cube forts and plaques marking where towns once existed. With two hours and a car or a full day and a bike, you can see the most stirring sights and appreciate the awesome scale of the battles. The town of Verdun is not your destination but a springboard into the nearby battlefields.

Tourist Information: The TI is on place Nation (May–Sept daily 8:30–18:30, otherwise closed 12:00–14:00 and at 18:00; closes at 17:30 in winter; tel. 03 29 86 14 18).

Arrival in Verdun

By Train: Walk straight out of the station and down avenue Garibaldi to the town center.

By Car: Follow signs to *centre-ville*, place Nation, and Porte Chatel and you'll pass the TI just before crossing the river.

Getting around the Verdun Battlefield

The TI has good maps of the battlefields. French-language mini-van tours of the battle sites are available June through September and leave the TI around 14:00 (occasionally in English—ask). You can rent a bike opposite Verdun's train station at **Cycles Flavenot** (tel. 03 29 86 12 43). To reach the battlefields by car or bike (about 20 miles round-trip), take the D-112 from Verdun (look for signs to Douaumont) and then take the D-913 to Douaumont.

The battlefield remains are situated on two sides of the Meuse

Verdun

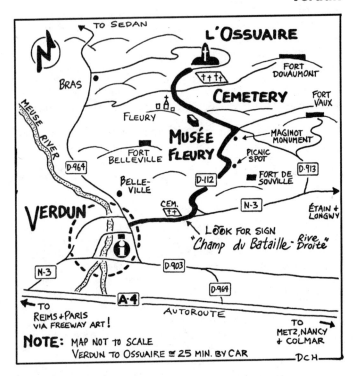

TO SEDAN

L'OSSUAIRE

N

FORT
DOUAUMONT

BRAS

† † ††

CEMETERY

FORT
VAUX

FLEURY

MEUSE RIVER

MAGINOT
MONUMENT

MUSÉE
FLEURY

FORT
BELLEVILLE

PICNIC
SPOT

D-964

D-913

D-112

FORT DE
SOUVILLE

BELLE-
VILLE

VERDUN

CEM.
††

N-3

ÉTAIN +
LONGWY

LOOK FOR SIGN
"*Champ du Bataille* - Rive Droite"

i

D-903

N-3

D-964

A-4

AUTOROUTE

TO
REIMS + PARIS
VIA FREEWAY ART!

TO
METZ, NANCY
+ COLMAR

NOTE: MAP NOT TO SCALE
VERDUN TO OSSUAIRE ≅ 25 MIN. BY CAR

— DCH—

River; the Rive Droite has more sights. By following signs to Fort Douaumont and the Ossuaire, you'll pass the Musée Fleury.

Sights—Verdun
▲▲**Battlegrounds**—The most compelling sights are the Mémorial-Musée de Fleury, the Ossuaire, and Fort Douaumont. Start with the **Mémorial-Musée de Fleury,** built around an impressive recreation of a battlefield, and its hard-hitting photos, weapon displays, and a worthwhile 15-minute movie narrated in English with headphones (20F, Mar–Dec 9:00–18:00, closes at 17:00 in winter). The museum is built on the site of a village (Fleury) that was obliterated during the fighting.

Don't miss **l'Ossuaire,** the tomb of the 130,000 French and Germans whose last homes were the muddy trenches of Verdun (Mar–early Sept daily 9:00–18:00, otherwise closes 12:00–14:00 and at 17:30). Look through the low windows for a bony memorial to those whose political and military leaders asked them to make the "ultimate sacrifice" for their countries. Enter the monument and experience a humbling and moving tribute. Ponder a war that left half of all the men in France aged 15 to 30 dead or wounded. See the thought-provoking 20-minute film (16F, theater in the basement, ask for the English version, closed Nov–Mar). You can climb the tower for a territorial view (6F). The little 1F picture boxes in the gift shop are worth a look if you don't visit the Mémorial-Musée de Fleury (turn through all the old photos before the time expires).

Before leaving, walk to the cemetery and listen for the eerie buzz of silence and peace. You can visit the nearby **Tranchée des Baionnettes**, where an entire company of soldiers was buried alive in their trench (the soldier's bayonets remained above ground until recently), or, even better, visit the nearby **Fort Douaumont**, a strategic command center for both sides at various times. It's more interesting from the outside than the inside (walk on top to appreciate the strategic setting of this fort and notice the round, iron-gun emplacements that could rise and revolve). A walk inside (15F) completes the picture, with long damp corridors and a German memorial where 1,600 Germans were killed by a single blast. Halfway between the Ossuaire and Fort Douaumont (on either side of the road) are fine trenches.

Citadelle Souterraine—This is a disappointing train ride through the tunnels of the French Command in downtown Verdun. While it tries to re-create the Verdun scene, it's not worth your time.

Transportation Connections—Verdun
By train to: Colmar (3/day, 5–7 hrs, transfers in Chalons-sur-Marne and Strasbourg), **Reims** (4/day, 3 hrs, transfer in Chalons-sur-Marne), **Paris'** Gare de l'Est (5/day, 3 hrs, transfer in Chalons-sur-Marne).

REIMS
Deservedly famous for its cathedral and champagne, contemporary Reims (rhymes with France) is a modern, bustling city with little character. Just 90 minutes from Paris by car or train, it makes a good day trip or handy stop for travelers en route elsewhere. Most sights of interest (champagne caves included) are within a 20-minute walk from the cathedral.

Tourist Information: The TI is just to the left of the cathedral as you face the front (Easter–June daily 9:00–19:30, less off-season, free map shows Champagne caves, tel. 03 26 77 45 25). Ask about tours of the cathedral in English (summer only, 90 min); self-guided Walkman tour available any time).

Arrival in Reims
By Train: Walk out of the station, look up, and follow the cathedral's spire. It's a 15-minute walk.

By Car: Just follow the *"cathédrale"* signs and park nearby (easiest behind the cathedral).

Sights—Reims

▲▲▲**Cathedral**—The cathedral of Reims is a glorious example of Gothic architecture, with the best west portal (inside and outside) anywhere. (Since medieval churches always face east, you enter the west portal.) The coronation place of French kings and queens for 800 years, it houses many treasures, great medieval stained glass, and a lovely modern set of Marc Chagall stained-glass windows from 1974 on the east end. Joan of Arc led a reluctant Charles VII here to be coronated in 1429; the event rallied the French to push the English out of France and end the Hundred Years' War. English explanations are along the right aisle (daily 7:30–19:30).

▲**Champagne Tours**—Reims is the capital of the Champagne region, and while the bubbly stuff's birthplace was closer to Epernay, you can tour a champagne cave right in Reims. All charge for tastings (20–30F, daily, most close 12:00–14:00 and at about 17:00). The **Taittinger Company** does a great job trying to convince you they're the best (walk 10 minutes up rue de Barbatre from cathedral to 9 place St. Nicaise, tel. 03 26 85 84 33). After seeing their movie (in comfortable theater seats), follow your guide down into some of the three miles of chilly chalk caves, many dug by ancient Romans. Popping corks signal when the tour's done and the tasting's begun (20F, includes tasting, 9:30–12:00 and 14:30–16:30).

One block beyond Taittinger, on place des Droits de l'Homme, are several other champagne caves. **Piper Heidsieck** offers a remarkable train-ride tour and tasting (35F, 51 boulevard Henri-Vasnier, call first, tel. 03 26 84 43 44).

Champagne purists may want to visit Epernay (26 km away, well-connected to Paris and Reims), where the granddaddy of champagne houses, **Moët et Chandon**, offers tours, except from 12:00 to 14:00 (35F with tasting, tel. 03 26 51 21 00). According to the story, it was near here that, in about 1700, the monk Dom Perignon, after much fiddling with double fermentation, stumbled onto this bubbly treat. On that happy day he ran through the abbey shouting, "Brothers, come quickly…. I'm drinking stars!"

Sleeping in Reims

Grand Hotel de l'Univers** is near the station and a small pedestrian plaza (Db-260–320F, easy parking, 41 boulevard Foch, 51100 Reims, tel. 03 26 88 68 08, fax 03 26 40 95 61).

Transportation Connections—Reims

By train to: Epernay (8/day, 30 min), **Verdun** (8/day, 3 hrs, transfer in Chalons-sur-Marne), **Paris'** Gare de l'Est (10/day, 90 min), **Colmar** (3/day, 5 hrs, transfer in Vitry and Strasbourg).

BELGIUM

- 12,000 square miles (a little larger than Maryland)
- 10 million people (833 people per square mile)
- 40 Belgian francs = about $1

Belgium falls through the cracks. Nestled between Germany, France, and Britain and famous for waffles, sprouts, and endive, it's no wonder many travelers don't even consider a stop here. But many who visit remark that Belgium is one of Europe's best-kept secrets. There are tourists—but not as many as the country's charms merit.

Belgium and the Netherlands

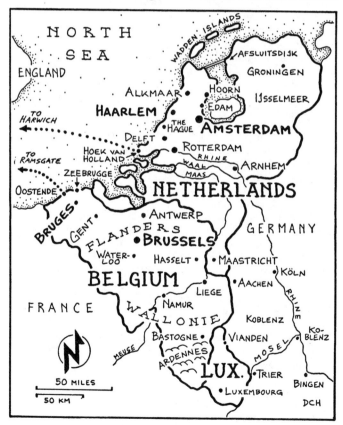

The country is split between the French-speaking Walloons in the south and the Dutch-speaking Flemish people (60 percent of the population) in the north. Talk to locals to learn how deep the cultural rift is. The capital city, Brussels, while mostly French speaking, is officially bilingual. There is a small minority of German-speaking people, and, because of Belgium's international importance, more than 20 percent of its residents are foreigners.

It is in Belgium that Europe comes together: where Romance languages meet Germanic languages, Catholics meet Protestants, and the Benelux union was established, planting the seed 40 years ago that today is sprouting into the unification of Europe. Belgium flies the flag of Europe more vigorously than any place in Europe.

Bruges and Brussels are the best two first bites of Belgium. Brussels is one of Europe's great cities and the capital of the European Community. Bruges is a wonderfully preserved medieval gem that expertly nurtures the tourist industry, bringing the town a prosperity it hasn't enjoyed since, as one of the biggest cities in the world, it helped lead northern Europe out of the Middle Ages 500 years ago.

Belgians brag that they eat as much as the Germans and as well as the French. They are the world's leading beer consumers and among the world's leading carnivores. In Belgium, never bring chrysanthemums to a wedding. And tweaking little kids on the ear is considered rude.

Ten million Belgians are packed into 12,000 square miles (roughly the size of Maryland). At 833 people per square mile, it's the second most densely populated country in Europe (after the Netherlands). This population concentration, coupled with a dense and well-lit rail and road system, causes Belgium to shine at night when viewed from space, a phenomenon NASA astronauts call the "Belgian Window."

Belgium's rail system is tops, and its various rail deals are worth considering. The second-class Multipass gives groups of three to five people any two trips in Belgium. Three people pay 1,260BF, four pay 1,420BF, and five pay 1,580BF; at least one of the Multipass users must be age 26 or older. People under age 26 can get a Go Pass: 1,420BF for 10 rides anywhere in Belgium. (The one-way Brussels–Bruges fare is 380BF per person.) Seniors age 60 plus can get any six rides for 1,260BF (2nd class) or 1,940BF (1st class). Expect a modest increase in pass prices as of February. Those traveling on the weekend should ask for the weekend discount for round-trips (40 percent off for 1 person, 60 percent off for any traveling companions).

BRUGES
(BRUGGE)

With Renoir canals, pointy gilded architecture, time-tunnel art, and stay-awhile cafés, Bruges is a heavyweight sightseeing destination as well as a joy. Where else can you ride a bike along a canal, munch mussels, wash them down with the world's best beer, savor heavenly chocolate, and see Flemish Primitives and a Michelangelo, all within 300 yards of a bell tower that rings out "Don't worry, be happy" jingles every 15 minutes? And there's no language barrier.

The town is Brugge (broo-gha) in Flemish…Bruges (broozh) in French and English. Before it was Flemish or French, the name was a Viking word for "wharf" or "embarkment." Right from the start, Bruges was a trading center. In the 11th century the city grew wealthy on the cloth trade. By the 14th century Bruges' population was 40,000, in a league with London and one of the largest in the world. At the time, Bruges was the most important cloth market in northern Europe. In the 15th century Bruges was the favored residence of the Dukes of Burgundy. Commerce and the arts boomed. Jan van Eyck and Hans Memling had studios here. But by the 16th century the harbor had silted up, and the economy collapsed. The Burgundian court left, Spain conquered Belgium in 1548, and Bruges' Golden Age was over. For generations Bruges was known as a mysterious and dead city. In the 19th century a new port, Zeebrugge, brought renewed vitality to the area. And 20th-century tourists discovered the town. Today Bruges prospers because of tourism: it's a uniquely well preserved Gothic city and a handy gateway to Europe. It's no secret, but even with the crowds it's the kind of city where you don't mind being a tourist.

Planning Your Time

Bruges needs at least two nights and a full, well-organized day. Even nonshoppers enjoy browsing here, and the Belgian love of life makes a hectic itinerary seem a little senseless. With one day, the speedy visitor could do this: 9:30—Climb the belfry, 10:00—Tour the Burg sights (visit the TI if necessary), 11:30—Take a boat tour, 12:15—Walk to the brewery, have lunch, and catch the 13:00 tour, 14:30—Walk through the Beguinage, 15:00—Tour the Memling Museum (six paintings), 15:45—See the Michelangelo in the church, 16:00—Tour the Groeninge Museum (closes at 17:00). Rent a bike for an evening ride through the quiet backstreets (or take a 900BF half-hour horse-and-buggy tour). Lose the tourists and find a dinner. (If this schedule seems insane, skip the belfry and the brewery—or stay another day.)

Orientation (tel. code: 050)

The tourists' Bruges (you'll be sharing it) is contained within a one-kilometer-square canal, or moat. Nearly everything of interest and importance is within a cobbled and convenient swath between the train station and Market Square (a 15-minute walk).

Tourist Information: The main office is on Burg Square (Mon–Fri 9:30–18:30, Sat–Sun 10:00–12:00, 14:00–18:30, off-season closes at 17:00, lockers and money exchange desk, tel. 050/448-686, public WC in courtyard). The other TI is at the train station (Mon–Sat 10:30–13:15, 14:00–18:30, closed Sun and off-season at 17:00, www.bruges.be). Both TIs sell a great 25BF all-inclusive Bruges visitors guide with a map and listings of all of the sights and services. The free *Exit* includes a monthly calendar of the many events the town puts on to keep its hordes of tourists entertained. It's in Dutch but almost readable (i.e., van Gershwin tot Clapton). Skip the TI's "combo" museum ticket. They also have train schedule information and specifics on the various kinds of tours available. Bikers will want the *5X on the Bike around Bruges* map/guide, which sells for 20BF and shows five routes through the countryside.

Internet Access: A cyber café is at Katelijnestraat 67, halfway between the station and Market Square near Walplein (60BF/15 min, also word processing and printing, Mon–Wed 9:30–21:30, Thu–Sat 9:30–17:30, tel. 050/349-352, e-mail: Kdenys@unicall.be).

Laundromat: You can wash clothes at Gentportstraat 28 (daily 7:00–22:00, English instructions, machines use 20BF coins; you'll need about 10 total) or at Mr. Wash (near Hotel Hansa on St. Jakobsstraat).

Arrival in Bruges

By Train: From the train (and from the TI near the station), you'll see the square belfry tower marking the main square. Upon arrival, stop by the station TI to pick up the Bruges visitors' guide (map in centerfold). There are no ATMs at the station, but you can change money at ticket windows. Buses marked "CENTRUM" go fast-as-a-taxi to the Market Square (40BF ticket, buy from driver, good for an hour). Buses #4 and #8 go farther, near the recommended Carmerstraat-area hotels. The taxi fare to most hotels is 250BF. It's a 20-minute walk from the station to the center: Cross the busy street and canal in front of the station, head up Oostmeers, and turn right on Steenstraat to reach Market Square. You could rent a bike at the station for the duration of your stay (325BF/day with a 500BF deposit, tel. 050/302-329), but other bike-rental shops are closer to the center (see below).

By Car: Park at the train station for just 100BF a day and pretend you arrived by train; show your parking receipt on the bus to get a free ride into town. The pricier underground parking garage at t'Zand costs 350BF/day.

Helpful Hints

You can change traveler's checks at Best Change (daily 9:00–21:00, until 19:00 in winter, just off Market Square on Steenstraat). The post office is on Market Square near the belfry (Mon–Fri 9:00–19:00, Sat 9:00–12:00). Shops are open 9:00–18:00, a little later on Friday. Grocery stores are usually closed on Sunday. Market day is Wednesday morning (Market Square) and Saturday morning (t'Zand). On Saturday and Sunday afternoons, there's a flea market along Dijver in front of the Groeninge Museum. October through March is off-season (when some museums close on Tuesday). A botanical garden blooms in the center of Astrid Park.

Sights—Bruges

Bruges' sights are listed here in walking order, from Market Square to the Burg to the cluster of museums around the Church of Our Lady to the Beguinage (a 10-minute walk from beginning to end). Like Venice, the ultimate sight is the town itself, and the best way to enjoy that is to get lost on the back streets away from the lace shops and ice-cream stands.

Market Square (Markt)—Ringed by banks, the post office, lots of restaurant terraces, great old gabled buildings, and the belfry, this is the modern heart of the city. Most city buses go from here to the station. Under the belfry are two great Belgian French-fry stands and a quadrilingual Braille description and model of the tower. In its day, a canal went right up to the central square of this formerly great trading center. Geldmuntstraat, just off the square, is a delightful street with many fun and practical shops and eateries.

▲▲**Belfry (Belfort)**—Most of this bell tower has stood over Market Square since 1300. In 1486 the octagonal lantern was added, making it 88 meters high—that's 366 steps (daily 9:30–17:00, Oct–Mar closed 12:30–13:30, ticket window closes 45 minutes

Bruges

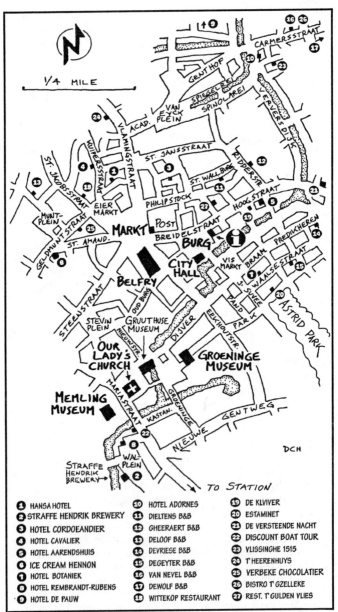

❶ HANSA HOTEL	❿ HOTEL ADORNES	⓳ DE KLUVIVER
❷ STRAFFE HENDRIK BREWERY	⓫ DIELTENS B&B	⓴ ESTAMINET
❸ HOTEL CORDOEANDIER	⓬ GHEERAERT B&B	㉑ DE VERSTEENDE NACHT
❹ HOTEL CAVALIER	⓭ DELOOF B&B	㉒ DISCOUNT BOAT TOUR
❺ HOTEL AARENDSHUIS	⓮ DEVRIESE B&B	㉓ VLISSINGHE 1515
❻ ICE CREAM HENNON	⓯ DEGEYTER B&B	㉔ T'HEERENHUYS
❼ HOTEL BOTANIEK	⓰ VAN NEVEL B&B	㉕ VERBEKE CHOCOLATIER
❽ HOTEL REMBRANDT-RUBENS	⓱ DEWOLF B&B	㉖ BISTRO T'GZELLEKE
❾ HOTEL DE PAUW	⓲ WITTEKOP RESTAURANT	㉗ REST. T'GULDEN VLIES

early, WC in courtyard). The view is worth the climb and the 100BF. Survey the town. On the horizon you can see the towns along the coast. Just before you reach the top, peek into the carillon room. The 47 bells can be played mechanically with the giant barrel and movable tabs (as they do on each quarter hour), or with a manual keyboard (as it does for regular concerts) with fists and feet rather than fingers. Be there on the quarter hour, when things ring. It's *bellissimo* at the top of the hour. Carillon concert times are listed at the base of the belfry (usually Mon, Wed, and Sat at 21:00 and Sun at 14:15). Back on the square, with your back to the belfry, turn right onto pedestrian-only Breidelstraat and thread yourself through the lace and *wafels* to Burg Square.

▲▲**Burg Square**—The opulent square called Burg is Bruges' civic center, historically the birthplace of Bruges and the site of the ninth-century castle of the first Count of Flanders. Today it's the scene of outdoor concerts and home of the TI (with a 10BF WC). It's surrounded by six centuries of architecture. Sweeping counterclockwise 360 degrees, you'll go from Romanesque (the round arches and thick walls of the brick basilica in the corner, best seen inside the lower chapel) to the pointed Gothic arches of the Town Hall (with its "Gothic Room") to the well-proportioned Renaissance windows of the Old Recorder's House (next door, under the gilded statues) and past the TI and the park to the elaborate 17th-century Baroque of the Provost's House. Complete your spin and walk to that corner.

▲**Basilica of the Holy Blood**—Originally the Chapel of Saint Basil, it is famous for its relic of the blood of Christ, which, according to tradition, was brought to Bruges in 1150 after the Second Crusade (and is displayed only during Friday worship services). The lower chapel (through the door labeled "Basiliek") is dark and solid— a fine example of Romanesque style (with some beautiful statues). The upper chapel (separate entrance, climb the stairs) is decorated Gothic and usually filled with appropriately contemplative music. A 10BF English flier tells about the relic, art, and history. The small but sumptuous Basilica Museum (well described in English) contains the gem-studded hexagonal reliquary (c. 1600) that carries the relic on its yearly Ascension Day trip through the streets of Bruges (museum is next to upper chapel, 40BF, daily 9:30–11:50, 14:00– 17:50; shorter hours and closed Wed afternoon off-season).

▲**City Hall's Gothic Room**—Your ticket gives you a room full of old town maps and paintings and a grand, beautifully restored "Gothic Hall" from 1400. Its painted and carved wooden ceiling features hanging arches (explained by an English flier). Notice the New Testament themes carved into the circular "vault keys." The wall murals are late-19th-century Romantic paintings of episodes from the city's history (described in the flier). The free ground-level lobby (closed on weekends) is a picture gallery of

Belgium's colonial history, from the Spanish Bourbon king to Napoleon (100BF, includes admission to Renaissance Hall, daily 9:30–17:00, closed 12:30–14:00 off-season, Burg 12).

Renaissance Hall (Brugse Vrije)—This is just one ornate room with an impressive Renaissance chimney. If you're into heraldry, the symbolism, explained in the free English flier, makes this worth a five-minute stop. If you're not, you'll wonder where the rest of the museum is (100BF, includes admission to City Hall, daily 9:30–12:30, 13:15–17:00, longer lunch—until 14:00—in winter, entry in the corner of the square).

From Burg to Fish Market to View—From Burg, walk under the Goldfinger family down Blinde Ezelstraat. Just after you cross the bridge, the persistent little fish market (Vismarkt, fresh North Sea catch sold Tue–Fri 6:00–13:00) is on your left. Take an immediate right to Huidevettersplein, a tiny, picturesque, and restaurant-filled square. Continue a few steps to Rozenhoedkaai Street, where you can get a great photo of the belfry reflected in the canal. Can you see its tilt? It leans about four feet. Down the canal (past a flea market on weekends) looms the huge spire of the Church of Our Lady (tallest brick spire in the Low Countries). Between you and the church are the next three museums.

▲▲▲Groeninge Museum—This diverse and classy collection shows off mostly Flemish art from Memling to Magritte. Rooms 1 through 18 take you from 1400 to 1945. While it has plenty of worthwhile modern art, the highlights are its vivid and pristine Flemish Primitives. (*Primitive* here means before the Renaissance.) Flemish art is shaped by its love of detail, its merchant patrons' egos, and the power of the Church. Lose yourself in the halls of Groeninge: Gaze across 15th-century canals, into the eyes of reassuring Marys, and through town squares littered with leotards, lace, and lopped-off heads (200BF, daily 9:30–17:00, Oct–Mar closed 12:30–14:00 and Tue, Dijver 12). The **Brangwyn Museum** (Arentshuis), next door, is only interesting if you are into lace or the early-20th-century art of Brangwyn (80BF, daily 9:30–17:00, off-season closed 12:30–14:00 and Tue, Dijver 16).

▲Gruuthuse Museum—A wealthy brewer's home, this is a sprawling smattering of everything from medieval bedpans to a guillotine. There's no information inside, so to understand the crossbows, dark old paintings, and what a beer merchant's doing with box seats peeking down on the altar of the Church of Our Lady next door, you'll have to buy or browse through the 600BF guidebook (130BF, daily 9:30–17:00, shorter hours off-season, Dijver 17). Leaving the museum, contemplate the mountain of bricks towering 120 meters above as they have for 600 years.

▲▲Church of Our Lady—The church stands as a memorial to the power and wealth of Bruges in its heyday. A delicate *Madonna and Child*, by Michelangelo, is near the apse (to the right if you're facing the altar). It's said to be the only Michelangelo statue to leave Italy in his lifetime (thanks to the wealth generated by Bruges' cloth trade). If you like tombs and church art, pay to wander through the apse (70BF, Michelangelo free, art-filled apse Mon–Fri 10:00–11:30, 14:30–17:00, closes at 16:00 on Sat, Sun 14:30–17:00, on Mariastraat).

▲▲**St. Jans Hospital/Memling Museum**—Across the street from the Church of Our Lady is a medieval hospital with six much-loved paintings by the greatest of the Flemish Primitives, Hans Memling. His *Mystical Wedding of St. Catherine* triptych deserves a close look. Catherine and her "mystical groom," the baby Jesus, are flanked by a headless John the Baptist and a pensive John the Evangelist. The chairs are there so you can study it. If you understand the Book of Revelations, you'll understand St. John's wild and intricate vision. The Reliquary of St. Ursula, an ornate little mini-church in the same room, is filled with impressive detail (100BF, daily 9:30–17:00, off-season closed 12:30–14:00 and Wed, Mariastraat 38).

▲▲**Straffe Hendrik Brewery Tour**—Belgians are Europe's beer connoisseurs. This fun and handy tour is a great way to pay your respects. The happy gang at this working family brewery gives entertaining and informative 45-minute, four-language tours (usually by friendly Inge, 140BF including a beer, piles of very steep steps, a great rooftop panorama, daily on the hour 11:00–17:00, Oct–Mar 11:00 and 15:00 only, 1 block past church and canal, take a right down skinny Stoofstraat to #26 on Walplein square, tel. 050/332-697). At Straffe Hendrik ("Strong Henry") they remind their drinkers: "The components of the beer are vitally necessary and contribute to a well-balanced life-pattern. Nerves, muscles, visual sentience, and a healthy skin are stimulated by these in a positive manner. For longevity and lifelong equilibrium, drink Straffe Hendrik in moderation!"

Their bistro, where you'll be given your included-with-the-tour beer, serves a quick and hearty lunch plate (the 150BF "bread with pâté and vegetables" is the best value, although the 250BF "meat selection and vegetables" is a beer-drinker's picnic for two). On sunny summer days they offer a barbecue and salad bar for 350BF. You can eat indoors with the smell of hops or outdoors with the smell of hops. This is a great place to wait for your tour or to linger afterward. From here the lacy cuteness of Bruges crescendos as you approach the Beguinage.

▲▲**Beguinage**—For military (and various other) reasons, there were more women than men in the medieval Low Countries. Towns provided Beguinages, dignified places in which these "Beguines" could live a life of piety and service (without having to take the same vows a nun would). You'll find Beguinages all over Belgium and Holland. Bruges' Beguinage—now inhabited not by

Beguines but by Benedictine nuns—almost makes you want to don a habit and fold your hands as you walk under its wispy trees and whisper past its frugal little homes. For a good slice of Beguinage life, walk through the simple museum (Beguine's House, left of entry gate, 60BF with English flier, daily 10:00–12:00, 13:45–17:00, shorter hours off-season).

Minnewater—Beyond the Beguinage is Minnewater, an idyllic, clip-clop world of flower boxes, canals, swans, and tour boats packed like happy egg cartons. Beyond that is the train station.

Almshouses—Walking from the Beguinage back to the center, you might detour along Nieuwe Gentweg to visit one of about 20 almshouses in the city. At #8, go through the door dated 1613 (free) into the peaceful courtyard. This was a medieval form of housing for the poor. The rich would pay for someone's tiny room here in return for lots of prayers. The Diamond Museum (at the start of Nieuwe Gentweg) is less interesting than an encyclopedia (200BF).

Bruges Experiences

Chocolate—Bruggians are connoisseurs of fine chocolate. You'll be tempted by chocolate-filled display windows all over town. Godiva is the best big-factory/high-price/high-quality local brand, but for the finest small-family operation, drop by **Maitre Chocolatier Verbeke**. While Mr. Verbeke is busy downstairs making chocolates, Mrs. Verbeke makes sure customers in the shop get the chocolate of their dreams. Ask her to assemble a bag of your favorites (The smallest amount sold is 100 grams—about seven pieces—for 90BF). Most are pralines, which means they're filled. While the "hedgehogs" are popular, be sure to get a "pharaoh's head." Pray for cool weather, since it's closed when it's very hot. (Open at least in the mornings on Tue, Wed, Fri, and Sat; open cooler afternoons as well; a block off Market Square at Geldmuntstraat 25; can ship overseas except during hot summer months, tel. 050/334-198.)

Lace and Windmills by the Moat—A 10-minute walk from the center to the northeast end of town brings you to four windmills strung out along a pleasant grassy setting on the "big moat" canal (between Kruispoort and Dampoort, on the Bruges side of the moat). One of the windmills (St. Janshuismolen) is open to visitors (40BF, daily 9:30–12:30, 13:15–17:00, closed Oct–Mar, at the end of Carmersstraat).

To actually see lace being made, drop by the nearby Lace Centre, where ladies toss bobbins madly while their eyes go bad (60BF includes afternoon demonstrations and a small lace museum called Kantcentrum, as well as the adjacent Jerusalem church; Mon–Fri 10:00–12:00, 14:00–18:00, until 17:00 on Sat, closed Sun, Peperstraat 3). The Folklore Museum, in the same neighborhood, is cute but forgettable (80BF, daily 9:30–17:00, less off-season, Rolweg 40). To find either place, ask for the Jerusalem church.

▲▲**Biking**—While the sights are close enough for easy walking, the town is a treat to bike through, and you can to get away from the tourist center. Consider a peaceful evening ride through the back streets and around the outer canal. Rental shops have maps and ideas. The TI sells a handy *5X on the Bike around Bruges* map/guide for 20BF; it narrates five different bike routes (18–30 kms) through the idyllic nearby countryside. The best trip is 30 minutes along the canal out to Damme and back. The Netherlands/Belgium border is a 40-minute pedal beyond Damme. Two shops rent bikes in the center of town (70BF for 1 hour, 150BF for 4 hours, or 250BF/day). Both offer free city maps and child seats. **Popelier Eric's** doesn't require a deposit and sells a good map of the countryside for 80BF (daily 9:00–21:00 in summer, 10:00–19:00 in winter, 50 meters from Church of Our Lady at Mariastraat 26, tel. 050/343-262). **'T Koffieboontje** asks for a 1,000BF deposit, your passport, or a credit-card imprint. They sell an annoying double-sided photocopy of the TI's biking brochure for 20BF; the map is on one side, and the directions are inconveniently on the other (Hallestraat 4, closer to the belfry, tel. 050/338-027). The less central **De Ketting** rents bikes for less (150BF/day, Gentpoortstraat 23, tel. 050/344-196).
Dolfinarium—At Boudewijnpark, just outside of town, dolphins make a splash at 11:15, 14:00, and 16:00 (280BF for the 40-min show, Debaeckestraat 12, call to confirm show times, tel. 050/383-838). The theme park's roller-skating rink is open in the afternoon (and turns into an ice-skating rink off-season). From Bruges, catch the "Sint Michiels" bus #7 or #17 from Kuipersstraat.

Tours of Bruges

Bruges by Boat—The most relaxing and scenic (if not informative) way to see this city of canals is by boat, with the captain narrating. Boats leave from all over town (190BF, 4/hrly, 10:00–18:00, copycat 30-min rides). Boten Stael (just over the canal from the Memling Museum) offers a 30BF discount with this book.
City Minibus Tours—"City Tour Bruges" gives 50-minute/380BF rolling overviews of the town in an 18-seat, two-skylight minibus with dial-a-language headsets and video support. The tour leaves hourly (on the hour, 9:00–19:00 in summer, until 18:00 in spring and fall, less in winter) from Market Square. The narration, while clean, is slow-moving and boring. But the tour is a lazy way to cruise by every sight I've described here.
Walking Tours—Local guides walk small groups through the core of town daily in July and August (150BF, depart from TI at 15:00). The tours, while earnest, are heavy on history and in two languages, so they may be less than peppy. Still, to propel you beyond the pretty gables and canal swans of Bruges, they are good medicine. A private guided tour costs 1,500BF (reserve at least 3 days in advance through a TI).

Bus Tours of Countryside—Quasimodo Tours offers those with extra time two excellent all-day tours through the rarely visited Flemish countryside. The "Flanders Fields" tour concentrates on World War I battlefields, trenches, memorials, and poppy-splattered fields (Sun, Tue, and Thu 9:00–16:30). The other is "Triple Treat": the port of Damme, a castle, a monastery, a brewery, and a chocolate factory as well as a sampling of the treats—a waffle, chocolate, and beer (Mon, Wed, and Fri 9:00–16:00). Hardworking Lote leads all the tours himself, in English only (1,500BF, 1,200BF for people under 26, CC:VM, 29-seat nonsmoking bus, lunch included, lots of walking, pickup at your hotel or the train station, tel. 050/370-470 to book, fax 050/374-960).

Bruges by Bike—The Backroad Bike Company leads daily bike tours through the nearby countryside (550–650BF, 30 km, 3 hrs, tel. 050/370-470). Shorter, longer, and evening tours are available.

Bus and Boat Tour—The Sightseeing Line offers a bus trip to Damme and a boat ride back (660BF, Apr–Jun daily at 14:00 and 16:00, 2 hrs, leaves from Market Square).

Sleeping in Bruges
(40BF = about $1, tel. code 050, zip code: 8000)
Sleep Code: **S** = Single, **D** = Double/Twin, **T** = Triple, **Q** = Quad, **b** = bathroom, **t** = toilet only, **s** = shower only, **CC** = Credit Card (**V**isa, **M**asterCard, **A**mex). Everyone speaks English.

Most places are located between the train station and the old center, with the most distant (and best) being a few blocks beyond Market Square to the north and east. B&Bs offer the best value. All include breakfast, are on quiet streets, and (with a few exceptions) keep the same prices throughout the year. Bruges is most crowded Friday and Saturday evenings Easter through October—with July and August weekends being worst. Otherwise, finding a room is easy.

Hotels
Hansa Hotel offers 20 rooms in a completely modernized old building. It's tastefully decorated in elegant pastels and has all the amenities. It's a great splurge (Db-4,360–5,770BF depending on room size, extra bed-1,250BF, CC:VMA, air-con, nonsmoking, elevator, Niklaas Desparsstraat 11, a block north of Market Square, tel. 050/338-444, fax 050/334-205, www.hansa.be, e-mail: information @hansa.be, cheery and hardworking Johan and Isabelle).

Hotel Aarendshuis, an old merchant's mansion, is well worn but comfortable. It's family run and has 25 spacious rooms, dingy carpets, chandeliered public places, and a small garden (prices vary with size and luxury: Sb-2,400BF, Db-3,000–4,000BF, Tb-4,000BF, Qb-4,500BF, kids under 10 free, car park-350BF, CC:VMA, elevator, 2 blocks off Burg Square at Hoogstraat 18, tel. 050/337-889, fax 050/330-816, e-mail: hotelaarendshuis@village.uunet.be).

Hotel Cordoeandier, another family-run place, rents 22 bright, simple, modern rooms on a quiet street two blocks off Market Square (Sb-1,950BF, Db-2,300BF, Tb-2,900–3,200BF, Qb-3,400BF, 5b-3,900BF, CC:VM, nearly free Internet access, Cordoeanierstraat 16, tel. 050/339-051, fax 050/346-111, www.cordoeanier.be, Kris and Veerie). Equally central and even cheaper but smoky and not the same value is **Hotel Nicolas** (Sb-1,600BF, Db-2,000BF, CC:VMA, elevator, next to Hotel Hansa at N. Desparsstraat 9, tel. 050/335-502, Chinese-run and decorated).

Hotel Cavalier, with less character and more stairs, serves a hearty buffet breakfast in a royal setting (Sb-1,900BF, Db-2,400BF, Tb-3,000BF, Qb-3,300BF, 2 lofty "backpackers' doubles" on the 4th floor-1,600BF or 1,800BF with WC, CC:VMA, Kuipersstraat 25, tel. 050/330-207, fax 050/347-199, e-mail: cavalier@skynet.be, run by friendly Viviane De Clerck).

Hotel Botaniek has three stars, nine small rooms, and a quiet location a block from Astrid Park. This friendly hotel is basic, small, and comfy (Sb-2,500BF, Db-2,900BF, Tb-3,500BF, CC:VMA, Waalsestraat 23, tel. 050/341-424, fax 050/345-939).

Hotel Rembrandt-Rubens has 15 rooms in a creaky 500-year-old building with tipsy floors, a mysterious floor plan, tacky rooms, ancient dippy beds, elephant tusks, a gallery of creepy old paintings, and probably the Holy Grail in a drawer somewhere (S-1,100BF, Ss-1,500BF, one D-1,600BF, Ds-2,100BF, Db-2,400BF, Tb-3,000BF, Qb-3,900BF, locked up at 24:00, on a quiet square between the Memlings and the brewery at Walplein 38, tel. 050/336-439). The breakfast room (which must have been the knights' hall) overlooks a canal (while Rembrandt and Rubens overlook you from an ornately carved and tiled 1648 chimney). There's a little warmth behind Mrs. DeBuyser's crankiness. The hotel has been in her family for 50 years.

Hotel Adornes is a great value and has 20 comfy new rooms in a 17th-century canalside house. They offer free parking and free loaner bikes; a cellar game and video lounge; and clean, simple rooms with full, modern bathrooms (Db-2,900–3,700BF depending upon size, CC:VMA, elevator, near Van Nevel B&B, below, and Carmersstraat at St. Annarei 26, tel. 050/341-336, fax 050/342-085, e-mail: hotel.adornes@proximedia.be, Nathalie runs the family business).

Hotel De Pauw is tall, skinny, and family run, with straightforward rooms on a quiet street across from a church (2 top-floor D-1,850BF, Db-2,100–2,450BF, CC:VMA, free and easy parking, cable TV and phones, Sint Gilliskerkhof 8, tel. 050/337-118, fax 050/345-140, info@hoteldepauw.be, Josine).

Hotel t'Keizershof is a dollhouse of a hotel that lives by its motto, "Spend a night, not a fortune." It's simple and tidy, with eight small, cheery old-time rooms split between two floors, a shower and toilet on each (S-950BF, D-1,400BF, T-2,100BF, Q-2,500BF, free and easy parking, laundry service-300BF, Oostmeers 126, a block in front of train station, tel. 050/338-728, e-mail: stefaan.persyn@skynet.be, run by Stefaan and Hilde).

Crowne Plaza Hotel Brugge is the most modern, comfortable, and central hotel option. Each of its 90 air-conditioned rooms comes with a magnifying mirror and trouser press (rack rate: Db-8,000BF, prices drop as low as 5,100BF on weekdays and off-season, CC:VMA, elevator, pool, Burg 10, tel. 050/345-834, fax 050/345-615, www.crowneplaza.com).

Bed-and-Breakfasts

These places offer the best value. Each is central and run by people who enjoy their work and offers lots of stairs and three or four doubles you'd pay 4,000BF for in a hotel. Parking is generally easy on the street.

Koen and Annemie Dieltiens are a friendly couple who enjoy getting to know their guests, who eat a hearty breakfast around a big table in their bright, homey, comfortable house. They are a wealth of information on Bruges (S-1,300BF, Sb-1,700BF, D-1,600BF, Db-1,900BF, T-2,100BF, Tb-2,400BF, Qb-2,900BF, 1-night stops pay 200BF extra per room, nonsmoking, Sint-Walburgastraat 14, 3 blocks east of Market Square, tel. 050/334-294, fax 050/335-230, e-mail: koen.dieltiens @skynet.be). The Dieltiens also rent a cozy studio and apartment for two to six people in a nearby 17th-century house (2 pay 13,300BF per week for studio, 14,700BF for apartment, prices higher for shorter stays and more people; cheaper off-season).

Paul and Roos Gheeraert live on the first floor, while their guests take the second. This neoclassical mansion with big, bright, comfy rooms is another fine value (Sb-1,600BF, larger Sb-1,700BF, Db-1,800BF, larger Db-1,900BF, Tb-2,400BF; rooms have coffeemakers and fridges; Ridderstraat 9, 4 blocks east of Market, tel. 050/335-627, fax 050/345-201, e-mail: paul.gheeraert@skynet.be). They also rent three modern, fully-equipped apartments and a large loft nearby (minimum 3 nights, view at http://users.skynet.be /brugge-gheeraert).

Chris Deloof's big, homey rooms are a good bet in the old center. The ones with showers are more elegant, but the upstairs A-frame lofty room is fun (Ss-1,400BF, D-1,500BF, Ds-1,900BF, pleasant breakfast room, free loaner bikes, nonsmoking, communal kitchen, Geerwijnstraat 14, tel. & fax 050/340-544, www.sin.be /chrisdeloof, e-mail: chris.deloof@ping.be). Chris also rents a nearby apartment, great for a family or group (Qb-3,500BF).

The **Van Nevel family** rents two attractive top-floor rooms with built-in beds in a 16th-century house (S-1,200–1,500BF, D-1,500–1,800BF, Carmersstraat 13, 10-min walk from Market

Square, tel. 050/346-860, fax 050/347-616, e-mail: robert.vannevel @advalvas.be). Robert enthusiastically shares the culture and history of Bruges with his guests.

Yvonne De Vriese rents three tidy but neglected B&B rooms on a corner overlooking two canals (1 S-1,000BF, D-1,500BF, Db-1,800BF, 500BF extra for 3rd or 4th person; breakfast served in your room; canal views come with mosquitoes; CC:VMA, Predik-herenstraat 40, 4 blocks east of Burg Square, take bus #6 or #16 from station and get off at the first stop on Predikheren Rei, tel. 050/334-224).

Jan Degeyter, a block away, rents two airy, spacious, wood-floored rooms on a quiet street (Db-1,800BF, Tb-2,300BF, Qb-2,800BF, CC:VMA, Waalsestraat 40, tel. 050/331-199, fax 050/347-857).

Arnold Dewolf's B&B is in a stately, quiet neighborhood (D-1,400BF, 1 big family room-1,400–2,200BF, depending on number of people, Oostproostse 9, 20-min walk from center, near windmills, tel. 050/338-366). Going down Carmersstraat, turn left on Peterseliestraat then right on Leestenburg to Oostprootse.

Hostels

Bruges has several good hostels offering beds for around 400BF in two- to eight-bed rooms (singles go for around 600BF). Pick up the hostel info sheet at the station TI. Smallest, loosest, and closest to the center are the dull **Snuffel Travelers Inn** (Ezelstraat 47, tel. 050/333-133), the **Bauhaus International Party Hotel** (Langestraat 135, tel. 050/341-093), and the funky **Passage** (Dweerstraat 26, tel. 050/340-232; its hotel next door rents 1,200BF doubles). The new, American-style **Charlie Rockets** bar and hostel is the liveliest and most central hostel (56 beds, 2 to 6 per room, 500BF per bed, Hoogstraat 19, tel. 050/330-660).

Eating in Bruges

Specialties include mussels cooked a variety of ways (one order can feed two people), fish dishes, grilled meats, and French fries. Touristy places on the square come with great views and are affordable; candle-cool bistros flicker on back streets. Don't eat before 19:30 unless you like eating alone. Tax and service are always included.

Wittekop is very Flemish—a cluttered, laid-back, old-time place specializing in the beer-soaked equivalent of beef bour-guignonne (600BF plates, Tue–Sat 18:00–24:00, closed Sun–Mon, terrace in the back, Sint Jakobsstraat 14, tel. 050/332-059).

The classy **'T Heerenhuys,** famous for its top-notch Flemish/French cooking, serves a much-raved-about 375BF lunch special (12:00–14:30, closed Thu and Sun, Vlamingstraat 53, tel. 050/346-178).

De Kluiver is a pub serving hot snacks, light 400BF meals, and great "seasnails in spiced bouillon" simmered in a whispering jazz ambience (Wed–Mon 18:00–01:00, closed Tue, Hoogstraat 12, tel. 050/338-927).

Pannekoekenhuisje, the little pancake house, is a cute restaurant serving delicious, inexpensive pancake meals (just off Geldmuntstraat at Helmstraat 3, tel. 050/340-086).

Lotus Vegetarisch Restaurant serves good veggie lunches only (300BF plates, Mon–Sat 11:45–13:45, closed Sun, just off the Burg at Wapenmakersstraat 5, tel. 050/331-078).

Two youthful, trendy, jazz-filled eateries: For hearty budget spaghetti (210BF), head for **Estaminet**, on the northern border of peaceful Astrid Park (open from 11:30 on, closed Mon afternoon and all day Thu, Park 5). Or try **De Versteende Nacht Jazzcafe** on Langestraat 11 (500BF meals, Tue–Sat 19:00–2:00, closed Sun–Mon).

Vlissinghe 1515, the oldest pub in town, serves hot snacks in great atmosphere (open from 11:30 on, closed Tue, Blekersstraat 2).

Bistro 't Gezelleke (next door to the Van Nevel B&B and near Bauhaus hostel) offers fine fresh food at bring-'em-in prices (300–400BF meals, Mon–Fri 12:00–24:00, Saturday from 18:00, closed Sun, Carmersstraat 15, tel. 050/338-102). **Restaurant 't Gulden Vlies**, just off Burg, is good for a late dinner (600BF plates, closed Mon–Tue, Mallebergplaats 17).

Picnics: Geldmuntstraat is a handy street when you're hungry. A block off Market Square, **Pickles Frituur** serves the best sit-down fries in town (Mon–Sat 11:00–24:00, closed Sun). A block farther, past the Verbeke chocolate shop, **Nopri Supermarket** is great for picnics (push-button produce pricer lets you buy as little as one mushroom, Mon–Sat 9:00–18:30, closed Sun). The small **Delhaize grocery** is on Market Square opposite the belfry (Mon–Sat 8:00–12:00, 13:30–18:00, closed Sun). **Selfi** has cheap sandwiches to go (Breidelstraat 16, between Burg and Market Square). For midnight munchies, you'll find Indian-run corner grocery stores.

Frietjes: These local French fries are a treat. Proud and traditional *frituurs* serve tubs of fries and various local-style shish kebabs. Belgians dip their *frietjes* in mayonnaise, but ketchup is there for the Yankees (along with spicier sauces). For a quick, cheap, and scenic meal, hit a *frituur* and sit on the steps or benches overlooking Market Square, about 50 yards past the post office.

Beer: Belgium boasts more than 350 types of beer. Straffe Hendrik ("Strong Henry"), a potent and refreshing local brew, is, even to a Bud Lite kind of guy, obviously great beer. Among the more unusual of the others to try: Dentergems (with coriander and orange peel) and Trappist (a dark, malty, monk-made beer). Non–beer drinkers enjoy Kriek (a cherry-flavored beer) and

Frambozen Bier (raspberry-flavored beer). Each beer is served in its own unique glass. Any pub carries the basic beers, but for a selection of more than 300 types, drink at **t'Brugs Beertje** (16:00–01:00, closed Wed, Kemelstraat 5). When you've finished those, step next door, where **Dreupel Huisje "1919"** serves more than 100 Belgian gins and liqueurs (closed Tue). Another good place to gain an appreciation of the Belgian beer culture is **de Garre**. Rather than a noisy pub scene, it has a sit-down-and-focus-on-your-friend-and-the-fine-beer ambience (huge selection, off Breidelstraat, between Burg and Markt, on the tiny Garre alley, daily 12:00–24:00).

Belgian Waffles: While Americans think of "Belgian" waffles for breakfast, the Belgians (who don't eat waffles or pancakes for breakfast) think of *wafels* as Leige-style (dense, sweet, eaten plain and heated up, served take-away) and Brussels-style (lighter, often with powdered sugar or whipped cream and fruit, served in teahouses). For the best Leige-style *wafels* in town, drop by **Ice Cream Hennon** for a Luikse Wafel (50BF, across from Nopri Supermarket, corner of Guldmuntstraat and Sind Amandstraat, daily 10:00–24:00). Hennon's *wafels* and ice cream (18 flavors) are extremely fresh…and tasty. Any number of teahouses serve Brussels-style *wafels*.

Transportation Connections—Bruges

From Brussels, all of Europe is at your fingertips (see "Brussels Connections," next chapter). Train info: tel. 050/382-382.

By train to: Brussels (2/hrly, 1 hr), **Ghent** (3/hrly, 20 min), **Oostende** (3/hrly, 15 min), **Köln** (6/day, 4 hrs), **Paris** (3 direct, high-speed Thalys trains/day, 2.5 hrs, 400BF supplement for Eurail), **Amsterdam** (hrly, 3.5 hrs).

Trains from England: Bruges is an ideal "welcome to Europe" stop after London. Take the Eurostar train from London to Brussels under the English Channel (6/day, 3 hrs), then transfer to Bruges (hrly, 1 hour). Or, if you'd prefer to cross the Channel by boat, catch the London–Dover train (2 hrs, from London's Victoria station), then the catamaran to Oostende (2 hrs; train station at Oostende catamaran terminal), then the Oostende–Bruges train (15 min). Five boats run daily (1,500BF one way, same price for the cheap five-day return ticket; call to reserve a seat and pay at the dock, CC:VMA, tel. 059/559-955).

BRUSSELS

Brussels, the capital of Belgium, is also the capital of Europe.
Since World War II it's been the convenient home of both
NATO and the "government of Europe," working busily to
move things towards unity. And it's Europe's linguistic hinge,
too (60 percent of all Belgians speak the Germanic Flemish, and
40 percent speak the Romantic French). It's easy to miss Brussels
as you zip from Amsterdam to Paris on the train, but those who
stop are pleasantly surprised. And in 2000, Brussels is a "cultural
capital" with even more arts and events than usual (check out
www.brussels2000.be).

Brussels, like Belgium, is officially bilingual. Most maps and
signs here list place-names in French and Flemish (Dutch). Since
80 percent of the people in Brussels speak French, I normally list
only the French names in this chapter.

Planning Your Time

Brussels is low on great sights and high on ambience. On a quick
trip, a day and a night are enough for a good first taste. It could
even be done as a day trip from Bruges (an hour away by train) or
a stopover on the Amsterdam–Paris ride (hrly trains). The main
reason to stop—La Grand Place—takes only a few minutes to see.
With very limited time, skip the indoor sights and enjoy a coffee
or a beer on the square. Even travelers not "into art" can spend an
enjoyable three hours at Brussels' ancient- and modern-art museums. If you do the auto and military museums (side by side), plan
on a three-hour trip from the town center. If you're in Brussels on
a Monday, when most sights are closed, consider the Auto World,
Atomium, shopping, a walking tour, or a minibus tour. Most
important, this is a city to browse and wander.

Brussels

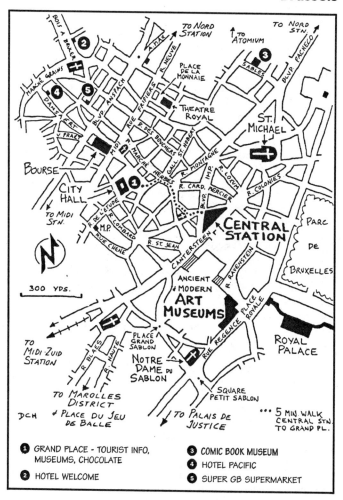

TO NORD STATION
TO NORD STN.
↑ TO ATOMIUM
BOIS A BRULER
PLACE DE LA MONNAIE
R. NEUVE
A TLAS
② HOTEL WELCOME
⊕
MARCHE GRAINS
④ ⑤
THEATRE ROYAL
SABLES
③
BLVD. PACHECO
ST. MICHAEL
⊕
DANSAERT
BLVD. ANSPACH
RUE FRIPIERS
R. DES BOUCHERS
GALL. ST. HUBERT
R. MONTAGNE
IMP. LOVUM
R. COLONIES
V. PRAL
MIDI
MARCHE HERBES
BOURSE
CITY HALL ← ①
R. CARD. MERCIER
CENTRAL STATION
PARC DE BRUXELLES
TO MIDI STN.
L'ETUDE
R. LOMBARD
M.P.
RUE CHENE
R. ST. JEAN
CANTERSTEEN
R. RAVENSTEIN
N
300 YDS.
ANCIENT & MODERN ART MUSEUMS
PLACE ROYALE
RUE REGENCE
ROYAL PALACE
⊕
PLACE GRAND SABLON
NOTRE DAME DU SABLON →
R. BLAES
R. HAUTE
TO MIDI-ZUID STATION
SQUARE PETIT SABLON
TO MAROLLES DISTRICT & PLACE DU JEU DE BALLE
DCH
↑ TO PALAIS DE JUSTICE
••• 5 MIN. WALK CENTRAL STN. TO GRAND PL.

① GRAND PLACE – TOURIST INFO, MUSEUMS, CHOCOLATE
② HOTEL WELCOME
③ COMIC BOOK MUSEUM
④ HOTEL PACIFIC
⑤ SUPER GB SUPERMARKET

Orientation (tel. code: 02)

Central Brussels is defined by a ring of roads (which replaced the old city wall) called the Pentagon. All hotels and nearly all the sights I mention are within this circle. The epicenter is the main square (La Grand Place), TI, and Central Station (three blocks away). To get to La Grand Place, walk downhill from the Central Station (through the arch in Le Meridien Hotel across the street) and turn right, and, after a block, you'll reach a small square with a fountain. For La Grand Place, turn left at the far end of the square; for the TI, continue straight past the square for one block. For the restaurant streets, take the first right (an alley) past the TI (see "Eating," below).

Tourist Information: Although the office at rue du Marche-aux-Herbes 63 is for all of Belgium, it does Brussels just fine (Mon–Fri 9:00–19:00, Sat–Sun 9:00–13:00, 14:00–19:00, closes off-season at 18:00, downhill three blocks from the Central Station, tel. 02/504-0390; two fun Europe stores are across the street). Another TI is in the city hall in La Grand Place (daily 9:00–18:00, closed on Sun off-season, tel. 02/513-8940). Among their countless fliers, pick up "Brussels, Yours to Discover," the weekly *What's On*, a city map, and a public transit map. The 70BF *Brussels Guide & Map* booklet is worthwhile if you want a series of neighborhood walks and a more complete explanation of the city's many museums. If your next destination is Bruges, get your Bruges map here.

Arrival in Brussels

By Train: Brussels can't decide which of its three stations (Central, Nord, and Midi) is the main one. Most international trains leave and land at the Nord and Midi Stations. The Eurostar leaves from Midi Station (also called Zuid or South), getting you to London in three hours. The area around the Midi Station is a rough-and-tumble immigrant neighborhood (with a towering Ferris wheel); the area around the Nord Station is a seedy red-light district. The Central Station has handy services (grocery store, fast food, a luggage storage, waiting rooms, and so on) and is nearest to the sights. Normally only Belgian and Amsterdam trains stop at Central. Don't assume your train stops at more than one station. Confirm your plan with the conductor.

Trains zip under the city, connecting all three stations every two minutes or so. It's a free and easy three-minute chore to connect from Nord or Midi to Central. As you wait on the platform for your train, look at the track notice board that tells which train is approaching. They zip in and out constantly. Anxious travelers often board the wrong train on the right track.

By Plane: Shuttle trains run between the three stations (Midi, Central, and Nord) and Brussels International Airport, 14 kilometers away (90BF, 4/hrly, 25 min). Airport info can connect you to your airline desk: tel. 02/753-3913.

Getting around Brussels

Most of Brussels' sights are walkable. For a few of the sights, like the auto and military museums, take the Métro. The TI's free "Métro Tram Bus Plan" is excellent. The integrated system uses

La Grand Place

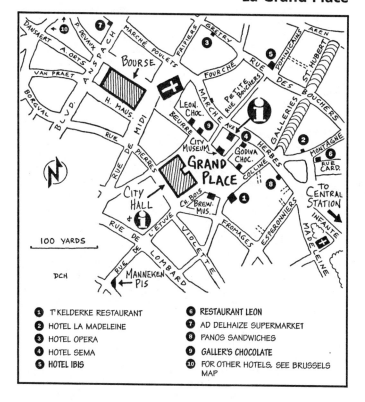

1 T'KELDERKE RESTAURANT
2 HOTEL LA MADELEINE
3 HOTEL OPERA
4 HOTEL SEMA
5 HOTEL IBIS
6 RESTAURANT LEON
7 AD DELHAIZE SUPERMARKET
8 PANOS SANDWICHES
9 GALLER'S CHOCOLATE
10 FOR OTHER HOTELS, SEE BRUSSELS MAP

one 50BF ticket that's good for one hour (notice the time when you first stamp it; buy tickets on the bus or at Métro stations). The deals (5 tickets/240BF, 10 tickets/340BF) are available at newsstands and Métro stations, and TIs sell the one-day ticket for 130BF (cheaper than three rides, transit info: tel. 02/515-2000).

Sights—Brussels

▲▲▲**La Grand Place**—Brussels' main square, aptly called La Grand Place, is the heart of the old town and Brussels' greatest sight. Any time of day it's worth swinging by to see what's going on. Concerts, flower markets, sound-and-light shows, endless people watching—it entertains (as do the streets around it).

The museums on the square are well-advertised but dull. The **Hôtel de Ville**, or city hall, with the tallest spire, is the square's centerpiece but no big deal to see (80BF, visits only by 30-min tours, Tue 11:30 and 15:15, Wed 15:15, and Sun 12:15). The **City Museum**, opposite the city hall, is in a neo-Gothic building (1875) called "the King's House" (in which no king ever lived). The top floor has an entertaining room full of costumes the *Manneken* statue has pissed through; the middle floor features maps and models of old Brussels; and the bottom floor has a few old paintings and tapestries (100BF, Tue–Fri 10:00–17:00, Sat–Sun 10:00–13:00, closed Mon). Opposite the King's House is the **Brewery Museum**, with one room of old brewing paraphernalia and one room of new (all explained in Flemish and French). It's pretty lame... but a good excuse for a beer (100BF including an unnamed local beer, daily 10:00–17:00). The **Chocolate Museum**, next door, is a delightful concept. But offering a meager set of displays, a second-rate video, a look at a "chocolate master" at work, and a choco-sample for 200BF, it's way overpriced (10:00–17:00, #13 Grand Place).

For many, the best thing about La Grand Place is **chocolate** at Godiva's, Leonidas, or Galler's. Each has an inviting display case of 20 or so chocolates and sells a minimum of 100 grams—your choice of six to eight pieces. Most consider Godiva the very best (handmade, 130BF/100 grams). But most locals sacrifice 10 percent in quality to double their take by getting their fix at Leonidas (machine-made, 50BF/100 grams, white is their specialty). Galler's chocolate, the royal favorite, rivals Godiva. Only their display includes English descriptions, so you'll know what you're enjoying (next to Leonidas at rue au Beurre #44, handmade, 100BF/100 grams).

Manneken-Pis—Brussels is a great city, but its mascot (apparently symbolizing the city's irreverence) is a statue of a little boy urinating. For the story about this little squirt, read a postcard stand. It's three short blocks off the Grand Place, but for exact directions, I'll let you ask a local, "*Où est le Manneken-Pis?*" He may be wearing some clever outfit. By tradition, costumes are sent to Brussels from around the world. Cases full of these are on display in the City Museum (described above).

Lace and Costume Museum—This has not a word of English and is worthwhile only to those who have devoted their lives to the making of lace (80BF, Mon–Tue, Thu–Fri 10:00–12:30, 13:30–17:00, Sat–Sun 14:00–16:30, closed Wed, Violette 6, a block off the square).

▲▲▲**Museum of Ancient Art and Modern Art**—These are two separate museums, now connected by a tunnel and covered by the same ticket. The Ancient Art museum, featuring Flemish and Belgian art of the 14th to 18th centuries, is packed with a dazzling collection of masterpieces by Van der Weyden, Breughel, Bosch, and Rubens. Start your visit with the free 30-minute video featuring a handful of Flemish masterpieces, enabling you to go through the museum understanding these as if you were an art historian. Consider the CD wand tour (100BF) and the 100BF *Twenty Masterpieces of the Art of Painting—A Brief Guided Tour* booklet. Tour the rooms of this museum in numerical order (starting with 10). Highlights are room 31—busy with Breugel—and rooms of Rubens (with delightful mini cartoons used as designs to produce the big canvases).

The Museum of Modern Art gives an easy-to-enjoy walk through the art of the 19th and 20th centuries. Highlights include David's famous neoclassical portrait of Marat (1793; two floors underground, press "-2" in elevator), the stirring Social Realism of the early industrial age, and the surreal fantasies of Rene and Georgette Magritte.

One ticket works for both museums (150BF, worthwhile 20BF map of ancient- and modern-art museums complex, Tue–Sun 10:00–17:00, closed Mon, half the rooms close for lunch 12:00–13:00, the other half close 13:00–14:00, decent cafeteria with salad bar, rue de la Regence 3, tel. 02/508-3211).

▲**Belgian Centre of the Comic Strip**—This strip joint is housed in an industrial warehouse designed by Horta, the local Art Nouveau great. It's free to get inside to visit the brasserie and bookstore. Upstairs the comics are interesting only to the Belgians (200BF, Tue–Sun 10:00–18:00, closed Mon, rue des Sables 20, tel. 02/219-1980).

▲**Park of the Cinquantenaire**—This park sprawls out from under a massive triumphal arch, which was built in 1880 to celebrate the 50th anniversary of Belgian independence. While precious few of the governmental buildings of the European Union (EU) are visually exciting, you can emerge from the Métro at the Schuman stop to be surrounded by the political headquarters of a more or less united Europe. The huge, star-shaped Berlaymont Building (built in 1963 to house the Commission of the European Union) was polluted by asbestos insulation and is now empty and awaiting renovation. From there, walk 10 minutes through the park to the AutoWorld and military museums (under the giant arch). The next Métro stop (Merode) is closer to the museums.

▲**AutoWorld**—Starting with Mr. Benz's motorized tricycle of 1886, you'll walk through a giant hall filled with 400 historic cars. It's well described in English. There's a one-hour/100BF Walkman tour available (200BF, daily 10:00–18:00, until 17:00 off-season, in the Palais Mondial, Parc du Cinquantenaire, Métro: Merode, tel. 02/736-4165).

▲**Royal Museum of the Army and Military History**—Wander through a vast collection of 19th-century weaponry and uniforms and a giant hall dedicated to airplanes of war (free, Tue–Sun 9:00–12:00, 13:00–16:30, closed Mon, tel. 02/737-7811). There's a good display from the Belgian struggle for independence (early 1800s).

Natural History Museum—Dinosaur enthusiasts come here for the world's largest collection of iguanodon skeletons (150BF, Tue–Fri 9:45–16:45, Sat–Sun 10:00–18:00, closed Mon, Chaussée de Wavre 260, Métro: Merode, tel. 02/627-4233).

Royal Museum of Central Africa—Remember the Belgian Congo? Brussels has an excellent museum of the Congo and much more of Africa (ethnography, sculptures, jewelry, colonial history, flora, and fauna) an hour from the center. Take Métro 1A to Montgomery and then take tram #44 to its final stop, Tervuren. From there walk 200 meters through the park to a palace (80BF, Tue–Fri 10:00–17:00, weekends until 18:00, closed Mon, tel. 02/769-5211).

Antoine Wiertz Museum—This 19th-century artist painted some of the world's largest canvases, with themes from biblical to political (free, 10:00–12:00, 13:00–17:00, closed Mon and every other weekend, rue Vautier 62, Métro: Troon, tel. 02/648-1718).

Atomium—This giant molecule, with escalators connecting the various "atoms" and a restaurant with a view in the top sphere, was the symbol of the 1958 Universal Exhibition held in Belgium (200BF, daily 9:00–20:00, until 18:00 off-season, Métro: Heizel, tel. 02/474-8977). Today it's the cheesy nucleus of a park on the edge of town that has the kid-pleasing **Mini-Europa**, with 1:25-scale models of 300 famous European buildings (420BF, discounts for kids, daily 9:30–20:00, closes earlier off-season, tel. 02/474-1311).

Tours of Brussels

Chatter Tour offers a youthful and creative 2.5-hour tour that mixes walking and public transport and makes hard-to-understand Brussels more than a collection of sights. The groups are small, and the guides expertly explain the delicate balance between French and Flemish through the architecture and art of the city. Starting with medieval and moving through modern styles, this is a study in how a region in an almost-perpetual state of flux until the last century somehow managed to find some cohesion and create a modern state. Of special interest is the late-19th-century Art Nouveau style, especially as pioneered by Belgian Victor Horta. You'll see several of his buildings (300BF, 250BF for hostelers who buy tickets at their hostel; mid-Jun–mid-Sept daily at 10:00; meet at Galeries Royales Saint-Hubert, rue Marche-aux-Herbes 90, near La Grand Place, tel. 02/673-1835). Ask about their other tours.

The **Human Profile of Brussels Minibus Tour** takes eight visitors on three-hour tours and has the same commitment to teaching an understanding of Brussels as Chatter Tours (1,000BF, mid-Mar–Oct daily at 10:00, 14:00, and 18:00, 10 Grand Place, tel. 02/715-9120).

De Boeck's City Tours—a typical three-hour, tape-recorded bus tour—provides the handiest way to get the grand perspective on Brussels (790BF, starts with a walk around La Grand Place before jumping on a tour bus at rue de la Colline 8, daily in season at 10:00, 11:00, 14:00, and 15:00; off-season at 10:00 and 14:00; buy tickets a block off La Grand Place at rue de la Colline 8, tel. 02/513-7744). You'll see (and learn about) the Royal Palace, Atomium, and the European Union Headquarters.

Sleeping in Brussels
(40BF = about $1, tel. code: 02, zip code: 1000)
Sleep Code: **S** = Single, **D** = Double/Twin, **T** = Triple, **Q** = Quad, **b** = bathroom, **t** = toilet only, **s** = shower only, **CC** = Credit Card (Visa, MasterCard, Amex). Everyone speaks English. Prices include breakfast unless noted otherwise.

Like everything else, hotel prices are high in central Brussels. You have three budget options: modern hostels with double rooms, safe but dingy old places, and business hotels offering summer or weekend specials. September is very crowded, and finding a room without a reservation can be impossible. In 2000 Brussels will host soccer's Europe Cup. Expect huge and rowdy crowds in late June.

Business Hotels with Summer Rates
The fancy (5,000–6,000BF) hotels of Brussels survive off the business and diplomatic trade. They are desperately empty in July and August (sometimes June, too) and on weekends (most Fri, Sat, and Sun nights). If you ask for a summer rate you'll save about a third. If you go through the TI, you'll save up to two-thirds. Four-star hotels in the center abound with summer rates between 2,500 and 3,000BF. If you are willing to sink as low as three stars, you'll probably get a double with enough comforts to keep a diplomat happy, including a fancy breakfast, for as low as 2,000BF.

While the TI assured me that every day in July and August there are tons of business-class hotel rooms on the push list, you can book in advance by calling the BTR room-booking service (tel. 02/513-7484). You will, however, get an even bigger discount by just showing up at the TI. In July and August I would arrive without a reservation, walk from the Central Station down to the TI, and let them book me a room within a few blocks. These seasonal rates apply only to business-class hotels. Because of this, budget accommodations, which charge the same throughout the year, go from being a good value one day to a bad value the next. I like the first three listings best.

Hotels near La Grand Place
Hotel Welcome is farthest away from the Grand Place (a 10-min walk) but is the best value. Just renovated by a bundle of hospitality energy named Meester Smeester, it offers small but business-class rooms. With just 10 rooms, it brags it's the smallest hotel in

Brussels (small Sb/Db-2,400BF, Db-2,800–3,400BF, larger Db-4,500BF rooms are draped in elegance and overlook the square, extra bed-500BF, breakfast-250BF, CC:VM, free parking, at Ste. Catherine Métro stop on a characteristic old square, 23 Quai au Bois a Bruler, tel. 02/219-9546, fax 02/217-1887, www .hotelwelcome.com, Sophie and Michael Smeester). Guests get a 5 percent discount at the pricey attached restaurant, La Truite d'Argent.

Hôtel La Madeleine, on the small square between the station and La Grand Place, is comfortable and hotelesque, with fine rooms (S-1,695BF, no shower at all for this room; Sb-2,995BF, Db-3,295BF, Tb-4,295BF, CC:VMA, elevator, rue de la Montagne 22, tel. 02/513-2973, fax 02/502-1350).

Hotel Pacific is gently run by Paul Powells, whose motto is "safe, clean, and cheap." While the charming breakfast room is 19th century, the ramshackle upstairs feels like a Jackson Pollock thrift shop. Even with the wrinkly linoleum and funky furnishings, Paul gives the place an enjoyable calmness (S-1,100BF, D-1,800BF, Ds-2,250BF, T-2,400BF, includes a cheese-omelet breakfast, nonsmoking, showers-100BF, elevator, 24:00 curfew, easy phone reservations, rue Antoine Dansaert 57, tel. 02/511-8459). To maintain the peace during the Europe Cup, Paul will accept only non–soccer fans in June 2000.

Hotel Ibis, perfectly situated halfway between the station and La Grand Place, is a huge modern place offering quiet, simple, industrial-strength yet comfy rooms with rates that stay the same every day (Db-4,200BF, extra person-500BF, breakfast-300BF, CC:VMA, air-con, elevator, smoke-free rooms, Grasmarkt 100, tel. 02/514-4040, fax 02/514-5067).

Hôtel Opera, on a great people-filled street near the Grand Place, is professional, dark, and classy, with street noise and boxy rooms (Sb-2,500BF, Db-2,900–3,000BF, Tb-3,650BF, Qb-4,200BF, CC:VMA, courtyard rooms are quieter, elevator, rue Gretry 53, tel. 02/219-4343, fax 02/219-1720).

Hotel Sema, with wood floors and some beamed ceilings, has 11 spacious and comfy rooms just off La Grand Place and right across from the TI (Sb-3,000–4,000BF, Db-3,500–4,500BF, Tb-4,000–5,000BF, CC:VMA, elevator, rooms have phones and cable TV, 24-hour desk, tel. 02/514-0760, fax 02/548-9039).

Hostels

Three classy and modern hostels, in buildings that could double as small, state-of-the-art, minimum-security prisons, are within a 10-minute walk of Central Station. Each accepts people of all ages, serves cheap hot meals, and charges about the same (S-695BF, D-1,140BF, beds in quads-470BF, beds in bigger dorms-405BF, sheets-125BF; nonmembers pay up to 100BF extra). All rates include breakfast and showers down the hall. **Breughel Hostel,** a fortress of cleanliness, is handiest and most comfortable. Twenty-two of its rooms are bunk-bed doubles (open 7:30–10:00, 14:00–01:00, CC:VM, midway between Midi and Central Stations, behind Notre Dame de la Chapelle church, rue de St. Esprit 2, tel. 02/511-0436, fax 02/512-0711, e-mail: jeugdherberg.bruegel @ping.be). **Sleepwell,** surrounded by high-rise parking lots, is also comfortable (offers Internet access and walking tours every morning at 10:00 for 100BF per person, rue de Damier 23, tel. 02/218-5050, www.sleepwell.be). **Jacques Brel** is a little farther out but still a reasonable walk from everything (rue de la Sablonniere 30, tel. 02/218-0187).

Eating in Brussels

Eat mussels in Brussels. They're served everywhere. You get a big-enough-for-two bucket and a pile of fries. Use one empty shell to tweeze out the rest of the mussels. When the mollusks are in season, from about July 15 through April, you'll get the big Dutch mussels. Locals take a break in May and June, when only the puny Danish variety is available. For an atmospheric cellar just off the Grand Place, step into the **t'Kelderke** (daily 12:00–2:00, La Grand Place 15, tel. 02/513-7344). It serves local specialties, including mussels (a splitable two-kilo bucket of *moules* for 625BF). Locals claim the best mussels are served at **Restaurant Leon,** which offers a small "Formula Leon" 445BF *menu* of a small bucket, fries, and a beer (daily from noon, rue des Bouchers 18, tel. 02/511-1415).

Brussels' restaurant streets are touristy but fun (exit left from TI on rue Marche-aux-Herbes and take the first right). Many of these restaurants take advantage of tourists by tacking on extra charges.

If Brussels puts you in an Art Nouveau mood, have a meal or coffee at the city's most atmospheric hangout, **De Ultieme Hallucinatie** (exotic 275–500BF meals, Mon–Fri 11:00–3:00, Sat–Sun from 16:00, beautiful patio, rue Royale 316, tel. 02/217-0614).

You'll find *frites* (French fries) and sandwich shops throughout Brussels. **Panos** has good, cheap sandwiches (on Grasmarkt, across from entrance of Galleries Royales St. Hubert).

Two **supermarkets** are about a block from the Bourse (Stock Exchange) and a few blocks from La Grand Place. The **AD Delhaize** is at the intersection of Anspachlan and Marche-aux-Poulets (Tue–Sat 9:00–20:00, Mon from 13:00, Sun 9:00–13:00), and the **Super GB** is a half block away at Halles and Marche-aux-Poulets (daily 9:00–20:00).

Transportation Connections—Brussels

By train to: Brugge (:03 and :30 past each hour, 50 min), **Amsterdam** (:44 after each hour, 3 hrs), **Berlin** (7/day, 9 hrs), **Bern** (4/day, 8 hrs), **Frankfurt** (9/day, 5 hrs), **Munich** (9/day,

8 hrs), **Rome** (4/day, 17–20 hrs), **Paris** (fast trains zip to Paris— 8/day, 90 min—but require booking by 20:00 the day before and come with a supplement of 420BF/2nd class, 630BF/1st class— even for railpass holders. There's one slow, 4-hr, no-supplement train a day). Train info: tel. 02/555-2525 (long wait); international train info: tel. 0900-95-777.

To London: Brussels and London are now just three 140-mile-per-hour hours apart by Eurostar train (under the English Channel in 20 min; 6/day). For the latest prices, call 800/ EUROSTAR in the United States or 0900-10366 in Belgium (www.eurostar.com). In 2000, "full-fare" tickets cost $239 for first class and $159 for second class. Full-fare tickets are exchangeable and fully refundable even after your departure date. The cheaper "Leisure" tickets cost $199 for first class and $119 for second class; these are nonexchangeable and 50 percent refundable up to three days before departure. You can buy your Eurostar tickets in the United States (800/EUROSTAR), at any major train station in Europe, or by phone in Europe (see below). If you buy tickets in person in Belgium, go to a major train station rather than a travel agency; you'll get your tickets immediately (travel agencies can't deliver until the next day). To order your ticket by phone in Belgium, call 0900-10366 for Eurostar information and 0900-10177 to reserve (expensive toll line costs 20BF/min from pay phone and 60BF/min from hotel); you can either pay with a credit card or simply reserve a seat (and pay at the station at least an hour before the train leaves).

Another option is the sloooow train and ferry combination (8/day, 4.5–7.5 hrs). Or save a little money by riding a Eurolines bus ($42 one way, $54 round-trip, tel. 02/203-0707 in Brussels).

By plane: Virgin Express flies cheap from Brussels to London (hrly, $60), Milan, Rome, Nice, Barcelona, Madrid, Ireland, and Copenhagen (tel. 02/752-0505, www.virgin-express.com). For airport information call 02/753-3913.

THE NETHERLANDS

- 14,000 square miles (a little larger than Maryland)
- 15 million people (1,150 per square mile, 15 times the population density of the United States)
- 1 guilder = about 50 cents

The Netherlands, Europe's most densely populated country, is also one of its wealthiest and best-organized. A generation ago, Belgium, the Netherlands, and Luxembourg formed the nucleus of a united Europe when they joined economically to form Benelux.

Efficiency is a local custom. The average income is higher than that in the United States. Though only 8 percent of the labor force is made up of farmers, they cultivate 70 percent of the land, and you'll travel through vast fields of barley, wheat, sugar beets, potatoes, and flowers.

"Holland" is just a nickname for the Netherlands. North Holland and South Holland are the largest of the 12 states that make up the Netherlands. The word *Netherlands* means "low-lands." Half the country is below sea level, reclaimed from the sea (or rivers). That's why the locals say, "God made the Earth, but the Dutch made Holland." Modern technology and plenty of Dutch elbow grease have turned much of the sea into fertile farm-land. While a new, 12th state—Flevoland, near Amsterdam—has recently been drained, dried, and populated, Dutch reclamation projects are essentially finished.

The Dutch generally speak English, pride themselves on their frankness, and like to split the bill. Traditionally, Dutch cities have been open-minded, loose, and liberal (to attract sailors in the days of Henry Hudson). And today, Amsterdam is a capital of alterna-tive lifestyles—a city where "victimless crime" is a contradiction in itself. While Amsterdam has its quiet sides, many enjoy more sedate Dutch evenings by sleeping in a small town nearby and side-tripping into the big city.

The Dutch guilder (f, for its older name, florin) is divided into 100 cents (c). There are about f2 in a U.S. dollar (f2 = $1). To roughly convert Dutch prices into dollars, simply divide the price in guilders by two (e.g., f60 = $30).

The country is so small, level, and well covered by trains and buses that transportation is a snap. Major cities are connected by speedy trains that come and go every 10 or 15 minutes. Connec-tions are excellent, and you'll rarely wait more than a few minutes. Round-trip tickets are discounted. Buses take you where trains don't, and bicycles take you where buses don't. Bus stations and bike-rental shops cluster around train stations. The national bus system, both within and between cities, runs on a uniform "strip card" system (though single-ride tickets are also available). You can buy various strip cards on the bus or more cheaply (15 strip cards, f11.75) at train stations, post offices, and some tobacco shops. If you're caught riding without a card, you have to take off your clothes.

Holland is a biker's dream. The Dutch, who average four bikes per family, have put small bike roads (with their own traffic lights) beside every big auto route. You can rent bikes at most train stations and drop them off at most others. (You can take bikes on trains, outside of rush hour, for f10.)

Smaller shops are open from 9:00 to 18:00 and until 21:00 on Thursdays (closed Sun). Larger stores and supermarkets are open weekdays from 8:00 to 20:00 and until 17:00 on Saturdays (closed Sun). The businesslike Dutch know no siesta, but many shopkeepers take Monday mornings off.

The best "Dutch" food is Indonesian (from the former colony). Find any Indisch restaurant and experience a rijsttafel ("rice table"). With as many as 30 spicy dishes, a rijsttafel can be split and still fill two hungry tourists. *Nasi rames* is a cheaper, smaller version of a rijsttafel. Local taste treats are cheese, pancakes (*pannenkoeken*), Dutch gin (*jenever*, pronounced "ya nayver"), light Pilsner beer, and "syrup waffles" (*stroopwafel*). Yogurt in Holland (and throughout northern Europe) is delicious and drinkable right out of its plastic container. *Broodjes* are sandwiches of fresh bread and delicious cheese—cheap at snack bars, delis, and *broodje* restaurants. For cheap fast food, try a Middle Eastern *shwarma*, roasted lamb in pita bread. Breakfasts are big by continental standards. Lunch and dinner are served at American times.

Experiences you owe your tongue in Holland: a raw herring (outdoor herring stands are all over), lingering over coffee in a "brown café," an old *jenever* with a new friend, and a giant rijsttafel. Tipping is not expected, but locals round the bill up (never more than 5 percent) as thanks for good service.

AMSTERDAM

Amsterdam is a progressive way of life housed in Europe's most 17th-century city. Physically, it's a city built upon millions of pilings. But, more than that, it's a city built on good living, cozy cafés, great art, street-corner jazz, stately history, and a spirit of live and let live. It has 800,000 people and as many bikes and has more canals than Venice—and as many tourists. While Amsterdam may box your Puritan ears, this great, historic city is an experiment in freedom.

Planning Your Time

While I'd sleep in nearby Haarlem, Amsterdam is worth a full day of sightseeing on even the busiest itinerary. While the city has a couple of must-see museums, its best sight is its own breezy ambience. The city's a joy on foot. It's a breezier and faster joy by bike. And the sights are conveniently laced together by the circular tram #20. Here are the essential stops for a day in Amsterdam:

Start the day with a circular orientation tour on tram #20 (described below). Break this morning overview with a stop at the city's two great art museums: Van Gogh and the Rijksmuseum (cafeteria for lunch). Pick up tram #20 where you got off and complete the circle back to the station (or walk to Spui from the museums via Leidsestraat).

Spend midafternoon taking a relaxing hour-long canal cruise (from the dock at Spui). Near Spui consider seeing the peaceful Begijnhof, the Amsterdam Historical Museum, and the flower market.

Visiting the Anne Frank House after 18:00 (it's open until 21:00) will save you an hour in line. On a balmy evening, Amsterdam has a Greek island ambience. Wander the Jordaan for the

Amsterdam Overview

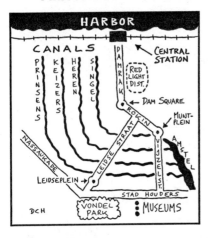

idyllic side of town and wander down Leidse-straat to Leidseplein for the roaring café and people scene. Wander the Red Light District while you're at it.

With extra time: With two days in Holland, I'd side-trip by bike, bus, or train to an open-air folk museum and visit Edam or Haarlem. With a third day I'd do the other great Amsterdam museums. With four days I'd do the "historic triangle" or visit The Hague.

Orientation (tel. code: 020)

Amsterdam's central train station is your starting point (TI, bike rental, and tram #20 and others fanning out to all points). Damrak is the main street axis, connecting the station with Dam Square (people-watching and hangout center) and its Royal Palace. From this spine the city spreads out like a fan, with 90 islands, hundreds of bridges, and a series of concentric canals (named "Prince's," "Gentleman's," and "Emperor's") laid out in the 17th century, Holland's Golden Age. Amsterdam's major sights are within walking distance of Dam Square.

Tourist Information

Avoid Amsterdam's inefficient VVV offices if you can (VVV is Dutch for tourist information office; TI in train station open Mon–Sat 8:00–20:00, Sun 9:00–17:00). Most people wait 30 minutes just to pick up information brochures and get a room. At the VVV in front of the station, avoid this line by studying the display of publications for sale and going straight to the sales desk (where everyone ends up anyway, since any information of substance will cost you). Consider buying a city map (f4), *What's On* (f4, monthly entertainment calendar), and any of the f4 walking-tour brochures ("Discovery Tour through the Center," "The Former Jewish Quarter," "Walks through Jordaan"). The Amsterdam Culture & Leisure Pass, offering free or discounted admissions to some sights and boat rides, isn't worth the clutter or cost (f40, doesn't include Anne Frank House). Nor does it make sense to stand in line at the VVV to buy prepaid same-cost admissions to various Amsterdam sights.

The TI on Leidsestraat is less crowded (Mon–Fri 9:00–19:00, closes at 17:00 Sat–Sun). But for f1 a minute, you can save yourself a trip by calling the tourist information toll line at 0900-400-4040 (Mon–Fri 9:00–17:00). If you're staying in nearby Haarlem, use the helpful Haarlem TI (see the Haarlem chapter) to answer most of your Amsterdam questions and provide you with the brochures.

At Amsterdam's Central Station, GWK Change has two hotel reservations windows that sell phone cards and cheaper city maps (f3) and answer basic tourist questions. The lines are shorter. They also change money, including coins, for a hefty f5 fee (near the lockers, at the right end of the station as you leave the platform).

Don't use the TI (or GWK) to book a room (you'll pay f5 and your host loses the 13 percent deposit). The phone system is easy, everyone speaks English, and the listings in this book are a better value than the potluck booking you'd be charged for at the TI.

Helpful Hints

Many shops close all day Sunday and Monday morning. A *plein* is a square, *gracht* means canal, and most canals are lined by streets with the same name. Handy telephone cards (f10, f25, or f50) are sold at the TI, the GVB public-transit office, tobacco shops, post offices, and train stations (calling the United States from a phone booth is now very cheap—you'll get about 5 minutes for a dollar). Internet access is easy at cafés all over town (Internet Café, a couple blocks from the station, is at Martelaarsgracht 11, f2.50 per 20 min, daily, long hours, waits 16:00–21:00, tel. 020/627-1052). Coffee-shops are also into surfing the Web. Tourists are considered green and rich, and the city has more than its share of hungry thieves—especially on the trams.

Arrival in Amsterdam

By Train: Amsterdam swings, and the hinge that connects it to the world is its perfectly central Central Station. Walk out the door and you're in the heart of the city. You'll nearly trip over trams ready to take you anywhere your feet won't. Straight ahead is Damrak Street, leading to Dam Square. With your back to the entrance of the station, the TI and GVB public-transit offices and circular tram #20A are just ahead and to your left.

By Plane: From Schiphol Airport, take the train to Amsterdam (6/hrly, 20 min, f6.25). If you're staying in Haarlem, take a direct express bus to Haarlem (#236 or #362, 2/hrly, 30 min, f7).

Getting around Amsterdam

The helpful GVB transit-information office is next to the TI (the glass building with the revolving sign in front of the train station). Its free multilingual *Tourist Guide to Public Transport* includes a transit map, explains ticket options and tram connections to all the sights, and describes the Circle Tram #20 route, listing all the stops (and nearby sights, #20A goes clockwise, #20B goes counter-clockwise).

By Bus, Tram, and Metro: Individual tickets cost f3 and give you an hour on the buses, trams, and metro system (on trams and buses pay as you board; buy metro tickets from machines). **Strip cards** are cheaper than individual tickets. Any downtown ride costs two strips (good for an hour of transfers). A card with 15 strips costs f12 at the GVB public-transit office, train stations, post offices, airport, or tobacco shops throughout the country; shorter strip tickets (two, three, and eight strips) are also sold on some buses and trams. Strip cards are good on buses all over Holland (e.g., six strips for Haarlem to the airport), and you can share them with your partner. An f10 **Day Card** gives you unlimited transportation on the buses and metro for a day in Amsterdam; you'll almost break even if you take three trips (valid until 6:00 the following morning; buy as you board or at the GVB public-transit office, which also sells a 2-day version for f15). If you get lost in Amsterdam, 10 of the city's 17 trams take you back to the central train station.

By Foot: The longest walk a tourist would take is 45 minutes from the station to the Rijksmuseum. Watch out for silent but potentially painful bikes, trams, and crotch-high curb posts.

By Bike: One-speed bikes, with "brrringing" bells and two locks (use them both; bike thieves are bold and brazen here), rent for f9.50 per day at the central train station (daily 8:00–22:00; deposit of f200 or your credit-card imprint and passport required; entrance to the left down the ramp as you leave the station, tel. 020/624-8391). In the summer, arrive early or make a telephone reservation (they hold bikes until 10:30).

By Boat: While the city is great on foot or bike, there is a "Museum Boat" and a similar "Canal Bus" with an all-day ticket that shuttles tourists from sight to sight. Tickets cost f25 (with discounts to sights worth about f5). The sales booths in front of the central train station (and the boats) offer handy free brochures with museum times and admission prices. The narrated ride takes 90 minutes if you don't get off (every 30 min in summer, every 45 min off-season, 7 stops, live quadrilingual guide, departures 10:00–17:00, discounted after 13:00 to f20, tel. 020/622-2181). If you're looking for a floating (nonstop) tour, the real canal tour boats (without the stops) give more information, cover more ground, and cost less (see below).

By Taxi: Amsterdam's taxis are expensive (f6 drop and f3 for each km). Given the fine tram system, taxis are only a good value for airport connections (Schiphol Airport to Amsterdam costs f55).

By Car: Forget it—frustrating one-ways, terrible parking.

Circle Tram #20 Orientation Tour

For a ▲▲ self-guided tour, orient yourself for f3 in less than an hour
by riding this designed-for-tourists circle route from the station.
Catch #20A (not #20B) from tram lane (or *spoor*) #2 on the left as you
leave the station. The free tourist guidebooklet—there's a stack on
the desk in the transit office 50 meters away—comes with a route
map and lists each stop. You could buy the f6 one-day tram #20 pass.
Tram #20 runs every 10 minutes from 9:00 to 18:00 only.

0. Train Station: Leaving the station you pass both the canal bus
and museum boat docks (left). *Rondvaart* sign (right) means round-
trip. Boats like these all over town offer similar one-hour city
tours. Gliding up the tacky commercial cancan called the Damrak
you're following the same route taken by boats loaded with spices
and goodies from the East Indies in the city's early trading days.
The buildings across the water are Amsterdam's oldest. Behind
them is the Red Light District and old sailor's quarter. The huge
redbrick Beurs building (left) is the Dutch stock exchange.

1. The Dam Square: This is the city center, where the original
dam was built across the Amstel River, giving the town its name.
To your right is the Royal Palace (1655); next to it is the New
Church, the coronation church of Dutch royalty. To your left is
the World War I Memorial (1956), now becoming a generic peace
memorial; behind that is a strip of head shops. Straight ahead is
one of many "diamond polishing centers." Beyond the Dam Square
you continue down Rokin. Parallel and a block to the right is the
thriving Kalverstraat pedestrian shopping mall.

2. Spui Square: This marked the end of the city in the 14th
century. It's near the Begijnhof and the University of Amsterdam's
archaeology museum, which has a fine Egyptian collection.

3. Muntplein: This lively area is marked by the Mint Tower from
1620 (on the right). Behind that a charming flower market lines
the Singel Canal (see the row of greenhouses, thriving Mon–Sat
9:00–17:00). Turning left you enter a noisy neon nightlife center.

4. Rembrandtplein: Look for Rembrandt's statue in the leafy park
(right). This is the center of gay Amsterdam. You'll pass lots of dis-
cos and a Planet Hollywood, and a bridge will take you over the
Amstel River. The modern brown and white building (left) is the
city hall. Adjacent is the round Opera House. Notice the charming
counterbalance bridges (right).

5. Waterlooplein: This is famous for its flea market (daily except
Sun, on left). The Jewish Quarter (right) features the impressive
new Jewish History Museum (renovated brick synagogues with
blue and white banner). Crossing the bridge (funny paintings
revealed when opened) you enter green Amsterdam (gardens and
hothouses of University of Amsterdam all around, zoo nearby).

6. Plantage Kerklaan: Immediately to the right of this tram
stop, the white facade of the old Dutch Theater (Hollandsche

Amsterdam

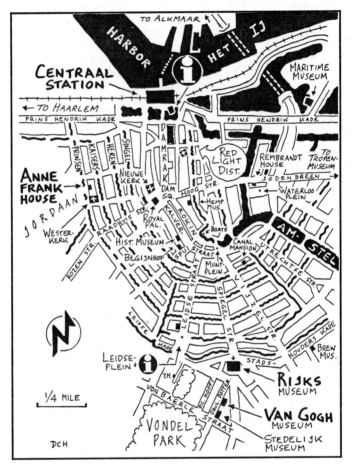

Schouwburg) survives. Used by Nazis as a holding zone for Jews being deported, today it's a memorial. The Dutch Resistance Museum and the zoo are half a block to the left. Passing through many University of Amsterdam buildings, notice the "XXX" symbol of the city (the three Xs stand for the adversities the Amsterdammers have overcome throughout their history: fire, plague, and floods). Crossing the Amstel River again, see the city hall and the opera house again in the distance (right), the palatial Amstel Hotel (behind on the left) and, in the distance, Holland's tallest skyscraper—the Phillips corporate headquarters.

7. Frederiksplein: Notice the houseboats; they're a common sight in Amsterdam. Also in Frederiksplein, you'll see the huge Albert Cuyp Market, perhaps the town's most interesting market, showing off the town's ethnic mix daily except Sunday. Now, passing through a nondescript area, notice how the city works: shops at street level—with homes above—keep neighborhoods vital, people-friendly, and safe. Bike lanes even have their own little traffic lights. New buildings still lean out and come with planks and pulleys for hoisting furniture past too-narrow stairways. Many of these are brick and built in the Art Deco "Amsterdam School" from the 1920s—a time when architects considered entire blocks as integrated works of art. Notice street signs with the district listed. You're in the *oud-zuid* (old south) quarter. Mail slots have green and orange decals saying yes or no to junk mail. And now public phone booths stand next to curbside computers for Internet access (locals use "chip cards"—the first step toward the cash-free society of the future—to access things like these).

8. Museumplein: A huge park (right) leads to the grand redbrick Rijksmuseum (built in 1885 by the same guy who designed Central Station). The new addition to the Van Gogh Museum (opened 1999) juts into the park in the foreground. The Concertgebouw (on the left) is Amsterdam's main concert hall. A huge underground parking lot keeps things uncluttered.

9. Van Baerlestraat: Rounding the corner, you stop at the Stedelijk Modern Art Museum (right) and the Van Gogh Museum (see crowd on right). An ice rink (right) faces the Coster Diamond House (left).

10. Hobbenmastraat: This is the stop for the Rijksmuseum (right). A fancy gate marks the entrance to the sprawling, in-love-with-life Vondelpark (left). Pass a casino (right) as you cross a canal and enter the noisy, people-filled Leidseplein area.

11. Leidseplein: Your tram just skirts Amsterdam's liveliest café, people-watching, and entertainment district. Be sure to loiter in Leidseplein later on. The huge modern parking lot (Texaco station, left) marks the line between the protected old town (right) and the anything-goes new one (left). Turning right you cut through the proud, fashionable, and trendy Jordaan district. Ahead stands the much-loved tallest church spire in town, marking the Westerkerk (West Church). Anne Frank hid out just down the street. As you continue ahead, the canal system is evident as you cross the Prince's, Keizers (kings), Herren (medieval business fat cats), and Singel canals and head toward the back side of the Royal Palace we saw at the Dam Square. Hop out here or glide back to your starting point at the Central Station.

Sights—Amsterdam's Museum Neighborhood

▲▲▲Rijksmuseum—Built to house the nation's greatest art, the Rijksmuseum packs several thousand paintings into 200 rooms.

To survive, focus on the Dutch masters: Rembrandt, Hals, Vermeer, and Steen. For a list of the top 20 paintings, pick up the cheap fl leaflet "A Tour of the Golden Age" and plan your attack (or follow the self-guided tour, one of 20, in my *Mona Winks* guidebook). CD tours are available, allowing you to dial up descriptions of over 200 paintings (f7.50).

Follow the museum's chronological layout to see painting evolve from narrative religious art to religious art starring the Dutch love of good living and eating to the Golden Age, when secular art dominated. With no local church or royalty to commission big canvases in the post-1648 Protestant Dutch republic, artists had to find different patrons. They specialized in portraits of the wealthy city class (Hals), pretty still lifes (Claesz), and non-preachy slice-of-life art (Steen). The museum has four quietly wonderful Vermeers. And, of course, a thoughtful brown soup of Rembrandt, including *Night Watch*. Works by Rembrandt show his excellence as a portraitist for hire (*De Staalmeesters*) and offer some powerful psychological studies, such as *St. Peter's Denial*—with a betrayed Jesus in the murky background (f15, daily 10:00–17:00, great bookshop, decent cafeteria; tram #2, #5, or #20 from the station; Stadhouderskade 42).

The Rijksmuseum celebrates 2000 with a year of special exhibits. Through most of the tourist season (Apr 15–Sept 17) the *Glory of the Golden Age* exhibit will amass an extravaganza of 17th-century Dutch art: the permanent collection—already the world's best—plus much much more. The result: too much art, long lines, and higher prices. Admission will jump to f25, and they threaten to dole out entry times only by advance reservation (for details: info@rijksmuseum.nl or call upon arrival, tel. 020/674-7000).

▲▲▲**Van Gogh Museum**—Next to the Rijksmuseum, this outstanding and user-friendly museum was opened in 1973 to house the 200 paintings owned by Vincent's younger brother Theo. Newly renovated in 1999, it's a stroll through a beautifully displayed garden of van Gogh's work and life (f12.50, daily 10:00–18:00, Paulus Potterstraat 7, tel. 020/570-5200). The museum also focuses on the late 19th-century art that influenced van Gogh (it happened to be in his brother Theo's collection). The new exhibition hall (included with admission) features art from 1840 to 1920. The f8.50 audio guide includes insightful commentaries about van Gogh's paintings along with related quotations from Vincent himself.

Stedelijk Modern Art Museum—Next to the Van Gogh Museum, this place is fun, far-out, and refreshing. It has mostly post-1945 art but also a sometimes-outstanding collection of Monet, van Gogh, Cézanne, Picasso, and Chagall and a lot of special exhibitions (f9, daily 11:00–19:00, closes at 17:00 Nov–Mar, tel. 020/573-2737).

Sights—Near Dam Square

▲▲**Anne Frank House**—A virtual pilgrimage for many, this house offers a fascinating look at the hideaway of young Anne when the Nazis occupied the Netherlands. Pick up the English pamphlet at the door. Recently expanded, the exhibit now offers more thorough coverage of the Frank family, the diary, the stories of others who hid out, and the Holocaust. Why do thousands endure hour-long daytime lines when they can walk right in by arriving after 18:00? Last entrance is 20:30. Visit after dinner (f10, Apr–Aug daily 9:00–21:00, closes daily at 19:00 Sept–Mar, 263 Prinsengracht, tel. 020/556-7100). For an interesting glimpse of Holland under the Nazis, rent the powerful movie *Soldier of Orange* before you leave home.

Westerkerk—Near the Anne Frank House, this landmark church has a barren interior, Rembrandt somewhere under the pews, and Amsterdam's tallest steeple. It's worth climbing for the view (f3, ascend only with a guide, departures on the hour, Apr–Sept Mon–Sat 10:00–17:00, closed Sun, tel. 020/612-6856).

Royal Palace (Koninklijk Paleis)—The palace, right on Dam Square, was built as a lavish city hall for Amsterdam, part of the proud new Dutch Republic. Amsterdam was awash in profit from trade, and, when it was built (around 1660), this building was one of Europe's finest. Today it's the official (but not actual) residence of the queen. Its sumptuous interior is worth a look (f5, Jun–Aug daily 12:30–17:00, less off-season).

▲**Begijnhof**—Step into this tiny, idyllic courtyard in the city center to escape into the charm of old Amsterdam. Notice house #34, a 500-year-old wooden structure (rare since repeated fires taught city fathers a trick called brick). Peek into the hidden Catholic church, opposite the English Reformed church, where the pilgrims worshiped while waiting for their voyage to the New World (marked by a plaque near the door). Be considerate of the people who live here (free, on Begijnensteeg Lane, just off Kalverstraat between #130 and #132, pick up flyer at office near entrance).

Amsterdam Historical Museum—Offering the town's best look into the age of the Dutch masters, this creative and hardworking museum features Rembrandt's paintings, fine English descriptions, and a carillon loft. The loft comes with push-button recordings of the town bell tower's greatest hits and a self-serve carillon "keyboard" to ring a few bells yourself (f11, Mon–Fri 10:00–17:00, Sat–Sun 11:00–17:00, good-value restaurant, next to Begijnhof, Kalverstraat 92, tel. 020/523-1822). Its free pedestrian corridor is a powerful teaser.

Sights—East Amsterdam

To reach these sights from the train station, ride tram #9, #14, or #20. The first six sights listed make an interesting walk.

Central Amsterdam

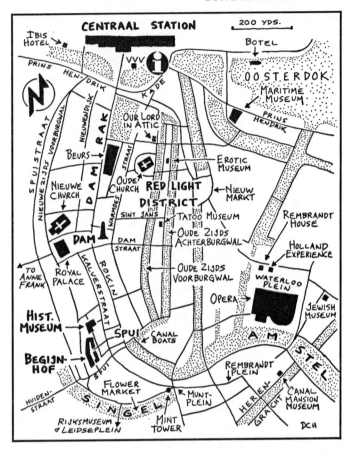

Rembrandt's House—Rembrandt's reconstructed house is filled with exactly what his bankruptcy inventory of 1656 said he owned. You'll find no paintings but 65 of his etchings (f12.50, Mon–Sat 10:00–17:00, Sun 13:00–17:00, 10-min English video upon request, Jodenbreestraat 4, tel. 020/638-4668).

Holland Experience—Bragging "Experience Holland in 30 minutes," this show takes you traveling with three clowns through an idealized montage of Dutch clichés. No words but lots of images and special effects as you rock with the boat and get spritzed with perfume while viewing the tulips (f17.50, 2 enter for the price of 1 with this book, or show this book and get f2.50 off the f25 combo Rembrandt's House/Experience ticket, daily 10:00–18:30, Jodenbreestraat 8, near Rembrandt's House and Waterlooplein street market, metro: Waterlooplein, tel. 020/422-2233). The men's urinal is a trip to the beach. Plan for it.

Waterlooplein Flea Market—For over a hundred years, the flea market of the Jewish Quarter has raged daily except Sunday behind the Rembrandt House.

Jewish History Museum—Four historic synagogues have been joined by steel and glass to make one modern complex telling the story of the Jews in Amsterdam through the centuries (f8, daily 11:00–17:00, good kosher café, Jonas Daniel Meijerplein 2, tel. 020/626-9945).

Dutch Theatre (Hollandsche Schouwburg)—This is a moving memorial. Once a great theater in the Jewish neighborhood, this was used as an assembly hall for local Jews destined for Nazi concentration camps. On the wall, 6,700 family names pay tribute to the 104,000 Jews deported and killed by the Nazis. There's little to actually see but plenty to think about (free, daily 11:00–16:00, Plantage Middenlaan 24, tel. 020/626-9945).

▲▲Dutch Resistance Museum (Verzetsmeuseum)—This is a new and impressive look at how the Dutch resisted their Nazi occupiers from 1940 to 1945. You'll see propaganda movie clips, study forged ID cards under a magnifying glass, and read of ingenious, clever, and courageous efforts to hide local Jews from the Germans (f8, Tue–Sun 12:00–17:00, closed Mon, well described in English, tram #9 or #20A from station, Plantage Kerklaan 61, tel. 020/620-2535). Amsterdam's famous zoo is just across the street.

▲Tropenmuseum (Tropical Museum)—As close to the Third World as you'll get without lots of vaccinations, this imaginative museum offers wonderful re-creations of tropical-life scenes and explanations of Third World problems (f12.50, Mon–Fri 10:00–17:00, Sat–Sun 12:00–17:00, tram #9 to Linnaeusstraat 2, tel. 020/568-8215).

Netherlands Maritime (Scheepvaart) Museum—This huge collection of model ships, maps, and sea-battle paintings fills the 300-year-old Dutch Navy Arsenal. Given the Dutch seafaring heritage, I expected a killer museum but found it lifeless and boring. Sailors may disagree, but—even with its re-creation of an 18th-century Dutch East India Company ship manned with characters in old costumes—the museum disappoints (f12.50, daily 10:00–17:00, closed Mon off-season, English explanations, don't waste your time with the 30-min movie, bus #22 or #32 to Kattenburgerplein 1, tel. 020/523-2222).

Sights—Red Light District
Our Lord in the Attic (Amstelkring)—Near the station, in the Red Light District, you'll find a fascinating hidden church

filling the attic of a hollowed-out row of 17th-century merchant's houses. This dates from 1661, when post-Reformation Dutch Catholics couldn't worship in public (f7.50, Mon–Sat 10:00–17:00, Sun 13:00–17:00, Oudezijds Voorburgwal 40, tel. 020/624-6604).

▲Red Light District—Europe's most touristed ladies of the night shiver and shimmy in display-case windows between the Oudezijds Achterburgwal and Oudezijds Voorburgwal, surrounding the Oude Kerk (Old Church). Druggies make the streets uncomfortable late at night, but it's a fascinating walk at any other time after noon (S&F, f50).

Amsterdam has two sex museums, one in the Red Light District and one a block in front of the train station on Damrak. While visiting one can be called sightseeing, visiting both is hard to explain. Here's a comparison:

The Red Light District sex museum is less offensive, with five sparsely decorated rooms relying heavily on badly dressed dummies acting out the roles that women of the neighborhood play. It also has videos, phone-sex phones, and a lot of uninspired paintings, old photos, and sculpture (f5, daily 11:00–24:00, along the canal at Oudezijds Achterburgwal 54).

The Damrak sex museum goes deeper and has more rooms. It tells the story of pornography from Roman times through 1960. Every sexual deviation is uncovered in its various displays, and the nude and pornographic art is a cut above the other sex museum's. Also interesting are the early French pornographic photos and memorabilia from Europe, India, and Asia. You'll find a Marilyn Monroe tribute and some S&M displays, too (f5, daily 10:00–23:30, Damrak 18, a block in front of the station).

More Sights—Amsterdam

▲Herengracht Canal Mansion (Willet Holthuysen Museum)—This 1687 patrician house offers a fine look at the old rich of Amsterdam, with a good 20-minute English introductory film and a 17th-century garden in back (f7.50, Mon–Fri 10:00–17:00, Sat–Sun 11:00–17:00, tram #1, #2, #4, #5, or #9 to Herengracht 605, tel. 020/523-1870).

Vondelpark—This huge and lively city park is popular with the Dutch—families with little kids, romantic couples, hippies sharing blankets and beers, and oldsters strolling. It's the scene of free concerts in the summer (tel. 020/523-7790).

Leidseplein—Brimming with cafés, this people- and pigeon-watching square is an impromptu stage for street artists, accordionists, jugglers, and unicyclists. Sunny afternoons are the liveliest. Stroll nearby Lange Leidsedwarsstraat (1 block north) for a taste-bud tour of ethnic eateries from Greece to Indonesia.

Shopping—Amsterdam brings out the browser even in those who were not born to shop. Ten general markets, open six days a week, keep folks who brake for garage sales pulling U-ies. Shopping highlights include Waterlooplein (the flea market); the huge Albert Cuyp street market; various flower markets (daily except Sun, along Singel Canal near the mint tower, or Munttoren); diamond dealers (free cutting and polishing demos at shops behind the Rijksmuseum and on Dam Square); and Kalverstraat, Amsterdam's teeming walking/shopping street (parallel to Damrak).

Tours of Amsterdam

▲▲**Canal-Boat Tour**—These long, low, tourist-laden boats leave continually from several docks around the town for a good, if uninspiring, one-hour quadrilingual introduction to the city (f13, 2/hrly, more frequent in summer). One very central company is at the corner of Spui and Rokin, about five minutes from Dam Square (daily 10:00–22:00, tel. 020/623-3810). No fishing allowed—but bring your camera for this relaxing orientation. Some prefer to cruise at night, when the bridges are illuminated.

Biking and Walking Tours—The Yellow Bike Tour company offers bike tours (f33 for 3-hour city tour; f42.50 for 6.5-hour, 35-kilometer countryside tour; daily Apr–Nov) and city walking tours for groups by arrangement (f200, 2 hrs, Nieuwezijds Kolk 29, 3 blocks from train station, tel. 020/620-6940).

Do-It-Yourself Bike Tour of Amsterdam—A day enjoying the bridges, bike lanes, and sleepy off-the-beaten-path canals on your own one-speed is the essential Amsterdam experience. The real joys of Europe's best-preserved 17th-century city are the countless intimate glimpses it offers: the laid-back locals sunning on their porches under elegant gables, rusted bikes that look as if they've been lashed to the same lamppost since the '60s, wasted hedonists planted on canalside benches, happy sailors permanently moored but still manning the deck.

For a good day, rent a bike at the station. Head west down Haarlemmerstraat, working your wide-eyed way down the Prinsengracht (along the canal) and detouring through the gentrified small streets of the Jordaan area before popping out at Westerkerk under the tallest spire in the city.

Pedal past the palace, through Dam Square, and down Kalverstraat (the city's bustling pedestrian mall) and poke into the sleepy Begijnhof. Catch the hour-long cruise at Spui. Continue down Rokin to the Mint Tower, biking along the Singel Canal flower market to Leidsestraat. Dodge trams and people down Leidsestraat. Enjoy the lush and peaceful Vondelpark. Then pedal back to the Dam Square. To detour through seedy, sexy, pot-smoking Amsterdam, roll down Damstraat and then turn left down Oudezijds Voorburgwal through the land of Rastafarian "coffee shops," red lights over black tights, and sailors lost without the sea. You'll pop out near the station.

To finish your day, escape into the countryside by hopping on the free ferry behind the Amsterdam station. In five minutes Amsterdam will be gone, and you'll be rolling through your very own Dutch painting. (See "Getting around Amsterdam," above, for info on bike rental).

Brewery Tour—The infamous Heineken brewery tours are in full slosh Monday through Friday at 9:30 and 11:00 (f2; tours also afternoons and Sat in summer; must be 18 years old, tram #16, #24, or #25, Stadhouderskade 78, near Rijksmuseum, tel. 020/523-9666). Try to arrive a little early.

Wetlands Safari, Nature Canoe Tours Near Amsterdam— If you'd like to "turn your back on Amsterdam" and get a dose of the *polder* country and village life along with some exercise, consider this tour. Majel Tromp, a village girl who speaks great English, takes groups of no more than 15. The program: Meet at the VVV tourist office outside the station, catch a bus, stop for coffee, take a canoe trip with several stops, munch a village picnic lunch (included), canoe, and bus back into the big city by 14:30 (f58, May–mid-Sept Mon–Fri, call to reserve, tel. 020/686-3445 or 06/53-552-669, http://members.xoom.com/wet_lands).

Sleeping in Amsterdam
(f1 = about 50 cents, tel. code: 020)
Sleep Code: **S** = Single, **D** = Double/Twin, **T** = Triple, **Q** = Quad, **b** = bathroom, **t** = toilet only, **s** = shower only, **CC** = Credit Card (**V**isa, **M**asterCard, **A**mex). Nearly everyone speaks English in the Netherlands, and prices include breakfast unless noted.

While I prefer sleeping in cozy Haarlem (see below), those into more urban charms will find that Amsterdam has plenty of beds. Summer weekends are booked well in advance.

Sleeping near the Station
Amstel Botel, the city's only remaining "boat hotel," is a shipshape, bright, and clean floating hotel with 175 rooms (Sb-f130, Db-f147, Tb-f180, worth the extra f10 for canal-side view, breakfast-f12, f33/ day parking pass, CC:VMA, elevator, 400 yards from the station, on your left as you leave station, you'll see the sign, Oosterdokskade 2-4, 1011 AE Amsterdam, tel. 020/626-4247, fax 020/639-1952).

Ibis Amsterdam Hotel is a modern and efficient 180-room place towering over the station. It's perfectly central but out of the bustle and quiet—all comfort and value without a hint of charm (Db-f274, family-f358, skip breakfast and save f22 per person, CC:VMA, book long in advance, air-con, smoke-free floors, Stationsplein 49, tel. 020/638-3080, fax 020/620-0156, www.ibishotel.com).

Amsterdam Hotels

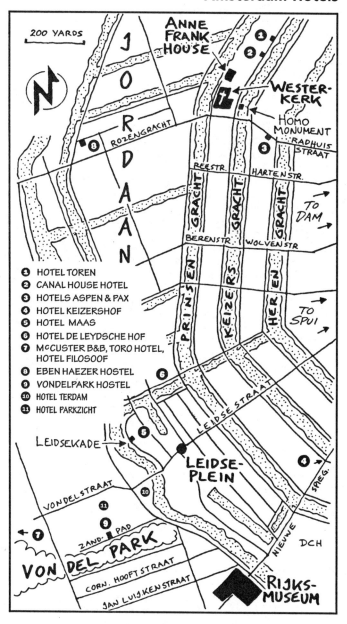

200 YARDS

N

JORDAAN

ANNE FRANK HOUSE

WESTER-KERK

Homo MONUMENT

RADHUIS STRAAT

ROZENGRACHT

REESTR.   HARTEN STR.

TO DAM

BERENSTR.   WOLVEN STR.

PRINSEN GRACHT

KEIZERS GRACHT

HEREN GRACHT

TO SPUI

❶ HOTEL TOREN
❷ CANAL HOUSE HOTEL
❸ HOTELS ASPEN & PAX
❹ HOTEL KEIZERSHOF
❺ HOTEL MAAS
❻ HOTEL DE LEYDSCHE HOF
❼ McCUSTER B&B, TORO HOTEL, HOTEL FILOSOOF
❽ EBEN HAEZER HOSTEL
❾ VONDELPARK HOSTEL
❿ HOTEL TERDAM
⓫ HOTEL PARKZICHT

LEIDSE STRAAT

LEIDSEKADE

LEIDSE-PLEIN

SPIEG.

VONDELSTRAAT

ZAND. PAD

VON DEL PARK

NIEUWE   DCH

CORN. HOOFT STRAAT

JAN LUIJKEN STRAAT

RIJKS-MUSEUM

Sleeping between Dam Square and the Anne Frank House

Hotel Toren is a chandeliered historic mansion in a pleasant canalside setting in downtown Amsterdam. This splurge is classy yet friendly, quiet, two blocks northeast of the the Anne Frank House and still run by the Toren family: Elsje, Lisa, and Eric (Sb-f200, Db-f225–350, Tb-f270; bridal suites for f310–410 make you want to get married; prices vary with view and Jacuzzi; 10 percent discount for 3 nights and cash with this book, CC:VMA, air-con, Keizersgracht 164, 1015 CZ Amsterdam, tel. 020/622-6352, fax 020/626-9705, e-mail: hotel.toren@tip.nl).

Well-heeled readers enjoy the similar 17th-century **Canal House Hotel**, a few doors down, with its beautiful antique interiors, candlelit evenings, and soft music (Db-f265–345, CC:VMA, elevator, Keizersgracht 148, 1015 CX Amsterdam, tel. 020/622-5182, fax 020/624-1317, e-mail: canalhousehotel @compuserve.com).

Cheap hotels line the convenient but noisy main drag between the town hall and the Anne Frank House. Expect a long, steep, and depressing stairway, with quieter rooms in the back. **Hotel Aspen**, a good value for a budget hotel, is tidy, stark, and well maintained (S-f55, D-f80, Db-f125, Tb-f130–150, Qb-f180, no breakfast, CC:MA, Raadhuisstraat 31, 1016 DC Amsterdam, tel. 020/626-6714, fax 020/620-0866, run by Esam). A few doors away, **Hotel Pax** has large, plain, but airy backpacker-type rooms (S-f55–75, D-f80–110, T-f110–130, Q-f120–150, no breakfast, prices vary with size and season, CC:VMA, 2 showers for 8 rooms, Raadhuisstraat 37, tel. 020/624-9735, run by 2 brothers: Philip and Peter).

Calendula Goldbloom's B&B, run by an American couple, offers two comfortable rooms in a classy old home in a quiet Jordaan neighborhood a 5 minute walk northwest of the Anne Frank House (D-f180, extra bed f50, 2-night minimum, good breakfasts, Goudsbloemstraat 132, tel. 020/428-3055, fax 020/ 776-0075, www.calendulas.com, Lynn and Dennis).

Sleeping in the Leidseplein Area

The area around Amsterdam's museum square (Museumplein) and the rip-roaring nightlife center (Leidseplein) is colorful, comfortable, convenient, and affordable. These three canalside places are 5 or 10 minutes from Leidseplein.

Hotel Keizershof is a wonderfully Dutch place, with six bright, airy rooms in a 17th-century canal house. A steep spiral staircase leads to rooms named after old-time Hollywood stars. The enthusiastic hospitality of the De Vries family has made this place a treat for 38 years (S-f75, D-f125, Ds-f135, Db-f150, T-f175, Tb-f200, CC:VM, nonsmoking, classy breakfast, nice garden; tram #16, #24, or #25 from station; where Keizers canal crosses Spiegelstraat at Keizersgracht 618, 1017 ER Amsterdam, tel. 020/622-2855, fax 020/624-8412, e-mail: keizershof@vdwp.nl).

Hotel Maas is a big, well-run, elegant, quiet, and stiffly hotelesque place (S-f110, 1 D-f135, Db-f250–275, suite-f375, prices vary with view and room size, extra person-f50, CC:VMA, hearty breakfast, air-con, elevator, tram #1, #2, #5, or #20 from station, Leidsekade 91, 1017 PN Amsterdam, tel. 020/623-3868, fax 020/622-2613, www.hotelmaas.nl).

Hotel De Leydsche Hof is canalside with simple, quiet rooms. Its peaceful demeanor almost helps you overlook the flimsy cots and old carpets (Ds-f110, Tb-f150, Qb-f200, no breakfast, near where Keizersgracht hits Leidsegracht, Leidsegracht 14, 10-minute walk from Leidseplein, 1016 CK Amsterdam, tel. 020/623-2148, run by friendly Mr. Piller).

Sleeping near Vondelpark

These options connect you with the sights via an easy tram ride, a pleasant 15-minute walk, or a short bike ride through Vondelpark.

Karen McCuster, a friendly Englishwoman, rents cozy rooms in her shoes-off home. Rooms are clean, white, and bright, with red carpeting and green plants; one room has a private rooftop patio (D-f90–120, depending on room size, little or no breakfast, tram #2 from station to Amstelveenseweg, Zeilstraat 22, third floor, 1075 SH Amsterdam, tel. 020/679-2753, fax 020/670-4578).

Toro Hotel, in a peaceful residential area at the edge of Vondelpark, is your personal turn-of-the-century hotel/mansion, with a plush lounge, elegant dining hall, and 22 rooms with TVs, safes, and phones. Rooms in the back overlook the park, canal, and garden, which is yours for relaxing. Mr. Plooy fusses over his guests (Ss-f165, Sb-f200, Db-f250, Tb-f300, CC:VMA, elevator, metered parking at the door, tram #2 from station to Koningslaan, then walk to intersection of Emmalaan and Koningslaan, Koningslaan 64, 1075 AG Amsterdam, tel. 020/673-7223, fax 020/675-0031).

Hotel Filosoof greets you with Aristotle and Plato in the foyer and classical music in its lobby. Its 25 rooms are decorated with themes; the Egyptian room has a frieze of hieroglyphics. Philosophers' sayings hang on walls as thoughtful travelers wander down the halls or sit in the garden, rooted deep in discussion. The rooms are small (and split between two buildings), but the hotel is endearing (Sb-f155, Db-f185, Tb-f235, Qb-f275, CC:VMA, cheaper off-season, all rooms have TV and phone, Anna Vondelstraat 6, 5-minute walk from tram #1 line, get off at Constantyn Huygenstraat, tel. 020/683-3013, fax 020/685-3750, e-mail: filosoof@sx4all.nl).

Best Western Hotel Terdam is a 90-room American-style hotel well situated on a quiet street just across the bridge from bustling Leidseplein (Db-f260–305, depending on season and air-con, CC:VMA, elevator, Tesselschadestraat 23, tel. 020/612-6876, fax 020/683-8313, www.hospitality.nl/ams).

Hotel Parkzicht is an old-time place with lots of extremely steep stairs and 14 big plain rooms on a quiet street bordering Vondelpark (S-f65, Sb-f95, Db-f140–170, as low as f100 in winter, Tb-f220, Qb-f250, CC:VMA, tram #1, #2 or #5 from station, Roemer Visscherstraat 33, tel. 020/618-1954, fax 020/618-0897).

Hostels

The Shelter Jordan (also known as Hostel Eben Haezer) is scruffy, friendly, well run, and in a great neighborhood. They offer Amsterdam's best budget beds in 20-bed dorms (f28 with sheets and breakfast, maximum age 35, nonsmoking, near the Anne Frank House, Bloemstraat 179, tel. 020/624-4717, www.shelter.nl, e-mail: jordan @shelter. nl). It serves hot meals, runs a snack bar, offers lockers, leads nightly Bible studies, and closes the dorms from 10:00 to 12:30. Its sister Christian hostel, **The Shelter City**, in the Red Light District, is similar but definitely not preaching to the choir (open to any traveler, f28 per bed, tel. 020/625-3230, e-mail: city@shelter.nl).

The city's two IYHF hostels are **Vondelpark**, Amsterdam's top hostel (f38 with breakfast, S-f85, D-f125, nonmembers pay f5 extra, lots of school groups, 6 or 8 beds per dorm, right on the park at Zandpad 5, tel. 020/589-8996, fax 020/589-8955), and **Stadsdoelen YH** (f29 with breakfast, f5 extra without YH card, f6.25 for sheets, just past Dam Square, closed Jan, Kloveniersburgwal 97, tel. 020/624-6832, fax 020/639-1035). Each accepts travelers only under 35. While generally booked long in advance, a few beds open up each day at 11:00.

Eating in Amsterdam

Dutch food is basic and hearty. *Eetcafés* are local cafés serving budget sandwiches, soup, eggs, and so on. Cafeterias, *broodje* (sandwich shops), and automatic food shops are also good bets for budget eaters. Picnics are cheap and easy. A central supermarket is **Albert Heijn**, at the corner of Koningsplein and Singel canal near the flower market (Mon–Sat 10:00–20:00, Sun 12:00–18:00).

Of Amsterdam's thousand-plus restaurants, no one knows which are best—especially me. I pick an area and wander. The major action is around Leidseplein. Wander along restaurant row: Leidsedwarsstraat. For fewer crowds and more charm, find something in the Jordaan. The best advice: your hotel's. Most keep a reliable eating list for their neighborhood. Here are a few handy places to consider:

Eating near Spui in the Center

The city university's **Atrium** is a great budget cafeteria (f9 meals, Mon–Fri 12:00–14:00, 17:00–19:30; from Spui, walk west down

Landebrug Steeg past the canalside Café 't Gasthuys 3 blocks to Oudezijds Achterburgwal 237, go through arched doorway on the right, tel. 020/525-3999). **Café 't Gasthuys**, one of Amsterdam's many "brown" cafés (named for their smoke-stained walls), makes good sandwiches and offers indoor or canalside seating (daily 12:00–01:00, walk west down Landebrug Steeg to Grimburgwal 7).

La Place, a cafeteria on the ground floor of the Vroom Dreesmann department store, has islands of entrées, veggies, fruits, desserts, and beverages (Mon–Sat 10:00–21:00, Thu until 22:00, Sun 11:00–21:00, near Mint Tower, corner of Rokin and Muntplein).

Eating in the Train Station
The train station has a surprisingly classy budget self-service **Stationsrestauratie** on platform 1 (Mon–Sat 7:00–22:00, Sun from 8:00).

Eating near the Anne Frank House
For pancakes in a family atmosphere, try the **Pancake Bakery** (f18 pancakes, splitting is OK, offers an Indonesian pancake for those who want 2 experiences in 1, daily 12:00–21:30, Prinsengracht 191, 1 block north of A.F. House, tel. 020/625-1333). Across the canal, **De Bolhoed** serves serious vegetarian food (daily 12:00–22:00, Prinsengracht 60, tel. 020/626-1803). **Dimitri's** is the place for a hearty salad (f18 main course salads, daily 8:00–22:00, reservations smart, Prinsenstraat 3, tel. 020/627-9393).

Eating near the Rijksmuseum, on Leidseplein
The Art Deco **American Hotel** dining room serves an all-you-can-eat f16 salad bar (available 12:00–14:30, 18:00–22:00, where Leidseplein hits Singel Canal). On the café-packed street called Lange Leidsedwarsstraat, **Bojo** is a reasonably-priced Indonesian restaurant at #51 (daily from 16:00, 020/622-7434). If hunger hits in the **Rijksmuseum**, head for the cafeteria in the west wing's ground floor.

Bars
Try a *jenever* (Dutch gin), the closest thing to an atomic bomb in a shot glass. While cheese gets harder and sharper with age, *jenever* grows smooth and soft. Old *jenever* is best.

Drugs
Amsterdam, Europe's counterculture mecca, thinks the concept of a "victimless crime" is a contradiction. While hard drugs are definitely out, marijuana causes about as much excitement as a bottle of beer. Throughout the Netherlands "coffee shops" are pubs selling marijuana. Menus dangling from strings look like the inventory of a drug

bust. Display cases show various joints or baggies for sale. The Dutch roll a little tobacco into their joints. To avoid that you need to get a baggie and papers. Baggies usually cost f25—smaller contents...better quality. Walk east from Dam Square on Damstraat for a few blocks and then down to Nieuwmarkt. While several touristy Bulldog Cafés are hits with tourists, less-glitzy neighborhood places (farther from the tourists) offer a better value and a more comfortable atmosphere.

Pot should never be bought on the street in Amsterdam. Well-established coffee shops are considered much safer. Up to five grams of marijuana per person per day can be sold in coffee shops. Minimum age for purchase: 18 years.

The tiny **Grey Area** coffee shop is a cool, welcoming, and smoky hole-in-the-wall appreciated among local aficionados as a seven-time winner of Amsterdam's Cannabis Cup award. Judging by the proud autographed photos on the wall, many of America's most famous heads have dropped in. You're welcome to just nurse a bottomless cup of coffee (open high noon to 21:00, closed Mon, between Dam Square and the Anne Frank House at Oude Leliestraat 2, tel. 020/420-4301, www. greyarea.nl, Steven and John).

Near the corner of Leidsestraat and Prinsengracht, **Tops** coffee shop has Internet access. **Homegrown Fantasy's** coffee shop and gallery, about two blocks northwest of Dam Square, has a gentle Dutch atmosphere and cosmic restroom (daily 9:00–24:00, Nieuwe Zijds Voorburgwal 87a, tel. 020/627-5683). They also have a grow shop next door.

▲**Marijuana and Hemp Museum**—This is a collection of dope facts, history, science, and memorabilia (f8, daily 11:00–22:00, Oudezijds Achterburgwal 148, tel. 020/623-5961). While small, it has a shocker finale: the high-tech grow room in which dozens of varieties of marijuana are cultivated in optimal hydroponic (among other) environments. Some plants stand five feet tall and shine under the intense grow lamps. The view is actually through glass walls into the neighboring "Sensi Seed Bank" Grow Shop (which sells carefully cultivated seeds and all the gear needed to grow them). It's an interesting neighborhood. The Cannabis College Foundation "dedicated to ending the global war against the cannabis plant through public education" is next door at #102 (www.cannabiscollege.org). As you wander, ponder the 400,000 Americans in jail because of U.S. marijuana laws.

Transportation Connections—Amsterdam

Amsterdam's train-information center requires a long wait. Save lots of time by getting train tickets and information in a small-town station or travel agency. For phone information, 0900-9292 for local trains or 0900-9296 for international trains (75 cents/min, daily 7:00–24:00, wait through recording and hold...hold...hold...).

By train to: Schiphol Airport (6/hrly, 20 min, f6.25), **Haarlem** (6/hrly, 15 min, f10.50 round trip), **The Hague** (4/hrly, 45 min), **Rotterdam** (4/hrly, 1 hr), **Brussels** (hrly, 3 hrs), **Oostende** (hrly, 4 hrs, change in Roosendaal), **Paris** (5/day, 5 hrs, required fast train from Brussels with f21 supplement; the only cheap no-supplement option is the overnight train), **London** (4/day, 10–12 hrs), **Copenhagen** (5/day, 11 hrs), **Frankfurt** (10/day, 5 hrs), **Munich** (8/day, 8 hrs, change in Mannheim), **Bonn** (10/day, 3 hrs), **Bern** (8/day, 9 hrs, change in Basel).

Amsterdam's Schiphol Airport: The airport, like most of Holland, is English speaking, user-friendly, and below sea level. Its banks offer fair rates (24 hours daily, in the arrival area). Schiphol Airport has easy bus and train connections (7 miles) into Amsterdam or Haarlem. The airport also has a train station of its own. (You can validate your Eurailpass and hit the rails immediately or, to stretch your train pass, buy the short ticket today and start the pass later.) Schiphol flight information (tel. 0900-0141) can give you flight times and your airline's Amsterdam number for reconfirmation before going home (f1 per minute to climb through its phone tree). KLM tel. 020/649-9123, Martainair tel. 020/601-1222.

HAARLEM

Cute, cozy, yet real and handy to the airport, Haarlem is a fine home base, giving you small-town, overnight warmth with easy access (15 minutes by train) to wild and crazy Amsterdam.

Haarlem is a busy Dutch market town buzzing with shoppers biking home with fresh bouquets. Enjoy Saturday (general) and Monday (clothing) market days, when the square bustles like a Brueghel painting with cheese, fish, flowers, and families. Make yourself at home here. Buy some flowers to brighten your hotel room.

Orientation (tel. code: 023)
Tourist Information: Haarlem's VVV, at the train station, is friendlier, more helpful, and less crowded than Amsterdam's. Ask your Amsterdam questions here (Mon–Fri 9:30–17:30, Sat 10:00–14:00, closed Sun, tel. 0900-616-1600, f1 a minute, their f4 *Haarlem* magazine is not necessary).

Arrival in Haarlem: As you walk out of the train station, the TI is on your right and the bus station is across the street. Two parallel streets flank the train station (Kruisweg and Jansweg). Head up either one and you'll reach the town square and church within 10 minutes. If you're uncertain of the way, ask a local person, "*Grote Markt?*" ("Main Square?"), and they'll point you in the right direction.

Helpful Hints: The handy GWK change office at the station offers fair exchange rates (Mon–Sat 8:00–20:00, Thu–Fri until 21:00, Sun 9:00–17:00). The train station rents bikes (f9.50/day, f100 deposit, Mon–Sat 6:00–24:00, Sun 7:30–24:00). For Internet access (f7.50/30 min), nonguests are welcome to use Hotel Amadeus' computer (facing market square), and nonsmokers are welcome at High Times (Lange Veerstraat 47). My Beautiful Launderette is handy, self-service, and cheap (f11 wash and dry, daily 8:30–20:30, bring coins, including 6 Dutch quarters to dry, near Vroom Dreesman department store at Boter Markt 20). The VVV and local hotels have a helpful parking brochure.

Sights—Haarlem

▲▲**Market Square (Grote Markt)**—Haarlem's market square is the town's delightful centerpiece. To enjoy a coffee or beer here simmering in Dutch good living is a quintessential European experience. In a recent study, the Dutch were found to be the most content people in Europe. And later, the people of Haarlem were found to be the most content in the Netherlands. Observe. Just a few years ago trolleys ran through the square and cars were parked everywhere. But today it's a people zone, with market stalls filling the square on some days and café tables on others. The local drunk used to hang out on the bench in front of the town hall, where he'd expose himself to newlyweds. The Dutch, rather than arrest the man, moved the bench. The big statue in the square is of Coster, the man only Haarlemers think invented printing. The little shops around the cathedral have long been church owned and rented to bring in a little cash. The fine building nearest the cathedral is the old meat hall—decorated with carved bits of early advertising.

▲**Church (Grote Kerk)**—This 15th-century Gothic church (now Protestant) is worth a look, if only for its Oz-like organ (from 1738, 30 meters high, its 5,000 pipes impressed both Handel and Mozart). Note how the organ, which fills the west end, seems to steal the show from the altar. Pick up the English flyer, which lists spots of interest, including Frans Hals tomb (under the black lantern in the choir). To enter, find the small *"Entrée"* sign behind the church (f2.50, Mon–Sat 10:00–16:00). Consider attending (even part of) a concert to hear Holland's greatest pipe organ (regular free concerts Tue mid-May–mid-Oct at 20:15; additional concerts Jul–Aug on Thu at 15:00; confirm schedule at TI).

▲▲**Frans Hals Museum**—Haarlem is the hometown of Frans Hals, and this refreshingly easy museum—an almshouse for old men back in 1610—displays many of his greatest paintings (f10, Mon–Sat 11:00–17:00, Sun 12:00–17:00, tel. 023/511-5775). Enjoy lots of Frans Hals group portraits (rooms 21, 26, 28) and take-me-back paintings of old-time Haarlem (room 22). Peter Brueghel the Younger's painting *Proverbs* (outside room 24) illustrates 72 old Dutch proverbs. To peek into old Dutch ways, identify some with the help of the English-language key.

History Museum—Across the street from the Frans Hals Museum, this small, free museum gives a peek into old Haarlem. Request the English version of the 10-minute video. Study the large-scale model of Haarlem in 1822 before the town's fortifications were demolished

Haarlem

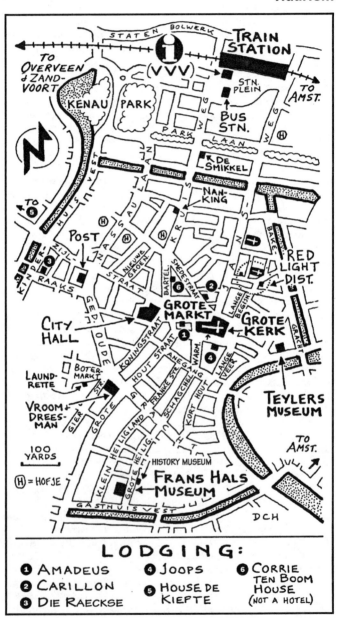

LODGING:

1. AMADEUS
2. CARILLON
3. DIE RAECKSE
4. JOOPS
5. HOUSE DE KIEFTE
6. CORRIE TEN BOOM HOUSE (NOT A HOTEL)

(Tue–Sat 12:00–17:00, Sun 13:00–17:00, closed Mon, Groot Heiligland 47, tel. 020/542-2427). The adjacent architecture museum (also free) is of conceivable interest to architects.

Corrie Ten Boom House—Haarlem is also home to Corrie Ten Boom, popularized by *The Hiding Place*, an inspirational book and movie about the Ten Boom family's experience hiding Jews from Nazis. The Ten Boom House is open for hourlong English tours (donation accepted, Tue–Sat 10:00–16:00, Nov–Mar Tue–Sat 11:00–15:00, 50 meters off market square at Barteljorisstraat 19; the clock shop people get all wound up if you go inside—wait at the door, where tour times are posted, tel. 023/531-0823). The Ten Boom family had for generations hosted a prayer meeting for peace here for Jews and Christians. On the 100th anniversary of the prayer meetings, the Gestapo came, looking for the hiding place. It's a great and inspirational story (although non-Christians may be put off by the preaching mixed in).

▲**Teylers Museum**—Famous as the oldest museum in Holland, it's interesting mainly as a look at a 200-year-old museum—fossils, minerals, and primitive electronic gadgetry. New exhibition halls (with rotating exhibits) have freshened up the place. Stop by if you enjoy mixing, say, Renaissance sketches with pickled coelacanths (f10, Tue–Sat 10:00–17:00, Sun 12:00–17:00, Spaarne 16, tel. 023/531-9010).

Canal Cruise—Making a scenic loop through and around Haarlem, these little trips are more relaxing than informative (f12.50, 70 min, 5/day, across from Teylers Museum at Spaarne 11a, tel. 023/535-7723).

Red Lights—For a little red-light district precious as a Barbie doll, wander around the church in Haarlem's cutest Begijnhof (two blocks northeast of big church, off Lange Begijnestraat, no senior or student discounts). Don't miss the mall marked by the red neon sign reading "*t'Steegje*." The nearby t'Poortje (office park) costs f7.50.

Global Hemp Museum—More a hemp-products store and hub of Haarlem's coffee-shop action, this friendly place runs a humble hemp museum out back (shop free, museum f5, Mon–Sat 11:00–18:00, summer Sun 12:00–18:00, down the canal from Teylers Museum at Spaarne 94, tel. 023/534-9939).

Amsterdam to Haarlem Train Tour

Since you'll be commuting from Amsterdam to Haarlem, here's a tour to keep you entertained. Departing from Amsterdam, grab a seat on the right (with your back to Amsterdam, top deck if possible). Everything is on the right unless I say on the left.

You're riding the oldest train line in Holland. Across the harbor behind the Amsterdam station, the tall brown skyscraper is the corporate office of Shell Oil. The Dutch had the first multinational corporation (the United East India Company back in the

17th century). And today this international big-business spirit survives with companies like Shell and Phillips.

Leaving Amsterdam you'll see the cranes and ships of its harbor—sizable but nothing like the world's biggest in nearby Rotterdam.

On your left find the old windmill. In front of it the little garden plots and cottages are escapes for big-city people who probably don't even have a balcony.

Coming into the Sloterdijk Station (where trains connect for Amsterdam airport), you'll see huge office buildings, such as Dutch Telecom KPN. These grew up after the station made commuting easy.

Half a mile past Sloterdijk Station, about 50 yards to the right of the tracks, a yellow sign says, "Tippel Zone—open 21:00." (*Tippel* is the sound a mouse makes when it runs through the house at night.) This is a drive-in brothel. See the oval driveway with pink "bus stops" for browsing, the lounge building, and the blue privacy stalls behind (including two for bikers). The lounge has a clinic with a nurse and counselors to keep the women healthy. If a prostitute is diagnosed with AIDS, she gets a subsidized apartment to encourage her to quit the business. Shocking as this may seem to some, it's a good example of a pragmatic solution to a problem—getting the most dangerous prostitutes off the streets and combating AIDS.

Passing through a forest and by some houseboats, you enter a *polder*—reclaimed land. This is an ecologically sound farm zone, run without chemicals. Cows, pigs, and chickens run free—they're not raised in cages. The train tracks are on a dike, which provides a solid foundation not susceptible to floods. This way the transportation system functions right through any calamity. Looking out at the distant dike, remember you're in the most densely populated country in Europe. On the horizon, sleek modern windmills whirl.

Passing the tall smokestack and the Sony Music Building, find a big, unnamed, beige and white building. This is where the Dutch currency is printed (top security, no advertising). This has long been a family business. Study a bill. Even today you can read who printed it: Johan Enschede en Zonen, imp. (Johan Enschede and Sons, Inc.).

As the train slows down, you're passing through Holland's biggest train-car maintenance facility and entering Haarlem. Look left. The domed building is a prison, built in 1901 and still in use. As you cross the Spaarne River you'll see the great church spire towering over Haarlem as it has since medieval times— back when a fortified wall circled the town. Hop out into one of Holland's oldest stations. Art Nouveau—decor from 1908— survives all around.

Nightlife in Haarlem

Haarlem's evening scene is great. The bars around the Grote Kerk and Lange Veerstraat are colorful and lively. You'll find plenty of music.

The best show in town: the café scene on the market square. In good weather, café tables tumble happily out of the bars.

For trendy local crowds, consider a drink at the **Studio** (on the square, next to Hotel Carillon) or **Café 1900** (across from the Corrie Ten Boom House (live music Sun night).

Coffee Shops: Haarlem has 16 "coffee shops," where marijuana is casually sold and smoked by easygoing noncriminal types. The **Frans Hals Coffee Shop** is one of the best established (in front of station at 46 Kruisweg). The display case–type "menu" explains what's on sale (f5 joints, f25 baggies, space cakes—but no alcohol, only soft drinks). At **High Times**, smokers can choose from 16 varieties of joints in racks behind the bar (neatly prepacked in trademarked "Joint Packs," f4-7.50, daily 12:00–23:00, Internet access, 47 Lange Veerstraat). If you don't like the smell of pot, avoid places sporting Rastafarian yellow, red, and green colors; wildly painted walls; or plants in the windows.

Crack is the wild and leathery place to go for loud music, pool, darts, and smoking (Lange Veerstraat 32). **Imperial Café and Bar** has live music every Monday, Wednesday, Thursday, and Friday (a few doors down from Crack, at Korte Veerstraat 3).

Sleeping in Haarlem
(f1 = about 50 cents, tel. code: 023)

Sleep Code: **S** = Single, **D** = Double/Twin, **T** = Triple, **Q** = Quad, **b** = bathroom, **t** = toilet only, **s** = shower only, **CC** = Credit Card (Visa, MasterCard, Amex).

The helpful Haarlem tourist office ("VVV" at the train station, Mon–Fri 9:30–17:30, Sat 10:00–14:00, tel. 0900-616-1600, f1/minute) can nearly always find you a f35 bed in a nearby private home (for a f10-per-person fee plus a cut of your host's money). Avoid this if you can; it's cheaper to call direct.

Haarlem is most crowded in April, on Easter weekend, in May, and in August. Nearly every Dutch person you'll encounter speaks English. The listed prices include breakfast (unless otherwise noted) and usually include the f3.50-per-person-per-day tourist tax. To avoid this town's louder-than-normal street noises, forgo views for a room in the back.

Hotel Amadeus, on the market square, has 15 small, bright, and basic rooms. Some have views of the square. This characteristic hotel, ideally located above a turn-of-the-century dinner café, is relatively quiet. Its lush old lounge/breakfast room, on the second floor, overlooks the square (Sb-f97.50, Db-f140, Tb-f180, Qb-f200, includes tax, 2-night stay and cash get you a 5 percent discount, a 12-min walk from train station, CC:VMA, steep climb to lounge, then an elevator, Grote Markt 10, 2011 RD Haarlem, tel. 023/532-4530, fax 023/532-2328, www.amadeus-hotel.com, Mike takes good care of his guests).

Hotel Carillon also overlooks the town square but comes with a little more traffic and bell-tower noise. Many of the well-worn rooms are small, and the stairs are ste-e-e-p. The front rooms come with great town-square views and street noise (22 rooms, tiny loft singles-f57.50, Db-f137, Tb-f180.50, Qb-f194, includes tax, no elevator, 12-min walk from train station, CC:VMA, Grote Markt 27, 2011 RC Haarlem, tel. 023/531-0591, fax 023/531-4909, e-mail: fra.baars@wxs.nl). The Carillon also runs the nearby **Die Raeckse Hotel**, which has fewer stairs, less character, more traffic noise, and decent rooms (Sb-f92.50–110, Db-f135–160, baths cost more than showers, CC:VMA, Raaks 1, 2011 VA Haarlem, tel. 023/532-6629, fax 023/531-7937).

Hotel Joops is an innovative concept. From a reception desk in his furniture store, just behind the cathedral, Mr. Joops administers a corral of 80 rooms, all within a block of the church. He has cheap, well-worn, spacious rooms (S-f75, D-f105, T-f140) and new suites with kitchenettes (Db-f122–152, depending upon size, Tb-f165–195, breakfast—with the furniture—is f17.50 extra, save about 5 percent with cash, CC:VM, Oude Groenmarkt 20, 2011 HL Haarlem, tel. 023/532-2008, fax 023/532-9549, e-mail: joops@hotelinformation.com).

Bed and Breakfast House de Kiefte, your get-into-a-local-home budget option, epitomizes the goodness of B&Bs. Marjet (mar-yet) and Hans, a fun-to-know Dutch couple who speak English fluently, rent four bright, cheery, nonsmoking rooms (with good breakfast and travel advice) in their quiet, 100-year-old home (Ds-f90, T-f130, Qs-f165, Quint/s-f190, cash only, minimum 2 nights, family loft sleeps up to 5, very steep stairs, kid-friendly, Coornhertstraat 3, 2013 EV Haarlem, tel. 023/532-2980, cellular 06-5474-5272). It's a 15-minute walk or f12 taxi ride from the train station and a five-minute walk from the center. From Grote Markt (market square), walk straight out Zijlstraat and over the bridge and take a left on the fourth street.

Hotel Lion D'Or is a classy business hotel with all the professional comforts and a handy location. Don't expect a warm welcome (34 rooms, Sb-f210, Db-f275, extra beds-f50, often 10 percent off on weekends and slow times, CC:VMA, elevator, some nonsmoking rooms, across the street from the station at Kruisweg 34, 2011 LC Haarlem, tel. 023/532-1750, fax 023/532-9543).

The 300-room, very American **Hotel Haarlem Zuid** is sterile but a good value for those interested only in sleeping and eating. It sits in an industrial zone, a 20-minute walk from the center on the road to the airport (Db-f153–173, depending upon size of room, add f10 each for a 3rd or 4th person, breakfast included or skip and save f15 each, CC:VMA, elevator, easy parking, inexpensive hotel restaurant, Toekenweg 2, 2035 LC Haarlem, tel. 023/536-7500, fax 023/536-7980). Buses #70, #72, and #75 connect the hotel to the station and market square every 10 minutes.

Sleeping near Haarlem

Pension Koning, a 15-minute walk north of the station or a quick hop on bus #71, has five simple rooms in a row house in a residential area (S-f45, D-f90, T-f120, 2-night minimum, includes breakfast, Kleverlaan 179, 2023 JC Haarlem, tel. 023/526-1456).

Hostel Jan Gijzen, completely renovated and with all the youth-hostel comforts, charges f34 for beds (breakfast) in six-bed dorms (f5 extra for nonmembers) and f6.50 for sheets (a few D-f82, daily 7:00–24:00, closed Nov–Feb, Jan Gijzenpad 3, 2 miles from Haarlem station—take bus #2, or a 5-minute walk from Santpoort Zuid train station, tel. 023/537-3793, fax 023/537-1176).

Eating in Haarlem

Eating between Market Square (Grote Markt) and Train Station

Enjoy an Indonesian rijsttafel feast at the **Nanking Chinese-Indonesian Restaurant** (daily 16:00–22:00, Kruisstraat 16, a few blocks off Grote Markt, tel. 023/532-0706). Couples eat plenty, heartily, and cheaply by splitting a f24.50 Indonesian "rice table" for one; each eater should order a drink. Say hi to gracious Ai Ping and her daughter, Fan. Don't let them railroad you into a Chinese (their heritage) dinner. They also do cheap and tasty takeout.

Pancakes for dinner? **Pannekoekhuis "De Smikkel"** serves a selection of over 50 dinner (meat, cheese, etc.) and dessert pancakes. The pancakes (f16 each) are filling. With the f2.50-per-person cover charge, splitting is OK (daily 16:00–22:00, closed Mon in winter, 2 blocks in front of station, Kruisweg 57, tel. 023/532-0631).

Eat well and surrounded by trains and 1908 architecture in the classy **Brasserie Haarlem** Station Restaurant (f30 for 3 courses, daily 12:00–23:00, between tracks #3 and #6).

Eating on or near Zijlstraat

Eko Eet Café is great for a cheery, tasty vegetarian meal (f19 *menu*, daily 17:30–21:30, Zijlstraat 39). Because they serve only fresh food, the menu gets sparse by 21:00.

Vincent's Eethuis serves the best cheap, basic Dutch food in town. This former St. Vincent's soup kitchen now feeds more gainfully employed locals than poor (f9, free seconds on veggies, friendly staff, Mon–Fri 12:00–14:00, 17:00–19:30, Nieuwe Groenmarkt 22).

The friendly **De Buren** offers handlebar-mustache fun and

traditional Dutch food (such as *draadjesvlees*—beef stew with applesauce—and *oma's kippetje*—grandmother's chicken) to happy locals (f25 dinners, Wed–Sun 17:00–22:00, closed Mon–Tue, outside the tourist area at Brouwersvaart 146, near the intersection with Zijlsingel, across the canal from Die Raeckse Hotel and close to House de Kiefte B&B, tel. 023/534-3364). Gerard and Marjo love their work. Enjoy their creative menu, made especially for you.

Eating between the Market Square and Frans Hals Museum

Jacobus Pieck Eetlokaal is popular with locals for its fine-value "global cuisine" (f18 plate of the day, Mon–Sat 10:00–22:00, Sun 12:00–22:00, Warmoesstraat 18, tel. 023/532-6144).

For a (f2) cone of old-fashioned French fries, drop by **Friethuis de Vlaminck** on Warmoesstraat 3 (Tue–Sat until 18:00). Notice the old-time shop sign cobbled into Warmoesstraat's brick sidewalk.

La Plume steak house is noisy with a happy, local, and very carnivorous crowd (f28 meals, daily from 17:30, CC:VMA, Lange Veerstraat 1).

Bastiaan serves good "Mediterranean" cuisine in a classy atmosphere (f30 dinners, Tue–Sun from 18:00, closed Mon, CC:VMA, Lange Veerstraat 8).

De Lachende Javaan ("The Laughing Javanese") serves the best real Indonesian food in town. Their f35 rijsttafel is great (light eaters can split this extravaganza—f5 for the extra plate, Tue–Sun from 17:00, closed Mon, CC:VMA, Frankestraat 25, tel. 023/532-8792).

For a candlelit dinner of cheese and wine, consider **In't Goede Uur** (Tue–Sun from 17:30, closed Mon, Korte Houtstraat 1).

For a healthy budget lunch with Haarlem's best view, eat at **La Place**, on the top floor or roof garden of the Vroom Dreesman department store (Mon–Sat 9:30–18:00, Thu until 21:00, closed Sun, on the corner of Grote Houtstraat and Gedempte Oude Gracht).

Picnic shoppers head to the **DekaMarkt** supermarket (Mon–Sat 8:30–20:00, closed Sun, Gedemple Oude Gracht 54, between Vroom Dreesman department store and post office).

Transportation Connections—Haarlem

By train to: Amsterdam (6/hrly, 15 min, f6 one way, f10.50 same-day return, ticket not valid on "Lovers Train," a misnamed private train that runs hrly), **Delft** (2/hrly, 38 min), **Hoorn** (4/hrly, 1 hr), **The Hague** (4/hrly, 35 min), **Alkmaar** (2/hrly, 30 min), **Schiphol Airport** (2/hrly, 40 min, f10, transfer at Amsterdam-Sloterdijk); the direct buses #236 (use a strip card) and #362 (local cash) to the airport are faster (2/hrly, 30 min, f6.25); by taxi it's f70.

Sights—Near Haarlem and Amsterdam

The Netherlands are tiny. The sights listed below are an easy day trip by bus or train from Haarlem or Amsterdam. Match your interest with the village's specialty: flower auctions, folk museums, cheese, Delft porcelain, beaches, or modern art.

▲▲**Enkhuisen's Zuiderzee Museum**—This lively, open-air folk museum in the salty old town of Enkhuizen has a "Living on Urk" village populated by people who do a convincing job of role-playing no-nonsense 1905 Dutch villagers. No one said "Have a nice day" back then. You can eat herring hot out of the old smoker and see barrels and rope made. Children enjoy the dress-up chest, the old-time game zone, and making sailing ships out of old wooden shoes (f17.50, early Apr–late Oct daily 10:00–17:00, free tours at 14:00, private guide for f80, tel. 0228/351-111). Train from Amsterdam direct to Enkhuisen, where a boat shuttles you to the museum, avoiding a pleasant 15-minute walk.

▲**Zaanse Schans**—This 17th-century Dutch village turned open-air folk museum puts Dutch culture—from cheese making to wooden-shoe carving—on a lazy Susan. Take an inspiring climb to the top of a whirring windmill (gather a group and ask for a tour). Located in the town of Zaandijk, this is your easiest one-stop look at traditional Dutch culture and the Netherlands' best collection of windmills (free, daily 8:30–18:00, until 17:00 in winter, parking f7.50/1 hr, f15/day, tel. 075/616-8218). Fifteen minutes by train north of Amsterdam: Take the Alkmaar-bound train to Station Koog-Zaandijk and then walk, following the signs—past a fragrant chocolate factory—for 10 minutes.

▲▲**Aalsmeer Flower Auction**—Get a bird's-eye view of the huge Dutch flower industry. Wander on elevated walkways (through what's claimed to be the biggest building on earth) over literally trainloads of freshly cut flowers. About half of all the flowers exported from Holland are auctioned off here in six huge auditoriums (f7.50, Mon–Fri 7:30–11:00; the auction wilts after 9:30, but the warehouse swarms; gift shop, cafeteria; bus #172 from Amsterdam's station, 2/hrly, 1 hr; from Haarlem take bus #140, 2/hrly, 1 hr, tel. 0297/393-939). Aalsmeer is close to the airport and a handy last fling before catching a morning weekday flight.

▲▲▲**Keukenhof**—This is the greatest bulb-flower garden on earth. Each spring 6 million flowers, enjoying sandy soil behind the Dutch dunes, conspire to make even a total garden hater enjoy them. This 100-acre park is packed with tour groups daily from about March 23 to May 21 for the spring show (f18, 8:00–19:30, last tickets sold at 18:00) and from August 18 to September 18 for the summer exhibition (f12.50, 9:00–18:00; bus #50 or #51 from Haarlem then transfer at Lisse; tel. 0252/465-555, www.keukenhof.nl). Go late in the day for the best light and the fewest groups.

Zandvoort—For a quick and easy look at the windy coastline in a

Day Trips from Haarlem and Amsterdam

RAIL
BUS
BOAT

NORTH
SEA

NOT TO SCALE
AMST.-HAARLEM ≈ 10 MI.

shell-lover's Shangri-La, visit the beach resort of Zandvoort, a breezy 45-minute bike ride or 8 minutes by train or car west of Haarlem (from Haarlem, follow signs to Bloemendaal). South of the main beach, bathers work on all-around tans.

▲**Hoorn**—This is an elegant, quiet, and typical 17th-century Dutch town north of Amsterdam. Its TI can rent you a bike or give you a walking-tour brochure. Any TI offers the flier describing the "Historic Triangle," an all-day excursion from Amsterdam that connects Hoorn, Medemblik, and Enkhuizen by steam train and boat (f30 plus f6.25 for the train back to Haarlem, 2/day, tel. 0229/214-862).

De Rijp—This sleepy town is worth visiting if you're driving north of Amsterdam.

Volendam, Marken, and Monnikendam—These famous towns are quaint as can be (although Volendam is too touristy).

▲**Delft**—Peaceful as a Vermeer painting (he was born here) and lovely as its porcelain, Delft is a typically Dutch town with a special soul. Enjoy it best by simply wandering around, watching people, munching local syrup-waffles, or daydreaming from the canal bridges. The town bustles during its Saturday antiques market (9:00–17:00). Its colorful Thursday food-and-flower market attracts many traditional villagers (9:00–17:00). The TI on the main square has a f3.50 brochure outlining Delft's sights, including a "Historical Walk through Delft" (Mon–Fri 9:00–18:00, Sat 9:00–17:30, Sun 10:00–15:00, tel. 015/212-6100). The town is a museum in itself, but if you need a turnstile, it has an impressive Army Museum (f6, Mon–Sat 10:00–17:00, Sun 13:00–17:00). Or tour the Royal Porcelain Works to watch the famous 17th-century blue Delftware turn from clay into art (f5, Mon–Sat 9:00–17:00, summer Sun 9:30–17:00, tel. 015/256-9214).

▲**Alkmaar**—Holland's cheese capital is especially fun (and touristy) during its weekly cheese market (Friday 10:00–12:00).

▲▲**Edam**—For the ultimate in cuteness and peace, make tiny Edam your home. It's sweet but palatable and 30 minutes by bus from Amsterdam (2/hrly). The Edam Museum is a small, quirky house offering a fun peek into a 400-year-old home and a floating cellar (f3.50, Tue–Sat 10:00–16:30, Sun 13:30–16:30, closed in winter, on the main square). Wednesday is the town's market day (9:00–13:00). In July and August, market day includes a traditional cheese market (10:30–12:30). TI tel. 0299/315-125.

Sleeping and Eating: Hotel De Fortuna, an eccentric canalside mix of flowers, a cat of leisure, a pet turtle, and duck noises, offers steep stairs and low-ceilinged rooms in several ancient buildings in the old center of Edam (Db-f185, includes breakfast, CC:VMA, garden patio, attached restaurant, Spuistraat 3, 1135 AV Edam, tel. 0299/371-671, fax 0299/371-469). The centrally located **Damhotel** (on a canal around the corner from the TI) has attractive, comfortable rooms with a plush feel (Sb-f90, Db-f140, Tb-f210, includes breakfast, CC:VMA, attached restaurant, Keizersgracht 1, 1135 AZ Edam, tel. 0299/371-766, fax 0299/374-031). The TI (tel. 0299/315125) has a list of cheaper rooms in private homes. **Tai Wah** has take-out Chinese/Indonesian (eat in De Fortuna garden) and indoor seating (13:00–21:45, closed Tue, Lingerzijde 62, tel. 0299/371-088).

▲**Rotterdam**—This city, the world's largest port, bounced back after being bombed flat in World War II. See its towering Euromast, take a harbor tour, and stroll its great pedestrian zone. (TI tel. 0900/403-4065, toll call—f1 per minute).

▲▲**The Hague (Den Haag)**—Locals say the money is made in Rotterdam, divided in The Hague, and spent in Amsterdam. The Hague is the Netherlands' seat of government and the home of several engaging museums. The Mauritshuis' delightful, easy-to-tour art collection stars Vermeer and Rembrandt (f12.50, Tue–Sat 10:00–17:00, Sun 11:00–17:00, Korte Vijverberg 8, tel. 070/302-3456). Across the pond, the Torture Museum (Gevangenpoort) shows the medieval mind at its worst (f6, Tue–Fri 10:00–16:00, Sat–Sun 12:00–16:00, closed Mon, required tours on the hour, last one at 16:00; confirm with the ticket taker if the film and talk will be in English before you commit, tel. 070/346-0861). For a look at the 19th century's attempt at virtual reality, tour Panorama Mesdag, a 360-degree painting of nearby Scheveningen in the 1880s with a 3-D sandy-beach foreground (f7.50, Mon–Sat 10:00–17:00, Sun 12:00–17:00, Zeestraat 65, tel. 070/310-6665). The nearby Peace Palace, a gift from Andrew Carnegie, houses the International Court of Justice (f5, Mon–Fri, required guided tours only at 10:00, 11:00, 14:00, or 15:00; closes without warning—call ahead or check at TI, tram #7 or #8 from the station, tel. 070/302-4137). Scheveningen, the Dutch Coney Island, is liveliest on sunny summer afternoons (take tram #7); and Madurodam, a mini-Holland amusement park, is a kid pleaser (f21, kids 4–11 f14, daily 9:00–18:00, until 20:00 in Jun, until 23:00 Jul–Aug, tram #1 or #9, tel. 070/355-3900). The Hague's TI is at the train station (Mon–Sat 9:00–17:30, later in summer, Sun 10:00–17:00, tel. 06/3403-5051, fl a minute).

Utrecht—The Museum von Speelklok tot Pierement has free and necessary guided 50-minute tours on the hour demonstrating its musical clocks, calliopes, and street organs (f9, Tue–Sat 10:00–17:00, Sun 12:00–17:00, closed Mon, last tour at 16:00, 10-minute walk from station, Buurkerkhof 10, tel. 030/231-2789).

▲▲Arnhem's Open-Air Dutch Folk Museum—An hour east of Amsterdam, Arnhem has Holland's first and biggest folk museum. You'll enjoy a huge park of windmills, old farms, traditional crafts in action, and a pleasant education-by-immersion in Dutch culture. The English guidebook (f7.50) explains each historic building (f18, Apr–Oct daily 10:00–17:00, tel. 026/357-6111). The park has several good budget restaurants and covered picnic areas. Its rustic Pancake House serves hearty (splittable) Dutch flapjacks.

Trains make the 70-minute trip from Amsterdam to Arnhem twice an hour (likely transfer in Utrecht). At Arnhem station, take bus #3 or, even better, #13 (faster, 4/hrly, 15 min) to the Openlucht Museum. By car from Haarlem, skirt Amsterdam to the south on E9, follow signs to Utrecht, and take A12 east to Arnhem. Just before Arnhem, take the Arnhem Nord exit "*Openluchtmuseum*" and follow signs to the nearby museum. For the Kröller-Müller Museum, follow white signs to Hoge Veluwe.

▲▲Kröller-Müller Museum and Hoge Veluwe National Park—Near Arnhem, the Hoge Veluwe National Park is Holland's largest (13,000 acres) and is famous for its Kröller-Müller Museum. This huge, impressive modern-art collection, including 55 paintings by van Gogh, is set deep in the forest. The park has hundreds of white bikes you're free to use to make your explorations more fun. After you pay f8.50 at the park entrance, the museum is "free" (Tue–Sun 10:00–17:00, easy parking, tel. 055/378-1441). Pick up information at the Amsterdam or Arnhem TI (tel. 026/442-6767). Bus #12 connects the Arnhem train station with the Kröller-Müller Museum (Mar–Oct). A visit to the park and the open-air museum makes a great day trip from Amsterdam.

APPENDIX

"La Marseillaise"
There's a movement in France to soften the lyrics of their national anthem. Sing it now . . . before it's too late.

Allons enfants de la Patrie, (Let's go, children of the fatherland,)
Le jour de gloire est arrivé. (The day of glory has arrived.)
Contre nous de la tyrannie (The blood-covered flagpole of tyranny)
L'étendard sanglant est levé, (Is raised against us,)
L'étendard sanglant est levé. (Is raised against us.)
Entendez-vous dans nos campagnes (Do you hear what's happening in our countryside?)
Mugir les féroces soldats? (The ferocious soldiers are howling)
Qui viennent jusque dans nos bras (They're coming nearly into our grasp)
Egorger nos fils et nos compagnes. (They're slitting the throats of our sons and our women.)
Aux armes citoyens, (Grab your weapons, citizens,)
Formez vos bataillons, (Form your battalions,)
Marchons, marchons, (March on, march on,)
Qu'un sang impur (So that their impure blood)
Abreuve nos sillons. (Will fill our trenches.)

French History in an Escargot Shell
Around the time of Christ, Romans "Latinized" the land of the Gauls. With the fifth-century fall of Rome, the barbarian Franks and Burgundians invaded. From this unique mix of Latin and Celtic cultures evolved today's France.

While France wallowed with the rest of Europe in medieval darkness, it got a head start in its development as a nation-state. In 507 Clovis established Paris as the capital of his Christian Merovingian dynasty. Clovis and the Franks would eventually become Louis and the French. Charles Martel stopped the spread of Islam by beating the Spanish Moors at the Battle of Poitiers. And Charlemagne, the most important of the "Dark Age" Frankish kings, was crowned Holy Roman Emperor in 800 by the pope. Charles the Great presided over the "Carolingian Renaissance" and effectively ruled a vast-for-the-time empire.

The Treaty of Verdun, which in 843 divided Charlemagne's empire among his grandsons, marks what could be considered the birth of Europe. For the first time, a treaty was signed in vernacular languages (French and German) rather than in Latin. While this split established a Franco/Germanic divide, it also heralded an age of fragmentation. While petty princes took the reigns, the Frankish king ruled only Île-de-France, a small region around Paris.

Vikings, or Norsemen, settled in what became Normandy. Later, in 1066, these "Normans" invaded England. The Norman king, William the Conqueror, consolidated his English domain, accelerating the formation of modern England. But his rule also muddied the political waters between England and France, kicking off a centuries-long struggle between the two nations.

In the 12th century, Eleanor of Aquitaine (a separate country in southwest France) married Louis VII, king of France, bringing Aquitaine under French rule. They divorced, and she married Henry of Normandy, soon-to-be Henry II of England. This marital union gave England control of a huge swath of land from the English Channel to the Pyrénées. For 300 years, France and England would struggle over control of Aquitaine. Any enemy of the French king would find a natural ally in the English king.

In 1328 a French king (Charles IV) died without a son. The English king (Edward III) was his nephew and naturally was interested in the throne. The French resisted. This pitted France, the biggest and richest country in Europe, against England, with the biggest army. They fought from 1337 to 1453, in what was modestly called the Hundred Years' War.

Regional powers from within France sided with England. Burgundy actually took Paris, captured the royal family, and recognized the English king as heir to the French thrown. England controlled France from the Loire north, and things looked bleak for the French king.

Enter Joan of Arc, a 16-year-old peasant girl driven by religious voices. France's national heroine left home to support the dauphin Charles VII (boy prince, heir to the throne but too young to rule). Joan rallied the French, inspiring them to ultimately throw out the English. In 1430 Joan was captured by the Burgundians, who sold her to the English, who convicted her of heresy and burned her at the stake in Rouen. But the inspiration of Jeanne d'Arc lived on, and by 1453, English holdings on the Continent had dwindled to the port of Calais.

By 1500, a strong centralized France had emerged, with borders similar to today's borders. Her kings (from the Renaissance François I through the Henrys and all those Louises) were model divine monarchs, setting the standards for absolute rule in Europe.

Outrage over the power plays and spending sprees of the kings, coupled with the modern thinking of the Enlightenment—whose leaders were the French *philosophes*—led to the French Revolution (1789) and the end of the Old Regime and its notion that some are born to rule while others are born to be ruled.

But the excesses of the Revolution led to the rise of Napoléon, who ruled the French empire as a dictator until his excesses ushered him into a south Atlantic exile. The French settled on a compromise role for their ruler. The modern French king was himself ruled by a constitution. Rather than dress in leotards and powdered wigs, he went to work in a suit with a briefcase.

The 20th century spelled the end of France's reign as a military and political superpower. Devastating wars with Germany in 1870, 1914, and 1940 and the loss of her colonial holdings have left France with not quite enough land, people, or production to be a top player on a global scale.

Still, France is the cultural capital of Europe and a leader in the push to integrate Europe into one unified economic power. When that happens, Paris will once again emerge as a superpower capital.

Camping

Here are some good campgrounds for the French destinations recommended in this book. All provide free hot showers and clean bathroom facilities and average 60F for two people per night. Campers should pack sleeping bags, a tent, a tarp, sleeping pads, thongs for the showers, a camping *gaz* stove (no Coleman fuel here), a light kettle, plastic plates, and silverware. Consider buying cheap fold-up camping chairs (40F), available at big French *supermarchés*.

Paris: Avoid camping here. It's too hard to reach the city center. Still, if you must, try Camp du Bois du Boulogne, allée du Bord de l'Eau in the Bois (woods) de Boulogne (tel. 01 45 24 30 00). It's the only campground "in" Paris, but it is not strong on security and is generally crowded. Open all year and fully equipped.

Rouen: Municipal Camping. Ten minutes by car or bus from Rouen, in Deauville, on the N-15 toward Le Havre (tel. 02 35 74 07 59). Nice but small area; immaculate bathrooms.

Honfleur: Camping du Phare. A scruffy facility with a great location—a few minutes' stroll from the heart of Honfleur. It's just outside the city as you head to Trouville (open Apr–mid-Oct). A far nicer facility, but a five-minute drive to town, is Camping Domaine Catinière, in Fiquefleur (tel. 02 32 57 63 51, open Apr–Sept).

Bayeux: Municipal Camping. Very friendly, small sites, but a terrific facility and a 10-minute walk to the city center (boulevard Eindhoven, tel. 02 31 92 08 43, open Mar–Oct).

D-day Beaches: You'll see small campgrounds everywhere. The area between Arromanches and the Pointe du Hoc is best.

Mont St. Michel: Camping du Mont St. Michel (Pb. 8/50116 Le Mont St. Michel, tel. 02 33 60 09 33, check in at Motel Vert). It's 1.5 miles from le Mont and 50 yards from great views of it. Otherwise, nothing to write home about. Open year-round.

Amboise: Camping de L'Île d'Or. On the island across the bridge from the city center—you can't miss it. Scenic location and easy walk into Amboise. Mini golf and pool (tel. 02 47 57 23 37).

Sarlat: Camping Les Perieres. A 15-minute walk downhill to Sarlat. This resort sports a pool, tennis courts, a store, a café, and a lovely setting. Call ahead in the summer or forget it (Rd. 47, tel. 05 53 59 05 84, open Apr–Sept).

Albi: Parc de Caussels. One mile east of town. Crowded but friendly, with a huge supermarket across the street (tel. 05 63 60 37 06, open Apr–Nov).

Carcassonne: Camping de la Cité. Brand-new site and facility; a 15-minute walk to la Cité. Inquire at TI for information or follow signs from the *ville basse*, the newer part of the city (tel. 04 68 25 11 77).

Arles: Camping City. The best and most convenient of several in the area. It's a 15-minute walk from the city center; they have a new pool, a poolside café, and hairy umbrellas (on the road to Crau, tel. 04 90 93 08 86, open Mar–Oct).

Avignon: Camping Bagatelle. Right across the Pont (bridge) Daladier from Avignon. Great city views, popular, lots of sites and a great café (tel. 04 90 86 30 39).

Cagnes-sur-Mer (Nice): Camping Panoramer. Meet the friendly owners and admire the best Riviera view around. It's a long walk to the Nice-bound bus stop, but buses run often (open Easter–Sept 20, chemin des Gros Buaux, follow chemin du Val Fleuri from the N-7 in Cagnes-sur-Mer, call ahead in summer, tel. 04 93 31 16 15).

Antibes: Camps are everywhere; you'll see signs. There's easy access to Nice via bus. Be sure to arrive by noon in the summer.

Annecy: Campgrounds line each side of the lake.

Chamonix: Camping les Rosières. Comfortable site, wonderful views, and a beautiful 20-minute walk to town—follow the stream. Funky trailers for rent one mile from Chamonix on route du Praz (open all year, tel. 04 50 53 10 42).

Beaune: Camping les Cent Vignes. This is my favorite campground in France, a 15-minute walk to the city center, fully equipped (great restaurant), individual sites, and campers from all over Europe (open mid-Mar–Oct, 10 rue Dubois, follow signs toward Dijon and watch for camping signs, tel. 03 80 22 03 91).

Dijon: Camping Municipal du Lac. Streamside location and a short waddle to the lake. Fine facilities (open Apr–mid-Nov, one mile from Dijon, follow signs from the station in the direction of Paris, tel. 03 80 43 54 72).

Colmar: Camping intercommunal de l'Île. A few miles from the city center but with a nice riverfront location and good facilities (Plage de L'Île, follow the N-415 toward Fribourg, open Feb–Nov, tel. 03 89 41 15 94).

Let's Talk Telephones

Dialing Direct

Here's a primer on making direct phone calls. For information specific to France and the Low Countries, see "Telephones and Mail" in the introduction.

Calling between Countries: Dial the international access code (of the country you're calling from), the country code (of the country you're calling), the area code (if it starts with zero, drop the zero), and then the local number. (For France, see "Europe's Exceptions," below.)

Calling Long Distance within a Country: First dial the area code (including its zero) and then dial the local number.

Europe's Exceptions: Some countries, such as France, Italy, Spain, Portugal, Norway, and Denmark, do not use area codes. To make an international call to these countries, dial the international access code (usually 00), the country code, and the local number in its entirety. Okay, so there's one exception: for France, drop the initial zero of the local number. To make long-distance calls within any of these countries, simply dial the local number. (For example, within France, dial the 10-digit telephone number direct throughout the country.)

International Access Codes

When dialing direct, first dial the international access code of the country you're calling from. For the United States and Canada, it's 011. Virtually all European countries use "00" as their international access code; the only exceptions are Finland (990), Estonia (800), and Lithuania (810).

Country Codes

After you've dialed the international access code, dial the code of the country you're calling.

Austria—43	Finland—358	Norway—47
Belgium—32	France—33	Portugal—351
Britain—44	Germany—49	Spain—34
Canada—1	Greece—30	Sweden—46
Czech Rep.—420	Ireland—353	Switzerland—41
Denmark—45	Italy—39	United States—1
Estonia—372	Netherlands—31	

Calling Card Operators

	AT&T	MCI	Sprint
France	0800 99 00 11	0800 99 00 19	0800 99 00 87
Belgium	0800-100-10	0800-100-12	0800-100-14
Netherlands	0800-022-9111	0800-022-9122	0800-022-9119

Telephone Directory
Useful Parisian Phone Numbers and Addresses

Emergency: Dial 17 for police, otherwise 01 42 60 33 22
Emergency Medical Assistance: 15
Paris & France Directory Assistance (some English spoken): 12
English Tourist Information Recording: 01 47 20 88 98
American Church: 01 47 05 07 99
American Express: 11 rue Scribe, Mo: Opéra, 01 47 77 77 07
American Hospital: 01 46 41 25 25
American Pharmacy: 01 47 42 49 40
Office of American Services (lost passports, etc.): 01 42 96 12 02
U.S. Embassy: 01 43 12 22 22
Sunday Banks: 115 and 154 avenue des Champs-Élysées

Numbers and Stumblers

- Europeans write a few of their numbers differently than we do. 1 = 1 , 4 = 4 , 7= 7. Learn the difference or miss your train.
- In Europe, dates appear as day/month/year, so Christmas is 25/12/00.
- Commas are decimal points and decimals commas. A dollar and a half is 1,50, and there are 5.280 feet in a mile.
- When pointing, use your whole hand, palm downward.
- When counting with fingers, start with your thumb. If you hold up your first finger to request one item, you'll probably get two.
- What we Americans call the second floor of a building is the first floor in Europe.
- Europeans keep the left "lane" open for passing on escalators and moving sidewalks. Keep to the right.

Climate

First line, average daily low; second line, average daily high; third line, days of no rain.

Paris

J	F	M	A	M	J	J	A	S	O	N	D
34°	34°	39°	43°	49°	55°	58°	58°	53°	46°	40°	36°
43°	45°	54°	60°	68°	73°	76°	75°	70°	60°	50°	44°
16	15	16	16	18	19	19	19	19	17	15	14

Nice

J	F	M	A	M	J	J	A	S	O	N	D
40°	41°	45°	49°	56°	62°	66°	66°	62°	55°	48°	43°
56°	56°	59°	64°	69°	76°	81°	81°	77°	70°	62°	58°
23	20	23	23	23	25	29	26	24	22	23	23

Amsterdam

J	F	M	A	M	J	J	A	S	O	N	D
31°	31°	34°	40°	46°	51°	55°	55°	50°	44°	38°	33°
40°	42°	49°	56°	64°	70°	72°	71°	67°	57°	48°	42°
8	11	14	14	16	16	13	12	11	10	9	9

Basic French Survival Phrases

For more user-friendly French phrases, check out *Rick Steves'*
French Phrase Book and Dictionary or *Rick Steves' French, Italian &*
German Phrase Book and Dictionary.

Hello (good day).	**Bonjour.**	bohn-zhoor
Do you speak English?	**Parlez-vous anglais?**	par-lay-voo ahn-glay
Yes. / No.	**Oui. / Non.**	wee / nohn
I'm sorry.	**Désolé.**	day-zoh-lay
Please.	**S'il vous plaît.**	see voo play
Thank you.	**Merci.**	mehr-see
Goodbye.	**Au revoir.**	oh vwahr
Where is...?	**Où est...?**	oo ay
...a hotel	**...un hôtel**	uhn oh-tehl
...a youth hostel	**...une auberge**	ewn oh-behrzh
	de jeunesse	duh zhuh-nehs
...a restaurant	**...un restaurant**	uhn rehs-toh-rahn
...a grocery store	**...une épicerie**	ewn ay-pee-suh-ree
...the train station	**...la gare**	lah gar
...the tourist info office	**...l'office du tourisme**	loh-fees dew too-reez-muh
Where are the toilets?	**Où sont les toilettes?**	oo sohn lay twah-leht
men / women	**hommes / dames**	ohm / dahm
How much is it?	**Combien?**	kohn-bee-an
Cheaper.	**Moins cher.**	mwan shehr
Included?	**Inclus?**	an-klew
Do you have...?	**Avez-vous...?**	ah-vay-voo
I would like...	**Je voudrais...**	zhuh voo-dray
...a ticket.	**...un billet.**	uhn bee-yay
...a room.	**...une chambre.**	ewn shahn-bruh
...the bill.	**...l'addition.**	lah-dee-see-ohn
one	**un**	uhn
two	**deux**	duh
three	**trois**	twah
four	**quatre**	kah-truh
five	**cinq**	sank
six	**six**	sees
seven	**sept**	seht
eight	**huit**	weet
nine	**neuf**	nuhf
ten	**dix**	dees
At what time?	**À quelle heure?**	ah kehl ur
Just a moment.	**Un moment.**	uhn moh-mahn
Now.	**Maintenant.**	man-tuh-nahn
today / tomorrow	**aujourd'hui / demain**	oh-zhoor-dwee / duh-man

Road Scholar Feedback for
FRANCE, BELGIUM & THE NETHERLANDS 2000

We're all in the same travelers' school of hard knocks. Your feedback helps us improve this guidebook for future travelers. Please fill this out (or use the on-line version at www.ricksteves.com/feedback), attach more info or any tips/favorite discoveries if you like, and send it to us. As thanks for your help, we'll send you our quarterly travel newsletter free for one year. Thanks! Rick

Of the recommended accommodations/restaurants used, which was:

Best _____

       Why? _____

Worst _____

       Why? _____

Of the sights/experiences/destinations recommended by this book, which was:

Most overrated _____

       Why? _____

Most underrated _____

       Why? _____

Best ways to improve this book:

_____

I'd like a free newsletter subscription:

____ Yes   ____ No   ____ Already on list

_____
Name

_____
Address

_____
City, State, Zip

_____
E-mail Address

Please send to: ETBD, Box 2009, Edmonds, WA 98020

Jubilee 2000—Let's Celebrate the Millennium by Forgiving Third World Debt

Let's ring in the millennium by convincing our government to forgive the debt owed to us by the world's poorest countries. Imagine spending over half your income on interest payments alone. You and I are creditors, and poor countries owe us more than they can pay.

Jubilee 2000 is a worldwide movement of concerned people and groups—religious and secular—working to cancel the international debts of the poorest countries by the year 2000.

Debt ruins people: In the poorest countries, money needed for health care, education, and other vital services is diverted to interest payments.

Mozambique, with a per-capita income of $90 and life expectancy of 40, spends over half its national income on interest. This poverty brings social unrest, civil war, and often costly humanitarian intervention by the U.S.A. To chase export dollars, desperate countries ruin their environment. As deserts grow and rain forests shrink, the world suffers. Of course, the real suffering is among local people born long after some dictator borrowed (and squandered) that money. As interest is paid, entire populations go hungry.

Who owes what and why? Mozambique is one of 41 countries defined by the World Bank as "Heavily Indebted Poor Countries." In total, they owe $200 billion. Because these debts are unlikely to be paid, their market value is only a 10th of the face value (about $20 billion). The U.S.A.'s share is under $2 billion.

How can debt be canceled? This debt is owed mostly to the U.S.A., Japan, Germany, Britain, and France either directly or through the World Bank. We can forgive the debt owed directly to us and pay the market value (usually 10 percent) of the debts owed to the World Bank. We have the resources. (Norway, another wealthy creditor nation, just unilaterally forgave its Third World debt.) All the U.S.A. needs is the political will . . . people power.

While many of these poor nations are now democratic, corruption is still a concern. A key to Jubilee 2000 is making certain that debt relief reduces poverty in a way that benefits ordinary people: women, farmers, children, and so on.

Let's celebrate the new millennium by giving poor countries a break. For the sake of peace, fragile young democracies, the environment, and countless real people, forgiving this debt is the right thing for us in the rich world to do.

Tell Washington, D.C.: If our government knows this is what we want, it can happen. Learn more, write letters, lobby legislators, or even start a local Jubilee 2000 campaign. For details, contact Jubilee 2000 (tel. 202/783-3566, www.j2000usa.org). For information on lobbying Congress on J2000, contact Bread for the World (tel. 800/82-BREAD, www.bread.org).

Faxing Your Hotel Reservation

Faxing is more accurate and cheaper than telephoning. Use this handy form for your fax (or find it online at www.ricksteves.com /reservation). Photocopy and fax away.

One-Page Fax

To: _____ @ _____
         hotel   *fax*

From: _____ @ _____
           name   *fax*

Today's date: ___ / ___ / ___
              day month year

Dear Hotel _____,

Please make this reservation for me:

Name: _____

Total # of people: _____   # of rooms: _____   # of nights: _____

Arriving: ___ / ___ / ___ My time of arrival (24-hr clock): _____
          day month year (I will telephone if I will be late)

Departing: ___ / ___ / ___
           day month year

Room(s): Single___ Double___ Twin___ Triple___ Quad___

With: Toilet___ Shower___ Bath___ Sink only___

Special needs: View___ Quiet___ Cheapest Room___

Credit card: Visa___ MasterCard___ American Express___

Card #: _____

Expiration date:_____

Name on card: _____

You may charge me for the first night as a deposit. Please fax or mail me confirmation of my reservation, along with the type of room reserved, the price, and whether the price includes breakfast. Thank you.

_____
Signature

_____
Name

_____
Address

_____
City   *State*   *Zip Code*   *Country*

_____
E-mail Address

INDEX